THE
TELEVISION
INDUSTRY

THE
TELEVISION
INDUSTRY

A HISTORICAL DICTIONARY

Anthony Slide

Greenwood Press

NEW YORK
WESTPORT, CONNECTICUT
LONDON

Library of Congress Cataloging-in-Publication Data

Slide, Anthony.
    The television industry : a historical dictionary / Anthony Slide.
      p. cm.
    Includes bibliographical references and index.
    ISBN 0-313-25634-9 (alk. paper)
    1. Television broadcasting—United States—History—Dictionaries.
  I. Title.
    PN1992.3.U5S57   1991
    384.55'4'0973—dc20   91-4363

British Library Cataloguing in Publication Data is available.

Library of Congress Catalog Card Number: 91-4363
ISBN: 0-313-25634-9

First published in 1991

Greenwood Press, 88 Post Road West, Westport, CT 06881
An imprint of Greenwood Publishing Group, Inc.

Printed in the United States of America

The paper used in this book complies with the
Permanent Paper Standard issued by the National
Information Standards Organization (Z39.48-1984).

10 9 8 7 6 5 4 3 2 1

Contents

Preface

Fred Allen once commented that "television is a triumph of equipment over people." Fred Allen would not appreciate this book—probably to the same extent that television viewers did not appreciate Fred Allen—for here is a volume that deals with "things" rather than people. *The Television Industry: A Historical Dictionary* completes the "trilogy" of historical dictionaries, which began in 1986 with *The American Film Industry* and continued, in 1989, with *The International Film Industry*.

The Television Industry: A Historical Dictionary is the first "what's what" of television, providing more than 1,000 entries on production companies, distributors, organizations, genres, technical terms, and much, much more. Following many of the entries is an address (if the company or organization is still active) and, where appropriate, a bibliography. A general bibliography of reference books on television appears at the end of the volume. An asterisk (*) following a name in any of the entries indicates that there is a separate entry for that subject.

Aside from the more obvious entries, the reader will find headings for such widely used television terms as Cue Cards, Residuals, and Telethons. There are also entries on a wide variety of genres, including Children's Programming, Detective Dramas, Homosexuality, News, Sitcoms, Soap Operas, and Sports. An appendix provides brief biographical essays on the three major network figures in American television history: Leonard H. Goldenson, William S. Paley, and David Sarnoff.

Headings are based on the best-known name of the company or technical innovation and are not necessarily the final names by which the subjects are known. However, all such alternative names are included in the index. Wherever feasible, birth and death years are noted for key figures mentioned in the entries.

The purpose of this book is not to provide an encyclopedia of television programming. Three volumes already serve that purpose: *The Complete Directory to Prime Time Network TV Shows, 1946–Present* by Tim Brooks and Earle Marsh, *Syndicated Television: The First Forty Years, 1947–1987* by Hal Erickson, and *Movies Made for Television: The Telefeature and the Mini-Series, 1964–1984* by Alvin H. Marill. Reference should also be made to Lucia Schultz's unpublished "Television Movies and Miniseries, January 1, 1987–June 30, 1990." All of these works proved invaluable in the preparation of this current volume.

The Television Industry: A Historical Dictionary is primarily concerned with all areas of the American television industry, both "free television" and cable. It does include entries on many foreign television networks and production companies. In particular, there is substantial coverage of the television industry in the United Kingdom, increasingly familiar to American television viewers thanks to programming on cable and public television. References to countries in the index provide access to entries on specific companies or organizations in those countries.

While the book answers a good many questions, two that remain unexplained are why on Steve Allen's *Meeting of the Minds* (PBS, 1976–1981) every female figure in history looked like Allen's wife, Jayne Meadows, and why has Lawrence Welk, one of the most enduring of television stars, not been inducted into the Television Academy Hall of Fame? These questions notwithstanding, the present volume should serve as an essential reference tool for any scholar, student, or librarian involved in the study of the television industry. It is also hoped that the book will prove entertaining for the casual reader who might wonder about the link between DuMont, the first fourth network, and Fox, the most recent fourth network; the origins of some of the more familiar company names on television, such as King World or Telerep; or the variety of programming offered by the more than fifty cable networks.

Basic research for this volume was undertaken at the following libraries, to the staffs of which I give my thanks: the Margaret Herrick Library of the Academy of Motion Picture Arts and Sciences, the Louis B. Mayer Library of the American Film Institute, the Hollywood Public Library, the Library of the Independent Broadcasting Authority (London), and the Westminster Central Reference Library (London).

Thanks are also due the following: Academy Film Productions (Bernard Howard); Action for Children's Television (Susan L. Edelman); Advanced Television Systems Committee (Christy Kehlbeck); The Arthur Company (Lisa Shaw); the Association of Independent Television Stations, Inc. (Laurence B. Laurent); Rudy Behlmer; Black Awareness in Television (David Rambeau); Alan Braun; Broadcast Pioneers; Cabletelevision Advertising Bureau; Cable Television Public Affairs Association; Canadian Association of Broadcasters; Canadian Cable Television Association (Kari-Anne Cullen); C & C Syndication; Chris-Craft Industries, Inc.; Community Antenna Television Association; Cox Enterprises, Inc.; Don Fedderson Productions; Sally Dumaux; Dan Einstein; the Federal Communications Commission (Stephen F. Sewell); Fox/Lorber Associates, Inc.;

Sandy Frank; Gannett; Robert Gitt; Alan L. Gleitsman; Robert D. Graff; Leo
A. Handel; Burt I. Harris; the International Television Association; Ronnie
James; John Blair Communications, Inc.; Jan Kacperek; King Broadcasting Company; KQED; MPO Vidtronics (Lynn Fidanza); National Association of College
Broadcasters (Glenn Gutmacher); National Association of Telecommunications
Officers and Advisors; National Broadcast Editorial Association; National Cable
Television Association; National Cable Television Institute (Ray Charest); National Coalition on Television Violence; National Council for Families & Television; National Federation of Local Cable Programmers; James B. Poteat;
Howard Prouty; Radio-Television News Directors Association; Ralph Edwards
Productions (Eddy Jo Bernal); Roncom Productions, Inc. (Mickey Glass); Horace
Schwerin; Scripps Howard Broadcasting Company; SECA; Society of Broadcast
Engineers, Inc. (Elberta Clayton); Society of Cable Television Engineers, Inc.
(Patricia B. Zelenka); Station Representatives Association; Teleklew; Telemated
Motion Pictures (Saul S. Taffet); TeleRep (Daniel R. Kelly); Television Index,
Inc. (Jonathan Miller); TVOntario; Videotex Industry Association; Walt Disney
Archives (Dave Smith); WGBH (Jeanne M. Hopkins); WNET; and Women in
Cable (Lora J. Di Padova).

At Greenwood Press, I would like to thank my editor, Marilyn Brownstein,
and my production editor, Arlene Belzer.

A

THE A&E CABLE NETWORK. Often compared to PBS* because of the cultural nature of its programming, A&E (the Arts & Entertainment) Network is a basic cable channel, which began broadcasting on February 1, 1984, and provides a varied range of programming twenty-four hours a day for approximately 44 million subscribers. Headed by Nickolas Davatzes, A&E is jointly owned by Capital Cities/ABC, NBC,* and the Hearst Corporation, and is the result of a merger between the ARTS cable network (owned by ABC* and Hearst) and The Entertainment Channel (owned by RCA*). The ARTS network was introduced on April 12, 1981, and The Entertainment Channel was extant between 1982 and 1983. The bulk of A&E's programming (60 percent in 1984 and 40 percent in 1989) comes from the BBC.*

Address: 555 Fifth Avenue, New York, NY 10017.

BIBLIOGRAPHY

Farber, Stephen, "A&E, the Arts Channel That Thrives," *New York Times*, August 5, 1985, p. 17.

Flinn, John, and Cecilia Capuzzi, "Programming for the New Cable Audience," *Channels of Communications*, vol. VIII, no. 3, March 1988, pp. 114–115.

Hickey, Neil, "Just What Cable Didn't Need—Another Cultural Network," *TV Guide*, August 2, 1986, pp. 34–37.

Kleinfield, N.R., "A&E: A Cable Success Story," *New York Times*, April 16, 1989, pp. H31, H39.

Schneider, Steve, "A&E Is Trying To Broaden Its Image," *New York Times*, October 19, 1986, section 2, p. 29.

Zoglin, Richard, "A Tough Sell for the Arts," *Time*, March 11, 1985, p. 64.

AARON SPELLING PRODUCTIONS, INC. was formed in June 1970 by popular television producer Aaron Spelling (born 1928). From its inception until September 1987, the company had an exclusive relationship with ABC,* for whom it produced a record number of ninety "movies of the week," as well as

The Love Boat (1977–1987), *Vega$* (1978–1981), *Dynasty* (1981–1989), *Strike Force* (1981–1982), *At Ease* (1983), and *Hotel* (1983–1988). Later, it produced *Nightingales* for NBC (1988–1989).

The company went public in 1986, and in February 1989 it merged with Laurel Entertainment, Inc. and Worldvision Enterprises* to form Spelling Entertainment. Worldvision was acquired by Spelling from Great American Communications Co.* (which, in turn, acquired 48.6 percent of the new company as part of the deal). In April 1991, Aaron Spelling sold his interest in Spelling Entertainment to Charter Co. for $47 million. At the same time, Charter Co. acquired all shares in the company held by Great American.

Address: 1041 North Formosa Avenue, Los Angeles, CA 90046.

BIBLIOGRAPHY

Drew, Clare L., "The Selling of Spelling," *Channels of Communications*, vol. X, no. 7, May 21, 1990, pp. 26–28.

See, Carolyn, "This Man Knows What America Wants to Watch," *Panorama*, vol. I, no. 5, June 1980, pp. 74–77.

ABC (AMERICAN BROADCASTING COMPANY). RCA* created ABC, under the original name of the American Broadcasting System, in 1941. In the spring of that year, the FCC* had ruled that no organization could maintain more than one network, a reference to NBC's* ownership of the Blue and Red radio networks. NBC's parent company, RCA, disposed of the 116 radio stations of the Blue Network for $8 million to Edward J. Noble, owner of the Life Savers Corporation. The name American Broadcasting Company was purchased from WOL-Washington, D.C., in 1944 for $10,000, and the network officially adopted the name in December 1944. However, in order to avoid confusion among listeners, the name Blue Network continued to be used as well until June 15, 1945.

ABC entered television in 1948, with its first program being *On the Corner*, starring Henry Morgan, and broadcast on April 19 of that year. ABC was very much the lesser of the three networks, and it was not until 1954 that it achieved its first major programming success with *Disneyland* (first seen on October 27, 1954), which later became *Walt Disney Presents* (in 1958), *Walt Disney's Wonderful World of Color* (in 1961), *The Wonderful World of Disney* (in 1969), and *Disney's Wonderful World* (in 1979). The most popular of the early series seen on ABC was *The Adventures of Ozzie and Harriet*, starring Ozzie and Harriet Nelson, and first seen on October 3, 1952.

A major change in ABC's corporate status took place in 1950 when Leonard H. Goldenson (born 1905) merged his company United Paramount Theatres (UPT) with ABC. UPT was formerly the theatre chain owned by Paramount Pictures, and with its merger with ABC, a new company, American Broadcasting–Paramount Theatres, Inc., was created early in 1952.

In 1955, Warner Bros.* began an exclusive production program with ABC. Three years later, in 1958, ABC began morning and early-afternoon television broadcasts, with the financial assistance of the Young & Rubicam advertising agency. The network introduced color* programming in 1962, with full color broadcasting beginning in 1966. ABC's first major attempt at late-night programming was *The Joey Bishop Show* (1967–1969).

Two takeover bids were made for ABC in the sixties. In 1965, ITT proposed a merger, but it was rejected by the Justice Department three years later. Also in 1968, Howard Hughes attempted an unfriendly takeover, but he dropped the proposal, perhaps because of the necessity of his appearing in person at the FCC public hearing. In April 1965, the network adopted the name of American Broadcasting Companies, Inc., and moved to its present corporate headquarters in New York.

In the past, ABC was the subject of numerous snide remarks because of its perennially poor ratings. It was often called the "Almost Broadcasting Company," and a favorite comment of Milton Berle was: "The way to end the Vietnam War is to schedule it on ABC. It'll be cancelled in thirteen weeks." One positive step in ABC's attempt to improve its ratings was the December 1970 teaming of Howard K. Smith and Harry Reasoner to present the *ABC Evening News*.

Elton Rule (1917–1990) was named president of the ABC Broadcast Group in 1970, after serving as president of the ABC TV Network since 1968. When he retired from ABC in 1984, he was its vice-chairman. In 1974, Frederick S. Pierce (born 1933) took over from Walter A. Schwartz as president of ABC-TV and executive vice-president of ABC Companies, Inc. He moved ABC from its usual third place in the ratings to first place in January 1976. Between 1976 and 1979, Pierce was also able to lure seventeen CBS* affiliates and nine NBC affiliates to ABC. On June 1, 1977, Pierce appointed Roone Arledge, the head of ABC Sports, to be the new head of the News Division, an appointment that created considerable controversy. (Arledge resigned as head of the Sports Division in January 1986.) Pierce also became the subject of controversy and some amusement, when, in 1981, it was revealed that he had placed psychic Beverlee Dean under contract as a consultant on programming. Pierce resigned in January 1986 and was replaced as president of the ABC Division by John B. Sias, a Capital Cities Communications* executive, who was placed in charge of ABC's entertainment, news, and sports divisions.

Anthony D. Thomopoulos (born 1938) resigned in November 1985 as president of the ABC Broadcast Group, a position he had held since 1983 (he had joined ABC ten years earlier), and he was replaced by Brandon Stoddard (born 1937). Stoddard resigned in March 1989, and was replaced by Robert Iger. Stoddard was subsequently placed in charge of a new production division.

On January 23, 1977, ABC began airing the mini-series *Roots*, which proved to be the most widely viewed program on television up to that time.

In July 1982, the ABC Entertainment Talent Development Program was created to place under a special development contract actors and actresses of great potential who did not fit immediate casting needs. The first twelve contractees included Arsenio Hall, Gordon Thomson, and Emma Samms. Later contractees included Ann Jillian, Tom Hanks, Emanuel Lewis, and Danny Pintauro. In 1984,

ABC invested $225 million for the rights to televise the Summer Olympic Games from Los Angeles. In November 1986, the Weintraub Entertainment Group incorporated its Pathé newsreel holdings with the ABC News Library to form ABC/Weintraub Pathé.

In 1985, Capital Cities Communications, Inc. negotiated the acquisition of ABC, a purchase that was completed in January 1986. The resultant company was named CapCities/ABC and headed by Thomas S. Murphy (born 1925), who was succeeded in 1990 by Daniel B. Burke (born 1929). Capital Cities instituted a cost-cutting program at the network, but even so, ABC lost $70 million in 1986 and $53 million in 1987. The loss in 1988 was only $14 million, and that was generally attributed to the heavy expenses involved in the production of the mini-series *The Winds of War* (1983), a successor to ABC's earlier mini-series *War and Remembrance* (1988–1989), and to the costs of covering the Winter Olympics in Calgary and the presidential election campaigns. In 1989, ABC announced a profit of $150 million.

The network owns twenty-one radio stations and the following television stations: KFSN-Fresno; KABC–Los Angeles; KGO–San Francisco; WLS-Chicago; WABC–New York; WTVD-Durham, North Carolina; WPVI-Philadelphia; and KTRK-Houston.

Addresses: 1300 Avenue of the Americas, New York, NY 10019; 4151 Prospect Avenue, Los Angeles, CA 90027.

BIBLIOGRAPHY

"ABC Never Stops Pioneering," *TV Guide*, January 1, 1966, p. 3.

Alter, Jonathan, "Taking the Knife to ABC," *Newsweek*, April 7, 1986, p. 58.

"A Bad Week for ABC," *Time*, May 12, 1980, p. 63.

"Big Media, Big Money," *Newsweek*, April 1, 1985, pp. 52–59.

Brown, Les, "ABC-TV Head Confident Network Is Ready for 80s," *New York Times*, October 18, 1979, p. C23.

Carter, Betsy, "ABC Goes a-Hunting," *Newsweek*, January 8, 1979, pp. 70–71.

DeMott, John S., "A Network Blockbuster," *Time*, April 1, 1985, pp. 60–63.

Fabrikant, Geraldine, "Not Ready for Prime Time?" *New York Times Magazine*, April 12, 1987, pp. 30–37.

Goldenson, Leonard H, with Marvin J. Wolf. *Beating the Odds*. New York: Charles Scribner's Sons, 1991.

"Happy Days Are Here at ABC," *Newsweek*, January 10, 1972, pp. 40–41.

Knoll, Steve, "Things May Never Be the Same Again," *TV Guide*, August 21, 1976, pp. 6–9.

Lewis, Grover, "The Greening of ABC-TV," *New West*, June 20, 1977, pp. 55–61.

Morgan, Thomas B., "We're in a Fight for Our Lives," *TV Guide*, December 8, 1962, pp. 7–9.

Quinlan, Sterling. *Inside ABC: American Broadcasting Company's Rise to Power*. New York: Hastings House, 1979.

Spence, Jim, "Stars and Strife at ABC Sports," *TV Guide*, June 4, 1988, pp. 2–9.

Waters, Harry F., "A Relish for Risks," *Newsweek*, June 15, 1987, p. 59.

Zoglin, Richard, "Battling Back from No. 3," *Time*, April 1, 1985, pp. 64–65.

———, "Tightening the Belts at ABC," *Time*, May 5, 1986, pp. 78–79.

ABC CIRCLE FILMS was an in-house production unit of ABC,* responsible for many important television movies and mini-series, as well as the co-production of the series *Moonlighting* (ABC, 1985–1989). Its first production was *The Man* (1971), which was intended as a two-hour television movie but was released theatrically by Paramount. Other major ABC Circle productions include *Love among the Ruins* (1975), *The Jericho Mile* (1979), *Ike* (1979), *The Day After* (1983), *Amerika* (1987), *Baby M* (1988), and *War and Remembrance* (1988–1989).

In the summer of 1989, ABC Circle Films became part of a new unit, ABC Entertainment, headed by Brandon Stoddard. Herb Jellinek, ABC Circle's vice-president of production, who had been with ABC since 1952 and in charge of ABC Circle Films since its inception, retired.

ABC FILMS, INC. was the ABC network's syndication arm. It was active in the fifties and sixties, distributing dozens of series, including *Kieran's Kaleidoscope* (Syndicated, 1952), *Passport to Danger* (Syndicated, 1954), *The Three Musketeers* (Syndicated, 1955), *The Life and Legend of Wyatt Earp* (ABC, 1955–1961), *The People's Court of Small Claims* (Syndicated, 1958), *Ben Casey* (ABC, 1961–1966), *The Fugitive* (ABC, 1963–1967), *Shindig* (ABC, 1964–1966), *The Addams Family* (ABC, 1964–1966), and *Dark Shadows* (ABC, 1966–1971). Henry G. Plitt (born 1918), who was later to head his own theatre circuit, was the president of ABC Films from 1959 to 1965. He was succeeded by Hal Golden and Kevin O'Sullivan. Following the FCC* ruling that networks must refrain from program syndication by June 1, 1973, ABC sold the subsidiary to a group of executives—Kevin O'Sullivan, Jerry Smith, Neil Delman, Colin Campbell, and Howard Lloyd—and they renamed the company Worldvision Enterprises.*

ACADEMY FILM PRODUCTIONS, INC. was founded in Chicago in April 1950 by Bernard Howard, who had produced his first television show for WBKB-Chicago in 1947. The company produced television commercials, together with educational and training films. It was also responsible for two local television series of the fifties, *Bob Elson Interviews of the Century* and *The Lovelier You*.

Address: 3918 Estes Avenue, Lincolnwood, IL 60645.

THE ACADEMY OF FAMILY FILMS AND TELEVISION was founded in 1980 by Dr. Donald A. Reed to recognize, through awards, the contributions made by films and television to family entertainment.

Address: 334 West 54 Street, Los Angeles, CA 90037.

THE ACADEMY OF TELEVISION ARTS AND SCIENCES was founded in Los Angeles as an organization similar to the Academy of Motion Picture Arts and Sciences in October 1946 by Syd Cassyd and a group of a half dozen industry associates. A year later, it elected Edgar Bergen (1903–1978) as its first president. In 1955, the academy merged with its New York equivalent to become the National Academy of Television Arts and Sciences. Unfortunately, the organization became increasingly splintered as biases were perceived by members on both coasts, and eventually, in 1977, it split again into two groups, the Hollywood Academy of Television Arts and Sciences in Los Angeles (the word Hollywood was soon dropped) and the National Academy of Television Arts and Sciences in New York.

The National Academy of Television Arts and Sciences (NATAS; 111 West 57 Street, Suite 1020, New York, NY 10019) maintains chapters in Arizona, Atlanta, Boston, Chicago, Cleveland, Columbus, Detroit, Miami, Nashville, New York, Philadelphia, St. Louis, San Diego, San Francisco, Seattle, and Washington. Attempts at a reunification of the two academies, headed by Diana Muldaur and Richard Frank, began in 1985, but were put on hold in January 1987.

The most prominent of the academy's activities is the presentation of the annual Emmy awards, honoring excellence in television. Aside from the Prime Time Emmy Awards, which are televised nationally, the academy also presents local Emmys and Emmys for daytime programming. A July 1977 agreement permitted the Hollywood Academy of Television Arts and Sciences (HATAS) to retain rights to the prime time Emmy Awards, while NATAS kept exclusive rights to the daytime and sports Emmy Awards. However, for many years, the daytime Emmy Awards have been sponsored by both groups.

The first Emmy Awards were presented on January 25, 1949, at the Hollywood Athletic Club, and were hosted by Walter O'Keefe. The award itself, designed by Louis McManus, was named "Emmy" by pioneering television engineer Harry Lubcke (president of the academy from 1949 to 1950), who coined the name as a derivative of "Immy" (a nickname for the image orthicon tube).

Aside from the Emmy Awards, the academy publishes a magazine, *Emmy*,* and is involved in various educational and cultural activities including forum lunches, at which prominent members of the industry speak; the UCLA Film and Television Archive;* and a Television Academy Hall of Fame (to which new members are elected annually). The academy foundation was restructured and reconstituted in February 1989, with Elton Rule as its first president. Plans for an academy library were announced in December 1987. In 1989, the academy began the construction of new headquarters in North Hollywood, which opened in 1991. Since September 1986, the academy has been active in the campaign against substance abuse, and to that end, it sponsored the animated special *Cartoon All-Stars to the Rescue*, televised simultaneously on ABC,* CBS,* NBC,* and Fox* on April 21, 1990.

James L. Loper, the former president of KCET,* has been executive director of the academy since December 1983.

Address: 5220 Lankershim Boulevard, North Hollywood, CA 91601.

BIBLIOGRAPHY

Kaufman, Dave, "TV Acads Detail Terms of Their Peace Agreement," *Daily Variety*, July 8, 1977, pp. 1, 16.

————, "TV Acad Could Use Some Spring Cleaning," *Daily Variety*, May 2, 1983, p. 14.

Link, Tom, "Dreams and Dissent: The Television Academy's Forty Years," *Emmy*, vol. VIII, no. 5, September/October 1986, pp. 32–57.

Loftus, Jack, "TV Acad Repair Work Underway," *Daily Variety*, April 14, 1983, pp. 1, 23.

Michael, Paul, and James Robert Parish. *The Emmy Awards: A Pictorial History*. New York: Crown, 1970.

Taub, Eric, "The Birth of Emmy," *Emmy*, vol. VIII, no. 5, September/October 1986, pp. 58–68.

ACADEMY PICTURES, INC. was a producer of animated commercials, active in the fifties. A number of prominent animators—including William Lightfield, William Tytla, and Arthur Babbitt—were associated with the company, which had offices in both New York and Los Angeles.

ACCESS (Alberta Educational Communications Corporation) was founded on April 1, 1974, to provide educational broadcasting for the Canadian province of Alberta. It has its origins in the Alberta Educational Communications Authority, founded in 1971 by the government of Alberta, and embraces the Calgary and Region Educational Television, CKUA-Radio, and the Metropolitan Edmonton Educational Television Association.

Address: 16930 114 Avenue, Edmonton, Alberta T5M 9Z9, Canada.

ACCURACY IN MEDIA, founded in 1969 by Reed Irvine, researches complaints regarding factual errors made by the news media and attempts to have such errors publicly corrected. It monitors television reporting and presents awards for accuracy in communications journalism.

Address: 1275 K Street, N.W., Suite 1150, Washington, DC 20005.

BIBLIOGRAPHY
Irvine, Reed. *Media Mischief and Misdeeds*. Chicago: Regnery Gateway, 1984.

THE ACE AWARDS are cable television's highest honors. So named because they are "Awards for Cablecasting Excellence," the spade-shaped trophies have been presented since 1979 (when eighteen awards were given out). Through 1986, the awards were administered by the National Cable Television Association,* and since 1987, they have been presented under the auspices of the National Academy of Cable Programming. The academy's claim is: "When you're the best at what you do, they call you an ace. When you're the best at what you do on cable TV, they give you an ACE." Up to and including the fourth year of the awards, they were given to the programs themselves and not to stars or individuals. The acronym ACE is also used by the American Cinema Editors for their awards, and this has led to some confusion and irritation on the part of the latter group.

Address: 1724 Massachusetts Avenue, N.W., Washington, DC 20036.

BIBLIOGRAPHY
Ross, Chuck, "ACE: The Show Grows Up under the National Academy of Cable Pro-
    gramming," *The Hollywood Reporter*, February 2, 1987, p. 12.

THE A.C. NIELSEN COMPANY is best known to the general public for its
measurement of the television audience and preparation of the Nielsen Ratings.
In reality, the company is involved in all aspects of market research, and only
10 percent of its business relates to television audience research. Founded in
1923 by engineer A.C. Nielsen with borrowed capital of $45,000, the A.C.
Nielsen Company became involved in broadcast ratings with the radio industry
in the thirties. Arthur Nielsen, Jr., became president of the company in 1957
and its chairman in 1976. A.C. Nielsen, Sr., died in 1980. Four years later, the
company was purchased by Dun & Bradstreet Corporation for $1.3 billion in
stock.

In 1942, Nielsen introduced the Audimeter, a box attached then to radio sets
and later to television receivers to record minute-by-minute listening or viewing
by sample households. A more sophisticated device, the Storage Instantaneous
Audimeter, was introduced in 1973. A further device, the People Meter,* was
introduced in 1987. In addition, Nielsen households maintain audilogs, which
are diaries indicating viewing habits. The A.C. Nielsen Company was selected
to conduct the surveys for *The People's Choice Awards*, which were first seen
on CBS* on March 4, 1975.

Address: 1290 Avenue of the Americas, New York, NY 10104.

BIBLIOGRAPHY
Alridge, Ron, "An Interview with A.C. Nielsen, Jr.," *Emmy*, vol. III, no. 2, Spring
    1981, pp. 8–10, 46.
Head, Sydney W., and Christopher H. Sterling, "Audience Measurement and Testing,"
    in *Broadcasting in America: A Survey of Electronic Media*. Boston: Houghton
    Mifflin, 1987, pp. 373–403.
Stavro, Barry, "Rating Nielsen," *Forbes*, December 17, 1984, pp. 100–105.
Traub, James, "The World According to Nielsen," *Channels of Communications*, vol.
    IV, no. 5, January/February 1985, pp. 26–32, 70–71.

ACTION FOR CHILDREN'S TELEVISION (ACT) is a non-profit organization "working to encourage diversity in children's TV, to discourage over-
commercialization of children's programming, and to eliminate deceptive advertising aimed at young viewers." It was founded in January 1968 by four
Massachusetts mothers, Peggy Charren, Evelyn Kaye Sarson, Lillian Ambrosino,
and Judy Chalfen, and by 1971 had its own offices with members in thirty-eight
states. ACT announced its first Achievement in Children's Television Awards
in 1972, and has long been active in petitioning (and even suing, in May 1982)
the Federal Communications Commission (FCC*) to adopt rules for children's
programming. It was instrumental in promoting the Children's Television Advertising Practices Act (H.R. 3288), introduced in the House in September 1987

and the Senate in February 1988, and limiting the amount of advertising time on television targeted to children.

Address: 20 University Road, Cambridge, MA 02138.

THE ACTS SATELLITE NETWORK. The Southern Baptist Convention entered television in 1981 with the creation of the American Christian Television Service, a satellite-linked network of 115 low power television stations. In June 1984, the network began broadcasting as a basic cable service under the name of ACTS, providing religious and family programming twenty-four hours a day.

Address: 6350 West Freeway, Fort Worth, TX 76150.

ACUS PICTURES CORPORATION was a minor New York–based distributor, with a library of eight feature films available to television, active in the fifties and early sixties.

"AD HOC" NETWORK is the term used to describe a group of television stations contracting to carry a specific program or series, such as Operation Prime Time* or "The Mobil Showcase Network."*

ADMIRAL CORP. was a major manufacturer of television receivers in the late forties and fifties. It was also the sponsor of *On the Corner*, the first program seen on ABC,* on April 19, 1948. The company was not particularly successful in marketing color television sets, garnering only 4 percent of the market. In 1972, it marketed a videotape-recording/playback system on behalf of Avco for $1,700 per machine. As a result of continuing financial problems, Admiral merged into Rockwell International on April 9, 1974.

BIBLIOGRAPHY
"Al Rockwell's Puzzle," *Forbes*, January 15, 1974, pp. 31–32.
"Playing It Straight," *Forbes*, November 1, 1972, p. 64.
"Show Goes On, and Production Perks: Admiral's New Color Tube Plant," *Business Week*, April 16, 1966, pp. 122–124.

ADVANCE FILM PRODUCTIONS, INC. was a minor New York–based producer of television programming, active in the early fifties, and owned by *Film Daily* and *Radio and Television Daily* executive Charles A. Alicoate.

ADVERTISERS' TELEVISION PROGRAM SERVICE, INC. was a Los Angeles–based distributor active in the early and mid-fifties. It handled some distribution for *Mr. and Mrs. North* (CBS, 1952–1953; NBC, 1954), but was not the primary distributor of the program. (The main distributor was the New York–based firm Bernard L. Schubert, Inc.)

ADVERTISING AGENCIES. In recent years, the power of the advertising agencies has somewhat diminished in that they can no longer afford to purchase the sole sponsorship of a radio or television series as they did in the days of live television in the forties and early fifties. However, their power does remain substantial. For example, in 1981, Leo Burnett U.S.A. controlled the placement of television commercials for twenty-six corporations. In 1958, Young & Rubicam helped finance the start of ABC's morning and early-afternoon television programming.

Much of the superior programming in live television can be attributed to the efforts of advertising agencies. Because J. Walter Thompson thought it could produce a series for television similar to its popular radio drama anthology *Lux Radio Theater*, it persuaded Kraft to sponsor *Kraft Television Theatre* (NBC, 1947–1958). According to Frank Sturcken in *Live Television: The Golden Age of 1948–1958 in New York* (Jefferson, N.C.: McFarland, 1990), J. Walter Thompson was also the first agency to produce a variety show on television (for Shell in 1940) and the first to telecast a baseball World Series (for Ford in 1947).

Advertising agencies also handled the syndicated distribution of many television series. Among those distributed by J. Walter Thompson (through JWT Syndication) were *Foreign Intrigue* (1951–1955), *Speakeasy* (1974), *David Niven's World* (1974), *Other People—Other Places* (1974), *Take Five with Stiller and Meara* (1977), and *Norm Crosby's Comedy Shop* (1978–1979).

Perhaps nothing better demonstrates the one-time power in television of advertising agencies than a listing of their clients and sponsored shows, published by Batten, Barton, Durstine & Osborn, Inc. (BBDO) in 1957:

The American Tobacco Company—*Trackdown, The Jack Benny Program, Your Hit Parade*

Armstrong Cork Company—*Armstrong Circle Theatre*

B.F. Goodrich—*The George Burns and Gracie Allen Show*

Bristol-Myers—*Arthur Godfrey Time, Playhouse 90, Arthur Murray Party*

Campbell's Soup—*Lassie, Joseph Cotten Show, Colt 45*

DeSoto-Plymouth Dealers of America—*You Bet Your Life*

E.I. DuPont De Nemours—*DuPont Show of the Month*

General Electric—*The General Electric Theater, Cheyenne*

General Mills—*Bob Crosby Show, Our Miss Brooks, The Lone Ranger, Disneyland*

Lever Brothers—*Art Linkletter's House Party, Joseph Cotten Show, Comedy Time, The Price Is Right, Truth or Consequences, Life of Riley, Have Gun Will Travel*

Minnesota Mining—*Mickey Mouse Club, Andy's Gang, Tic Tac Dough, Queen for a Day*

Revlon—*The $64,000 Question, The $64,000 Challenge, 20th Century–Fox Hour, Walter Winchell*

Timken Roller Bearing—*Telementaries*

United States Steel—*United States Steel Hour*

Wildroot Company—*The Adventures of Robin Hood, All-Star Golf*

ADVERTISING INFORMATION SERVICES, INC., headed by Jack Safir-stein, is an aircheck service providing, for research purposes, more than 60,000 television commercials recorded off the air from 1976 to the present.

Address: 353 Lexington Avenue, New York, NY 10016.

AFFILIATED PROGRAM SERVICE, INC. (Paul F. Adler, president) was a New York–based television distributor, active in the fifties and early sixties.

AFFILIATED STATIONS are television stations affiliated with one of the three networks, ABC,* CBS,* or NBC,* under standard two-year affiliate agreements. Affiliated stations have the right of first refusal to the approximately eighty hours per week of network programming that they are offered. In return, they are paid an agreed amount of "network compensation" in return for allowing the networks to use their programming time. Aside from network programming, affiliates broadcast local news, local programming, and syndicated programming. According to the Scripps Howard Broadcasting Company,* approximately 30 percent of an affiliate station's advertising revenue is generated by local news and information programming. Approximately three-quarters of all television stations are affiliated with a network.

BIBLIOGRAPHY
Finnegan, Joseph, "Give Me a 'A'! Give Me a 'B'! Give Me a 'C'!" *TV Guide*, July 31, 1971, pp. 20–22.
Head, Sydney W., and Christopher H. Sterling, "Commercial Broadcast Networks and Affiliates," in *Broadcasting in America: A Survey of Electronic Media*. Boston: Houghton Mifflin, 1987, pp. 198–205.
Knoll, Steve, "Showdown at Clearance Gap," *TV Guide*, April 10, 1976, pp. 2–7.
————, "Affiliate Power," *TV Guide*, April 17, 1976, pp. 29–32.
Nicholas, David, "We Regret That 'Maude' Will Not Be Seen . . . ," *TV Guide*, March 3, 1973, pp. 6–8.

AFTRA (The American Federation of Television and Radio Artists) is the union representative for all performers in television and radio (including actors, news-casters, disc jockeys, announcers, weathermen, singers, and dancers). It was founded in August 1937 as AFRA (The American Federation of Radio Artists), and comedian Eddie Cantor was elected its first president. The name change took place on September 17, 1952, when AFRA merged with the Television Authority, led by George Heller, a temporary group formed by performers' unions in April 1950 to protect their interests while working in television. AFRA had 2,000 members in 1937, and fifty years later, AFTRA had 70,000 members. In the late eighties and after, discussions took place concerning a merger between AFTRA and SAG (the Screen Actors Guild).

Addresses: 1350 Avenue of the Americas, New York, NY 10019; 1717 North Highland Avenue, Hollywood, CA 90028.

BIBLIOGRAPHY
Eaker, Sherry, "AFTRA Celebrates the First 50 Years," *Back Stage*, November 6, 1987,
     pp. 1, 23–34.

THE A.H. BELO CORP. is a publisher of Dallas/Fort Worth area newspapers
(notably the *Dallas Morning News*), originally incorporated in 1926 and reincorporated in March 1987. Through its subsidiary, Belo Broadcasting Corp.,
it owns WFAA-Dallas, WTVC-Chattanooga, and KFDM-Beaumont, Texas. In
June 1983, it acquired the television stations of the former Corinthian Broadcasting Group: KHOU-Houston; KXTV-Sacramento; KOTV-Tulsa; WISH-
Indianapolis; WAVE–Fort Wayne, Indiana; and WVEC–Hampton and Norfolk,
Virginia.

The Corinthian Broadcasting Group was formed in 1957 to manage the broadcast assets of John Hay Whitney. The group was acquired in 1971 by Dun &
Bradstreet Companies, Inc. for $134 million.

The A.H. Belo Corp. is also involved in the syndication of a number of self-
produced programs, including *Mr. Peppermint*, *Texas Country Reporter*,
Scratch, and *Pulse*.

Address: P.O. Box 655237, Communications Center, Dallas, TX 75265.

ALADDIN TELEVISION PRODUCTIONS, INC. was a Los Angeles–based
production company, founded in 1953 by Harry M. Popkin. It produced the
1954 *Kid Magic* series for local television.

ALAN ENTERPRISES, INC. was founded in 1970 by Alan Gleitsman, a
former sales representative for the Walter Reade Organization, and was incorporated in 1971. A smaller, independent television distributor, it specialized in
classic and foreign feature films and also handled the controversial series *Vietnam: The 10,000 Day War* (Syndicated, 1981). The company was sold in 1986
to Color Systems Technology.

ALAN LANDSBURG PRODUCTIONS, INC. was founded in 1970 by Alan
Landsburg (born 1933). From 1971 to 1975, it was partnered with Tomorrow
Entertainment, Inc.* (a subsidiary of General Electric), but in September 1978,
the company was purchased by Reeves Communications Corp.* (which has
extensive postproduction facilities in New York), and which at that time was
known as Reeves Teletape. Specializing primarily in entertainment programming
with a documentary approach, the Los Angeles–based Alan Landsburg Productions was responsible for the series *In Search of...* (Syndicated, 1976–1982),
That's Incredible! (ABC, 1980–1984), *Those Amazing Animals* (ABC, 1980–
1981), and *Life's Most Embarrassing Moments* (ABC, 1983); together with a
number of made-for-television movies, including *The Savage Bees* (NBC, 1976),
The Jayne Mansfield Story (CBS, 1980), *Bill* (CBS, 1981), and *Adam* (NBC,
1983).

Alan Landsburg Productions, Inc. ceased operations as an independent unit of Reeves when Landsburg resigned from the company on April 1, 1985, and formed the Landsburg Company (11811 West Olympic Boulevard, Los Angeles, CA 90064) in association with Cox Communications, Inc.*

ALBERT BLACK TELEVISION PRODUCTIONS was a New York–based producer, primarily of television commercials, active in the fifties.

THE ALBET COMPANY was formed by Allen Ludden and his wife, actress Betty White, for the production of *Win with the Stars* (Syndicated, 1968) and *The Pet Set* (Syndicated, 1971).

AL BUFFINGTON PRODUCTIONS was a Los Angeles–based producer, primarily of television commercials, active in the fifties.

THE ALFRED I. DUPONT–COLUMBIA UNIVERSITY AWARDS IN BROADCAST JOURNALISM honor outstanding achievements in radio and television journalism. They were established in 1942 by Jessie Ball duPont to honor her husband's memory, and since 1977 (when the networks ceased to cover the annual fall event) they have been televised on PBS.*
Address: Columbia University, Graduate School of Journalism, New York, NY 10027.

ALIEN PRODUCTIONS, headed by Bernie Brillstein and Tom Patchett, was formed for the production of *Alf* (NBC, 1986–1990).
Address: 8860 Hayden Place, Culver City, CA 90232.

ALLEGRO PICTURES, INC. was a Los Angeles–based producer of filmed television series, founded by William Lava, and active in the fifties.

ALLEN A. FUNT PRODUCTIONS was the New York–based company responsible for the production of the original filmed episodes of *Candid Camera* (ABC, 1948; NBC, 1949; CBS, 1949–1950; NBC, 1953), and for the segments of *Candid Camera* seen on *The Garry Moore Show* during 1959 and 1960.

ALLEN AND ALLEN PRODUCTIONS, founded by George E. Allen, was a Los Angeles–based producer, active in the fifties and sixties, and responsible for the filming of some episodes of the syndicated series *Wild Life in Action*.

ALLEND'OR PRODUCTIONS, INC. was founded in 1953 by Algernon G. Walker. Based in Los Angeles, it was a producer of commercials and industrial films, active through 1988.

THE ALLIANCE OF TELEVISION FILM PRODUCERS, INC. was founded in 1951. In 1964, it merged with the Association of Motion Picture Producers to become what is now called the Alliance of Motion Picture and Television Producers, to which all major television and film producers belong.
Address: 14144 Ventura Boulevard, 3rd Floor, Sherman Oaks, CA 91423.

ALL-SCOPE PICTURES, INC. was a Los Angeles–based producer of television commercials, founded by Gordon S. Mitchell in July 1946 (at which time it was producing industrial and sports films). In the sixties, it relocated to the Fox Western Avenue Studios lot, and functioned as the television commercial film division of 20th Century–Fox. At this time, a number of studios, including M-G-M, Universal, and Columbia–Screen Gems, operated divisions strictly for the production of filmed television commercials. In the seventies, 20th Century–Fox operated Wylde Films, Inc. for this purpose.

ALPHA TELEVISION PRODUCTIONS, INC. Founded by Chester Erskine, Alpha Television Productions, Inc. was the Los Angeles–based producer of *TV Reader's Digest* (ABC, 1955–1956).

ALPHAVENTURE was the company responsible for the production, between 1974 and 1978, of the children's series *The Big Blue Marble*, created by Harry Fownes and sponsored by ITT. In later years, the program was produced by the Blue Marble Co.

ALTERNATIVE VIEW NETWORK is a cable network, broadcasting religious programming from 7:30 A.M. to 1:00 P.M. on Sundays only. It was launched in October 1985.
Address: 400 Common Street, Shreveport, LA 71101.

ALTO BROADCASTING introduced television to the Philippines in 1953 on DZAQ-TV. Later, it joined with Chronicle Broadcasting to form ABS-CBN, the country's leading television network. (Broadcasting in the Philippines comes under the National Telecommunications Commission, Ministry of Transport and Communications, David Gutierrez Building, Scout Reyes Corner, Panay Avenue, Quezon City 3008, Philippines.)
Address: Mother Ignacia Avenue, Quezon City, 3008, Philippines.

ALTON ALEXANDER PRODUCTIONS, INC. was a minor New York–based producer of television programming (chiefly commercials), active in the fifties and early sixties.

ALUMINUM CO. OF AMERICA, represented by the advertising agency of Fuller, Smith & Ross, sponsored four different dramatic anthology series: *The Alcoa Hour* (NBC, 1955–1957), *Alcoa Theatre* (NBC, 1957–1960), *Alcoa Pre-*

sents (ABC, 1959–1961), and *Alcoa Premiere* (ABC, 1961–1962). The first was one of the major drama series from "the Golden Age of Television."* The company also sponsored Edward R. Murrow's *See It Now*, and supported him, despite threats of a boycott, in his March 9, 1954, attack on Senator Joseph R. McCarthy.

AMEN (American Music Entertainment Network) was a short-lived Christian-music cable network, based in Louisville, Kentucky, and active only in 1986. It was created by Al Gannoway and Bill Airy, and its programming was seen only in Southern states.

AMERICAN-BRITISH TV MOVIES, INC. was a New York–based distributor of British features and television series (including *Muffin the Mule* and *Case Histories of Scotland Yard*), active in the fifties. It was owned by Nat Kramer.

THE AMERICAN FAMILY BROADCAST GROUP, INC. is a division of American Family Corp. (incorporated 1973) as a successor to American Family Life Assurance Co. (incorporated 1955). It owns seven television stations: WAFF-Huntsville, Alabama; WTVM-Columbus, Georgia; WTOC-Savannah, Georgia; KWWL-Waterloo, Iowa; WAFB–Baton Rouge; KFVS–Cape Girardeau, Missouri; and WITN-Washington, North Carolina. In 1980, it acquired the Blackhawk Broadcasting Co.

   Address: 375 Macon Road, Suite 15, Columbus, GA 31907.

AMERICAN FILM PRODUCERS/PRODUCTIONS, INC. was a New York–based producer of television commercials and distributor of television programs, founded in 1946 by Robert Gross. Active through 1988, it was, according to the 1953 *Television Yearbook*, one of the first companies to standardize the packaging and labeling of commercials.

AMERICAN MOVIE CLASSICS is the only national cable network devoted to the exclusive programming with no commercial interruptions of Hollywood feature films and short subjects from the thirties through the seventies. Since the channel's inception, its films have been hosted by former actor Bob Dorian. A division of Rainbow Programming Services Corp.,* American Movie Classics (AMC) was launched on October 1, 1984, with 300,000 original subscribers. Its original principal owners were CBS* and Cablevision Systems Corp. In 1986, CBS sold its share to Rainbow, which resold it to Tele-Communications, Inc.* In 1985, AMC became involved in a major legal dispute with Turner Broadcasting System, Inc.* and MGM/UA over its $45 million exclusive cable-licensing agreement for 1,600 films from MGM/UA, to be aired over a ten-year period. The lawsuits were dropped, and MGM/UA paid Rainbow $50 million.

   In December 1989, AMC announced plans for the production of original programming with an initial budget allocation of $20 million. American Movie

Classics broadcasts approximately sixty feature films a month, and is offered to subscribers as a bonus to basic cable.

Address: 150 Crossways Park West, Woodbury, NY 11797.

BIBLIOGRAPHY

Beermann, Frank, "American Movie Classic [sic] To Get Basic Cable Play," *Daily Variety*, September 9, 1985, p. 6.

Daniels, Bill, "$50 Mil Windfall Primes Rainbow Pic-Service Pump," *Daily Variety*, November 27, 1985, pp. 1, 29.

Girard, Tom, "Movie Classics Pay Service Lines Up Pix," *Daily Variety*, September 13, 1984, pp. 1, 17.

Knoll, Steve, "New Service Shops for Vintage Films," *New York Times*, July 15, 1984, section 2, p. 22.

Mitchell, Kim, "American Movie Classics Counts 6 Mil Subscribers for its Vintage Films," *Daily Variety*, June 15, 1987, pp. 116, 120.

THE AMERICAN SOCIETY OF TV CAMERAMEN is a fraternal organization for working cameramen, offering seminars and promoting professionalism within the industry, and founded in 1974. A related organization (with the same address) is the International Society of Videographers, founded in 1981.

Address: Box 296, Sparkill, NY 10976.

THE AMERICAN SPORTSCASTERS ASSOCIATION, founded in 1979, is a fraternal organization of more than 500 radio and television sports commentators. It sponsors seminars, maintains information on its membership, and holds the annual Sportscasters Hall of Fame.

Address: 150 Nassau Street, New York, NY 10038.

AMERICAN TV ENTERPRISES (Louise DeWitt, president) was a Los Angeles–based producer of television commercials, active in the fifties.

AMERICAN WOMEN IN RADIO AND TELEVISION was founded in 1951 as a professional organization for women holding creative, administrative, and executive positions in the industry. With more than 3,000 members, its activities include an educational foundation, awards presentations, and a publications program.

Address: 1101 Connecticut Avenue, N.W., Suite 700, Washington, DC 20036.

AMPEX, a major name in the introduction of audio magnetic tape-recording, was founded in 1944 by the Russian-born Alexander Mathew Poniatoff (1892–1980)—the first three letters of the company name are his initials. In December 1951, the company authorized research into a professional videotape-recording system for television. The six-man team involved consisted of Charles E. Anderson, Ray Dolby, Alex Maxey, Shelby Henderson, Charles Ginsberg, and Fred Pfost. On April 14, 1956, Ampex introduced the first practical videotape recorder, Mark IV, at the National Association of Radio and Television Broadcasters convention in Chicago. CBS* was the first network to use the new machine on the air, for the November 30, 1956, broadcast of *Douglas Edwards and the News*. In 1968, in association with ABC,* Ampex introduced a two-tube color camera, the only competitor at the time to a similar camera created in 1964 by Toshiba.

On January 15, 1981, Ampex merged into Signal Companies, Inc., which in turn merged into Allied-Signal, Inc. on September 19, 1985. Allied-Signal discontinued the operations of Ampex Corp. on March 31, 1987.

ANALOG and DIGITAL. The two terms most commonly used in the field of audio tape-recording for radio and television are analog and digital. Analog sound recording is an audio recording system wherein the electrical sound signal fluctuates exactly like (*analog*ous to) the original sound stimulus over its entire range. The digital recording system, which has a better signal-to-noise ratio, is an audio recording system that translates original sound stimuli into many computer-like on–off pulses. Digital recording is sometimes called "transparent" because it does not pick up superfluous or system-induced noise.

ANGLIA TELEVISION is the independent ("commercial") television network for the east of England (covering Norfolk, Suffolk, Cambridgeshire, Bedfordshire, Northamptonshire, most of Essex, and parts of Hertfordshire, Buckinghamshire, Leicestershire, and south Lincolnshire). It was formed by a group that included *The Guardian* and Romulus Films, under the leadership of Lord Townshend, and began broadcasting on October 27, 1959.

While American viewers may be familiar with the P.D. James mysteries from Anglia, the best known of the more than 500 hours of independent programming produced each year by the network is the *Survival* series. The latter, produced by the subsidiary company, Survival Anglia Ltd., is Britain's most successful television export, and was the first British program to be seen in China. *Survival* originated in a fifteen-minute series, *Countryman*, started in June 1960. The first *Survival* program was *The London Scene*, broadcast in January 1961, with Aubrey Buxton narrating. That same year, Colin Willock joined Anglia as the head of its Natural History Unit, and guided and expanded the *Survival* series.

Address: Anglia House, Norwich NR1 3JG, United Kingdom.

BIBLIOGRAPHY

Davis, Anthony, editor. . . . *the first twenty-one years*. Norwich, U.K.: Anglia, 1980.
Patterson, Richard, "The Perfect International Project: Anglia Television's *Survival*," in *International TV & Video Guide 1987*. London: Tantivy Press, 1988, pp. 29–31.

ANIK, which means "little brother" in the language of the Inuit Indians, was the first Canadian communications satellite, launched from Cape Canaveral on November 9, 1972. Five channels of ANIK were leased in 1982 by United

Satellite Communication Incorporated to provide the first satellite, direct-to-home television service.

ANIMALS have been featured in all genres of American television. The more popular of the wildlife/nature series have been *Animal Express* (Syndicated, 1986); *Lorne Greene's Last of the Wild* (Syndicated, 1974–1979); *Safari to Adventure*, with Bill Burrud (Syndicated, 1969–1975); *Wild Kingdom*, starring Marlin Perkins until his death in 1986 (NBC, 1968–1971; Syndicated, 1971 to present); and *The Wild, Wild World of Animals*, with William Conrad (Syndicated, 1973–1978). *Mr. Ed* (CBS, 1961–1965) featured a talking horse, and a 1951 syndicated series, *The Chimps*, had a cast of chimpanzees starring in an ongoing detective drama. Betty White welcomed animals and their pets on *The Pet Set* (Syndicated, 1971), produced by her husband Allen Ludden. An earlier program, *Pet Shop* (DuMont, 1951–1953) was hosted by Gail Compton, and encouraged the adoption of homeless animals. Major drama series that have starred animals are *The Adventures of Champion*, Gene Autry's horse (CBS, 1955–1956); *The Adventures of Rin Tin Tin* (Syndicated, 1954–1959); *Elephant Boy* (Syndicated, 1973); *Flipper* (NBC, 1964–1967); *Fury* (NBC, 1955–1966); *Lassie* (CBS, 1954–1971), and *Sergeant Preston of the Yukon*, with the dog Yukon King (Syndicated, 1958).

Other series featuring animals are *Animals, Animals, Animals* (ABC, 1976–1981); *Animal Clinic* (ABC, 1950–1951); *Animal Secrets* (NBC, 1966–1967); *Daktari* (CBS, 1966–1969); *Jambo* (NBC, 1969–1971); *The Life and Times of Grizzly Adams* (NBC, 1977–1978); *McDuff, the Talking Dog* (NBC, 1976); *Me and the Chimp* (CBS, 1972); *Meet Me at the Zoo* (CBS, 1953); *My Friend Flicka* (CBS, 1956–1957); *Sunday at the Bronx Zoo* (ABC, 1950); *Those Amazing Animals* (ABC, 1980–1981); *Your Pet Parade* (ABC, 1951); and *Zoorama* (CBS, 1965).

Mrs. Barbara Woodhouse became a household name on both British and American television with her various programs: *Training Dogs the Woodhouse Way* (BBC, 1980), *The Woodhouse World of Animals* (BBC, 1980), *Barbara Woodhouse Goes to Beverly Hills* (Yorkshire Television, 1981), *Barbara's World of Horses and Ponies* (BBC, 1981), and *Barbara Woodhouse's Roadshow* (BBC, 1982).

BIBLIOGRAPHY

"The Orangutan Upstaged Jimmy Stewart," *TV Guide*, December 4, 1971, pp. 43–45.

ANIMATED PRODUCTIONS, INC. is a New York–based producer of animated television programs and commercials, founded in 1946 by Al Stahl (who had commenced his career with Max Fleischer).

Address: 1600 Broadway, New York, NY 10019.

ANIMATION, INC. was a Los Angeles–based producer of animated television commercials, founded in 1955 by Earl Klein, and active through the mid-sixties.

ANSO PRODUCTIONS was formed by Ann Sothern (born 1909) to produce *The Ann Sothern Show* (CBS, 1958–1961). A few years earlier, Miss Sothern had created Vincent Productions (named for her patron saint) to take care of financial matters relating to her earlier television success, *Private Secretary/Susie* (CBS, 1953–1957).

THE "ANTI-SIPHONING" RULE was introduced by the FCC* in 1970. It prevented cable television operators from offering feature films to their subscribers unless such films had been rejected by "free television" broadcasters. It also introduced fines for cable operators airing games involving sports that had been seen on a broadcast station in the same community in the past two years, and forbade cable operators from airing syndicated programs. These discriminatory rulings against the cable television industry were struck down by the U.S. Court of Appeals for the District of Columbia in 1977.

THE ARAB STATES BROADCASTING UNION was founded in February 1969 as an intergovernmental body within the League of Arab States.
Address: 22a Taha Hussein Street, Zamalek, Cairo, Egypt.

ARBITRON was the only major competitor of A.C. Nielsen* in offering a television ratings system from the fifties through the present. The Arbitron ratings system was introduced in January 1958 after being developed by the American Research Bureau. It gave network executives and advertising agencies immediate information about what a viewer was watching and when he or she switched channels or turned off the set. It was initially operational in New York, Chicago, and Los Angeles. The company also introduced the ADI (Area of Dominant Influence), which defines dominant areas of television viewing concentrated on a central city or town. Somewhat obviously, the No. 1 ADI is New York City, with 7,043,900 television households (as of 1989–1990). The smallest ADI is Alpena, Michigan, No. 209, with 15,500 television households. Arbitron's ADI information is published each year in *The Broadcasting Yearbook*.
    The Arbitron Ratings Co. is a subsidiary of Control Data Corporation.
    Address: Metropolitan Tower, 142 West 57 Street, New York, NY 10019.
BIBLIOGRAPHY
Head, Sydney W., and Christopher H. Sterling, "Audience Measurement and Testing," in *Broadcasting in America: A Survey of Electronic Media*. Boston: Houghton Mifflin, 1987, pp. 373–403.
"Instant Ratings," *TV Guide*, February 22, 1958, pp. 10–11.

ARD is the acronym for Arbeitsgemeinschaft der öffentlich-rechtlichen Rundfunkanstalten der Bundesrepublik Deutschland (The Association of Public Broadcasting Corporations in the Federal Republic of Germany). One of two German nationwide public networks—the other is ZDF*—ARD was established in June 1950, and began broadcasting in 1952. It is financed through advertising and license fees, and its members are: Bayerischer Rundfunk (Munich), Hessischer

Rundfunk (Frankfurt am Main), Norddeutscher Rundfunk (Hamburg), Radio Bremen (Bremen), Saarländischer Rundfunk (Saarbrucken), Sender Freies Berlin (West Berlin), Süddeutscher Rundfunk (Stuttgart), Südwestfunk (Baden-Baden), Westdeutscher Rundfunk (Cologne), Deutsche Welle (Cologne), and Deutsch- landfunk (Cologne).

Address: Arnulfstrasse 42, Munich 2, D–8000 Germany.

BIBLIOGRAPHY

Brack, Hans. *German Radio and Television: Organization and Economic Basis*. Geneva: EBU, 1968.

Collins, Richard, and Vincent Porter. *WDR and the Arbeiterfilm: Fassbinder, Ziewer and Others*. London: British Film Institute, 1981.

ARGYLE TELEVISION FILMS, INC. was a New York–based distributor of minor features for television, usually British, founded in 1952 by Louis Gold- stein, and active through 1957.

THE ARMED FORCES BROADCASTING ASSOCIATION is a fraternal organization for former and current military broadcasters, founded in 1982.

Address: P.O. Box 12013, Arlington, VA 22209.

THE ARMED FORCES RADIO AND TELEVISION SERVICE. The Armed Forces Radio Service was formed in 1942 as part of the Information and Edu- cation Division of the War Department, when Col. Thomas H.A. Lewis was requested by President Franklin D. Roosevelt to organize a service providing radio entertainment to service personnel throughout the world. Lewis was a former vice-president of the Young & Rubicam advertising agency and the husband of Loretta Young, and with his connections was able to secure major creative talent for the new service. The Armed Forces Radio Service became the Armed Forces Radio and Television Service in 1954, following experimental tests with television broadcasts at Limestone Air Force Base in Maine; by 1956, twenty television stations were operational.

Address: 10888 La Tuna Canyon, Sun Valley, CA 91352.

BIBLIOGRAPHY

Kirby, Edward M., and Jack W. Harris. *Star-Spangled Radio*. Chicago: Ziff-Davis, 1948.

Link, Tom, "The GI Joe Network," *Emmy*, vol. XII, no. 4, July/August 1990, pp. 70– 74.

[J. (JOSEPH)] ARMSTRONG & CO. was a New York–based producer of television commercials, active in the fifties and sixties.

THE ARMY-MCCARTHY HEARINGS, which began on April 22, 1954, were seen in their entirety on ABC* and in substantial part on CBS,* DuMont,* and NBC.* The unedited televising of the hearings presented such a negative impression of Senator Joseph McCarthy to the American people that they became largely responsible for his political downfall. Public opinion was also influenced by Edward R. Murrow's "A Report on Senator Joseph R. McCarthy," on *See It Now*, broadcast on CBS on March 9, 1954.

ARNOLD SHAPIRO PRODUCTIONS, INC. was founded in 1981, and is best known for its production of *Scared Straight*, first seen on KTLA–Los Angeles* on November 2, 1978. Two sequels followed: *Scared Straight!: Another Story* (CBS, 1980) and *Scared Straight!: 10 Years Later* (Syndicated, 1987). The company is also responsible for *Rescue 911* (CBS, 1989-   ).
   Address: 5800 Sunset Boulevard, Hollywood, CA 90028.

ARROWHEAD PRODUCTIONS was a Los Angeles–based company, active in the fifties and early sixties, and founded by Ed Beloin. It was responsible for the 1955 syndicated series *So This Is Hollywood*.

THE ARTHUR COMPANY was formed in 1983 by Arthur L. Annecharico, and as of June 1, 1986, entered into a production partnership with MCA, Inc. Since its inception, the Arthur Company has produced *Down to Earth* (Cable, 1984), *Safe at Home* (Cable, 1985), *Rocky Road* (Cable, 1985), *Comedy Challenge* (Pilot, 1986), *The O'Brians* (Pilot, 1986), *Here To Stay* (Pilot, 1986), *Airwolf* (Syndicated, 1987), *The Munsters Today* (Syndicated, 1988–1990), *The New Adam–12* (Syndicated, 1989–1990), *The New Dragnet* (Syndicated, 1989–1990), and *What a Dummy* (Syndicated, 1990).
   Address: 100 Universal City Plaza, Universal City, CA 91608.
BIBLIOGRAPHY
Girard, Tom, "MCA-Arthur Prod'n Partnership," *Daily Variety*, May 6, 1986, pp. 1, 14.

ARTISTS' TELEVISION ACCESS was founded in 1983 to provide low-cost and subsidized access to VHS video facilities and access to exhibition space for video artists.
   Address: 992 Valencia Street, San Francisco, CA 94110.

THE ARTS CHANNEL was a short-lived British cable network, owned by the WH Smith Group plc, Television South, and others, which began broadcasting on September 29, 1985. It was taken over by United Programming in 1988 and ceased operations at the beginning of 1989.

THE ASIA-PACIFIC BROADCASTING UNION was founded in 1964 as an association of broadcasters in forty-seven countries; it presents the annual Asiavision Awards.
   Address: P.O. Box 1164, 59700 Kuala Lumpur, Malaysia.

ASSOCIATED ARTISTS PRODUCTIONS, INC. was a New York–based distribution company, founded in 1949 by Eliot Hyman (1904–1980) and others. Hyman bought out his partners and acquired sole ownership of the company in

1950. Inactive for a couple of years, Associated Artists Productions (AAP) was revived in 1953, and three years later purchased the Warner Bros. library of approximately 1,500 short subjects, 750 features, and 337 cartoons. These were the first major studio films available to television; in addition, AAP distributed *Johnny Jupiter* (DuMont, 1953; Syndicated, 1954) and *Candid Camera* (NBC, 1953). In 1958, AAP was purchased by United Artists, and Hyman became president of the new company, which was renamed United Artists Associated, Inc.

ASSOCIATED BROADCAST ADVERTISING CO. was a Los Angeles–based producer of television commercials, founded by Irwin T. and Gertrude T. Porter, and active in the fifties and early sixties.

ASSOCIATED ENTERPRISES was a Los Angeles–based producer of television commercials and packager of television shows. Founded by Robert Struble, it was active in the early fifties.

ASSOCIATED PROGRAM SERVICE was a New York–based division of Muzak Corp., distributing television programs (usually of an educational nature), together with 1,186 feature films for television. It was active in the early fifties.

ASSOCIATION FILMS, INC. Founded in 1953 by J.R. Bingham, Association Films, Inc. was a New York–based distributor of public service films and programs for television. It became Association Sterling Films in 1970 and ceased operations in 1981. A related company was Sterling Movies U.S.A., Inc.

THE ASSOCIATION FOR COMPETITIVE TELEVISION was a Washington, D.C.–based trade organization, active in the sixties.

THE ASSOCIATION OF INDEPENDENT TELEVISION STATIONS, INC. was formed in 1972 through the efforts of Roger Rice. It was created to represent the interests of television stations that are not affiliated with the three major networks. Initially based in New York, it moved to Washington, D.C., in 1981.
   Address: 1200 18 Street, N.W., Suite 502, Washington, DC 20036.
BIBLIOGRAPHY
Gunther, Noel, "INTV: The Mouse That Roared," *Channels of Communications*, vol. VIII, no. 1, January 1988, pp. 66–68.

THE ASSOCIATION OF MAXIMUM SERVICE TELECASTERS, INC. was founded in 1956, dedicated, according to contemporary publicity, "to insuring maximum television service to the American people. Consistent with this objective it favors efforts to expand and develop television service throughout the United States but opposes any compromise or deterioration of the technical quality or service now being provided.'' The association continues to operate, determined to assure the maintenance and development of a free, over-the-air nationwide television system.

Address: 1730 M Street, N.W., Suite 713, Washington, DC 20036.

THE ASSOCIATION OF RADIO-TELEVISION NEWS ANALYSTS is a defunct organization, which was founded in 1942. Many famous names, including Robert Trout, H.V. Kaltenborn, and Chet Huntley, were involved with the association, which, according to contemporary publicity, was formed ''to maintain the independence and prestige of the profession and to improve the standards of analytical broadcasting and to protect the best interests of the public and the industry.''

ATLANTIC TELEVISION CORP. was created in the late forties by Astor Pictures Corporation to distribute its 200 feature films to television. Like Astor, Atlantic was owned by Robert M. Savini; both companies were purchased by Franklin F. Bruder in 1959, and both filed for bankruptcy in 1963.

ATLAS TELEVISION CORPORATION was a New York–based company, active in the fifties, which was founded in 1948 by Henry Brown (a former exhibitor and theatre owner) to distribute a library of minor American and British Westerns, comedies, and musical shorts.

AUDIENCE TESTED PRODUCTIONS was a Los Angeles–based producer of television programs and commercials. Founded by Bernard D. Cirlin, it was active in the fifties.

AUDIO-ONLY CABLE NETWORKS. The following is a listing of audio-only cable networks, with their addresses and the years in which they first commenced broadcasting. All can be heard twenty-four hours a day:

Cable Radio Network (10487 Sunland Boulevard, Sunland, CA 91040; 1982)

Classical (AEI Music Network, 3717 National Drive, Suite 109, Raleigh, NC 27612; 1989)

C-SPAN Audio 1 (400 North Capitol Street, N.W., Washington, DC 20001; 1989)

C-SPAN Audio 2 (400 North Capitol Street, N.W., Washington, DC 20001; 1989)

Debut (AEI Music Network, 3717 National Drive, Suite 109, Raleigh, NC 27612; 1989)

Galactic Radio (9697 East Mineral Avenue, Englewood, CO 80112; 1987)

Greek Radio Network of America (60 Old State Road, Media, PA 19063; 1983)

The Jazz Network (KKJZ/United Video, 3801 South Sheridan Road, Tulsa, OK 74145; 1983)

Lifestyle (AEI Music Network, 3717 National Drive, Suite 109, Raleigh, NC 27612; 1979)

Moody Broadcasting Network (820 North LaSalle Drive, Chicago, IL 60610; 1982)

Startracks (AEI Music Network, 3717 National Drive, Suite 109, Raleigh, NC 27612; 1984)

Tempo Sound (ICT, 342 Madison Avenue, Suite 505, New York, NY 10173; 1984)

WFMT (United Video, 3801 South Sheridan Road, Tulsa, OK 74145; 1979)

AUDIO PRODUCTIONS, INC. was a New York–based producer of television commercials, founded in 1933 as an industrial film producer by Frank K. Speidell. Later, it became a division of Visualscope Inc. and then became a division of Reeves Teletape, Inc. in 1977.

Address: 227 East 45 Street, New York, NY 10017.

AURORA FILM DISTRIBUTORS, INC. was an Omaha, Nebraska–based distributor of feature films and shorts to television, owned by Keith T. Smith, and active in the fifties and early sixties. It also handled the thirty-minute syndicated series *Sleepy Joe* (1956). A related and still active company owned by Smith is Modern Sound Pictures, Inc., which distributes to television, forty-five feature films, primarily British-produced, but also including Cecil B. DeMille's *King of Kings* (1927), to which it owns all rights.

Address: Modern Sound Pictures, Inc., 1402 Howard Street, Omaha, NE 68102.

THE AUSTRALIAN BROADCASTING CORPORATION (ABC) was founded in June 1932 as the Australian Broadcasting Commission, financed through license fees paid by radio listeners. In 1942, the government introduced the Broadcasting and Television Act to regulate all radio and television broadcasting in Australia; the act was amended in 1948 to permit the creation of the Australian Broadcasting Control Board (later renamed the Australian Broadcasting Tribunal) and to allow for additional funding of ABC.

Experimental television was first seen in Australia in Brisbane in 1934. Australia's first television station was TCN–9 (Sydney), which began broadcasting on July 13, 1956, and became the first television station in Australia to commence official transmission, on October 2, 1956. In 1968, ABC adopted the PAL* color system, and color television was introduced in March 1975. *AUSSAT*, Australia's first communications satellite, was launched in 1985. The Australian Broadcasting Corporation was reconstituted under the Australian Broadcasting Corporation Act 1983, and is responsible to the Parliament through the minister for communications.

Address: 145–153 Elizabeth Street, Sydney 2001, Australia.

BIBLIOGRAPHY

Allen, Yolanda, and Susan Spencer. *The Broadcasting Chronology, 1809–1980*. North Ryde, Australia: Australian Film and Television School, 1983.

Beilby, Peter, editor. *Australian TV: The First 25 Years*. Melbourne: Nelson/Cinema Papers, 1981.

Hall, Sandra. *Super Toy: Twenty Years of Australian Television*. Melbourne: Sun Books, 1977.

Inglis, K.S., assisted by Jan Brazier. *This Is the ABC: The Australian Broadcasting Commission, 1932–1983*. Carlton, Australia: Melbourne University Press, 1983.

Kippax, Susan, and John P. Murray. *Small Screen Big Business*. Melbourne: Angus & Robertson, 1979.

AUTHORS PLAYHOUSE, INC., owned by Eugene Solow and Brewster Morgan, was the producer of *Dr. Hudson's Secret Journal* (Syndicated, 1955–1956), starring John Howard as the character created by Lloyd C. Douglas. The company also produced three dramas under the collective title of ''John Steinbeck's The Pastures of Heaven'' for the CBS series, *Omnibus*, in 1954. These dramas, together with others, were released in syndication under the series title of ''Curtain Call Theatre.'' Additional dramas produced by Authors Playhouse, Inc. were released in syndication under the collective title of ''Authors Playhouse.''

AVASTA PRODUCTIONS was responsible for *Alcoa Premiere* (ABC, 1962–1963).

AVCO BROADCASTING CORP. was a major owner of television stations, which it had acquired from Crosley Broadcasting (founded in 1922 by Powell Crosley). The corporation was headed by John T. Murphy (born 1913), who had been vice-president in charge of television at Crosley from 1951 to 1957. The stations that Avco owned from 1966 to 1977 were WLWT-Cincinnati; WLWD-Dayton, Ohio; WLWC-Columbus, Ohio; WLWI-Indianapolis; and WMOL–San Antonio, Texas.

AWARD TELEVISION CORP., founded by Milton J. Salzberg, was a New York–based producer of television programming and commercials, active in the fifties. Its best-known production was *The Jimmy Demaret Show* (CBS, 1954), on which the golfer interviewed prominent personalities.

B

[ALBERT R.] BAILEY FILMS, INC. was a Los Angeles–based packager of minor television programs and educational films, active in the fifties and early sixties.

THE [TED] BAILEY ORGANIZATION, INC. was a major New York television-oriented public relations company, active from the forties through the sixties. In its early years, it was also involved in television production.

BAIRD TELEVISION LTD. was formed in June 1925 to exploit the thirty-line mechanical television* system of Scottish inventor John Logic Baird (1888–1946). Two other companies were later floated to exploit the invention, Baird Television Development Company (April 1927) and Baird International Television (June 1928). The three companies were merged in March 1930.

The first license for a television station in the United Kingdom (2TV-London) was issued to Baird in August 1926, and on September 30, 1929, the BBC* began the transmission of the Baird programs. However, the BBC dropped the Baird system in 1936, and Baird's company quickly disappeared.

BIBLIOGRAPHY

Baird, John Logie. *Sermons, Soap and Television: Autobiographical Notes*. London: Royal Television Society, 1988.

Baird, Margaret. *Television Baird: The Story of the Man Who Invented Television*. Cape Town, South Africa: Haun, 1973.

Hallet, Michael. *John Logie Baird and Television*. London: Priory Press, 1978.

McArthur, Tom, and Peter Waddell. *The Secret Life of John Logie Baird*. London: Hutchinson, 1986.

———. *Vision Warrior: The Hidden Achievement of John Logie Baird*. Kirkwall, Orkney, U.K.: The Orkney Press, 1990.

Tiltman, Ronald F. *Baird of Television: The Story of John Logie Baird*. London: Seeley Service, n.d.

BALLET. Despite the success of *Barishnikov on Broadway* (ABC, 1980), ballet has held little, if any, appeal to network television. Anton Dolin and Alicia Markova were seen in early experimental broadcasts by NBC* in the mid-thirties. Perhaps the first ballet to be seen on network television was the Royal Ballet Company's production of *The Sleeping Beauty*, starring Michael Soames and Margot Fonteyn, and shown as part of NBC's *Producer's Showcase* on December 12, 1955. Aside from occasional brief appearances by ballet dancers and companies, such as those by the New York City Ballet and Ballet Espagnol on *Bell Telephone Hour* (NBC, 1959), ballet on television has been limited to presentations on PBS.*

The first complete televised ballet on British television was William Walton's *Façade*, danced by Margot Fonteyn and Robert Helpmann, and seen on the BBC* on December 8, 1936.

BIBLIOGRAPHY

Sorgen, Carol, "Pas de Tube," *Emmy*, vol. VI, no. 5, September/October 1984, pp. 24–28, 62.

B & R ENTERPRISES, INC. was formed by Ray Bolger and Jerry Bresler for the production of *The Ray Bolger Show* (ABC, 1953–1955).

THE BANFF TELEVISION FESTIVAL was founded in 1979 to recognize "excellence in television films and programs" with trophies and cash awards. It is held each summer.

Address: Banff Centre, St. Julien Road/Box 1020, Banff, Alberta, Canada T0L O6O.

BANNER FILMS, INC. was owned by Sol and Julian Lesser and was active in the fifties and sixties as both a producer and a distributor for television. Its most successful production was *Bold Journey* (ABC, 1956–1959), with other series including *I Search for Adventure* (Syndicated, 1954), *Night Court USA* (Syndicated, 1958), and *Crime and Punishment* (Syndicated, 1961). Among the series that Banner distributed were *Judge Roy Bean* (Syndicated, 1955) and *Big World of Little Adam* (Syndicated, 1964); it also distributed many features, cartoons, and serials to television (including the Pine-Thomas–produced features). A related company was Julian Lesser's Television Adventure Films Corp.

BARNABY PRODUCTIONS is the production company of singer Andy Williams, responsible for *The Andy Williams Show* (ABC 1958; NBC, 1962–1967, 1969–1971), and a number of television specials.

BARRIS INDUSTRIES, INC./BARRIS PRODUCTIONS, INC. The producer who most disturbed television critics in the sixties with his tasteless, but extremely popular, series was Chuck Barris (born 1929). It is perhaps difficult to believe that television could offer anything worse than *The Dating Game*

(ABC, 1965–1973; Syndicated, 1973–1974, 1977–1980), and *The Newlywed Game* (ABC, 1966–1974; Syndicated, 1977–1980), but Chuck Barris proved it possible with *The Gong Show* (Syndicated, 1976–1980), which he hosted, and *The $1.98 Beauty Contest* (Syndicated, 1978–1979), hosted by Rip Taylor. Barris revived his two ABC series through his Bel Air Productions: *The New Newlywed Game* (Syndicated, 1985-   ) and *The All-New Dating Game* (Syndicated, 1986-   ).

BARRY & ENRIGHT PRODUCTIONS, INC. was founded in New York in 1946 by Jack Barry (1918–1984), who served as president, and Don Enright, who was vice-president. The company produced many popular game shows, some of which were first introduced on radio, and many of which had Jack Barry as their host: *Juvenile Jury* (NBC, 1947–1953; CBS, 1954), *Life Begins at 80* (NBC, 1950; ABC, 1950–1952; DuMont, 1952–1955; ABC, 1955–1956), *Twenty-One* (NBC, 1956–1958), *High Low* (NBC, 1957–1958), *Tic-Tac-Dough* (NBC, 1957–1958), *Dough Re Mi* (NBC, 1958–1960), and *Concentration* (NBC, 1958–1973). The rights to the last show were acquired by NBC.*

The company was badly affected by the quiz show scandals of 1957 to 1959 and ceased operations in the latter year. The partnership was revived in 1975. It owns 50 percent of Colbert TV Sales, which distributes its product, and is active as a theatrical producer (*Private Lessons* [1981], *Next of Kin* [1989], and others); it has also produced a number of made-for-television movies, including *The Cover Girl and the Cop* (NBC, 1988).

Address: 1888 Century Park East, Suite 1100, Los Angeles, CA 90067.

THE BARTER SYSTEM permits sponsors or syndicators to provide programs to television stations either at no cost or at a minimal charge in return for free advertising space. The idea first gained prominence in 1955, when the California soft drink manufacturer Cantrell & Cochrane distributed the RKO features to television on this basis. The three most successful shows distributed on the barter system are *The Lawrence Welk Show*, *Hee Haw*, and *Wild Kingdom*. In 1989, Paramount distributed nine feature films on a barter system, with the split being ten-and-a-half minutes of advertising time retained by Paramount and eleven-and-a-half minutes for the television stations involved. *Daily Variety* (May 3, 1989) estimated that Paramount would gross $700,000 for each title.

Cash/Barter is a form of the barter system whereby the distributor or syndicator receives some cash payment for the show but also retains some advertising time.

THE BBC (THE BRITISH BROADCASTING CORPORATION). The initials most synonymous with integrity and quality of broadcasting are those of the British Broadcasting Corporation, the BBC, often referred to in the United Kingdom as "the Beebe." As of 1990, the BBC transmitted 11,000 hours of television and 30,000 hours of radio programming each year. It carries no advertising and no sponsored programming, and is almost entirely funded through license fees paid by owners of television receivers. Additional government funding is made available to finance the twenty-four-hour English-Language World Service of BBC Radio, and the BBC's radio broadcasts in thirty-six languages of news, current affairs, and other programming.

The British Broadcasting Company Ltd. was formed in 1922, and began daily radio broadcasts on November 14 of that year, under license from the Post Office. The company was dissolved in December 1926, and on January 1, 1927, the British Broadcasting Corporation was established by Royal Charter, with J.C.W. Reith (1889–1971) as its first director-general. (Reith had been appointed the company's general manager in 1922, and resigned in 1938.)

The first transmission of television in the United Kingdom was of the thirty-line experimental system from John Logie Baird's Long Acre, London, studio, on August 20, 1929, and the first experimental television play was *The Man with the Flowers in His Mouth*, broadcast on July 14, 1930. While the BBC was required to carry the Baird signals, it originated its own experimental program from Studio BB at Broadcasting House on August 22, 1932. The first experimental transmission from the BBC's Alexandra Palace in North London took place on August 26, 1936, with Leslie Mitchell as the first television announcer. Later that same month, Elizabeth Cowell became the BBC's, and the world's, first female television announcer.

Official inauguration of a regular television service by the BBC, from Alexandra Palace, using both the 240-line Baird and the 405-line Marconi-EMI systems, took place on November 2, 1936. The Baird system was abandoned within three months. Alexandra Palace remained the BBC's main transmitter until 1956, when it was replaced by the Crystal Palace in South London.

With the outbreak of World War II, the BBC abandoned regular television transmission for defense reasons, on September 1, 1939. Service was resumed on June 7, 1946, but was still limited to London and its environs. It was not until December 1949 that a second transmitter was opened at Sutton Coldfield, just outside Birmingham, and serving the Midlands regions. On August 27, 1950, the BBC televised its first broadcast from outside the United Kingdom, when Richard Dimbleby (a popular BBC current affairs personality) hosted the celebration of the centenary of the first cross-Channel telegraph cable in Calais, France. In 1960, the purpose-built BBC Television Centre in West London was opened, and on April 20, 1964, a second television channel, BBC2, was introduced. On July 1, 1967, the BBC introduced Europe's first color television service, utilizing the PAL* system.

The BBC maintains a number of divisions. BBC Enterprises is its commercial arm, publishing and marketing programming and program-related materials throughout the world. *Radio Times** and *BBC Wildlife*, a monthly natural-history magazine, are published by BBC Magazines. A subsidiary company, Redwood Publishing, is responsible for an additional group of magazines, including *Intercity*, published as a promotional tool for British Rail. BBC Books publishes more than one-hundred new titles each year, while the Home Entertainment

Department, created in June 1987, handles BBC Video and BBC Records. In the fifties, the BBC acquired the Hulton Picture Library, one of the largest photographic archives in the world, and including all the photographs published in the popular magazine *Picture Post*. The library was sold by the BBC in May 1988 to Brian Deutsch. In the summer of 1990, the corporation announced plans for an affiliated production company, BBC Films, which would finance theatrical features whose budgets were between $4 and $10 million.

Address: Television Centre, Wood Lane, London W12 7RJ, United Kingdom.

BIBLIOGRAPHY

Black, Peter. *The Biggest Aspidistra in the World: A Personal Celebration of Fifty Years of the BBC*. London: BBC, 1972.

Bloomfield, Paul. *B.B.C.* London: Eyre & Spottiswoode, 1941.

Boyle, A. *Only the Wind Will Listen: Reith of the BBC*. London: Hutchinson, 1972.

Briggs, Asa. *The BBC: The First Fifty Years*. Oxford: Oxford University Press, 1985.

Burns, Tom. *The BBC: Public Institution and Private World*. London: Macmillan, 1977.

Green, Hugh C. *The Third Floor Front: A View of Broadcasting in the Sixties*. London: Bodley Head, 1969.

Horner, Rosalie. *Inside BBC Television*. London: BBC, 1983.

Inside BBC Television: A Year behind the Camera. Exeter, Devon, U.K.: Webb & Bower, 1983.

Leapman, Michael. *The Last Days of the Beeb*. London: Allen & Unwin, 1986.

McCabe, Colin, and Olivia Stewart, editors. *The BBC and Public Service Broadcasting*. Manchester, U.K.: Manchester University Press, 1986.

Simon, Ernest. *The BBC from Within*. London: Victor Gollancz, 1953.

Tracey, Michael. *A Variety of Lives: A Biography of Sir Hugh Greene*. London: Bodley Head, 1983.

Trethowan, Ian. *Split Screen*. London: Hamish Hamilton, 1984.

Wolfe, Kenneth M. *The Churches and the British Broadcasting Corporation, 1922–1956: The Politics of Religious Broadcasting*. London: SCM Press, 1984.

BBC LIONHEART TELEVISION INTERNATIONAL, INC. is a wholly owned subsidiary of the BBC,* and responsible for the distribution of all BBC programming in North America. It was founded in May 1981 as Lionheart Television International, a subsidiary of Public Media Inc., another of whose subsidiaries, Films Inc., handled 16mm distribution of the BBC product. The company was formed, following the end of the BBC's contract with Time-Life Films, Inc.,* by six former executives of the latter: Wynn Nathan, Frank Miller, Bob Greenstein, Floyd Osburn, Mark Feldman, and Mary Miller. The BBC's financial interest in the company gradually increased until it became sole owner.

Address: 630 Fifth Avenue, Suite 2220, New York, NY 10111.

BIBLIOGRAPHY

"Ex-T-L Exex Start Lionheart for Yank Syndication of BBC Product," *Daily Variety*, May 8, 1981, p. 4.

BELL PICTURES CORPORATION/BELL FILM EXCHANGE (Sidney Kulick, president) was a New York–based television distributor, active in the fifties and sixties.

BELMAR PRODUCTIONS was responsible for *The Joey Bishop Show* (NBC, 1961–1964; CBS, 1964–1965).

BEMILLER PRODUCTIONS, operated by the Bemiller family (Richard, Ted, and Robert), was a Los Angeles–based producer of live and animated television commercials, active in the fifties.

BILL BURRUD PRODUCTIONS, INC. The best known producer of wildlife adventure series, Bill Burrud Productions, Inc., was organized in 1954 by Bill Burrud (1925–1990), who remained head of the company until 1985, when his son John became president and chief operating officer and he became chairman of the board. The most popular of Burrud's series was *Animal World* (also known as *Animal Kingdom*; NBC, 1968; CBS, 1969; ABC, 1970; CBS, 1971; Syndicated, 1973–1980). Other Burrud series are *Wanderlust* (Syndicated, 1957, 1965), *True Adventure* (Syndicated, 1960–1961), *Island in the Sun* (1965), *The Challenging Seas* (1968), and *Safari to Adventure* (Syndicated, 1971–1973).

In 1959, Burrud co-created Teldynamics as a company to distribute *Treasure* (Syndicated, 1959). In 1978, he founded Communications, Inc. to provide programming for the cable and educational market, and in 1985, Burrud founded The New Company to produce commercials and home videos.

Address: 15922 Pacific Coast Highway, Suite 200, Huntington Harbor, CA 92649.
BIBLIOGRAPHY
McComb, Gordon, "Bill Burrud Productions Places Accent on Adventure," *Millimeter*, July 1979, pp. 140–143, 178–180.

BILL MELENDEZ PRODUCTIONS was founded in 1964 by the highly regarded animator (born 1916), who had earlier been associated with Walt Disney and UPA. It has animated all the Charles M. Schulz/"Charlie Brown" programs, beginning with *A Charlie Brown Christmas*, first seen on CBS on December 9, 1965, and including the series *The Charlie Brown and Snoopy Show* (CBS, 1983–1986); as well as *It's the Great Pumpkin, Charlie Brown* (CBS, 1966) and *A Charlie Brown Thanksgiving* (CBS, 1973).

Address: 439 North Larchmont Boulevard, Los Angeles, CA 90004.

BING CROSBY ENTERPRISES, INC. was founded in 1946 by Harry L. "Bing" Crosby (1904–1977), who served as chairman of the board. It was extremely active in the introduction of magnetic tape into the United States, and helped finance the early activities of Ampex.* On November 11, 1951, the company's Electronic Division, headed by John Mullin, introduced the first working magnetic videotape recorder. The company also produced Crosby's radio show. Basil F. Grillo (born 1910), who had been Crosby's business manager in 1945, served as president of Bing Crosby Enterprises, and, later, became president of the related company, Bing Crosby Productions, Inc., from 1957 to

1969. Bing Crosby Enterprises was dissolved in the early sixties, but the production company remains in existence, and, for many years, was managed by Crosby's brother Everett. Among its productions are *Royal Playhouse* (DuMont, 1951–1952), *The Chimps* (Syndicated, 1951), *Rebound* (ABC, 1952; DuMont, 1952–1953), and *Crown Theater* (Syndicated, 1953). Curiously, Crosby did not use his own production company for his first television series *The Bing Crosby Show* for CBS in 1954. Bing Crosby Productions had an active syndication division in the early seventies, at which time it was "A service of Cox Broadcasting Corp."

Address: Bing Crosby Productions, Inc., 610 South Ardmore Avenue, Los Angeles, CA 90038.

BIOGRAPH TELEVISION CO., INC. was created by Paul Killiam (born 1916) in 1952, when he acquired the rights and the original negatives for all the films of the American Biograph Company. Working in association with Saul J. Turell, Killiam produced the *Movie Museum* series of 176 ten-minute shorts, originally offered for syndication in 1954 and 1955. Each episode consisted of a shortened version of an American Biograph or Edison film, together with a news or actuality item.

Address: 6 East 39 Street, New York, NY 10016.

BIBLIOGRAPHY

"Movie Museum," in *Films on Film History* by Anthony Slide. Metuchen, N.J.: Scarecrow Press, 1979, pp. 136–139.

BLACK AWARENESS IN TELEVISION (BAIT) was founded in Detroit by David Rambeau in 1970 to lobby for black representation in television through training programs and access to broadcasting facilities. It produces the radical black weekly program *For My People*, first seen from 1971 to 1981 on WDET-Detroit, and subsequently on WKDB-Detroit.

Address: 13217 Livernois, Detroit, MI 48238.

BLACK ENTERTAINMENT TELEVISION (BET) is a basic cable network, which dubs itself "The Urban Contemporary Channel" and provides programming for black audiences. As of 1990, it had 27.5 million subscribers. BET was founded by Robert L. Johnson, with a $15,000 personal bank loan and a $500,000 investment from Tele-Communications, Inc.* Totally supported by advertising revenue, it was launched on January 25, 1980, with two hours of programming a week. By 1983, the network was offering six hours of programming a day, and a year later, it introduced twenty-four hour a day programming.

A private company, BET is 48 percent owned by Tele-Communications, Inc., HBO,* and the Great American Broadcasting Company. In the first six years of its operation, it lost $10 million, and it only began to break even in 1986. In September 1990, it entered into a fifty-fifty limited partnership with actor/pro-

ducer Tim Reid to produce black-oriented programming through a new company
called United Image Entertainment.

Address: 1899 9 Street, N.E., Washington, DC 20018.

BIBLIOGRAPHY

Beck, Kirsten, "BET Faces Music, Comes up with Talk," *Channels of Communications*,
vol. 8, no. 6, June 1989, pp. 58–60.

Shiver, Jube, Jr., "Building a Network," *Los Angeles Times*, August 27, 1989, part IV,
pp. 1, 4.

Smith, Sally Bedell, "Cable Network for Blacks Is Marking 5 Years on the Air," *New
York Times*, January 24, 1985, p. 19.

Williams, Christopher C., "A Black Network Makes Its Move," *New York Times*,
September 17, 1989, p. F4.

BLACKLISTING. The anti-Communist hysteria and witch-hunt of the late
forties and early fifties was not limited to the American film industry. As a result
of the publication of their names as individuals with supposed Communist ties
in *Counterattack: The Newsletter of Facts on Communism* and *Red Channels:
The Report of Communist Influence in Radio and Television*, a number of prominent figures in early television were blacklisted and/or fired.

Ireene Wicker saw the cancellation of her popular children's program *The
Singing Lady* (ABC, 1948–1950) because of what were, as it happened, inac-
curate claims of her association with left-wing causes published in *Red Channels*.
Over the objections of the star, Gertrude Berg, Philip Loeb was fired from the
role of Jake Goldberg (on *The Goldbergs*), which he had played on CBS* from
1949 to 1951. Jean Muir was to have played the mother on the television version
of *The Aldrich Family* (NBC, 1949–1953), but was removed at the last minute
because of threats of a boycott against the show's sponsor, General Foods.

Because General Foods was threatened from both sides, both by those who
opposed Jean Muir's appearance and by those who saw General Foods' dismissal
of the actress as a threat to freedom of speech, the company decided that in the
future it would maintain a veil of secrecy over casting decisions involving performers on the anti-Communist blacklist. Advertising agencies and networks
appointed executives as "security officers" to investigate an actor's political
ties, with the most notorious of such figures being Jack Wren of Batten, Barton,
Durstine & Osborn (BBDO).

For a while, the popular series *I Love Lucy* was threatened as a result of
accusations against its star, but in 1953, Lucille Ball appeared before the House
Un-American Activities Committee and cleared her name. "There's nothing red
about Lucy but her hair," claimed her husband, Desi Arnaz.

On August 10, 1955, AFTRA* passed a national referendum stating that if a
member refused to answer the question as to whether he or she was or ever had
been a Communist, he or she would "be subject to the charge that he is guilty
of conduct prejudicial to the welfare of AFTRA" and could be censured or
expelled from membership.

BIBLIOGRAPHY
Cogley, John. *Report on Blacklisting, II: Radio-Television*. New York: The Fund for the
      Republic, 1956.
Navasky, Victor S. *Naming Names*. New York: The Viking Press, 1980.

THE BLACK/MARLENS COMPANY was formed by producers Carol Black and Neal Marlens and is responsible for the production of *The Wonder Years* (ABC, 1988-   ), in association with New World Television. In November 1990, the Black/Marlens Co. signed a four-year contract with Walt Disney Studios.

BLACKS ON TELEVISION. There can be little argument that blacks have only gained a moderate degree of prominence on American television series in recent years, but the reality also is that the first black performers ever to be seen on television were the American vaudeville team of Buck and Bubbles, who appeared on the first BBC* television presentation from Alexandra Palace on November 2, 1936.

On early American television, blacks were reduced to portraying maids— Ethel Waters (1950–1952) and Louise Beavers (1952–1953) on the ABC* series, *Beulah*; or handymen—Willie Best on *The Stu Erwin Show* (ABC, 1950–1955). The first major breakthrough for black performers on television came with *The Nat "King" Cole Show* (NBC, 1956–1957). Earlier black entertainers seen on television include Harry Belafonte on *Sugar Hill Times* (CBS, 1949), Hazel Scott in a show of the same name (DuMont, 1950), and Bob Howard on *Sing It Again* (CBS, 1950–1951).

Bill Cosby made the breakthrough for black Americans in a non-variety series with *I Spy* (NBC, 1965–1968). It was followed by *Julia* (NBC, 1968–1971), with Diahann Carroll; *Barney Miller* (ABC, 1975–1982), with Ron Glass; *The Jeffersons* (CBS, 1975–1985), with Sherman Hemsley and Isabel Sanford; *Diff'rent Strokes* (NBC, 1978–1985; ABC, 1985–1986), with Gary Coleman and Todd Bridges; *WKRP in Cincinnati* (CBS, 1978–1982), with Tim Reid; and *Benson* (ABC, 1979–1986), with Robert Guillaume. Guillaume had earlier been featured on the ABC comedy series *Soap* (1977–1981).

One of the earliest nationwide information programs geared toward black audiences was *Tony Brown's Journal*, first seen on PBS* in 1970. In 1978, Max Robinson became one of the four anchormen for ABC's *World News Tonight*. Three years later, Robinson made a speech at Smith College accusing all three networks of racism. Bryant Gumbel co-hosted *Games People Play* (NBC, 1980–1981) before becoming co-host of NBC's *Today Show* in 1982. Ed Bradley joined CBS's *60 Minutes* in 1981; earlier, he had been a regular on *CBS News* (1976–1981).

Two major made-for-television movies that dealt with historic aspects of black America were *The Autobiography of Miss Jane Pitman* (CBS, 1974), starring Cicely Tyson, and *Roots* (ABC, 1977). *Soul Train*, produced and hosted by Don Cornelius, was first seen on Chicago television in 1970 and has been syndicated since 1971. The first and only game show to be hosted by a black American is *Musical Chairs* (CBS, 1975), with Adam Wade.

Later series featuring blacks include *The Flip Wilson Show* (NBC, 1970–1974); *Redd Foxx* (ABC, 1977–1978); *Private Benjamin* (CBS, 1981), with Hal Williams; *The Cosby Show* (NBC, 1984-), with Bill Cosby and Phylicia Rashad; *227* (NBC, 1985-), with Marla Gibbs, Hal Williams, and Jackee [Harry]; and *Amen* (NBC, 1986-), with Sherman Hemsley, Clifton Davis, and Anna Maria Horsford. *The Lenny Henry Show* (BBC, 1987–1988) has found an American audience on the Bravo! (U.S.)* cable network.

Harry Belafonte was the first black American to win an Emmy, which was awarded in 1959 for Best Performance in a Variety or Musical Program. The first black-owned television station was WGPR-Detroit, which began broadcasting as a UHF* station in 1975. The first black-owned VHF station was WAEO-Rhinelander, Wisconsin, which was purchased in 1979 by Seaway Communications and owned by Jasper Williams and a group of black businessmen. That same year, TV3, a majority–black-owned company, took over the license for WLBT-Jackson, Mississippi, following a fifteen-year struggle led by the Office of Communication of the United Church of Christ, which claimed the station's former owners were racist, and which eventually won a 1969 landmark Supreme Court decision.

BIBLIOGRAPHY

Daniel, Therese, and Jane Gerson. *The Colour Black: Black Images in British Television*. London: British Film Institute, 1989.

Hill, George H. *Ebony Images: Black Americans and Television*. Carson, Calif.: Daystar, 1986.

Hill, George H., and Sylvia Saverson Hill. *Blacks on Television: A Selectively Annotated Bibliography*. Metuchen, N.J.: Scarecrow Press, 1985.

How Blacks Use Television for Entertainment and Information. Washington, D.C.: Booker T. Washington's Cable Communications Resource Center, n.d.

Jackson, Anthony W. *Black Families and the Medium of Television*. Ann Arbor, Mich.: University of Michigan Bush Program in Child Development and Social Policy, 1982.

MacDonald, J. Fred. *Blacks and White TV: Afro-Americans in Television since 1948*. Chicago: Nelson-Hall, 1983.

Miller, Randall N., editor. *Ethnic Images in American Film and Television*. Philadelphia: Balch Institute, 1978.

Noble, Gil. *Black Is the Color of My TV Tube*. Secaucus, N.J.: Lyle Stuart, 1981.

Poindexter, Paula, and Carolyn Stroman, "Blacks and Television: A Review of the Research Literature," *Journal of Broadcasting*, vol. XXV, no. 2, Spring 1981, pp. 103–122.

Smith, Ronald L. *Cosby*. New York: St. Martin's Press, 1986.

Snorgrass, J. William, and Gloria T. Woody. *Blacks and Media: A Selected, Annotated Bibliography, 1962–1982*. Tallahassee, Fla.: A and M University Press, 1985.

Warner, Malcolm-Jamal. *Theo and Me: Growing Up Okay*. New York: Dutton, 1988.

Watkins, Mel, "Beyond the Pale," *Channels of Communications*, vol. I, no. 1, April/May 1981, pp. 56–60.

BLINKEY PRODUCTIONS, INC. was the New York company responsible for the children's puppet series *The Adventures of Blinkey* (Syndicated, 1952), created and written by Lucille Emerick.

BOB BANNER ASSOCIATES, INC. was formed in 1958 when Banner (born 1922) left NBC,* for whom he had produced and directed *The Dinah Shore Show* (NBC, 1951–1957). The company took over production of *The Garry Moore Show* (CBS, 1958–1967) and also helped develop the new version of *Candid Camera* (CBS, 1960–1967). Noted for its production of variety programming, Bob Banner Associates, Inc. produced a number of Carol Burnett specials, and was also responsible for many made-for-television movies, including *My Sweet Charlie* (NBC, 1970), *Mongo's Back in Town* (CBS, 1971), *Lisa, Bright and Dark* (NBC, 1973), *Journey from Darkness* (NBC, 1975), *Bud and Lou* (NBC, 1978), *My Husband Is Missing* (NBC, 1978), *The Darker Side of Terror* (CBS, 1979), and *If Things Were Different* (CBS, 1980).

In June 1989, in association with ML Media Opportunity Partners (one of whose owners was former ABC* president Elton H. Rule) and the Gary L. Pudney Company, it formed Paradigm Entertainment as a separate production entity.

Address: 132 South Rodeo Drive, Suite 402, Beverly Hills, CA 90212.

BOCHCO, STEVEN PRODUCTIONS, INC. See STEVEN BOCHCO PRODUCTIONS, INC.

BORDER TELEVISION plc is the independent ("commercial") British television network for the Isle of Man, the Scottish borders, and most of Cumbria. It is owned and controlled by individuals and corporations active in the transmission area, with the largest group of shares owned by Cumbrian Newspapers Group Limited, whose chairman, Sir John Burgess, is chairman of the board of Border Television. The company, which began broadcasting on September 1, 1961, produces a number of programs, such as the children's series *Ghost Train on Sunday*, which have enjoyed success in the United Kingdom, but none of its programming has been seen in the United States.

Address: The Television Centre, Carlisle CA1 3NT, United Kingdom.

THE BRAND NAMES FOUNDATION, INC. was a New York–based organization, active in the fifties and sixties. According to contemporary publicity, it "conduct[ed] a year 'round promotional program in radio, TV, and other media which emphasize[d] to the public the benefits and services of manufacturers' brand names, brand competition and brand advertising."

BRANDT ENOS ASSOCIATES was a minor New York–based producer of television programming and documentaries, active in the early fifties.

BRAVO! (U.K.) is a British cable channel, which began broadcasting in September 1985. Operating twenty-four hours a day, it specializes in "old" feature films and television series.

Address: Communications House, Unit 3, Blue Riband Estate, Roman Way, Croydon, Surrey CR9 3RA, United Kingdom.

BRAVO! (U.S.) is the cultural cable network, featuring American and foreign films, interview programs, performing arts specials, documentaries, and musical and comedy series. Two of its more popular series are *The Lenny Henry Show* and *The South Bank Show*, both purchased from British television. Bravo! was founded by Charles Dolan, the head of Cablevision Systems Corp., one of the network's original owners, along with Cox Communications, Inc.* and Daniels & Associates. First seen in December 1980, Bravo! is a division of Rainbow Programming Services Corp.,* which originally alternated Bravo! with the Escapade adult-movie service on a nightly basis. Bravo! currently broadcasts from 8.00 P.M. to 6.00 A.M., Mondays through Fridays, and 5.00 P.M. to 6.00 A.M. on Saturdays and Sundays. It has 4 million subscribers.

The network was highly criticized when it bowed to protests and cancelled the July 2, 1988, telecast of Jean-Luc Godard's *Hail Mary*. In 1989, it teamed with the Center for the Book in the Library of Congress to sponsor the Bravo for Books project.

Address: 150 Crossways Park West, Woodbury, NY 11797.

BIBLIOGRAPHY

Brewin, Bob, "Bravo for Bravo!" *Village Voice*, January 10, 1984, pp. 22–23.

Knoll, Steve, "Can Bravo Make Culture Pay?" *New York Times*, February 26, 1984, section 2, p. 31.

Polskin, Howard, "Bravo!" *TV Guide*, May 21, 1988, pp. 8–9.

Schneider, Steve, "Movies out of the Mainstream Find a Home on Bravo," *New York Times*, October 27, 1985, section 2, p. 26.

———, "Bravo Thrives on Culture," *New York Times*, December 15, 1985, section 2, p. 36.

BRISKIN PRODUCTIONS, INC. was responsible for the series *Casey Jones* (Syndicated, 1959), and other television programming produced in association with Screen Gems.* The company was organized in 1956 by Irving Briskin (born 1903), whose relationship with Columbia dated back to 1935, when the studio purchased his company, Meteor Pictures.

BRISTOL-MYERS was the first company to sponsor a network television series, *Geographically Speaking*, first seen on NBC* on October 27, 1946. The series, which ran through December 1, 1946, consisted of travel films narrated by Mrs. Carveth Wells.

THE BRITISH BROADCASTING CORPORATION. See THE BBC

BRITISH SATELLITE BROADCASTING LIMITED is the United Kingdom's most recently created national broadcaster, which launched its first satellite on August 10, 1989. Created by Anglia Television,* the Granada Group, Pearson Bond Corporation, Chargeurs, Invest International, London Merchant Securities, Next, Reed International, and Trinity International, British Satellite Broadcasting Limited (BSB) began its licensed satellite television service in the spring of 1990, providing five national channels: The Movie Channel (offering six feature films a day); Now: The Channel For Living (providing informational programming, much of it provided by New Era Television, and created by the *Daily Mail* and Yorkshire Television Limited*); The Galaxy Channel (with family programming); The Sports Channel (with much of its programming provided by Champion Television, a division of Mark McCormack's Trans World International); and The Power Station (providing rock and popular music).

Address: The Marcopolo Building, Chelsea Bridge, Queenstown Road, London SW8 4NQ, United Kingdom.

BIBLIOGRAPHY

Clarke, Genevieve, "From One to Five," *Airwaves,* no. 22, Spring 1990, pp. 4–5.

BRITISH TELECOM. British Telecommunications plc, better known as British Telecom, has replaced the Post Office in the United Kingdom as the terrestrial transmission network for radio and television. British Telecom also operates cable television systems and has a financial interest in Premiere (U.K.),* MTV Europe, and the Children's Channel.*

Address: 81 Newgate Street, London EC1A 7AJ, United Kingdom.

THE BROADCAST EDUCATION ASSOCIATION provides specialized training in radio and television broadcasting for individuals, colleges and universities, and television and radio stations belonging to the National Association of Broadcasters. It was founded in 1955 as the Association for Professional Broadcasting Education, "to secure mutual advantages that will flow from a continuing relationship between the nation's broadcasters and institutions of higher education which offer a high standard of training and guidance for those planning to enter the broadcasting profession." The name was changed in 1973.

Address: 1771 N Street, N.W., Washington, DC 20036.

BROADCASTERS' AUDIENCE RESEARCH BOARD is a limited company, formed in August 1980 by the BBC* and the independent television companies to provide measurement of the television audience. It superceded JICTAR (Joint Industry Committee for Television Advertising Research), which had been formed in 1961 by the Independent Television Companies Association, the Incorporated Society of British Advertisers, and the Institute of Practitioners in Advertising to provide figures of audience viewing of independent television.

Such figures were given to JICTAR by TAM (Television Audience Measurement), founded in 1954 and the first official ratings contractor to ITV;* and later by Audits of Great Britain, which took over from TAM in July 1968.

Address: Knighton House, 56 Mortimer Street, London W1N 8AN, United Kingdom.

THE BROADCAST FINANCIAL MANAGEMENT ASSOCIATION was founded in 1961 to further the interests of those in the financial administration of the radio and television industries. It has a publications program, presents the annual AVATAR award, conducts seminars, and maintains a variety of committees. In 1972, it created the Broadcast Credit Association to provide credit information on advertising agencies.

Address: 701 Lee Street, Suite 1010, Des Plaines, IL 60016.

BROADCASTING is the most important of trade papers devoted to the radio and television industry. First published on October 15, 1931, it was edited by Sol Taishoff until his death in 1982, at which time Lawrence Taishoff became editor. Since 1941, it has been published as a weekly.

Address: 1735 DeSales Street, N.W., Washington, DC 20036.

BIBLIOGRAPHY

The First 50 Years of Broadcasting. Washington, D.C.: Broadcasting Publications, 1982.

Slide, Anthony, editor. *International Film, Radio, and Television Journals*. Westport, Conn.: Greenwood Press, 1985.

THE BROADCASTING AND ENTERTAINMENT TRADES ALLIANCE (BETA), with more than 45,000 members, is the largest U.K. trade union of broadcast employees. It was founded in 1984 with the merger of the Association of Broadcasting and Allied Staffs (founded in 1940) and the National Association of Theatrical, Television and Kinematograph Employees (founded in 1890).

Address: 181–185 Wardour Street, London W1V 4BE, United Kingdom.

THE BROADCASTING ORGANIZATIONS OF NON-ALIGNED COUNTRIES/ORGANISMES DE RADIODIFFUSION DES PAYS NON ALIGNÉS is an association of broadcasters from 101 non-aligned nations, founded in 1977.

Address: Generala Zdanova 28, 1100 Belgrade, Yugoslavia.

BROADCAST PIONEERS is a society of professional broadcasters, to which anyone in the radio, television, or cable industry may belong. It was founded in 1942 as an association of radio pioneers titled The Twenty Year Club, reorganized in 1947 as The Radio Pioneers Club, and given its present name in 1957. The purposes of the organization, as specified in its constitution, are:

To establish a membership organization of persons who, by their long years of service in the field of Broadcasting, desire to become associated for the purposes of friendship and education. The Club shall be a central clearing house for the exchange of information and historical data about the industry and shall record, in form to be determined, facts and data about the history of the industry and its traditions for use by this and future generations. It is felt that this organization, with the resultant exchange of information, would make a valuable contribution to the public interest.

A Broadcasters Hall of Fame was created in 1950, and the group also sponsors the luncheons for the annual George Foster Peabody Awards.* On April 19, 1972, the Broadcast Pioneers Library (1771 N Street, N.W., Washington, DC 20036) was dedicated.

Address: 320 West 57 Street, New York, NY 10019.

BROADCAST PROMOTION AND MARKETING EXECUTIVES was founded in 1956 as the Broadcasters' Promotion Association. It promotes professionalism in its members' fields, together with an awareness of broadcast promotion, through publications and workshops.

Address: 6255 Sunset Boulevard, Suite 624, Los Angeles, CA 90028.

BRT (Belgische Radio en Televisie) is the Dutch–Flemish Belgian television company, which (along with RTBF*) began broadcasting in October 1953 as a division of the National Institute of Radio. In 1960, it became an independent public broadcasting service; color was introduced in 1971, and a second channel became operational in 1977. BRT is administered by a board of directors appointed by the Flemish Cultural Community Council, and it is financed through license fees paid to the government. It does not carry advertising. The structure of the system is governed by a decree dated December 28, 1979.

Address: Boulevard Reyers 52, 1040 Brussels, Belgium.

THE BRUCE CHAPMAN CO., founded in 1953, was a New York–based producer and distributor, primarily of television commercials, but also responsible for the fifteen-minute syndicated series *The Answer Man* (1955) with Albert Mitchell.

BUENA VISTA TELEVISION is an operating unit of the Walt Disney Company. Among the syndicated series that it distributes to television are *Siskel & Ebert* (1986-   ), *DuckTales* (1987-   ), *Win, Lose or Draw* (1987-   ), *Live with Regis & Kathie Lee* (1988-   ), and *Chip 'n' Dale's Rescue Rangers* (1989-   ). In August 1988, a separate division, Buena Vista Television Productions, was created, headed by senior vice-president Jamie Bennett. In October of the same year, Bob Jacquemin, who had been with Buena Vista since 1985 as senior vice-president, was named to the new post of president of Buena Vista Television. The company was criticized in October 1989 by independent television stations for the overly high prices that it was asking for its feature packages, and as a result, the "Touchstone 1" package of twenty-six features was sold to a cable network, USA.*

Address: 500 South Buena Vista Street, Burbank, CA 91521.

THE BURT AND BERT COMPANY was formed by Burt Reynolds and Bert Convy to co-produce *Win, Lose or Draw* (Syndicated, 1987-   ).

[EDWARD A.] BYRON PRODUCTIONS was a New York–based distributor of packaged television programming, active in the fifties.

C

THE CABLE ALLIANCE FOR EDUCATION (CAFE) was created in 1989 as a non-profit organization, matching the resources of the cable television industry with the needs of America's schools. The alliance provides free programming, curriculum-based support materials, and copyright clearances for the replay of selected programs on videotape. By December 1992, twenty-nine cable channels will provide free installation and basic service to all public junior and senior high schools reached by cable.

Address: 1900 North Beauregard, Suite 108, Alexandria, VA 22311.

THE CABLE AUTHORITY was established, under the Cable and Broadcasting Act 1984, to promote, license, and regulate the cable industry in the United Kingdom.

Address: Gillingham House, 38–44 Gillingham Street, London SW1V 1HU, United Kingdom.

THE CABLE COMMUNICATIONS POLICY ACT OF 1984 (Public Law 98–549) was adopted by the Senate in 1983 and the House of Representatives in 1984, and signed into law by President Ronald Reagan on October 30, 1984. It amends the Communications Act of 1934, and provides a national policy with regard to cable television. Its purposes are to: assure that cable communications provide the widest possible diversity of information sources and services to the public; establish guidelines for the conduct of federal, state, and local authorities with respect to the regulation of cable systems; establish franchise procedures and standards that encourage the growth and development of cable systems and that assure that cable systems are responsive to the needs and interests of the local community; establish an orderly process for franchise renewal that protects cable operators against unfair denials of renewal where the operator's past performance and proposal for future performance meet the statutory standards;

promote competition in cable communications; and minimize unnecessary regulation that would impose an undue economic burden on cable systems.

THE CABLE JUKEBOX is an interactive music-video cable channel, seen in the United Kingdom twenty-four hours a day. Owned by the WH Smith Group plc, it began broadcasting in November 1987.

Address: The Quadrangle, 180 Wardour Street, London W1V 4AE, United Kingdom.

CABLE TELEVISION. Initially known as CATV (Community Antenna Television), cable television has become a major entertainment force in the United States, with more than 9,000 cable systems serving 50 million households as of 1990.

Cable television dates from 1948, when areas that could not receive over-the-air television were serviced through mountaintop antennas connected by wires to homes wishing to receive the broadcast signals. The first CATV systems were introduced by Ed Parsons (Astoria, Oreg.), John Watson (Mahoney City, Pa.), Robert Tarlton (Lansford, Pa.), and Martin Malarkey, Jr. (Pottsville, Pa.). It was in Pottsville that the National Community Television Council, the forerunner to the National Cable Television Association,* was created in 1951. The technical expansion of cable television systems in the fifties was made possible through the work of Henry "Hank" Diambra, C-Cor Electronics, Blonder-Tongue, Henry "Hank" Abajian, and Jerrold Electronics Corporation.

The FCC* granted the first common-carrier microwave construction permit to J.E. Belknap & Associates of Poplar Bluff, Missouri, in 1954, but four years later decided that CATV systems were not common carriers and that the agency had no jurisdiction over them. However, the FCC reconsidered its decision, and in 1966 issued a report and order requiring cable systems to carry all local television station programs, prohibiting duplication of programming carried on local television, and placing restrictions on the ability of cable operators to import broadcast signals from outside their immediate areas. In 1968, the Supreme Court affirmed the FCC's authority to impose such rulings. The cable industry basically marked time until 1972, when the FCC modified its restriction against the importation of distant broadcast signals, and that same year, HBO* began operation.

The cable industry, as it exists today, came into being in 1973 with the development of a domestic communications satellite (DOMSAT), approved by the FCC that year and launched in 1974. In December 1975, HBO became the first cable programmer to distribute its signals via satellite. Federal policy governing the cable industry was introduced through the Cable Communications Policy Act of 1984,* which was signed by President Ronald Reagan on October 30, 1984.

The question of "must carry" rules, requiring cable operators to carry all local broadcast signals, was a major source of dispute within the industry. The rules were first implemented by the FCC in 1966, but were struck down by the U.S. Court of Appeals, D.C. Circuit, in July 1985 on the grounds that they were a violation of the cable operators' First Amendment rights. A new set of must carry rules were introduced by the FCC in December 1985, under pressure from Congress, and the cable industry agreed to the compromise rules in March 1986. However, in December 1987, the U.S. Court of Appeals, D.C. Circuit, again struck down the must carry rules, insisting they were incompatible with the First Amendment.

According to information provided by the National Cable Television Association, the number of cable systems in the United States has increased from 4,225 in 1980 to 9,010 in 1989. Cable industry revenues have increased from $2.6 billion in 1980 to $15.4 billion in 1989, and cable advertising revenue has increased from $58 million in 1980 to $2 billion in 1989. As of 1989, cable operators were spending $2.6 billion on programming, and cable networks have increasingly become involved in original programming, with, for example, TNT* producing thirty original shows in 1990.

BIBLIOGRAPHY

Baldwin, Thomas F., and D. Stevens McVoy. *Cable Communication*. Englewood Cliffs, N.J.: Prentice-Hall, 1983.

Beck, Kirsten. *Cultivating the Wasteland: Can Cable Put the Vision Back in TV?* New York: American Council for the Arts, 1983.

Brenner, Daniel L., and Monroe E. Price. *Cable Television and Other Nonbroadcast Video: Law and Policy*. New York: Clark Boardman, 1986.

Cable Television in a New Era. New York: Practising Law Institute, 1983.

Cable Television: Retrospective and Prospective. New York: Practising Law Institute, 1985.

Chin, Felix. *Cable Television: A Comprehensive Bibliography*. New York: Plenum, 1978.

Delson, Donn, and Edwin Michalove. *Delson's Dictionary of Cable, Video and Satellite Terms*. Thousand Oaks, Calif.: Bradson Press, 1983.

Dolan, Edward V. *TV or CATV? A Struggle for Power*. Port Washington, N.Y.: Associated Faculty Press, 1984.

Epler-Wood, Gregory, and Paul D'ari, editors. *Cable Programming Resource Directory*. Washington, D.C.: Broadcasting Publications, 1987.

Ferris, Charles D., Frank W. Lloyd, and Thomas J. Casey. *Cable Television Law: A Video Communications Practice Guide*. New York: Matthew Bender, 1986.

Garay, Ronald. *Cable Television: A Reference Guide to Information*. Westport, Conn.: Greenwood Press, 1988.

Grant, William. *Cable Television*. Reston, Va.: Reston Press, 1983.

Hamburg, Morton I. *All About Cable: Legal and Business Aspects of Cable and Pay Television*. New York: Law Journal Seminars Press, 1984.

Hollins, Timothy. *Beyond Broadcasting: Into the Cable Age*. London: British Film Institute, 1984.

Hollowell, Mary Louise, editor. *The Cable/Broadband Communications Book*. White Plains, N.Y.: Knowledge Industry Publications, 1983.

Howard, Herbert H. *Ownership Trends in Cable Television*. Washington, D.C.: National Association of Broadcasters, 1985.

The Interactive Cable TV Handbook. Bethesda, Md.: Phillips, 1983.

Jones, Glenn R. *Jones' Dictionary of Cable Television Technology, Including Related Computer & Satellite Definitions*. Englewood, Colo.: Jones International, 1988.

Jones, Kensinger, Thomas F. Baldwin, and Martin P. Block. *Cable Advertising: New Ways to New Business*. Englewood Cliffs, N.J.: Prentice-Hall, 1986.

Kaatz, Ronald B. *Cable Advertiser's Handbook*. Lincolnwood, Ill.: Crain Books, 1985.

Kellough, Patrick Henry. *Cable Television and Censorship: A Bibliography*. Monticello, Ill.: Vance Bibliographies, 1985.

Kenney, Brigitte L., editor. *Cable for Information Delivery: A Guide for Librarians, Educators and Cable Professionals*. White Plains, N.Y.: Knowledge Industry Publications, 1984.

LeRoy, David, and Judith M. LeRoy. *The Impact of the Cable Television Industry on Public Television*. Washington, D.C.: Corporation for Public Broadcasting, 1983.

Nadel, Mark, and Eli Noam, editors. *The Economics of Cable Television (CATV): An Anthology*. New York: Columbia University Graduate School of Business, 1983.

Negrine, Ralph M., editor. *Cable Television and the Future of Broadcasting*. New York: St. Martin's Press, 1985.

The New Era in CATV: The Cable Franchise Policy and Communications Act of 1984. New York: Practising Law Institute, 1985.

Orton, Barry, editor. *Cable Television and the Cities: Local Regulation and Municipal Uses*. Madison: University of Wisconsin Extension, 1982.

Parsons, Patrick. *Cable Television and the First Amendment*. Lexington, Mass.: Lexington Books, 1987.

————, editor. *Milestones in Cable Television USA*. University Park, Pa.: National Cable Television Center and Museum, 1990.

Pepper, Robert. *Competition in Local Distribution: The Cable Television Industry*. Cambridge, Mass.: Harvard University Program on Information Resources Policy, 1983.

Phillips, Mary. *CATV: A History of Community Antenna Television*. Evanston, Ill.: Northwestern University Press, 1972.

A Practical Guide to the Cable Communications Policy Act of 1984. New York: Practising Law Institute, 1985.

Rice, Jean, editor. *Cable TV Renewals and Refranchising*. Washington, D.C.: Communications Press, 1983.

Roman, James W. *Cable Mania: The Cable Television Sourcebook*. Englewood Cliffs, N.J.: Prentice-Hall, 1983.

Seiden, Martin H. *Cable Television U.S.A.: An Analysis of Government Policy*. New York: Praeger, 1972.

Shakeout: The Year in Cable Programming. Washington, D.C.: Television Digest, 1983.

Shapiro, George H., Philip B. Kurland, and James P. Mercurio. *"Cablespeech": The Case for First Amendment Protection*. New York: Harcourt Brace Jovanovich, 1983.

Smith, Ralph Lee. *The Wired Nation—Cable TV: The Electronic Communications Highway*. New York: Harper & Row, 1972.

Thorpe, Kenneth E. *Cable Television, Market Power and Regulation*. Santa Monica, Calif.: Rand Corporation, 1985.

Townsend, George R., and J. Orrin Marlowe. *Cable: A New Spectrum of Communications*. New York: Spectrum, 1974.

Webb, G. Kent. *The Economics of Cable Television*. Lexington, Mass.: Lexington Books, 1983.

Webster, James G. *The Impact of Cable and Pay Cable Television on Local Station Audiences.* Washington, D.C.: National Association of Broadcasters, 1982.
Weinstein, Stephen B. *Getting the Picture: A Guide to CATV and the New Electronics Media.* New York: Institute of Electrical and Electronics Engineers, 1986.

THE CABLE TELEVISION ADMINISTRATION AND MARKETING SOCIETY (CTAM), founded in 1975, conducts seminars and disseminates information among its members regarding cable television marketing and operating.
Address: 635 Slaters Lane, Suite 250, Alexandria, VA 23314.

THE CABLETELEVISION ADVERTISING BUREAU is a non-profit association, founded in 1981, providing information to both the cable and advertising industries in an effort to promote advertising as a major revenue source for cable television.
Address: 757 Third Avenue, 5th Floor, New York, NY 10017.

THE CABLE TELEVISION ASSOCIATION promotes the development of the cable television industry in the United Kingdom. It was founded in 1932 as the Relay Services Association of Great Britain.
Address: 50 Frith Street, London W1V 5TE, United Kingdom.

THE CABLE TELEVISION INFORMATION CENTER was formed in 1972 to promote the industry through the supply of information to consumers and government agencies.
Address: P.O. Box 1205, Annandale, VA 22003.

THE CABLE TELEVISION PUBLIC AFFAIRS ASSOCIATION was founded in 1985 by a group of public relations professionals within the cable television industry. Through workshops, newsletters, and similar means it tries to provide members of the industry with the necessary skills and techniques to manage their companies' public affairs programs.
Address: P.O. Box 9185, Rosslyn, VA 22209–9998.

CABLE VIDEO STORE is a twenty-four hour a day cable network, with almost 1 million subscribers (as of 1990), offering between twenty and thirty new and recent feature films each month. It was launched in April 1986.
Address: 2200 Byberry Road, Hatboro, PA 19040.

CALIFORNIA NATIONAL PRODUCTIONS, INC. was NBC's* production subsidiary, active from the mid-fifties through the mid-sixties. From 1958 to 1960, it was headed by president Earl H. Rettig. Among the syndicated series with which it was associated are *Boots and Saddles* (1957), *The Blue Angels* (1960), *The Funny Manns* (1960), *The Jim Backus Show* (1960), and *Pony Express* (1960).

CAMBRIA was a producer of "limited-animation" series for television in the sixties. It was responsible for the following syndicated series: *Clutch Cargo* (1960), *Space Angel* (1961), *Captain Fathom* (1965), and *The New Three Stooges* (1965).

CAMERA CRAFT was a Los Angeles producer of television commercials in the fifties, which became an equipment rental house, servicing the television industry, in the sixties and seventies.

THE CAMERA TUBE, also known as the pick-up tube, is what makes television broadcasting possible. The tube picks up the image of the scene being televised and breaks up and converts that image into electrical energy. The breakthrough invention was the Iconoscope camera tube, created by Vladimir Zworykin in 1935. It was superceded by the Orthicon in 1939, and by the Image Orthicon (for studio and field applications) in 1954, and the vidicon (for film transmission) in 1950. A major breakthrough in camera tubes for color cameras came with the Plumbicon, introduced in 1965 by the Dutch-based company N.V. Philips Gloeilampenfabrieken. A further improvement was the Saticon, developed in 1976 by Hitachi and NHK* in Japan and introduced into the United States by RCA* the following year.
BIBLIOGRAPHY
Benson, K. Blair, "A Brief History of Television Camera Tubes," *SMPTE Journal*, vol. LXXXI, no. 8, August 1981, pp. 708–712.
Neuhasuer, Robert G., "Television Camera Tubes—A History but Not Yet an Obituary," *SMPTE Journal*, vol. LXXXXIX, no. 9, September 1990, pp. 708–722.
Zworykin, V.K., "Iconoscopes and Kinescopes in Television," *Journal of the Society of Motion Picture Engineers*, vol. XXVIII, no. 5, May 1937, pp. 473–497.

THE CANADIAN ASSOCIATION OF BROADCASTERS (CAB), incorporated in 1926, represents the interests of Canada's private broadcasters to the House of Commons, the Canadian Radio-Television and Telecommunications Commission, and the Department of Communications. It has created the Canadian Broadcast Standards Council to give uniform structure to industry self-regulation. As of 1990, the association's membership consisted of 260 AM stations, 113 FM stations, 67 television stations, and 3 networks.
Address: P.O. Box 627, Station B, Ottawa, Ontario, Canada K1P 5S2.

CANADIAN CABLE TELEVISION. Cable television was first introduced in Canada in the fifties; in 1952, E.R. Jarmain experimented with a rhombic antenna at his London, Ontario, home and formed London Cable TV; Rediffusion developed a cable system in Montréal; Tru Vu Television was formed by George Chandler in Vancouver; and Télévision de Grand-Mère and Télédistribution Asbestos were active on the Canadian west coast. In 1968, the Canadian Radio-Television and Telecommunications Communication (CRTC) was created by the Broadcasting Act, and commenced regulation of cable television (licenses for which had previously been issued by the Department of Transport). It was not until the mid-seventies that substantial regulations for the cable television industry were issued.

In 1979, the proceedings of the House of Commons created the first full-time satellite service, delivered by cable, and that same year a cable satellite network, La SETTE, was formed in Québec. MuchMusic, a music channel, and TSN, a sports network, were introduced in 1984, and the following year The Life Channel, a twenty-four hour health and life-style network, commenced operations. On November 30, 1987, licenses were granted for three new English specialty services (Vision TV, WeatherNow, and YTV) and five French specialty services (TV5, MétéoMedia, Musique Plus, Canal Famille, and Le Reseau des Sports), together with The Family Channel.

THE CANADIAN CABLE TELEVISION ASSOCIATION was created in Montréal in 1957 as the National Community Antenna Television Association, representing the interests of cable operators to various government departments. The name was changed in 1968, when a Revised Letters Patent was issued, and in 1970 the association moved its headquarters to Ottawa.

Address: Suite 1010, 360 Rue Albert Street, Ottawa, Canada K1R 7X7.

CANADIAN TELEVISION LIMITED was Canada's first television company, founded in Montréal in 1932 by a British engineer named Douglas West. Its first research engineer was Alphonse Ouimet (who later became president of the CBC*), and the company promoted the parallel inventions of mechanical television* by John Logie Baird and C. Francis Jenkins. Canadian Television Limited demonstrated its system by broadcasting a picture image to a receiver in Montréal's Ogilvie Department Store in October 1932, but shortly thereafter, the company ceased operations.

C & C TELEVISION CORP. At the end of 1955, Matty Fox (1911–1964) acquired the television rights to the library of 740 RKO features and RKO's short subjects on behalf of C & C Television Corp., which was named for soft drink manufacturer Cantrell & Cochrane (C & C Soda). In acquiring the films, C & C gained complete copyright ownership of the short subjects, but did not own theatrical rights to the features for the United States and Canada, and was also prohibited from broadcasting the films in six markets where General Teleradio, Inc.* owned television stations.

C & C Television removed the RKO logo from the films, substituting its own name, and introduced the title ''Movietime USA'' to the package of films. It provided the films free of charge or for a nominal sum to television stations in return for free advertising time. The deal earned for Matty Fox the description of ''Hollywood's own version of the wheeler-dealer'' from *Time* (June 12, 1964).

C & C was recapitalized in June 1958 as Television Industries, Inc. The name was changed to Trans-Beacon Corp. in May 1966, and the company was adjudicated bankrupt on March 22, 1971. C & C Syndication (4501 Greengate Court, Westlake Village, CA 91361), which distributed *Best of Groucho* in syndication, has no connection with C & C Television Corp., and was established in 1974.

CANNELL, STEPHEN J. PRODUCTIONS. See STEPHEN J. CANNELL PRODUCTIONS

CAPCITIES/ABC. See ABC; CAPITAL CITIES COMMUNICATIONS, INC.

CAPITAL CITIES COMMUNICATIONS, INC. was founded in 1954 by Tennessee businessman Frank Smith and broadcaster Lowell Thomas with the acquisition of WROW-Albany, New York. A second television station, WTVB-Raleigh, North Carolina, was acquired, and the company was given its name because its two stations were in the capital cities of their respective states. In its year of formation, the company hired Thomas S. Murphy (born 1925) as its first employee. He became president in 1964 and chairman and chief executive officer in 1966. With Murphy's guidance, Capital Cities expanded not only in the broadcast field but also in publishing—in 1968, for example, it acquired Fairchild Publications Inc. (publisher of *Women's Wear Daily*). Capital Cities remained little known until March 1985, when it acquired ABC,* which was four times its size, for $3.5 billion. Murphy negotiated the acquisition with ABC chairman Leonard H. Goldenson, and with financial help from Berkshire Hathaway Inc. (headed by Warren E. Buffet). As of the ABC purchase, Capital Cities owned fifty-three cable television systems (which it sold to the Washington Post Company in August 1985), seven television stations, twelve radio stations, twenty-seven weekly newspapers, ten daily newspapers, and forty-five other publications.

The purchase of ABC was completed in January 1986, and to comply with FCC* regulations as to the number of media outlets that a single company can own, Capital Cities, which was now renamed CapCities/ABC, sold WFTS-Tampa; WTNH–New Haven, Connecticut; WKBW-Buffalo; and WXYZ-Detroit, together with eight radio stations. The FCC granted CapCities/ABC a permanent waiver, permitting it to maintain ownership of multiple television and radio stations in New York, Chicago, Los Angeles, and San Franciso. As of June 1, 1990, Thomas S. Murphy retired, and his second in command, Daniel B. Burke (born 1929) was named chief executive officer, in addition to president (a position he had held since 1969).

Address: 77 West 66 Street, New York, NY 10023.

BIBLIOGRAPHY

Carter, Bill, "Capital Cities Chief Plans To Yield Post," *New York Times*, February 2, 1990, pp. C1, C14.

DeMott, John, "A Network Blockbuster," *Time*, April 1, 1985, pp. 60–63.

Hollie, Pamela G., "An Empire Builder without Usual Ego," *New York Times*, March 20, 1985, pp. 31, 38.

Kleinfield, N.R., "ABC To Be Bought by Capital Cities; Price $3.5 Billion," *New York Times*, March 19, 1985, pp. 1, 54.
Lippman, John, "CapCities/ABC Chairman Murphy Calls It Quits," *Daily Variety*, February 2, 1990, pp. 1, 29.
Rosenstiel, Thomas B., "Cap Cities Style Is Lean, Profitable," *Los Angeles Times*, March 19, 1985, part IV, pp. 1, 11.

CARAVEL FILMS, INC. was founded in 1923 by David J. Pincus as a producer of educational and industrial films. It was active throughout the fifties as a producer of commercials and other television programming.

[KEN] CARLSON TV FILMS was a Los Angeles–based producer of television commercials, active in the fifties.

THE CARNEGIE COMMISSION ON EDUCATIONAL TELEVISION was created in 1965 by the Carnegie Corporation. It released its report in February 1967, urging the creation of a Corporation for Public Television, to be funded by a federal excise tax on television receivers. A second panel, the Carnegie Commission on the Future of Public Broadcasting, released its report, known as *Carnegie II*, in January 1979. It urged a 300 percent increase in funding for public television through the payment by viewers of commercial licenses, the replacement of the Corporation for Public Broadcasting (CPB),* and an end to government control of public broadcasting. The first report led to the creation of the CPB; none of the findings of the second commission were implemented.
BIBLIOGRAPHY
Carnegie Commission on Educational Television. *Public Television: A Program for Action*. New York: Harper & Row, 1967.
Carnegie Commission on the Future of Public Broadcasting. *A Public Trust*. New York: Bantam Books, 1979.

CARSEY-WERNER PRODUCTIONS, INC. is responsible for two of the most popular shows on American television: *The Cosby Show* (NBC, 1984-   ) and *Roseanne* (ABC, 1988-   ). It was created in 1981 by Marcia Carsey (born 1944) and Tom Werner (born 1951), who had first joined forces at ABC* in 1979, when Werner became vice-president and senior executive of prime time development, and Carsey became senior vice-president of comedy and variety programs. Other series created by the company are *Love and Marriage* (ABC, 1983–1984), *Weekends* (ABC, 1983–1984), *Oh, Madeline* (ABC, 1983–1984), *A Different World* (NBC, 1987-   ), and *Chicken Soup* (ABC, 1989).

CARSON PRODUCTIONS, INC. was founded in June 1980 as the independent production company of television personality Johnny Carson (born 1925), with John H. McMahon (who had previously been president of Rastar Television) as its president. It had close ties to NBC,* which had first refusal on all its programs and to which Carson Productions was committed to turning out a minimum of three series over a three-year period. The company has been only relatively successful. Three of its series—*Lewis & Clark* (NBC, 1981–1982), *Cassie & Company* (1982), and *Teachers Only* (NBC, 1982)—proved critical failures, while only *Amen* (NBC, 1982-   ) and *Mr. President* (Fox, 1987–1988) have been popular with both critics and viewers. Carson Productions is also co-producer of the occasional series *The World's Greatest Bloopers, Practical Jokes and Commercials*, has a financial interest in *Late Night with David Letterman*, and controls all post-1980 editions of *The Tonight Show*.

A feature film division, Carson Films, was established in 1981, and it enjoyed success with its first production, *The Big Chill* (1983). Carson Productions is also active in the production of TV movies, with *The Star Maker* (NBC, 1981) and *Fire on the Mountain* (NBC, 1981).

Address: 5300 Melrose Avenue, Suite 309, Los Angeles, CA 90038.

BIBLIOGRAPHY

Boyer, Peter J., "Carson Productions: 3 Wishes Down and 1 To Go," *Los Angeles Times Calendar*, March 8, 1983, pp. 1, 5.
Farber, Stephen, "Carson Outfit Gains," *New York Times*, March 6, 1984, p. C18.
Kaufman, Dave, "Carson Prods. Beats Prod'n Odds," *Daily Variety*, September 21, 1981, p. 11.

CASCADE PICTURES OF CALIFORNIA, INC. was a Los Angeles–based producer of television commercials, founded by B.J. Carr, and active in the fifties and sixties.

THE CATHODE-RAY TUBE, invented in 1897 by Karl Ferdinand Braun, is the most important part of the television receiver. The face end of the bottle-shaped tube is the screen, on the inner surface of which the television picture appears.

BIBLIOGRAPHY

Lachenbruch, David, "A Guided Tour of Your Picture Tube," *TV Guide*, May 3, 1975, pp. 7–10.

CATV. See CABLE TELEVISION

CAVALCADE TELEVISION PROGRAMS, INC. was the television subsidiary of Cavalcade Pictures, Inc., founded in 1945 by Harvey Pergament. Among the programs it distributed was the fifteen minute *Tales of the Old West* (Syndicated, 1955).

CAVALIER PRODUCTIONS, INC. was the Los Angeles–based production company of Robert Young and Eugene B. Rodney, responsible for *Father Knows Best* (CBS, 1954–1955; NBC, 1955–1958; CBS, 1958–1962; ABC, 1962–1963). Its logo was "Ars Pro Multis."

THE CBC (THE CANADIAN BROADCASTING CORPORATION). Following the establishment of the first Royal Commission on Broadcasting in Canada in 1929, the Broadcasting Act of 1936 was enacted. It created the Canadian Broadcasting Corporation, to be financed from both license fees and advertising. In 1958, the Broadcasting Act was revised and the Board of Broadcast Governors was established; a further revision in 1968 created the Canadian Radio-Television Commission.

Television was introduced in Canada by the CBC in 1952, with separate broadcasts in French (from Montréal) beginning on September 6, and in English (from Toronto) beginning on September 8. One of the first television series to be produced by the National Film Board of Canada was *On the Spot/Sur le vif*, a weekly program created by Bernard Devlin, and first seen in 1953. CBC began color television broadcasting in Canada in the fall of 1966.

Address: 1500 Bronson Avenue/P.O. Box 8478, Ottawa, Ontario K1G 3J5, Canada.

BIBLIOGRAPHY

Ellis, David. *Evolution of the Canadian Broadcasting System: Objectives and Realities, 1928–1968.* Ottawa: Canadian Minister of Supply and Services, 1979.

Hallman, E.S., with H. Hindley. *Broadcasting in Canada.* London: Routledge & Kegan Paul, 1977.

McLean, Ross, "Anniversary Angst," *Channels of Communications*, vol. V, no. 1, May/June 1985, pp. 38–40.

Peters, Frank W. *The Public Eye: Television and the Politics of Canadian Broadcasting, 1952–1968.* Toronto: University of Toronto Press, 1979.

Troyer, Warner. *The Sound & the Fury: An Anecdotal History of Canadian Broadcasting.* Toronto: Personal Library, 1982.

Weir, E. Austin. *The Struggle for National Broadcasting in Canada.* Toronto: McClelland & Stewart, 1964.

CBS (COLUMBIA BROADCASTING SYSTEM). In 1927, a concert tour manager named Arthur Judson formed his own radio network, United Independent Broadcasters, Inc., with sixteen affiliated stations. The network received financial support from the Columbia Phonograph Company, which changed the network's name to the Columbia Phonograph Broadcasting System, under which the new network made its debut on September 19, 1927. The name was shortened to the Columbia Broadcasting System when two brothers, Leon and Isaac Levy, took it over in 1928—Leon remained on the board of CBS until 1977. Finally, later that same year, William S. Paley (1901–1990), using money from his family business, Congress Cigars, acquired a controlling interest in CBS, and became its president on September 16, 1928. In 1929, Paley moved the company to new headquarters at 485 Madison Avenue, New York City, where CBS remained until 1965, when it located to its present corporate offices at 51 West 52 Street.

The radio network grew in prominence in the thirties, thanks to the presence of stars such as Kate Smith, Bing Crosby, Bob Hope, and Major Bowes. In 1938, it broadcast Orson Welles' famous *War of the Worlds* presentation.

CBS entered television broadcasting in 1931, with regular scheduled programming over W2XAB, and ten years later began regular television broadcasting on WCBS–New York. Color* television was first demonstrated by CBS in 1940, using a system developed by Peter G. Goldmark. The CBS television network is generally dated from 1948, when it had thirty affiliated stations. The first network affiliate was WCAU-Philadelphia. In 1951, CBS began broadcasting the most popular television series of the decade, *I Love Lucy*, and a year later opened its Hollywood production facility, Television City. Also in 1951, CBS introduced its logo, the CBS eye, designed by Bill Gordon. The fifties may also be considered the decade in which CBS introduced some of the most popular soap operas to television, beginning in 1951 with *Search for Tomorrow*, and continuing with *The Guiding Light* (in 1952) and *As the World Turns* (in 1956).

Captain Kangaroo was the longest running children's show on television, seen on CBS from 1955 to 1981. *All in the Family*, first seen on CBS on January 12, 1971, is perhaps the most famous sitcom of all time, with the name of its central character, Archie Bunker (played by Carroll O'Connor), becoming a common term for bigot. *M*A*S*H* (1972–1983) was another successful sitcom on CBS, and its last episode, broadcast on September 19, 1983, was the most-watched television program up to that time. In the field of network news, Walter Cronkite (born 1916), with his closing remark, "And that's the way it is," became the most respected figure on television. He anchored the *CBS Evening News* from 1962 to 1981, and was succeeded by Dan Rather (born 1931).

As a result of the network's diversification, the CBS/Broadcast Group was formed in 1966. It consists of eight divisions: Television Network, Entertainment, News, Sports, Television Stations, Radio, Operations & Engineering, and Productions. The CBS News Archive was founded in 1969. In 1975, the CBS Engineering Research and Development Laboratories, created in 1938 with the mandate to develop "a practical television system," was renamed the CBS Technology Center.

In the early seventies, Fred Silverman received high praise as head of programming, but he left in 1975 to join ABC.* Robert A. Daly served as president of CBS Entertainment from 1977 until 1980, when he resigned and was replaced by B. Donald (Bud) Grant.

In March 1981, CBS Theatrical Films was formed, headed by Michael Levy, but it closed down operations a year later, and became a division of the Broadcast Group, headed by William Self. In June 1982, CBS/Fox Video was created as a joint venture between CBS and 20th Century–Fox. Also that same year, CBS, HBO,* and Columbia formed Tri-Star Pictures, but CBS sold its interest in 1985. The 1982 "CBS Reports" documentary *The Uncounted Enemy: A Vietnam Deception* resulted in a $120 million libel suit against the network brought by General William C. Westmoreland. The discontinuance of the suit was announced jointly by Westmoreland and CBS on February 18, 1985.

William S. Paley ran CBS starting in 1928, and groomed several successors, including Frank Stanton (who was named president in 1964 and retired in 1971), Arthur Taylor (who was president from 1972 to 1976), and John D. Blacke (who became president in 1976 and resigned in 1980). Eventually, Paley stepped down as chairman in 1983, and Thomas H. Wyman (born 1931) was named to replace him. (Wyman had served as president of CBS since 1980.)

In April 1985, Wyman was successful in fighting an unfriendly takeover bid by Ted Turner. That same year, he also faced an attack from Senator Jesse Helms, who led a campaign, titled Fairness in Media,* to acquire sufficient CBS stock in order to change a perceived liberal bias in *CBS News*. However, on September 10, 1986, Wyman resigned, and Paley returned to CBS as acting chairman, together with Laurence Tisch (born 1923) as acting chief executive officer. Tisch had acquired 9.9 percent of CBS stock the previous year. Nineteen eighty-six ended with lower profits for the network and CBS News no longer in first place in the ratings. The first change ordered by Tisch, who was the billionaire chairman of Loews, Inc., was the departure of Van Gordon Sauter (born 1935) as head of *CBS News*. Sauter had joined CBS in 1981; he was replaced by Howard Stringer. The latter was named president of the CBS Broadcast Group in July 1988, replacing Gene F. Jankowski (born 1934), who was named Broadcast Group chairman.

In order to make the network more profitable, Tisch has sold off a number of assets. CBS had entered the record business in 1938 with the purchase of the American Record Company, renamed Columbia Recording Corp. In 1988, CBS Records was sold for $2 billion. CBS entered publishing in 1967 with the purchase of Holt, Rinehart and Winston. In 1986, CBS Educational and Professional Publishing was sold for $500 million. In addition, CBS Music Publishing was sold in 1986 for $68.2 million, and CBS Magazines was sold in 1987 for $650 million.

In April 1977, CBS lost its perennial position as number one in the ratings to ABC.* Since then, it has failed to achieve its former dominance on a permanent basis. In recent years, the two most popular programs on CBS have been *60 Minutes* (1968-) and *Murder, She Wrote* (1984-).

CBS owns twenty radio stations and the following television stations: KCBS–Los Angeles, WCIX-Miami, WBBM-Chicago, WCBS–New York, and WCAU-Philadelphia.

Addresses: 51 West 52 Street, New York, NY 10019; 7800 Beverly Boulevard, Los Angeles, CA 90036.

BIBLIOGRAPHY
Alter, Jonathan, "The Struggle for the Soul of CBS News," *Newsweek*, September 15, 1986, pp. 52–54.
Auletta, Ken, "Gambling on CBS," *New York Times Magazine*, June 8, 1986, pp. 34–37, 106–110, 116.
Bedell, Sally, "What's Gone Wrong at Black Rock," *New York Times*, October 31, 1982, section 3, pp. 1, 8.
"Behind the Purge at CBS," *Time*, October 25, 1976, p. 52.

Boyer, Peter J., "CBS News in Search of Itself," *New York Times Magazine*, December 28, 1986, pp. 15, 18, 26, 34.

———. *Who Killed CBS?* New York: Random House, 1988.

"CBS: The First 60 Years," *The Hollywood Reporter*, 1987–88 TV Preview, pp. 79–104.

Joyce, Ed. *Prime Times, Bad Times*. New York: Doubleday, 1988.

Leonard, Bill. *In the Storm of the Eye: A Lifetime at CBS*. New York: G.P. Putnam, 1987.

McCabe, Peter. *Bad News at Black Rock*. New York: Arbor House, 1987.

Masring, Michael, "CBS under Siege," *The New Republic*, May 6, 1985, pp. 16–18.

Metz, Robert. *Reflections in a Bloodshot Eye*. Chicago: Playboy Press, 1975.

Paley, William S. *As It Happened: A Memoir*. Garden City, N.Y.: Doubleday, 1979.

Paper, Lewis J. *Empire: William S. Paley and the Making of CBS*. New York: St. Martin's Press, 1987.

Powell, Bill, and Jonathan Alter, "Civil War at CBS," *Newsweek,* September 15, 1986, pp. 46–50.

———, "The Showdown at CBS," *Newsweek*, September 22, 1986, pp. 54–59.

Reston, James, "Two Cheers for CBS," *New York Times*, September 14, 1986, section 4, p. 25.

Ruby, Michael, "CBS Plays Executive Suite," *Newsweek*, October 25, 1976, pp. 83, 86.

Russell, George, "A Cut above the Ordinary," *Time*, December 22, 1986, pp. 53, 56.

Sanoff, Alvin P., "CBS Struggles To Get Its Act Together," *U.S. News & World Report*, June 11, 1990, pp. 48–49.

Schwartz, Tony, "How CBS Is Changing Channels," *New York Times*, October 18, 1981, section 3, pp. 1, 17.

Slater, Robert. *This . . . Is CBS: A Chronicle of 60 Years*. Englewood Cliffs, N.J.: Prentice-Hall, 1988.

Smith, Sally Bedell, "Sharing the Throne at Black Rock," *New York Times*, September 14, 1986, section 3, pp. 1, 28.

———. *In All His Glory: William S. Paley, the Legendary Tycoon and His Brilliant Circle*. New York: Simon & Schuster, 1990.

THE CBS AWARDS were organized in 1950 by CBS* and World Video, Inc. Intended to encourage the emergence of new television writers, the awards consisted of monthly prizes of either $500 or $250 to the best dramatic television scripts submitted by college students. The judging was undertaken by Charles M. Underhill, director of programs at CBS-TV; Donald Davis, producer of *Actors' Studio*; and novelist John Steinbeck, vice-president of World Video, Inc.

BIBLIOGRAPHY

Steinbeck, John, "The Written Word Is Here To Stay," *International Photographer*, April 1950, p. 21.

CBS CABLE. In the spring of 1980, CBS* created a cable division, which was responsible for the short-lived CBS Cable network, airing from October 1981 through December 1982. Programming was devoted to culture and the performing arts, and each evening's shows were introduced by Patrick Watson. Created at a cost of $30 million and available in 5 million homes, it is generally agreed that CBS Cable failed because its advertising rates were too high and its emphasis on quality programming led to an excessive budget.

BIBLIOGRAPHY

Brown, Les, "Who Killed CBS Cable?" *Channels of Communications*, vol. II, no. 4, November/December 1982, pp. 12–13.

"CBS Gets a Sliver of the Cable Pie," *Newsweek*, August 17, 1981, p. 58.

Nicholson, Tim, and Peter McAlevey, "Cable TV's First Casualty," *Newsweek*, September 27, 1982, p. 66.

CBS FILMS, INC. was the network's syndication arm, organized in 1950 by Fred J. Mahlstedt. It was active in the fifties and sixties, distributing dozens of series, including *Amos 'n' Andy* (CBS, 1951–1953), *I Love Lucy* (CBS, 1951–1959), *Our Miss Brooks* (CBS, 1952–1956), *The Whistler* (Syndicated, 1954), *Fabian of Scotland Yard* (Syndicated, 1955), *Long John Silver* (Syndicated, 1955), *The Honeymooners* (CBS, 1955–1956), *Gunsmoke* (CBS, 1955–1975), *The Whirlybirds* (Syndicated, 1957–1959), *Perry Mason* (CBS, 1957–1966), *United States Border Patrol* (Syndicated, 1959), *The Twilight Zone* (CBS, 1959–1965), *The Beverly Hillbillies* (CBS, 1962–1971), *Petticoat Junction* (CBS, 1963–1970), and *Hogan's Heroes* (CBS, 1965–1971). Merle S. Jones (born 1905) was the company's president from 1958 to 1968, in which year the name was changed to CBS Enterprises, Inc. Following the FCC* ruling that networks must refrain from program syndication by June 1, 1973, CBS disposed of the subsidiary in 1971 after renaming it Viacom, Inc.*

CCTV (China Central Television) began, on an experimental basis, as Beijing Television in May 1958. Color* transmissions commenced in 1973, and satellite service to the entire country (which had an estimated 120 million television sets in 1988) began in February 1987. CCTV operates three channels, one of which (dating from 1986) is for Beijing only. The service is financed to a large extent by the government, but does rely in part on revenues from television commercials.

   Address: 11 Fuxing Road, Beijing, People's Republic of China.

BIBLIOGRAPHY

Michie, Laurence, "Television in China: Untapped Market Grows by Leaps and Bounds," *Daily Variety*, March 28, 1988, pp. 18, 28.

CEEFAX and ORACLE are teletext* services, permitting viewers in the United Kingdom to use their television receivers for the display of news and other printed information. Ceefax and Oracle are also used to subtitle programs for the hearing-impaired. Ceefax was developed by the BBC* and first demonstrated in 1974. Oracle (Optional Reception of Announcements by Coded Line Electronics) was developed by IBA* engineers in 1973. Oracle's use of live subtitling of the news began in July 1987. The Oracle subscription teletext service is provided by Air Call Teletext Ltd., formed by Oracle (which is jointly owned by the British independent television networks) and Air Call plc.

BIBLIOGRAPHY
Edwardson, S.M., and A. Gee, "CEEFAX: A Proposed New Broadcasting Service,"
    SMPTE Journal, vol. LXXXIII, no. 1, January 1974, pp. 14–19.
McKenzie, G.A., "ORACLE—An Information Broadcasting Service Using Data Trans-
    mission in the Vertical Interval," *SMPTE Journal*, vol. LXXXIII, no. 1, January
    1983, pp. 6–10.

CELEBRITY RIGHTS laws are applicable in many states, including California
and New York. They require that celebrities be paid if their images are used to
endorse a product, and most such laws apply also to the heirs up to fifty years
after the death of the personality. The first major use of a celebrity image to
promote a product was by IBM. In 1983, it hired Lord, Federico and Einstein
to construct a campaign for its microcomputers based around Charlie Chaplin's
tramp image. A reported $1 million was paid to the Chaplin estate for the use
of the tramp character.

The two most prominent agencies representing personalities and their estates
in the field of celebrity endorsement are Curtis Management Group (1000 Water-
way Boulevard, Indianapolis, IN 46202) and the Roger Richman Agency (9777
Wilshire Boulevard, Suite 815, Beverly Hills, CA 90212). Among the clients
or their estates represented by Curtis are Abbott and Costello, Fred Astaire,
James Dean, and Judy Garland. Richman's major clients are the estates of Charlie
Chaplin, Marilyn Monroe, and Mae West.

BIBLIOGRAPHY
Burstein, Daniel, "Using Yesterday To Sell Tomorrow," *Advertising Age*, April 11,
    1983, p. M–4.
Teicholz, Tom, "The Rights of the Living Dead," *Channels of Communications*, vol.
    II, no. 6, March/April 1983.

THE CENTER FOR NEW TELEVISION was founded in 1977 as a non-
profit organization, promoting innovation in video. It publishes a quarterly newsletter, *Scan*.

Address: 912 South Wabash Avenue, Chicago, IL 60605.

CENTRAL INDEPENDENT TELEVISION is the British independent ("commercial") television network for the midlands area. It started as the Associated
Broadcasting Company/Associated Television (ATV), which was launched as
the weekend television network for the London area on September 24, 1955,
and as the weekday television network for the Midlands on February 17, 1956.
Central Independent Television began broadcasting on January 1, 1982. It is
best known to American television viewers for the controversial puppet series
Spitting Image, *The Bretts*, and the "Inspector Morse" series. See also ZENITH
PRODUCTIONS LTD.

Address: Central House, Broad Street, Birmingham B1 2JP, United Kingdom.

CENTURY PRODUCTIONS, INC. was a packager of live television shows, founded in 1952 by John F. Tobin, and active through 1954, when Tobin joined NBC Films, Inc.* Century had offices in both Los Angeles and San Francisco.

CENTURY TOWER PRODUCTIONS is a wholly owned subsidiary of Orion Television, responsible for *Just Men!* (NBC, 1983) and the 1986–1989 syndicated edition of *Hollywood Squares*.

CHAD [GROTHKOPF] ENTERPRISES/CHAD ASSOCIATES, INC. was a New York–based producer of television commercials, active in the fifties.

CHANNEL 4, as its name implies, is the fourth national television network in the United Kingdom, after the two BBC* services and the group of advertiser-funded networks of independent television. The Channel 4 service was authorized by the Broadcasting Act of 1981, and was launched on November 2, 1982. Operated by the Channel Four Television Company Limited, Channel 4 is financed by subscriptions from the independent television networks levied by the IBA, of which the Channel Four Television Company is a wholly owned subsidiary. In return for funding Channel 4, the independent television networks have the right to sell advertising time on Channel 4 in their own regions.

Apart from a weekly "answerback" show for viewers, titled *Right To Reply*, Channel 4 makes none of its own programming but buys shows from independent producers and distributors and from the other independent television networks. It is particularly noted for its "Films on Four" seasons of feature films, which it has helped to finance in whole or part, and which include, among many others, *My Beautiful Laundrette* (1985) and *Dance with a Stranger* (1985). Channel 4's feature films demonstrate its concern for quality programming, and the network's philosophy has often been described as the "publishing" of programs by "authors." Channel 4 has also demonstrated a commitment to Britain's ethnic minorities in its programming.

Address: 60 Charlotte Street, London W1P 2AX, United Kingdom.
BIBLIOGRAPHY

Blanchard, Simon, and David Morley, editors. *What's This Channel Fo(u)r?: An Alternative Report*. London: Comedia, 1982.

Lambert, Stephen. *Channel Four: Television with a Difference?* London: British Film Institute, 1982.

McRobbie, Angela, editor. *Four on 4: Transcriptions from Four Open Forums on the New Television Channel*. Stafford, U.K.: Birmingham Film Workshop and West Midland Arts, 1982.

O'Connor, John J., "Britain's Channel 4—Where Commerce Serves Culture," *New York Times*, June 22, 1986, section 2, pp. 27, 29.

Tauber, Amy, "The Other Channel Four," *Village Voice*, July 1, 1986, pp. 55–56.

Thomas, Jo, "He Sees to It That Britain's Channel 4 Stays Innovative," *New York Times*, May 18, 1986, section 2, p. 27.

Watkins, Roger, "Channel 4 Cumbersome Compromise, But Indie Producers Happy," *Daily Variety*, January 26, 1983, pp. 34, 40.
Watson, Neil, "Five Innovative Years in Great Britain," *The Hollywood Reporter*, February 5, 1988, pp. 83–90.
Wyver, John, "The English Channel 4," *American Film*, vol. XI, no. 9, July/August 1986, pp. 46–49.
Zoglin, Richard, "Channel Snore to the Fore," *Time*, September 1, 1986, p. 73.

CHANNEL 1. A question that is often asked by television viewers is why there is no channel 1. The answer is that, immediately following the end of the World War II, the FCC* determined to reserve channel 1 as a national emergency channel. As a result of the FCC's action, stations operating on the channel 1 frequency were moved to channel 2, and all other channel users were moved up one frequency. For example, in Los Angeles, W6XAO-TV, which was channel 1, became channel 2. W6XAO later became the CBS* network's owned-and-operated station in Los Angeles, KCBS.

CHANNELS OF COMMUNICATIONS is one of the oldest of serious journals devoted to the television industry. It was founded in 1981 by the Media Commentary Council, Inc., and has been edited since its inception, in April/May of that year, by Les Brown. The journal ceased publication in December 1990, when Norman Lear's Act III Communications, which had purchased Channels of Communications in 1985, was unable to find a buyer for it.
    Address: 1515 Broadway, New York, NY 10036.
BIBLIOGRAPHY
Slide, Anthony, editor. *International Film, Radio, and Television Journals*. Westport, Conn.: Greenwood Press, 1985.

CHANNEL TELEVISION is the smallest of the British independent ("commercial") television networks, serving the Bailiwicks of Jersey and Guernsey and the other smaller islands that make up the Channel Islands group. It began broadcasting on September 1, 1962, and did not introduce color television until 1976.
    Address: Television Centre, La Pouquelaye, St. Helier, Jersey, Channel Islands, United Kingdom.

CHARLES BURROWS CHARLES PRODUCTIONS was formed by two brothers, Glen and Les Charles, and by Jim Burrows, who had first met the brothers when all three were with MTM Enterprises.* In association with Paramount, the company produced two major series, *Taxi* (ABC, 1978–1982; NBC, 1982–1983) and *Cheers* (NBC, 1982-). It was also responsible for *The Tortellis* (NBC, 1987) and *All Is Forgiven* (NBC, 1986).
    Address: 5555 Melrose Avenue, Los Angeles, CA 90038.
BIBLIOGRAPHY
Koch, Neal, "Bartenders with Class," *Channels of Communications*, vol. VIII, no. 10, November 1988, pp. 59–63.

CHARTER OAK TELE-PICTURES, founded in 1954, was a New York–based producer and distributor, operated by Louis Cavrell.

CHERYL-TV CORP. (Simon Lipson, president) was a distributor of twenty feature films to television, with offices in New York and Los Angeles, and active in the fifties and sixties.

[HARRY V.] CHESHIRE AND ASSOCIATES was a minor Los Angeles–based television producer of the fifties.

THE CHILDREN'S CHANNEL is a European cable network, specializing, as its name suggests, in programming for children. Owned by British Telecom,* Thames Television plc,* Central Independent Television,* and D.C. Thompson, the channel began broadcasting on September 1, 1984. It is seen in the United Kingdom, Scandinavia, the Republic of Ireland, and the Netherlands, and broadcasts in English with Dutch, Norwegian, or Swedish subtitling.
  Address: 9–13 Grape Street, London WC2H 8DR, United Kingdom.
BIBLIOGRAPHY
Coopman, Jeffrey, "The Children's Channel Gaining Subscribers," *Variety*, November 12, 1990, p. 58.

THE CHILDREN'S MEDIA LAB was created in 1982 to produce local television programming with and for children.
  Address: P.O. Box 9237, Berkeley, CA 94307.

CHILDREN'S PROGRAMMING. The one area in which American television had failed to adequately provide a public service has been children's programming. Despite the efforts of Action for Children's Television* and others, the FCC* and the networks have been unwilling to put aside the profit motive in programming shows for children, and have continued to permit the sponsorship of such shows by cereal manufacturers and other children-oriented companies. Only PBS,* with *Sesame Street* (1969-   ) and other programming from the Children's Television Workshop,* has demonstrated a commitment to quality entertainment for children.
  One of the earliest children's programs was *The Small Fry Club*, seen on the DuMont* network on Tuesdays, beginning in March 1947, and hosted by "Big Brother" Bob Emory. "Buffalo Bob" Smith (born 1917) introduced his string puppet Howdy Doody on NBC's *Puppet Playhouse* on December 27, 1947, and the following year, *Howdy Doody Time* began to air on NBC.* It remained on the network through 1960, changing its name to *The Howdy Doody Show* in 1956, and was revived as a syndicated series in 1975.
  Local children's programming proliferated in the late forties and early fifties, with two series gaining an eventual nationwide audience. From Los Angeles, animator Bob Clampett produced *Time for Beany* (Syndicated, 1949–1958), and

from Chicago, Burr Tillstrom introduced the Kuklapolitan Players and Fran Allison in *Kukla, Fran and Ollie* (seen on NBC from 1948 to 1954 and on ABC from 1954 to 1957, and later seen in syndication and on public television). Tillstrom is perhaps the first children's entertainer to have appeared on television, having broadcast from the New York World's Fair in 1939.*

Children's television shows that gained popularity in the fifties include *The Pinky Lee Show* (NBC, 1954–1956), *The Soupy Sales Show* (ABC, 1959–1961), and *The Shari Lewis Show* (NBC, 1960–1963). CBS* introduced *Captain Kangaroo* as an early-morning weekday program in 1955, starring Robert Keesham (born 1927). In 1954, *Disneyland* began airing on ABC,* and was broadcast between 7:30 and 8:30 P.M., as were most supposedly children's shows, such as *The Adventures of Rin Tin Tin* (ABC, 1954–1959). A year later, ABC introduced *The Mickey Mouse Show*.

The first major commitment by PBS to children's programming came in 1967 with *Mister Rogers' Neighborhood*, hosted by Fred Rogers (born 1928), and first seen on January 2, 1967. Since 1971, the series has been produced by Rogers' non-profit corporation, Family Communications.

As early as 1955, CBS was airing the Terrytoon cartoons that it owned under the title of *Mighty Mouse Playhouse*. Between 1964 and 1968, cartoons on Saturday mornings increased in program time from three to six hours, and in 1966, ABC, followed by CBS the following year, began Sunday-morning airing of cartoons. ABC began afterschool specials in 1972. However, efforts to designate 8:00 to 9:00 P.M. as a family viewing hour by the FCC in 1975 were declared illegal the following year by the U.S. District Court.

On October 1, 1990, Congress approved legislation to limit commercials on children's programs to ten-and-a-half minutes an hour on weekends and twelve minutes an hour on weekdays. It also established a National Endowment for Children's Educational Television Programming.

BIBLIOGRAPHY

Barcus, F. Earle. *Images of Life on Children's Television: Sex Roles, Minorities, and Families*. New York: Praeger, 1983.

Barcus, Francis Earle, and Rachel Wolkin. *Children's Television*. New York: Praeger, 1977.

Barlow, Geoffrey, and Alison Hill, editors. *Video Violence and Children*. New York: St. Martin's Press, 1985.

Belson, William A. *Television Violence and the Adolescent Boy*. Farnborough, U.K.: Saxon House, 1978.

Berry, Gordon L., and Claudia Mitchell-Kernan, editors. *Television and the Socialization of the Minority Child*. New York: Academic Press, 1982.

Brown, Ray, editor. *Children and Television*. Beverly Hills, Calif.: Sage Publications, 1976.

Bryant, Jennings, and Daniel R. Anderson, editors. *Children's Understanding of Television: Research on Attention and Comprehension*. New York: Academic Press, 1983.

Cater, Douglass, and Stephen Strickland. *TV Violence and the Child*. New York: Russell Sage Foundation, 1975.

The Child and Television Drama: The Psychosocial Impact of Cumulative Viewing. New York: Mental Health Materials Center, 1982.

Cullingford, Cedric. *Children and Television*. New York: St. Martin's Press, 1984.

Doney, Ruane L. *Guide to Innovative Children's Programs for Television*. Washington, D.C.: National Association of Broadcasters, 1984.

Dorr, Aimee. *Television and Children: A Special Medium for a Special Audience*. Beverly Hills, Calif.: Sage Publications, 1986.

Durkin, Kevin. *Television, Sex Roles and Children: A Developmental Social Psychological Account*. Milton Keynes, U.K.: Open University Press, 1985.

Fischer, Stuart. *Kid's TV: The First 25 Years*. New York: Facts on File, 1983.

Garry, Ralph, F.B. Rainsberry, and Charles Winick. *For the Young Viewers*. New York: McGraw-Hill, 1962.

Howe, Michael I. *Television & Children*. Hamden, Conn.: Shoe String Press, 1977.

Huesmann, L. Rowell, and Leonard D. Eron, editors. *Television and the Aggressive Child: A Cross National Comparison*. Hillsdale, N.J.: Lawrence Erlbaum Associates, 1986.

Johnston, Jerome, and James S. Ettema. *Positive Images: Breaking Stereotypes with Children's Television*. Beverly Hills, Calif.: Sage Publications, 1982.

Kaye, Evelyn. *The Family Guide to Children's Television: What To Watch, What To Miss, What To Change*. New York: Pantheon, 1974.

Kelley, Michael R. *A Parent's Guide to Television: Making the Most of It*. New York: John Wiley and Sons, 1983.

Liebert, Robert M., Joyce N. Sprafkin, and Emily S. Davidson. *The Early Window: Effects of Children's Television on Children and Youth*. Elmsford, N.Y.: Pergamon Press, 1982.

Melody, William. *Children's Television: The Economics of Exploitation*. New Haven, Conn.: Yale University Press, 1973.

Meyer, Manfred, editor. *Children and the Formal Features of Television: Approaches and Findings of Experimental and Formative Research*. New York: K.G. Saur, 1983.

Moody, Kate. *Growing Up on Television*. New York: Times Books, 1980.

Morris, Norman S. *Television's Child*. Boston: Little, Brown, 1971.

Mukerji, Rose. *Television Guidelines for Early Childhood Education*. Bloomington, Ind.: National Instructional Television, 1969.

Murray, John P., and Gavriel Salomon, editors. *The Future of Children's Television: Results of the Markle Foundation/Boys Town Conference*. Boys Town, Nebr.: Boys Town, 1984.

Noble, Grant. *Children in Front of the Small Screen*. Beverly Hills, Calif.: Sage Publications, 1975.

Palmer, Edward L. *Television and America's Children: A Crisis of Neglect*. New York: Oxford University Press, 1989.

Palmer, Patricia. *The Lively Audience: A Study of Children around the TV Set*. Sydney: Allen and Unwin, 1986.

Postman, Neil. *The Disappearance of Childhood*. New York: Delacorte Press, 1982.

Rainsberry, F.B. *A History of Children's Television in English Canada, 1952–1986*. Metuchen, N.J.: Scarecrow Press, 1988.

Rutstein, Nat. *"Go Watch TV!" What and How Much Should Children Really Watch*. New York: Sheed & Ward, 1974.

Schramm, Wilbur, Jack Lyle, and Edwin B. Parker. *Television in the Lives of Our Children*. Stanford, Calif.: Stanford University Press, 1961.

Schwarz, Meg, editor. *TV and Teens: Experts Look at the Issues*. Reading, Mass.: Addison-Wesley, 1982.

Shayon, Robert Lewis. *Television and Our Children*. New York: Longmans, 1951.

Wilkins, Joan Anderson. *Breaking the TV Habit*. New York: Charles Scribner's Sons, 1982.

Winick, Charles, Lorne G. Williamson, Stuart F. Chuznis, and Mariann P. Winick. *Children's Television Commercials: A Content Analysis*. New York: Praeger, 1973.

Winick, Mariann P., and Charles Winick. *The Television Experience: What Children See*. Beverly Hills, Calif.: Sage Publications, 1979.

Winn, Marie. *The Plug-In Drug: Television, Children, and the Family*. New York: Penguin Books, 1985.

Woolery, George. *Children's Television: The First Thirty-Five Years, 1946–1981. Part I: Animated Cartoon Series*. Metuchen, N.J.: Scarecrow Press, 1983.

————. *Children's Television: The First Thirty-Five Years, 1946–1981. Part II: Live, Film, and Tape Series*. Metuchen, N.J.: Scarecrow Press, 1985.

THE CHILDREN'S TELEVISION WORKSHOP (CTW) was formulated in 1966 as a result of discussions between Joan Ganz Cooney and Lloyd Morrisett of the Carnegie Corporation. It was launched in 1969 as an independent, non-profit corporation, initially funded by foundation and government grants. Its founder and chairman, Joan Ganz Cooney, was an Emmy-award winning producer with WNET,* and Jim Henson worked with the workshop from its conception, creating "Big Bird" and other popular characters for its *Sesame Street* series. The latter, first seen on PBS* in 1969, is the best known and most popular of the workshop's series for children. It was followed by *The Electric Company* (PBS, 1971–1981), produced for older children, and *3–2–1 Contact!* (PBS, 1980-   ). Additionally, CTW produced one season of the adult-oriented, family health show *Feeling Good* (PBS, 1975–1976).

A subsidiary, Palm Productions, was created in 1973 to develop movies for commercial television. The only production in its five years of existence was *Beauty and the Beast* (NBC, 1976). A second commercial production subsidiary, CTW Productions, was formed in May 1974. It produced the comedy special *Out to Lunch*, seen on ABC* on December 10, 1974. It also produced the animated special *The Lion, the Witch and the Wardrobe* (CBS, 1979). On September 19, 1988, CTW introduced its first production for cable television, *Encyclopedia*, on HBO,* with each episode featuring a different letter of the alphabet.

In 1979, the Children's Television Workshop was criticized by *Washington Post* columnist Jack Anderson for exorbitant expense accounts and various wasteful practices. He urged an end to government funding of the workshop. A year later, CTW opened an amusement park, Sesame Place, in Langhorne, Pennsylvania, which was indicative of where it would derive most of its current and future income—from the franchising of *Sesame Street*–related items.

Address: One Lincoln Plaza, New York, NY 10023.

BIBLIOGRAPHY

Cooney, Joan Ganz, "Sesame Street: The Experience of One Year," *Television Quarterly*, vol. IX, no. 3, Summer 1970, pp. 9–13.

Cowan, Alison Leigh, "CTW Romps onto Cable with 'Encyclopedia,' " *New York Times*, September 18, 1988, section H, pp. 31, 38.

Hennessee, Judith, "Can Children's TV Workshop Recapture Its Youth?" *New York Times*, April 1, 1979, section 2, pp. 35, 39.

Kalter, Joanmarie, "Survival Isn't Child's Play," *TV Guide*, July 25, 1987, pp. 36–39.

Kendig, Frank, "CTW's '3–2–1 Contact' Aims at Sparking an Interest in Science," *New York Times*, January 13, 1980, section 2, pp. 27–28.

Lesser, Gerald S. *Children and Television: Lessons from Sesame Street*. New York: Random House, 1975.

Meyers, William. "The Nonprofits Drop to 'Non,' " *New York Times*, November 24, 1985, section 3, pp. 1, 8.

Polsky, Richard M. *Getting to Sesame Street: Origins of the Children's Television Workshop*. New York: Praeger, 1974.

Powers, Ron, "Say It Ain't So, Snuffle-Upagus!" *TV Guide*, May 19, 1979, pp. 6–8.

Yin, Robert K. *The Workshop and the World: Toward an Assessment of the Children's Television Workshop*. Santa Monica, Calif.: Rand Corp., 1973.

CHRIS-CRAFT INDUSTRIES, INC. is a diversified company, with two major divisions devoted to television and to the industrial manufacture of plastic flexible films and non-woven fiber products (marketed in part through a subsidiary, M.D. Industries, Inc.). It has its origins in the latter industry, being incorporated on January 23, 1928, as a consolidation of the Automobile Batting Department of California Cotton Mills Co. and the Little Falls (N.Y.) Fibre Co., under the name of National Automotive Fibres, Inc. The name was changed to NAFI Corp. on April 24, 1959, and to Chris-Craft Industries, Inc. on April 30, 1962.

The company's involvement in television is handled through its majority-owned (61.4 percent as of February 1990) subsidiary, BHC Communications, Inc., which owns 100 percent of Chris-Craft Television, Inc. and, as of February 1990, 50.7 percent of United Television, Inc. (which Chris-Craft acquired from 20th Century–Fox in June 1981). BHC operates the following television stations: KCOP–Los Angeles, KPTV-Portland, Oregon, KMSP–Minneapolis/St. Paul, KTVX–Salt Lake City, KMOL–San Antonio, KBHK–San Francisco, and KUTP-Phoenix. KCOP and KPTV are owned by Chris-Craft Television, and the remainder are owned by United Television, Inc.

BHC Communications, Inc. was the largest shareholder in Warner Communications, Inc. from 1984 until 1989, when Time Warner became the majority shareholder. In August of that year, BHC received $1.6 billion for shares accepted by Time Warner in its tender for Warner Communications, Inc. shares and for additional shares sold to WCI. As a result of the Warner and Time merger, BHC holds, as of 1990, Time Warner 8.67 percent cash-pay stock and 11 percent pay-in-kind convertible preferred stock with an aggregate market value of $712 million. Chris-Craft Industries has been headed since 1983 by chairman of the board and president Herbert J. Siegel.

Address: 600 Madison Avenue, New York, NY 10022.

THE CHRISTIAN TELEVISION MISSION was founded in 1956 to produce and distribute "Christian-oriented" programming; it also publishes *Christian TV News*.

Address: 1918 South Ingram Mill Road, Springfield, MO 65804.

"CHURNING" is the name given by the pay-television cable industry to the problem of subscribers who sign up for a cable service and then, promptly, cancel it.

CIGARETTE ADVERTISING. In February 1969, the FCC* first proposed a ban on cigarette advertising for both radio and television. Such advertising had been abolished in the United Kingdom in 1965. Congressional legislation made cigarette advertising illegal on both radio and television after January 1, 1971. The legislation was resisted by both the tobacco industry and by broadcasters, who perceived a potential revenue loss, and it only came about as a result of considerable public pressure. At the same time, the Television Code* of the National Association of Broadcasters* was rewritten to warn against the gratuitous depiction of cigarette smoking as "glamorous, romantic [or] heroic."
BIBLIOGRAPHY
"Last Drag: Ban on Broadcast Advertising," *Newsweek*, January 4, 1971, p. 65.
"Snuffing Out Commercials," *Newsweek*, March 16, 1970, p. 69.

CINEGRAPHICS, INC., operated by Francis C. Thayer, was a New York–based producer, primarily of television commercials, active in the fifties and early sixties.

CINEMA-VUE CORPORATION, founded by Joseph P. Smith, was active in the fifties and sixties as a New York–based distributor to television of over 100 British features, 100 cartoons, and 300 Hal Roach and Mack Sennett comedies.

CINEMAX, a division of HBO,* is a cable network offering feature films, documentaries, and selected music and comedy programming to its more than 6 million subscribers. The twenty-four hour a day service began broadcasting on August 1, 1980, and unlike HBO, it does not specialize in current feature films. Prior to 1983, the network concentrated on the airing of feature films only, but since then it has included original programming. That year, NBC* cancelled *SCTV* (which had been seen on the network since 1981), and Cinemax added the series to its schedule. Cinemax is known in the industry simply as "Max."

Address: 1100 Avenue of the Americas, New York, NY 10036.

BIBLIOGRAPHY
Bierbaum, Tom, "Cinemax Seeks 'More With-It' Cable Audience," *Daily Variety*, May 18, 1983, pp. 1, 10.
Crook, David, "Cinemax—Another But Different, Pay Channel," *Los Angeles Times*, September 28, 1982, part VI, p.1.
Dougherty, Philip H., "Cinemax Campaign by Bates," *New York Times*, June 5, 1984, p. 45.
Graham, Jefferson, "Cinemax Now 3rd-Largest Pay Service; Time Has 2 of Top 3," *The Hollywood Reporter*, July 5, 1983, pp. 1, 8, 28.

CINE-TEL PRODUCTIONS, operated by Harry J. Lehman, was a Los Angeles–based producer and distributor, active in the fifties, and responsible for the thirty-minute syndicated series *Caliente Faces* (1955).

CINETUDES FILM PRODUCTIONS, LTD. is a New York–based producer of television commercials, founded in 1976 by Christine Jurzykowski. Related companies are Cinetudes Cable Programming Association and Atelier Cinema Video Stages, both formed in 1981.
   Address: 295 West 4 Street, New York, NY 10014.

THE CITIZENS COMMUNICATIONS CENTER OF THE INSTITUTE FOR PUBLIC REPRESENTATION was founded in 1971 to represent individuals and community groups seeking to remind television and radio stations that they are trustees of the communications media for the public.
   Address: c/o Georgetown University Law Center, 600 New Jersey Avenue, N.W., Washington, DC 20001.

CLAMPET-TOON COMMERCIALS, INC. was a Los Angeles–based producer of animated commercials, founded by former Warner Bros. animator Bob Clampett (1915–1985) in 1956. It remained active through 1961.

CLARION PRODUCTIONS is the production subsidiary of the advertising agency Foote, Cone & Belding Communications, Inc., and is responsible for the production of a number of made-for-television movies.
   Address: 101 Park Avenue, New York, NY 10178.

CLAYTON W. COUSENS PRODUCTIONS was a New York–based producer of television commercials and fashion shows, active from 1953 to 1956.

CLEAR CHANNEL COMMUNICATIONS, INC. was founded in 1972 by its president and chief executive officer, Lowry Mays. It owns sixteen radio stations, two radio networks, and four television stations: WPMI-Mobile, Alabama; KTTU-Tucson; WAWS-Jacksonville, Florida; and KOKI-Tulsa. In 1974, it merged San Antonio Broadcasting, Inc. into the company, and in 1984, it acquired Broad Street Communications Corp. Subsidiary companies are Clear Channel Sports, Inc. and Clear Channel Television, Inc.

Address: 175 East Houston Street, Suite 500, San Antonio, TX 78205.

THE CLIO AWARDS, named after the muse of history in Greek mythology, are competitive, annual awards for the best television commercials in various categories. The national awards have been presented since 1960 and the international awards since 1966; the judging is by a panel of advertising professionals.

Address: 336 East 59 Street, New York, NY 10022.

CLOSED CAPTIONING FOR THE DEAF. "Closed Captioning" means that subtitles are encoded in the video signal and can only be seen on a television receiver through the use of a decoder. The technical system used was first proposed by the National Bureau of Standards in 1971, and ABC* and NBC* demonstrated its application at a National Conference for the Hearing Impaired at the University of Tennessee at Knoxville in December 1971 and at Gallaudet College in Washington, D.C., in February 1972. The use of line 21 of the vertical blanking interval for the transmission of captions was approved by the FCC* on December 8, 1976, and decoders manufactured by Sanyo for Sears, Roebuck and Co. became commercially available in March 1980. The captions or subtitles are prepared by the National Captioning Institute, which was incorporated in March 1979. As of 1990, it was estimated that 1 million viewers used closed captioning.
BIBLIOGRAPHY
Wells, Daniel R., "Captioning for the Deaf—A PBS Progress Report," *SMPTE Journal*, vol. LXXX, no. 9, September 1980, pp. 656–658.

CNBC is a basic cable channel, operating twenty-four hours a day. The channel was created as a consumer news and business service by NBC,* under the presidency of Michael Eskridge. With 15 million subscribers, CNBC began broadcasting at 6:00 A.M. on April 17, 1989, with its first program being *World Business*. CNBC came about as a result of NBC's long-term lease, in 1988, of Tempo Television from Tele-Communications, Inc.*

Address: 2200 Fletcher Avenue, Fort Lee, NJ 07024.
BIBLIOGRAPHY
Huff, Richard, "NBC Bets Big Bucks on Biz Channel; CNBC To Take Off Next Week," *Variety*, April 12, 1989, pp. 82, 86.
Lierberman, David, "Attack of the Peacock," *Business Week,* No. 3068, September 5, 1988, p. 26.

CNN (CABLE NEWS NETWORK) is a twenty-four hour a day basic cable service, providing news, business reports, weather, and sports information. The world's first twenty-four hour news service was created by Robert E. "Ted" Turner (born 1938), with an original operating budget of $25 million and a staff of 225. It was first seen by 1.7 million subscribers at 6:00 A.M. Eastern Time on June 1, 1980, and interrupted its first commercial break to report the attempted assassination of civil rights leader Vernon Jordan. CNN's original newscasters were Bill Zimmerman, Mary Alice Williams, and Bernard Shaw. Daniel Schorr was its senior correspondent.

Among the major stories that CNN has covered live are the 1985 Beirut hijacking, the 1986 *Challenger* disaster, and the 1989 student revolt in Beijing. CNN's most impressive achievement has been the weekly *CNN World Report*, consisting of three-minute segments from ninety foreign television networks.

A separate Headline News channel, providing round-the-clock, regularly updated, thirty-minute news programs, was introduced by CNN in January 1982. As of 1990, CNN claimed 55 million subscribers in the United States (42 million for *Headline News*) and 150 million viewers worldwide in seventy-five countries. American tourists have found CNN a welcome attraction at most foreign hotels. CNN operates twenty news bureaus and has a staff of 1,720.

CNN added to its prestige with the outbreak of war in the Persian Gulf. The network provided the most comprehensive coverage of the fighting, and it was watched by 10.8 million households in the United States. In addition, many millions more watched independent television stations utilizing the CNN feed. It was the only U.S. network to have reporters in Baghdad providing live coverage of the first day of the allied air attack on the city, January 16, 1991. The pictures of the bombing, together with the commentary by Peter Arnett, John Holliman, and Bernard Shaw is believed to be the most watched event in television history.

Address: 1 CNN Center, Atlanta, GA 30303.

BIBLIOGRAPHY

Baker, Stephen, "The Cable News Networks Set Sail," *Panorama*, vol. I, no. 3, April 1980, pp. 44–47, 50.

Crook, David, "CNN Is Opening Some Eyes in News Coverage," *Los Angeles Times Calendar*, November 6, 1984, pp. 1, 4–5.

Diamond, Edwin, "All Day and All Night the Upstart Challenges the Establishment," *Panorama*, vol. I, no. 8, September 1980, pp. 68–73.

Gelman, Morrie, "Ted Turner's Global Village," *Daily Variety*, March 10, 1989, pp. 1, 59.

Goldstein, Richard, "How Good Is CNN?" *Village Voice*, April 30, 1985, p. 35.

Hall, Jane, "CNN: Far from Broken, But They're Fixing It," *Los Angeles Times Calendar*, April 1, 1990, pp. 5, 96.

Henry, William A., III, "Shaking Up the Networks," *Time*, August 9, 1982, pp. 50–56.

Kleinfield, N.R., "Cable News Network Wins Praise and Viewers," *New York Times*, April 19, 1987, section 3, pp. 1, 8–9.

Knoll, Steve, "Turner's Cable News Net Enters '81 with Strong Lead," *Daily Variety*, January 9, 1981, pp. 56, 58.

Leiser, Ernest, "The Little Network That Could," *New York Times Magazine*, March 20, 1988, pp. 30–38.

O'Connor, John J., "TV: The Early Days of 24-Hour News," *New York Times*, June 5, 1980, p. C23.

Robins, J. Max, "The Soul of a News Machine," *Channels of Communications*, vol. X, no. 3, March 1990, pp. 26–30.

Safchik, Irwin, "CNN at Ten: A Higher Station," *Emmy*, vol. XII, no. 3, May/June
     1990, pp. 36–40.
Schwartz, Tony, "The TV News Starring Ted Turner," *New York Times*, May 25, 1980,
     section 3, pp. 1, 4.
———, "Cable News Network—In Search of an Identity," *New York Times*, June 29,
     1980, pp. 27–28.
"Ted's Global Village," *Newsweek*, June 11, 1990, pp. 48–52.
"Ted Turner Tackles TV News," *Newsweek*, June 16, 1980, pp. 58–66.
"Terrible Ted vs. the Networks," *Time*, June 9, 1980, p. 68.
Van Horne, Harriet, "Night and Day, Play by Play—It's the News," *Television Quar-
     terly*, vol. XVII, no. 2, Summer 1980, pp. 19–21.
Whittemore, Hank. *CNN: The Inside Story*. Boston: Little, Brown, 1990.

COALITION FOR BETTER TELEVISION. See THE NATIONAL FED-
ERATION FOR DECENCY

COALITION FOR NO SOAP was a coalition of church groups formed in 1977
to oppose the televising of the comedy series *Soap* (ABC, 1977–1981).

THE COALITION OPPOSING SIGNAL THEFT was formed in 1986 to
disseminate information regarding signal theft and piracy within the cable television industry.
     Address: 1724 Massachusetts Avenue, N.W., Washington, DC 20036.

THE COAXIAL CABLE is the line of transmission for carrying television
signals. Its principal conductor is either a copper or copper-plated wire, sur-
rounded by insulation and encased in aluminum. Most sources discussing the
first coaxial cable are referring to the cable linking the East and West coasts,
which became operational in September 1951. However, in reality, the first
coaxial cable linked New York and Washington, D.C., in 1946, and made it
possible for viewers in both cities and surrounding areas to view the Joe Lewis–
Billy Conn fight on June 24, 1946.
BIBLIOGRAPHY
Ives, Herbert E., "Transmission of Motion Pictures over a Coaxial Cable," *Journal of
     the Society of Motion Picture Engineers*, vol. XXXI, no. 3, September 1938,
     pp. 256–272.
Osborne, H.S., "Coaxial Cables and Television Transmission," *Journal of the Society
     of Motion Picture Engineers*, vol. XXXXIV, no. 6, June 1945, pp. 403–418.

COCA-COLA TELEVISION was created in November 1986 by the Entertainment Business Sector of the Coca-Cola Company, which had acquired Columbia Pictures in 1982, as an umbrella organization for all of that studio's
television operations, including Columbia Pictures Television, Embassy Communications (acquired in 1985), and Merv Griffin Enterprises.* In March 1987,
Coca-Cola decided to split its television production into two distinct parts; Embassy would handle all television comedy and Columbia Pictures Television

would be responsible for television drama. In October 1987, the television division of the Entertainment Business Sector was merged with Tri-Star Television to become Columbia Pictures Television (the name under which Columbia's television division had operated in a previous incarnation after the demise of Screen Gems*). Merv Griffin Enterprises remained intact.

COLEX was a company created by Columbia Pictures Television and Lexington Broadcast Services/LBS Communications, Inc.,* with its first release being the syndicated situation comedy *What's Happening Now!!* (1985–1986).

COLOR. The battle over which network would introduce color to television was waged between CBS* and NBC,* with the latter the ultimate winner. The CBS system was field-sequential and mechanical, while the NBC system, developed by RCA,* was dot-sequential.

The CBS color system was developed by Dr. Peter Goldmark, the head of the network's research laboratories. The first color broadcast took place on August 27, 1940, from the Chrysler Building in New York, and for three months in the spring of 1941, CBS maintained a regular schedule of color programming. After initially rejecting the CBS color system in 1945, the FCC* adopted its use on November 20, 1950. RCA filed suit to delay the adoption, but on May 20, 1951, the Supreme Court upheld the FCC. The first network color programs were seen on CBS in June 1951, but because of the Korean War, production of color television receivers was suspended by the government. By the war's end in 1953, NBC and RCA were in the ascendancy.

In 1949, RCA developed a high-definition, all-electronic color television system, operating on a six-megacycle channel, and compatible with existing black-and-white television. The system was first demonstrated to the FCC in 1950. In 1952, NBC conducted compatible color television tests during regular broadcasting hours, and that same year, it equipped New York's Colonial Theatre as the first American studio ready for color production. On October 3, 1953, *NBC TV Opera Theatre* presented an hour-long television production of *Carmen* in color, and on November 3, 1953, a live show from the Colonial Theatre was transmitted by RCA Compatible Color Television, via radio relay, to Burbank, California, in the first transcontinental color television demonstration.

On October 7, 1953, RCA made available full details of its color television receiver at a New York symposium; earlier, it had made available to competing manufacturers information on the design and production of its improved color-television picture tube. The FCC approved NBC's plans for an "Introductory Year" of color television, beginning December 17, 1953, with one of the first telecasts being of the Tournament of Roses in Pasadena, California, which was seen in color on twenty-one stations and was the first West Coast origination of a color program. In March 1954, RCA began production of television sets with fifteen-inch color picture tubes, and in December of the same year it began manufacture of sets with twenty-one-inch color picture tubes.

NBC's first studio specifically designed for color broadcasting was dedicated in Burbank on March 27, 1955. Dwight D. Eisenhower was the first U.S. president to be seen on color television, from West Point, on June 7, 1955. The first dramatic show in color was *NBC Matinee Theatre*, broadcast on October 31, 1955. The first color television presentations of sporting events were Davis Cup Tennis on June 26–28, 1955; Georgia Tech versus Miami University football on September 17, 1955; and the Dodgers versus the Yankees in baseball on September 28, 1955. The largest audience up to that time—46 million—for a daytime television presentation was for the telecast, in color, of Sir Laurence Olivier's 1955 feature film production of *Richard III*, seen on NBC on March 11, 1956.

The advent of color television proved the foresight of Ziv Television Programs, Inc.,* which had filmed its 1950–1955 syndicated series, *The Cisco Kid*, in color, and thus assured its continued airing on television. (In fact, some episodes of *The Cisco Kid* were filmed in both black-and-white and color.)

BIBLIOGRAPHY

Coleman, Howard W., editor. *Color Television: The Business of Colorcasting*. New York: Hastings House, 1968.

Eddy, William C., "Color Television," in *The Eyes of Tomorrow*. New York: Prentice-Hall, 1945, pp. 129–142.

Goldmark, Peter C., with Lee Edson. *Maverick Inventor: My Turbulent Years at CBS*. New York: Saturday Review Press, 1973.

Goldmark, P.C., J.W. Christensen, and J.J. Reeves, "Color Television—U.S.A. Standard," *Journal of the Society of Motion Picture and Television Engineers*, vol. LVII, no. 4, October 1951, pp. 336–381.

Goldmark, P.C., J.N. Dyer, E.R. Piore, and J.M. Hollywood, "Color Television," *Journal of the Society of Motion Picture Engineers*, vol. XXXVIII, no. 4, April 1942, pp. 311–352.

Monroe, Robert B., "CBS Television Color Studio 72," *Journal of the Society of Motion Picture and Television Engineers*, vol. LXIV, no. 10, October 1955, pp. 542–549.

COLORAMA FEATURES was founded in 1957 by Jules B. Weill in recognition of television's imminent need for color material. Based in New York, it distributed twenty-six color feature films to television, and was active through 1967.

COLOR BARS appear at the beginning of a video to help the viewer obtain the best possible colors from the monitor. The NTSC* color bar signal has seven bars, generated at the prescribed luminance or brightness, chroma phase angle or hue, and chroma amplitude or saturation. From left to right, the vertical color bars are gray (of which 75 percent is white), yellow, cyan, green, magenta, red, blue, and black.

BIBLIOGRAPHY

Palmer-Benson, Timothy B., "What Color Bars Can Tell You," *The Perfect Vision*, vol. I, no. IV, Spring/Summer 1988, p. 70.

COMBINED TELEVISION PICTURES, INC. (John A. Byers, president) was a Beverly Hills–based television distributor, active in the fifties and early sixties.

COMEDIC PRODUCTIONS, INC. was the production company owned by comedians Tom and Dick Smothers, and responsible for *The Smothers Brothers Show* (CBS, 1965–1966) and *The Smothers Brothers Comedy Hour* (CBS, 1967–1969; ABC, 1970; NBC, 1975).

THE COMEDY CHANNEL was introduced on cable by HBO* on November 15, 1989, under the supervision of president Richard Beahrs. As its name indicates, the twenty-four hour a day channel is devoted exclusively to comedy, competing with MTV's Ha!* One of its first series was a group of silent comedies featuring Chaplin, Buster Keaton, and others, and hosted by Robert Klein, under the title *Dead Comics Society*. In April 1991, the Comedy Channel merged with Ha! to form CTV: The Comedy Network.
Address: 1100 Avenue of the Americas, New York, NY 10036.
BIBLIOGRAPHY
Rubin, Rosina, "Take My Channel, Please!" *Emmy*, vol. XII, no. 4, July/August 1990, pp. 90–94.

COMMODORE PRODUCTIONS AND ARTISTS, INC. (Walter White, Jr., president) was a Los Angeles–based television distributor, active in the fifties and early sixties.

THE COMMONWEALTH BROADCASTING ASSOCIATION is an organization of public broadcasting companies in the countries of the British Commonwealth, founded in 1945 as the Commonwealth Broadcasting Conference.
Address: Broadcasting House, London W1A 1AA, United Kingdom.

COMMONWEALTH FILM & TELEVISION, INC. was a New York–based distributor of over 100 features and 300 cartoons to television, founded by Mortimer D. Sackett, and active in the fifties and sixties.

THE COMMUNITY ANTENNA TELEVISION ASSOCIATION (CATA) was founded in 1974 to represent the interests of small and independent cable operators to the federal government and elsewhere.
Address: P.O. Box 1005/3977 Chain Bridge Road, Fairfax, VA 22030.

THE COMMUNITY TV NETWORK, founded in 1974, trains low-income, minority youth in video, in part through the production of the Chicago public-access television news program *Hard Cover*.
Address: 1105 West Lawrence Avenue, Suite 210, Chicago, IL 60640.

COMSAT (The Communications Satellite Corporation) is a private company, created by the Communications Satellite Act of 1962, and organized the following year with a board of representatives from AT&T, RCA,* Western Union International, and IT&T. COMSAT's founding followed the July 1962 launch of the communication satellite *Telstar 1*, and clearly indicated that international satellite communication was not to be a government-controlled industry in the United States. On an international level, COMSAT works with INTELSAT* (the International Telecommunications Satellite Consortium), formed in 1964.

Address: 950 L'Enfant Plaza, S.W., Washington, DC 20024.

CONDOR PICTURES, INC. is a producer of commercials and television programming (often pilots), owned by Milton Simon, and active from the fifties through the present.

Address: 1536 Viewsite Terrace, Hollywood, CA 90069.

CONSOLIDATED TELEVISION SALES was a Beverly Hills–based television distributor, active in the early fifties.

COOGA MOOGA PRODUCTIONS was owned by singer Pat Boone and produced his 1967 syndicated series *Pat Boone in Hollywood*.

COOKING SHOWS. While Julia Child is the best known of television chefs, with her PBS* series *The French Chef* (1963–1973) and *Julia Child and Company* (1978–1979), she was not the first to introduce viewers to the art of cooking. On NBC,* from 1946 to 1947, James Beard presented *I Love To Eat*; Beard later hosted a 1963 syndicated series. Also on NBC, from 1947–1948, Alma Kitchell hosted *In the Kelvinator Kitchen*. On CBS,* from 1948 to 1949, Dione Lucas hosted *To the Queen's Taste*. From New Zealand, Graham Kerr hosted *The Galloping Gourmet* (Syndicated, 1968–1971) and *Take Kerr* (Syndicated, 1975); and from Canada came *Celebrity Cooks* (Syndicated, 1978). The short-lived *Mama Malone* (CBS, 1984) was a sitcom* about a cooking show host, played by Lila Kaye.

Cooking series on British television have included *Cook's Night Out*, with Marcel Boulestin (BBC, 1937); *Philip Harben* (BBC, 1946–1954); *Fanny's Kitchen*, with Fanny and Johnny Cradock (Associated Rediffusion, 1955); *Family Fare*, with Delia Smith (BBC, 1973); and *Food, Wine and Friends*, with Robert Carrier (HTV, 1980).

CORNELL FILMS, INC., founded by Milton J. Salzburg, was a New York–based producer and distributor, active in the fifties and early sixties.

CORNWALL PRODUCTIONS was formed in 1953 by actress Ella Raines and executive William M. Dozier. The following year, it produced the syndicated series *Janet Dean, Registered Nurse*, starring Raines. The company ceased operations in 1956.

THE CORPORATION FOR ENTERTAINMENT AND LEARNING, INC. was founded in 1963 by Mert Koplin, and has been responsible for a number of prestigious television documentary series, including *Creativity with Bill Moyers* (PBS, 1982), *A Walk through the 20th Century with Bill Moyers* (PBS, 1982), and *The Animal Express* (USA Cable, 1986).

CORPORATION FOR PUBLIC BROADCASTING. See THE CPB

COSMAN PRODUCTIONS, INC. was created by comedian Lou Costello to produce the 1953 syndicated series *I'm the Law*.
BIBLIOGRAPHY
Costello, Lou, with Raymond Strait. *Lou's on First: A Biography*. New York: St. Martin's Press, 1981.

COSMOS BROADCASTING CORP., a division of the Liberty Group, was founded in 1931 by W. Frank Hipp. It owns the following television stations: WSFA-Montgomery, Alabama; KAIT-Jonesboro, Arkansas; WFIE-Evansville, Indiana; WAVE-Louisville; KPLC–Lake Charles, Louisiana; WTOL-Toledo; and WIS-Columbia, South Carolina.
   Address: Box 789, Greenville, SC 29602.

COSTUME DRAMA. Apart from various series on "Masterpiece Theatre,"* costume dramas have never been very popular with American television audiences. Indeed, aside from a few mini-series, there have been no costume drama series seen on American network television since the sixties, and the majority of such shows date from the previous decade. The following series were either filmed or produced in the United Kingdom: *The Adventures of Robin Hood*, with Richard Greene (CBS, 1955–1958); *The Adventures of Sir Francis Drake*, with Terence Morgan and Jean Kent (NBC, 1962); *The Adventures of Sir Lancelot*, with William Russell (NBC, 1956–1957); *The Buccaneers*, with Robert Shaw (CBS, 1956–1957); *Ivanhoe*, with Roger Moore (Syndicated, 1958); and *The Scarlet Pimpernel*, with Marius Goring (Syndicated, 1956). *The Adventures of William Tell*, with Conrad Phillips (Syndicated, 1958) was filmed in Switzerland; *Sword of Freedom*, with Edmund Purdom (Syndicated, 1957), and *The Three Musketeers*, with Jeffrey Stone (Syndicated, 1955), were filmed in Italy; *Tales of the Vikings*, with Jerome Courtland (Syndicated, 1959), was filmed in West Germany; and *Long John Silver*, with Robert Newton (Syndicated, 1955), was filmed in Australia. The only costume series to be filmed in the United States or Canada (often the latter) were *The Count of Monte Cristo* (Syndicated, 1955–1956), *Hawkeye and the Last of the Mohicans* (Syndicated, 1957), *Hudson's Bay* (Syndicated, 1958), and *Northwest Passage* (NBC, 1958–1959).

COUCH POTATOES is a derogatory term for those who spend too many hours watching television. It is also the name of a society, founded in 1976, to promote such activity and to encourage "a state of lengthy vegetation." The society has a membership of more than 8,500, all of whom must prove their devotion to television watching.

Address: P.O Box 249, Dixon, CA 95620.

COUNTRY MUSIC TELEVISION is a basic cable network, providing twenty-four hour a day programming of country music videos, interviews, and specials to more than 10 million subscribers (as of 1990). It was launched in February 1983.

Address: 704 18 Avenue South, Nashville, TN 37203.

COX COMMUNICATIONS, INC. is one of the largest communications companies in the United States, owning a considerable number of daily and weekly newspapers (including the *Atlanta Constitution*), twenty-three cable systems, twelve radio stations, and seven television stations as of 1990: KTVU–San Francisco; WFTV-Orlando; WHIO-Dayton, Ohio; WKBD-Detroit; WPXI-Pittsburgh; WSB-Atlanta; and WSOC-Charlotte, North Carolina.

The company has its origins in the 1898 purchase of the *Dayton Evening News* by James M. Cox. It entered the broadcast field in 1934, when James M. Cox, then governor of Ohio, acquired WHIO-Dayton, the first radio station in the area. The company moved its base of operations from Ohio to Atlanta in 1939, along with its acquisition of the *Atlanta Journal*. Cox Broadcasting Corporation was established as a public company in 1964, and the newspaper interests were organized into a private company, Cox Enterprises, Inc., in 1968. In 1982, Cox Broadcasting became Cox Communications, Inc., and in 1985 it was merged back into Cox Enterprises, Inc.

Address: 1400 Lake Hearn Drive, Atlanta, GA 30319.

THE CPB (THE CORPORATION FOR PUBLIC BROADCASTING) was founded in 1968, pursuant to the Public Broadcasting Act of 1967,

to stimulate diversity and encourage innovation and excellence in programs; advance the technology and application of delivery systems; safeguard the independence of local licensees and the freedom of expression within a decentralized public broadcasting community; and act as the trustee for the funds appropriated by the Congress or contributed to CPB by other sources.

The act specifically stated that the Corporation for Public Broadcasting "will not be an agency or establishment of the United States government," despite its reliance upon Congress for funding and the corporation's fifteen-person board being appointed by the president of the United States.

PBS* was initially answerable to the CPB until 1972, and there has always been a general uneasiness in the relationship between the two organizations. Frank Pace was the first CPB chairman (he left in 1972), and the first CPB grant, of $150,000, went to NET* for *Black Journal*. In 1980, the CPB created The Program Fund, to solicit, evaluate, and select programs for CPB funding, and among the best-known series that it has sponsored are *Great Performances*

(1973-), *American Playhouse* (1982-), *Frontline* (1983-), *The MacNeil/Lehrer NewsHour* (1983-), and *WonderWorks* (1984-). While primarily funded by Congress, the CPB has received a number of non-governmental grants, notably a gift of $150 million in 1981 from Walter H. Annenberg for the development of college-level radio and television courses.

Despite the efforts of Congress, the CPB became a highly political organization. In 1972, President Nixon vetoed a multi-year funding appropriation because of perceived bias in public broadcasting. Serious charges of politicization of the corporation began in 1984 with the election of Reagan appointee Sonia Landau as chairman. In 1985, Edward J. Pfister, president of the CPB since 1981, was forced to resign because of Landau's opposition to a trip by him to the USSR, where he was to consider the suitability of Soviet programming for PBS. Pfister's successor, Martin Rubenstein, resigned in November 1986 after only ten months in office, following a disagreement with Landau. In its early years, the CPB tried to keep its board meetings private, and it was not until November 1975 that it held its first public meeting, in Atlanta. In addition to charges of politicization, since 1982 the CPB has also been criticized by independent film and television producers with regard to its funding policies.

In 1988, the Public Television Financing Bill required the CPB and PBS to end their long-time feud over the control of public broadcasting in the United States. The following year, a proposal was worked out by PBS, CPB, and the National Association of Public Television Stations,* to take effect in 1991, whereby the CPB would have responsibility for the Independent Television Service and the Minority Initiatives producing group (both created in 1988). Two hundred million dollars in programming funds would be split between the CPB and PBS, and the latter would take over such well-established programs as *The MacNeil/Lehrer NewsHour* and *Great Performances*.

Address: 1111 16 Street, N.W., Washington, DC 20036.

BIBLIOGRAPHY

Hickey, Neil, "Public TV in Turmoil," *TV Guide*, July 23, 1977, pp. 2–9.
———, "Who's in Charge Here?" *TV Guide*, July 30, 1977, pp. 20–24.
———, "It All Comes Down to Money," *TV Guide*, August 6, 1977, pp. 29–32.
"A Simple Explanation of CPB, PBS and NET," *TV Guide*, December 5, 1970, p. 4.
Wharton, Dennis, "CPB Needs a Miracle Man as Prez," *Daily Variety*, January 27, 1986, pp. 1, 18.

See also PBS Bibliography.

[THOMAS] CRAVEN FILM PRODUCTIONS/CRAVEN FILM CORPORATION is a New York–based producer of commercials and television programming, which at one point also maintained an office in Toronto. Active from 1952 through the present, it was responsible for two syndicated shows of the mid-fifties, *The World through Stamps* and *The World around Us*.

Address: 5 West 19 Street, New York, NY 10011.

CREATIVISION, operated by Seymour Posner, was a New York–based producer of live and animated television commercials, active in the fifties.

CREST PRODUCTIONS, INC. (Joe Graham, president) was a New York–based producer of television commercials, active in the fifties.

CREST TELEVISION PRODUCTIONS, founded in 1954 by Lloyd Friedgen, was a Los Angeles–based producer and distributor of features to television. It remained active through the sixties.

CRIME GLORIFICATION by television was first considered an issue in the spring of 1958. J. Edgar Hoover, director of the Federal Bureau of Investigation, issued a bulletin on May 1, 1958, to all his agencies across the country, in which he warned industry executives that if they did not

take the initiative to correct the ominous trend of crime glorification, they [might] be assured it [could] be accomplished by the strong pressure of public opinion. . . . Certainly law enforcement officials have no right to dictate what should or should not be shown on the rectangular screens. They do have, however, the obligation to insist on the observance of the moral law which binds men in all matters. They also have the right to speak out when law enforcement is held up to ridicule and the criminal is elevated to heroic proportions.

BIBLIOGRAPHY
Carlson, James M. *Prime Time Law Enforcement: Crime Show Viewing and Attitudes towards the Criminal Justice System.* New York: Praeger, 1985.
"NAB Denies TV 'Glorifies Crime,' " *The Hollywood Reporter*, May 2, 1958, pp. 1, 11.

CROSBY, BING ENTERPRISES, INC. See BING CROSBY ENTERPRISES, INC.

CROSS-OWNERSHIP or Multiple-Ownership is the term used to describe ownership by a corporation or an individual of two or more mass media properties (radio stations, television stations, or newspapers) in the same community. Such cross-ownership was prohibited by the FCC* (73.3555) in 1975 and this was ultimately upheld by the Supreme Court in 1978. Most combinations in existence when the rule was adopted were not required to be divested, with the owners of such combinations having so-called "grandfather" status. However, if those companies were to sell their properties, the cross-ownership rules would apply. In 1970, the FCC adopted a rule forbidding network television companies from ownership of cable systems.

BIBLIOGRAPHY
Baer, Walter S., Henry Geller, and Joseph A. Gundfest. *Newspaper-Television Station Cross-Ownership: Options for Federal Action.* Santa Monica, Calif.: Rand Corporation, 1974.
Gormley, William T., Jr. *The Effects of Newspaper-Television Cross-Ownership on News Homogeneity.* Chapel Hill: University of North Carolina Press, 1976.

C-SPAN and C-SPAN II are the cable-satellite public affairs networks, providing twenty-four hour a day coverage of the House of Representatives and Senate activities, congressional hearings, press conferences, and selected debates of the British and Canadian Houses of Parliament. C-SPAN (which stands for Cable-Satellite Public Affairs Network) was formed in 1977 by Brian Lamb (born 1941) through voluntary contributions from various cable television companies. The first $25,000 was put up by Robert Rosencrans, C-SPAN's chairman and president of UA-Columbia Cablevision.

C-SPAN began broadcasting on March 19, 1979, with the first live televised session from the House of Representatives. Initially, that was all that was available to its 3.5 million subscribers, and when the House adjourned, C-SPAN went off the air. However, by 1984, the network was operating twenty-four hours a day, and also offering live viewer call-in programs, committee hearings, and National Press Club speeches.

A second channel, C-SPAN II, was introduced in June 1986. It has more than 20 million subscribers (as of 1990), while the original C-SPAN has almost 50 million. In 1988, C-SPAN signed an agreement with the National Archives and Records Service to allow for 2,000 selected master tapes to be given to the National Archives; subsequent donations were to follow. A year earlier, the Purdue University Public Affairs Video Archives (Stewart Center, G–39, West Lafayette, IN 47907) had started to tape and catalog all the C-SPAN broadcasts.

Address: 400 North Capitol Street, N.W., Suite 650, Washington, DC 20001.

BIBLIOGRAPHY

Brewin, Bob, "C-SPAN in New York: Shutting the Window on Washington," *Village Voice*, November 2, 1982, pp. 22–23.

Cory, John, "C-Span: Electronic Sunshine," *New York Times*, February 21, 1988, p. H31.

Crook, David, "Brian Lamb Is Bullish on Outlook for C-Span," *Los Angeles Times Calendar*, June 21, 1983, pp.1, 4.

"C-SPAN's Beat Keeps Web Busy in Nation's Capitol," *Daily Variety*, September 29, 1982, pp. 2, 6.

Davis, Douglas, "The Confessions of a C-Span Addict," *New York Times*, July 10, 1988, p. 31.

Geltner, Sharon, "Matching Set: Brian Lamb and Cable's C-SPAN," *Washington Journalism Review*, September 1984, pp. 29–33.

Gladstone, Brooke, "Cable's Own Public Television Network," *Channels of Communications*, vol. IV, no. 3, September/October 1984, pp. 32–35.

Goldsmith, Tom, "Cable's New Season Kicks Off with C-SPAN's Real-Life TV," *Variety*, September 29, 1982, p. 36.

Herbers, John, "The World According to C-Span," *New York Times*, August 13, 1985, p. 10.

Ivins, Molly, "Attention, News Junkies: You Don't Have To Rely on the Brokaw/Jennings/Rather Versions," *TV Guide*, December 3, 1988, pp. 49–52.

Kaplan, Peter W., "The Congressional Network," *Esquire*, May 1983, pp. 128–129.

Kerr, Gregory, "Lights, Camera . . . Congress!" *Emmy*, vol. IX, no. 3, May/June 1987, pp. 41–47.

Knoll, Steve, "C-SPAN Strives To Expand," *New York Times*, April 8, 1984, section 2, p. 28.

O'Daniel, Michael, "Cable Has a Secret," *Channels of Communications*, vol. V, no. 6, November/December 1983, pp. 48–51, 67.

Ornstein, Norman J., "Yes, Television *Has* Made Congress Better," *TV Guide*, July 25, 1987, pp. 4–8.

Rosenthal, Andrew, "C-SPAN Illuminates the Quiet Corners of '88 Campaigning," *New York Times*, October 22, 1987, p. 10.

Shear, Michael D., "10 Years of C-SPAN Coverage and the House Still Stands," *Los Angeles Times*, April 5, 1989, part VI, pp. 1, 9.

Stanley, Alessandra, "Tip Topped!" *Time*, May 28, 1984, p. 36.

Weaver, Warren, Jr., "C-Span on the Hill: 10 Years of Gavel to Gavel," *New York Times*, March 28, 1989, p. A10.

CUE CARDS, also known, for obvious reasons, as "Idiot Cards," are placed just out of camera range, and are read by actors or others experiencing problems in memorizing dialogue. Initially written by hand on large cards, they were later typed and unrolled on a teleprompter.* (The disadvantage with the latter is that it can only stay in one place, while cue cards can easily be arranged, out of sight, around a set, permitting the actor to allow his eyes apparently to wander, and thus make his delivery more natural.) The concept of such a form of prompt cards for actors was first introduced by John Barrymore on the stage in the thirties. The use of cue cards in television originated with *The Ed Wynn Show*, aired live in 1949. Wynn had used cue cards placed in the orchestra pit to help him with his monologues in vaudeville, and brought the technique to television, with the first cue cards being prepared by Barney McNulty.

BIBLIOGRAPHY

Fearn-Banks, Kathi, "It's All in the Cards," *Emmy*, vol. XII, no. 3, May/June 1990, pp. 42–44, 46.

D

DANNY THOMAS PRODUCTIONS was active in the seventies, following the demise of Thomas & Leonard Productions* and Thomas/Spelling Productions.* It was responsible for the series *Fay* (NBC, 1975–1976) and a number of made-for-television movies, including *Second Chance* (ABC, 1972), *Blood Sport* (ABC, 1973), *Remember When* (NBC, 1974), *The Gun and the Pulpit* (ABC, 1974), *High Risk* (ABC, 1976), and *Samurai* (ABC, 1979).

DANZIGER PRODUCTIONS, LTD. was the British-based company of two American brothers, Edward J. and Harry Lee Danziger, who had produced films in New York in the forties, and who came to England in the early fifties. They were responsible for a considerable amount of filmed television programming, including *Saber of London* (NBC, 1957–1960) and *The Cheaters* (Syndicated, 1961). In 1956, the Danzigers founded the New Elstree Studios.

DAPHNE PRODUCTIONS is the production company of Dick Cavett (born 1936), responsible for the various incarnations of *The Dick Cavett Show* on ABC,* PBS,* and cable television,* and for various other Dick Cavett–hosted programs.

Address: 1 West 67 Street, Suite 204, New York, NY 10023.

BIBLIOGRAPHY

Cavett, Dick, and Christopher Porterfield. *Cavett*. New York: Harcourt Brace Jovanovich, 1974.

———. *Eye on Cavett*. New York: Arbor House, 1983.

DAVID GERBER PRODUCTIONS was formed in 1976 by the former vice-president in charge of television at 20th Century–Fox. It was responsible for a number of made-for-television movies, as well as *Police Story* (NBC, 1973–1977), *Police Woman* (NBC, 1974–1978), and *David Cassidy—Man Undercover*

(NBC, 1978–1979). The company became inactive in 1985, when Gerber joined MGM/UA TV as head of worldwide production.

DAYTON PRODUCTIONS was a wholly owned subsidiary of Four Star Television,* with offices in Beverly Hills, and operational from 1957 to 1963. Its most important production was *Richard Diamond, Private Detective* (CBS, 1957–1959; NBC, 1959–1960). One of the owners of Four Star, Dick Powell (1904–1963), had played Diamond on radio from 1949 to 1952, but the television character was portrayed by David Janssen.

DBS is a direct broadcast satellite, which transmits signals directly to a rooftop receiving dish on a house or other building. It is cable television without wires, a system that makes affiliate stations obsolete. In 1980, COMSAT* created a subsidiary company, Satellite Television Corporation (STC), to promote corporate use of DBS. The first DBS able to handle direct-to-home service was Communications Technology Satellite (CTS), a joint venture between the United States and Canada, launched in 1976. Earlier, in 1977, the Japanese had launched the experimental DBS satellite *Yuri*.

BIBLIOGRAPHY

Countdown II: Jockeying at the DBS Starting Gate. Washington, D.C.: Television Digest, 1983.

The DBS Summit Conference. Washington, D.C.: Television Digest, 1983.

Morningstar, Gersh, "DBS: TV's Inevitable Future?" *Emmy*, vol. IV, no. 6, November–December 1982, pp. 35–38, 50.

Morse, Leon, "Insight: DBS," *Television Quarterly*, vol. XIX, no. 4, Winter 1983, pp. 69–74.

Nadel, Mark, and Eli Noam, editors. *The Economics of Direct Broadcast Satellites (DBS): An Anthology*. New York: Columbia University Graduate School of Business, 1983.

Oderman, Mark. *Current Trends in the Direct Broadcast Satellite Business*. Bethesda, Md.: Phillips, 1984.

DEMBY PRODUCTIONS, INC. was a New York–based production house headed by Emanuel Demby, who had been active in radio since 1936. From the fifties through the seventies, it produced minor television programming, including a fifteen-minute syndicated series, *Hollywood to Broadway*, produced in the mid-fifties.

DENA PICTURES, INC., co-owned by Danny Kaye; his wife, Sylvia Fine; Melvin Frank; and Norman Panama, was responsible, among other projects, for the production of *The Danny Kaye Show* (CBS, 1963–1967).

DENTISTS may not be the most popular of people, but they have been the leading characters in at least two television series: *Doc Corkle* (NBC, 1952), with Eddie Mayehoff in the title role, and *I'm a Big Girl Now* (ABC, 1980–

1981), with Danny Thomas as Dr. Benjamin Douglass. Peter Bonerz played the continuing character of dentist Dr. Jerry Robinson on *The Bob Newhart Show* (CBS, 1972–1978).

DEPICTO FILMS, INC. is a producer of television commercials and industrial films, active from the fifties through the present. It was initially headed by John Hans, and later by J.R. von Maur.

Address: 504-A Aspen Lane, Wyckoff, NJ 07481.

DESILU was formed by Lucille Ball and Desi Arnaz for the production of *I Love Lucy* (CBS, 1951–1961). Following the success of that show, the company began production of *Our Miss Brooks* (CBS, 1952–1956), starring Eve Arden. Later Desilu-produced series include *Willy* (CBS, 1954–1955), *Those Whiting Girls* (CBS, 1955–1957), *The Whirlybirds* (Syndicated, 1956–1959), *Desilu Playhouse* (CBS, 1958–1960), *The Ann Sothern Show* (CBS, 1958–1961), *Grand Jury* (Syndicated, 1959), *Guestward Ho!* (ABC, 1960–1961), *Harrigan & Son* (ABC, 1960–1961), and *Ben Casey* (ABC, 1961–1966).

The initial productions were filmed at the General Service Studios in Hollywood, but in January 1958, Desilu acquired two studios from RKO Teleradio Pictures, Inc. for a reported $6.15 million. The first was the RKO lot in Hollywood, and the second was the Culver City Studios, also owned by RKO but usually associated with David O. Selznick's productions. A third studio, the former Motion Picture Center Studios, was also purchased. The company labeled the studios Desilu-Culver (with thirteen sound stages), Desilu-Gower (with fourteen sound stages), and Desilu-Cahuenga (with nine sound stages). The studios were utilized for the filming of series by other companies (including *Lassie*, *Fury*, *The Gale Storm Show*, and *Frontier Correspondent*), and Desilu also provided production facilities for series that it filmed but in which it had no ownership (including *The Betty Hutton Show*, *The Jack Benny Show*, *The Danny Thomas Show*, *The Millionaires*, *The Real McCoys*, and *The Life and Legend of Wyatt Earp*). So prosperous did Desilu become that in 1958 it established the Desilu Workshop, with payments to young actors for training under its guidance.

In 1963, following his divorce from Lucille Ball, Desi Arnaz sold his share of Desilu to her for a reported $2.5 million. By the mid-sixties, Miss Ball had found the running of the company to be an arduous task, frequently having to face angry shareholders and defend the high salary that she was drawing as head of the company. It was, therefore, with some relief that she supported the acquisition of Desilu by Gulf + Western Industries, Inc. in July 1967 for $16.6 million of the latter's stock.

BIBLIOGRAPHY

Andrews, Bart, and Thomas J. Watson. *Loving Lucy*. New York: St. Martin's Press, 1980.

Higham, Charles. *Lucy: The Life of Lucille Ball*. New York: St. Martin's Press, 1986.

"$30 Million Desilu Gamble," *Life*, October 6, 1958, pp. 24–31.

DETECTIVE DRAMAS. The following is a listing of the more popular detective dramas featuring private investigators and non-police personnel on American television: *Martin Kane, Private Eye* (NBC, 1949–1954), *The Adventures of Ellery Queen* (DuMont, 1950–1951; ABC, 1951–1952; NBC, 1958–1959, 1975–1976), *Boston Blackie* (Syndicated, 1951–1952), *Craig Kennedy, Criminologist* (Syndicated, 1951), *Dick Tracy* (Syndicated, 1952), *Ellery Queen* (Syndicated, 1954), *The Lone Wolf* (Syndicated, 1954), *The Thin Man* (NBC, 1957–1959), *Mickey Spillane's Mike Hammer* (Syndicated, 1958–1959), *Peter Gunn* (NBC, 1958–1960; ABC, 1960–1961), *77 Sunset Strip* (ABC, 1958–1964), *Hawaiian Eye* (ABC, 1959–1963), *International Detective* (Syndicated, 1959), *Shannon* (Syndicated, 1961), *Mannix* (CBS, 1967–1975), *Cannon* (CBS, 1971–1976), *Barnaby Jones* (CBS, 1973–1980), *Harry-O* (ABC, 1974–1976), *The Rockford Files* (NBC, 1974–1980), *Switch* (CBS, 1975–1978), *Charlie's Angels* (1976–1981), *Vega$* (ABC, 1978–1981), *Magnum, P.I.* (CBS, 1980–1988), and *Nero Wolfe* (NBC, 1981).
BIBLIOGRAPHY
Meyers, Richard. *The TV Detectives*. San Diego: A.S. Barnes, 1981.

DEVILLIER DONEGAN ENTERPRISES was formed in 1981 by Ron Devillier and Brian Donegan as a theatrical and television distributor. It handles North American distribution of material from Channel Four, Film Australia, ABC Australia, and Television New Zealand, and is perhaps best known to American television audiences as the distributor of *Monty Python's Flying Circus*.
Address: 1608 New Hampshire Avenue, N.W., Washington, DC 20006.

THE DIAMOND HEAD STUDIO in Hawaii, built on land owned by the University of Hawaii's Kapiolani Community College, was created in the late seventies by CBS* for the filming of *Hawaii Five-O* (CBS, 1968–1980). It has also been used for the filming of many other television productions, including *Magnum, P.I.* (CBS, 1980–1988), *Tour of Duty* (CBS, 1987–), *War and Remembrance* (ABC, 1988–1989), many television commercials, and several feature films (in whole or part).
BIBLIOGRAPHY
Wood, Ben, "Hawaii Upgrades Diamond Head Studio," *Daily Variety*, June 20, 1988,
    p. 76.

DIC ENTERPRISES is a major producer of animated children's programming for television. It was founded in 1976 by French entrepreneur Jean Chalopin, with backing from Radio-Television Luxembourg. Andy Heyward joined the company in 1981, and in the winter of 1986 arranged a buy-out of DIC from its founders. Among DIC's syndicated series are *Inspector Gadget* (1983), *Heathcliffe* (1984), *GI Joe: A Great American Hero* (1985), *Dennis the Menace* (1986), and *The Real Ghostbusters* (1987).
Address: 3601 West Olive Avenue, Burbank, CA 91505.

BIBLIOGRAPHY
Bauer, Patricia E., "Babe in Toyland," *Channels of Communications*, vol. VII, no. 7, July/August 1987, pp. 48–51.

DICK CLARK PRODUCTIONS, INC. is the production company of ever-youthful popular music entrepreneur Dick Clark (born 1929). It was created to produce *American Bandstand* (ABC, 1957; Syndicated, 1957-   ), and its other productions include *The Dick Clark Show* (ABC, 1958–1968), *Dick Clark's World of Talent* (ABC, 1959), *Dick Clark's Live Wednesday* (NBC, 1978), *Inside America* (ABC, 1982), and *TV's Bloopers & Practical Jokes* (NBC, 1984-   ). In addition, the company has been responsible for many specials, and has handled television production of a number of award shows, including the American Music Awards, the Golden Globe Awards, and the Soap Opera Awards.

The company went public in January 1987, and Clark now serves as its chairman and chief executive officer.

Address: 3003 West Olive Avenue, Burbank, CA 91505.

BIBLIOGRAPHY
Clark, Dick, and Michael Shore. *The History of American Bandstand: It's Got a Great Beat and You Can Dance to It*. New York: Ballantine Books, 1985.
Snyder, Adam, "Dick Clark Grows Up," *Channels of Communications*, vol. VII, no. 5, May 1987, pp. 28–35.

THE DISCOVERY CHANNEL broadcasts non-fiction programming in the areas of nature, science, technology, world exploration, history, and human adventure from 9:00 A.M. through 3:00 A.M. daily. The first hour, *Assignment Discovery*, is intended for classroom use. A basic cable network, the Discovery Channel was founded by John Hendricks, a fund-raising consultant, with financing from Tele-Communications, Inc.,* United Cable, Cox Cable, and Newhouse Broadcasting. It began broadcasting in June 1985 with twelve hours of programming daily. In 1987, the Discovery Channel offered the first major U.S. look at Soviet television by airing sixty-six hours of that country's programming. In 1989, it signed a three-year contract with the BBC* to air the latter's most popular non-fiction programming beginning in the fall of 1990. In February 1991, the Discovery Channel acquired the Learning Channel.*

Address: 8201 Corporate Drive, Suite 1200, Landover, MD 20785.

BIBLIOGRAPHY
Brewin, Bob, "Another New Cable Net?" *Village Voice*, July 16, 1985, p. 44.
"Discovery Channel Seeks Success Where Others Failed," *Daily Variety*, June 27, 1985, p. 8.
Haithman, Diane, "Discovery Channel Finds Its Niche," *Los Angeles Times*, April 29, 1988, part VI, pp. 1, 30.
Safchik, Irwin, "True-Life TV: Cable's Discovery Channel," *Emmy*, vol. XI, no. 3, May/June 1989, pp. 34–37.
Schneider, Steve, "A Channel with a Difference," *New York Times*, June 16, 1985, section 2, p. 28.

THE DISNEY CHANNEL. The Walt Disney Company was the first studio to own and operate its own pay-cable television network, The Disney Channel, which began broadcasting on April 18, 1983. Appropriately, Mickey Mouse pulled the switch to launch the new network at 4:00 A.M. Pacific Coast Time. From 40,000 initial subscribers when it was launched, the network added 1 million subscribers in its first year of operation, and had 5 million by 1990. It began showing a profit as early as January 1985. Twenty-four hour a day programming was introduced on December 7, 1986, with children-oriented shows airing until 9:00 P.M. However, The Disney Channel has always tried to promote an image of being more than a children's television service, and bills itself as "America's Family Network."

The Disney Channel began with an ambitious program of thirteen original series. It produces made-for-television features with an average budget of between $2 and $3 million, and its first original film was *Tiger Town*, starring Roy Schneider, and broadcast in October 1983. In addition to films from the Disney organization, The Disney Channel has acquired selected features from Paramount, 20th Century–Fox, and the Samuel Goldwyn Company. The Disney Channel was headed by James P. Jimirro until June 1985, when John Cooke was named president; he revamped the operation, offering more family-oriented fare.

Address: 3800 West Alameda, Burbank, CA 91505.

BIBLIOGRAPHY

Crook, David, "The Disney Channel Does It Walt's Way," *Los Angeles Times Calendar*, April 17, 1983, pp. 3–4.

Davidson, Bill, "From Pinocchio to Prairie Home Companion to Profitability," *TV Guide*, June 18, 1988, pp. 41–46.

Ellis-Simons, Pamela, "The Disney Channel," *Channels of Communications*, vol. VII, no. 9, October 1987, pp. 43–45.

Gelman, Morrie, "Disney Ties Future to Cable TV," *Daily Variety*, December 28, 1981, pp. 1, 6.

Girard, Tom, "Disney Previews Pay-TV Channel," *Daily Variety*, April 13, 1983, pp. 1, 11.

———, "$100 Mil Commitment to Space-Age Media Bows Monday for Walt Disney," *Daily Variety*, April 15, 1983, pp. 1, 43.

———, "Disney Doubling Fevee Effort," *Daily Variety*, December 26, 1984, pp. 1, 9.

Graham, Jefferson, "Disney Channel Launched with 'Bang-Up' Cable Sales Reported," *The Hollywood Reporter*, April 25, 1983, p. 12.

———, "Disney's Answer to Subscriber's Pleas: More Cartoons, Features," *The Hollywood Reporter*, August 8, 1983, p. 6.

———, "The Disney Channel: A Creative Appraisal," *The Hollywood Reporter*, February 27, 1984, p. 8.

Hayes, Thomas C., "Disney's Cable TV Challenge," *New York Times*, February 15, 1985, pp. 31, 33.

Knoll, Steve, "The Disney Channel Has an Expensive First Year," *New York Times*, April 29, 1984, section 2, p. 28.

Mitchell, Kim, "Disney Redefines Channel as 'America's Family Net,' " *Daily Variety*, November 16, 1987, p. 3.

Sansweet, Stephen J., "Disney Has Big Hopes for Pay-TV," *Wall Street Journal*, April 17, 1983, pp. 1, 37.

Schneider, Steve, "Disney Channel Sticks to Family Fare," *New York Times*, October 7, 1984, section 2, pp. 26, 33.

Waters, Harry F., and Joe Contreras, "Wishing upon a Satellite," *Newsweek,* April 25, 1983, p. 93.

D.L. TAFFNER/LIMITED was founded in 1963 by Don Taffner (born 1930), primarily for the importation of foreign product for American television. The company owes its initial success to an early arrangement with Thames Television plc,* whereby D.L. Taffner/Limited had the U.S. rights to various Thames productions, including *The World at War* (Syndicated, 1974) and *The Benny Hill Show* (Syndicated, 1979-   ). However, it has also imported product from other countries, such as Canada's *Wayne and Shuster* (Syndicated, 1980).

D.L. Taffner/Limited is also responsible for the "Americanization" of several Thames productions, which became *Three's Company* (ABC, 1977–1984), *The Ropers* (ABC, 1979–1980), *Too Close for Comfort* (ABC, 1980–1983), and *The Ted Knight Show* (Syndicated, 1986). The company was formerly known as Gottlieb-Taffner.

Address: 31 West 56 Street, New York, NY 10019.

BIBLIOGRAPHY

Snyder, Adam, "After 25 Years, Still Doing It Don's Way," *Channels of Communications*, vol. VIII, no. 3, March 1988, pp. 73–75.

A DOCU-DRAMA is a television drama that is based on a historical event, and that blends elements of both documentary and theatre. Recent examples of the genre are *The Taking of Flight 847: The Uli Derickson Story* (NBC, 1988), *Terrorist on Trial: The U.S. vs. Salim Ajami* (CBS, 1988), *Everybody's Baby: The Rescue of Jessica McClure* (ABC, 1989), *Guts and Glory: The Rise and Fall of Oliver North* (CBS, 1989), *The Hijacking of the Achille Lauro* (NBC, 1989), *The Ryan White Story* (ABC, 1989), *Tailspin: Behind the Korean Airline Tragedy* (HBO, 1989), and *The Plot To Kill Hitler* (CBS, 1990).

A DOMSAT is a distribution or domestic satellite, relaying signals on a local or nationwide basis rather than on an international level. The use of domsats was approved by the FCC* in 1972, and one of the first to be launched was Western Union's *Westar 1* in 1974.

DON FEDDERSON PRODUCTIONS, INC. One of the most energetic of companies in the early years of television, Don Fedderson Productions, Inc. was founded in 1953 by the former general manager of KLAC–Los Angeles and KYA–San Francisco. Fedderson created two syndicated series, *The Liberace Show* (1953–1955) and *Life with Elizabeth* (1953–1955), starring Betty White, which introduced two new personalities to television. The first two series were followed by *The Millionaire* (CBS, 1955–1960) and *Do You Trust Your Wife?* (CBS, 1956–1957). *The Millionaire* was sold to CBS* for $3 million, and with that money, Fedderson was able to create *Date with the Angels* (ABC, 1957–1958), *My Three Sons* (ABC, 1960–1965; CBS, 1965–1972), *Family Affair* (CBS, 1966–1971), *To Rome with Love* (CBS, 1969–1971), and *The Smith Family* (ABC, 1971–1972).

In 1954, Fedderson, in association with Sam J. Lutz, created *The Lawrence Welk Show* (ABC, 1955–1971), and following its network cancellation, Fedderson arranged for that show's production as a syndicated series (1971–1982). In 1961, Don Fedderson Productions acquired the lease to the Hollywood Palladium, and ten years later purchased the property. Since the mid-eighties, the company has been inactive in the entertainment field.

Address: 16255 Ventura Boulevard, Suite 1117, Encino, CA 91436.

DON LEE BROADCASTING SYSTEM. Don Lee was a wealthy Los Angeles Cadillac dealer, who entered broadcasting in 1926 with the purchase of radio station KFRC–San Francisco. A year later, he acquired KHJ–Los Angeles. Lee became interested in television in 1930, and hired an electrical engineering student from the University of Southern California named Harry R. Lubcke (born 1905), who was given the title of director of television. On December 23, 1931, Don Lee began broadcasting from station W6XAO, located in the Don Lee Building at Seventh and Bixel Streets in downtown Los Angeles, utilizing a primitive cathode-ray tube camera invented by Lubcke. W6XAO presented programming one hour per day for six days a week, on a frequency of 44.5 megacycles.

On October 14, 1939, Los Angeles Mayor Fletcher Bowron opened W6XAO as a semi-commercial television station in a broadcast on both radio and television over the Don Lee Pacific Coast Network. Other participants were Morton Downey and Betty Rhodes. In 1939, the company acquired land on a mountaintop on the boundary of Griffith Park in Hollywood. Here, the new transmitter was located. The mountain was renamed Mount Lee, and is best known as the site of the Hollywood sign.

In 1950, the Don Lee Broadcasting System was purchased for $12.3 million by the company that became RKO General Broadcasting, and was operated as the Don Lee Division. Willet Henry Brown was named president of the division— he had joined Don Lee as the system's assistant general manager in 1932. In December 1950, CBS* acquired W6XAO, which was now known as KNXT and was eventually to be renamed KCBS. A year later, the Don Lee Division took over KHJ–Los Angeles (which was a DuMont* affiliate).

Don Lee was a pioneer in many areas of television. On May 21, 1932, the system broadcast television signals from its transmitter to a Western Air Express tri-motored plane flying over the city of Los Angeles. On March 10, 1933, it broadcast the feature film *The Crooked Circle* as it was concurrently showing in Los Angeles theatres. On March 23, 1933, it began three days of live coverage of the Long Beach earthquake. On April 15, 1938, it began broadcasting *Vine Street*, which is believed to have been the first television serial. On March 24, 1940, it broadcast the Easter Sunrise Service from the Hollywood Bowl for the first time. On April 1, 1948, it presented the first broadcast in the western United States of a symphony concert, by the Los Angeles Philharmonic orchestra, with Yehudi Menuhin as soloist.

BIBLIOGRAPHY

Lubcke, Harry R., "Television on the West Coast," in *We Present Television*, editors John Porterfield and Kay Reynolds. New York: W.W. Norton, 1940.

Stambler, Mark, "And in LA," *Emmy*, vol. VII, no. 4, July/August 1985, p. 87.

DONLEVY DEVELOPMENT ENTERPRISES was the production company of actor Brian Donlevy (1901–1972), and was responsible for the 1952 syndicated television series *Dangerous Assignment*.

DOUGFAIR CORPORATION was owned by Douglas Fairbanks, Jr. (born 1909), and operational from 1952 to 1961. It produced two syndicated television series, *Terry and the Pirates* (1952) and *Douglas Fairbanks Presents* (1952–1955).

THE DOUGLAS S. CRAMER COMPANY was formed following Cramer's resignation as production head of Paramount Television* in April 1971. Initially located on the Columbia lot, it later moved to the Warner-Hollywood Studios. The company merged with Aaron Spelling Productions, Inc.* in 1977, but resumed independent production in August 1989, while remaining part of Spelling Entertainment.

Among Cramer's many movies-for-television are *The Cat Creature* (ABC, 1973), *QB VII* (ABC, 1974), *The Sex Symbol* (ABC, 1974), *The Dead Don't Die* (NBC, 1975), *Who Is the Black Dahlia?* (NBC, 1975), *Search for the Gods* (ABC, 1975), *Cage without a Key* (CBS, 1975), *The New, Original Wonder Woman* (ABC, 1975), *Dawn: Portrait of a Teenage Runaway* (NBC, 1976), *Snowbeast* (NBC, 1977), and *Alexander: The Other Side of Dawn* (NBC, 1977).

Address: 1041 North Formosa Avenue, West Hollywood, CA 90046.

DOWNTOWN COMMUNITY TELEVISION CENTER was founded in 1972 as a non-profit organization providing free media services to producers, performers, and community organizations. Its first production was *Cuba: The People* (1974).

Address: 87 Lafayette Street, New York, NY 10013.

D.P.M. PRODUCTIONS, INC. (the initials stand for Dorothy P. Maulsby) was a New York–based producer of television commercials, active in the fifties and sixties. In the latter decade, the name was changed to Clifton Productions, Inc., and the company was operated by Maurice T. Groen.

DUDLEY TV CORP. was a division of the Beverly Hills–based Dudley Pictures Corp., founded in 1944 by Carl Ward Dudley (1910–1973). Dudley had been a writer in the shorts department at Warner Bros., and he formed his company for the production of industrial films and travelogs, beginning with a documentary for the Association of American Railroads. Among Dudley's theatrical productions is the 1958 Cinerama travelog *South Seas Adventures*. Dudley TV Corp. produced a number of minor syndicated travel series; it also produced the commercials for *I Love Lucy* and other shows, and distributed but did not produce the 1968 syndicated series *The Great Adventure*.

DUMONT. The fourth network, DuMont was active from 1947 to 1955, with its most popular programs being *The Original Amateur Hour* (1948–1949), starring Ted Mack; *Cavalcade of Stars* (1950–1952), starring Jackie Gleason in his first network series; *Captain Video and His Video Rangers* (1949–1955); and *Life Is Worth Living* (1952–1955), with Bishop Fulton J. Sheen.

A division of the Allen B. DuMont Laboratories, the network had its origins in station W2XWV, in Passaic, New Jersey, which began as an experimental television station in 1939, and which moved to New York to become WABD in 1944. DuMont acquired WTTG-Washington, D.C., in 1946, and became a fully fledged, if small, network the following year when it took over WDTV-Pittsburgh. Paramount Pictures had acquired a half interest in DuMont in 1938, and it linked up some, but not all, of the stations that it owned to bolster the DuMont network. However, the company remained under the control of Dr. Allen B. DuMont (1901–1965), as a division of the Allen B. DuMont Laboratories, Inc. (founded in 1931).

The Allen B. DuMont Laboratories were involved in the manufacture of a wide range of television tubes and cameras. In 1950, the company introduced the world's largest television receiver, the DuMont thirty-inch model.

Despite building up a group of over one hundred affiliate stations, DuMont was never able to provide satisfactory programming. As soon as it built up a television personality, such as Jackie Gleason or Ted Mack, he was stolen away by one of the other networks. Despite an impressive opening of its new corporate headquarters at 515 Madison Avenue, New York City, in 1954, hosted live by Gertrude Berg (whose series *The Goldbergs* ended its television life on DuMont that same year), DuMont was fighting a losing battle against NBC* and CBS.* The two networks controlled all the prominent VHF stations, and the FCC* rejected DuMont's proposal that some of those stations become affiliated to DuMont in exchange for DuMont's UHF* stations.

In May 1955, the DuMont network was dissolved, with the Allen B. DuMont Laboratories retaining control of WABD and WTTG. In May 1958, the company was renamed the Metropolitan Broadcasting Corporation. The following year, the stations were sold to John Kluge, to become part of Metromedia, Inc.,* and later to form the basis for a new fourth network, Fox Broadcasting Co.* In 1960, the Allen B. DuMont Laboratories were acquired by Fairchild Camera and Instrument Corporation.

BIBLIOGRAPHY

Hess, Gary Newton. *An Historical Study of the DuMont Television Network*. New York: Arno Press, 1979.

Kerr, Peter, "A Network of the Past Could Be a Model for the Future," *New York Times*, June 3, 1984, section 2, pp. 27–28.

Krampner, Jon, "The Death of the DuMont Network: A Real TV Whodunit," *Emmy*, vol. XII, no. 4, July/August 1990, pp. 96–103.

"Metromedia and the DuMont Legacy," *Museum of Broadcasting Newsletter*, vol. IX, no. 1, Winter 1985, pp. 16–18.

DYNAMIC FILMS, INC., founded by Nathan Zucker, was primarily a producer of industrial films. It made the occasional television commercial and television program, such as *On Stage with Monty Woolley* (Syndicated, 1954).

E

EARLY BIRD was the first commercial communications satellite, launched on April 6, 1965. Built by Hughes Aircraft, it remained in service for almost four years.

EDGAR J. SCHERICK ASSOCIATES is owned by independent producer Scherick, who has been active since 1967 with both theatrical and made-for-television movies. Among the latter are *Raid on Entebbe* (NBC, 1977), *A Circle of Children* (CBS, 1977), *Panic in Echo Park* (NBC, 1977), *Zuma Beach* (NBC, 1978), *Mother and Daughter: The Loving War* (ABC, 1980), *Revenge of the Stepford Wives* (CBS, 1980), *Thou Shalt Not Kill* (NBC, 1982), *Little Gloria. . . . Happy at Last* (NBC, 1982), and *The Scarlet Pimpernel* (CBS, 1982).

Address: 4000 West Alameda, Burbank, CA 91505.

EDIAD PRODUCTIONS was Edie Adams' production company, responsible for *Here's Edie* (ABC, 1963–1964).

"EDITED FOR TELEVISION" is a familiar subtitle that appears at the commencement of many feature films seen on television. It was first used by NBC* in the fall of 1970, in response to concerns expressed by the Federal Trade Commission (FTC) that television viewers were not being advised of cuts or re-editing in the films they were watching, and that as a result, television stations might be guilty of unfair or deceptive practices. The FTC revealed that between June and November 1969, of the 164 feature films seen on television, 57 percent were cut by two minutes or more.

BIBLIOGRAPHY

"As We See It," *TV Guide*, September 19, 1970, p. 4.

EDITORIAL FILMS, INC. was a New York–based production company, founded in 1952 by Babette J. Doniger, who had been a producer of live daytime women's programs for local television. The company was active in local New York television production for a couple of years.

EDWARDS, RALPH PRODUCTIONS. See RALPH EDWARDS PRODUCTIONS

E! ENTERTAINMENT TELEVISION is the new name given to the basic cable network, Movietime, as of June 1, 1990. The name change took place because of a perceived confusion by the audience that the network limited its programming to movies, when in reality, its twenty-four hour a day programming is devoted to coverage of film and other personalities. Founded by Larry Namer and Alan Mruvka, Movietime Channel, Inc. was launched on July 31, 1987, by HBO,* Warner Communications, American Television & Communications, Continental Cablevision, Cox Cable, News Channels Corp., United Cable, and Warner Cable. Jack Valenti, president of the Motion Picture Association of America, pulled the switch that brought Movietime on the air for its 2 million original subscribers. In the summer of 1989, HBO assumed management control of the network, and the founders resigned in August of that year.

In February 1989, Movietime launched a monthly magazine, *Movies USA*, which was distributed free of charge in movie theatres. In April 1989, a radio division was created to produce entertainment-related programming for syndication. As of 1990, Movietime had 14 million subscribers.

Address: 1800 North Vine Street, Hollywood, CA 90028.

BIBLIOGRAPHY

Gansberg, Alan L., "Focus on Movietime: A Basic Cable Service Whose Time Has Come," *The Hollywood Reporter*, May 2, 1988, pp. S1-S14.

Mitchell, Kim, "Movietime Joins Cable-TV Roster," *Daily Variety*, August 3, 1987, p. 12.

———, "Movietime Launches Newsy Showbiz Channel July 31," *Daily Variety*, August 7, 1987, p. 24.

Parisi, Paula, "HBO's Plan for Movietime: 'CNN of Entertainment,' " *The Hollywood Reporter*, July 9, 1989, pp. 1, 6.

———, "HBO Gains Control of Movietime Net," *The Hollywood Reporter*, August 8, 1989, pp. 1, 6.

———, "HBO Temp Team To Direct Movietime," *The Hollywood Reporter*, August 22, 1989, pp. 1, 134.

———, "HBO Team Begins Movietime Overhaul," *The Hollywood Reporter*, October 6, 1989, pp. 1, 49.

Richmond, Ray, "Diary of a Relaunch," *Channels of Communications*, vol. X, no. 10, July 16, 1990, pp. 38–41.

Weinstein, Steve, "HBO Plans To Give Movietime Channel a New Identity," *Los Angeles Times*, August 22, 1989, part VI, p. 1.

THE EIDOPHOR was a large-screen television projector, invented by the Swiss researcher Dr. Fritz Fischer in 1939, and first demonstrated in December 1943. The projector continues to be marketed by Eidophor Limited (Althardstrasse 70, CH–8105, Regansdorf, Switzerland).

BIBLIOGRAPHY

Sponable, Earl I., "Eidophor System of Theater Television," *Journal of the Society of Motion Picture and Television Engineers*, vol. LX, no. 4, April 1953, pp. 337–343.

[RAPHAEL] ELAN–[RALPH] PORTER PRODUCTIONS, INC. was a New York–based producer, primarily of television commercials, active in the fifties through the seventies.

ELECTRIC TOY BOX is a cable television network offering 104 different computer games per year. It was first broadcast in December 1989, and is seen two days a week.

Address: X*PRESS Information Services, 4643 South Ulster Street, Denver, CO 80237.

ELECTRONIC ARTS INTERMIX is a non-profit media arts organization, founded in 1971 by Howard Wise as a follow-up to his 1969 exhibition "TV as a Creative Medium."

Address: 536 Broadway, 9th Floor, New York, NY 10012.

THE ELECTRONIC MEDIA RATING COUNCIL was formed in 1964 as the Broadcast Rating Council to establish minimum standards for electronic media ratings surveys.

Address: 420 Lexington Avenue, New York, NY 10017.

ELECTRONIC NEWS GATHERING (ENG), also known as Electronic Journalism, was introduced in 1973, following the development of a time-base corrector, which permits the mixing of live material at a television studio with videotaped items. ENG replaced the former method of news coverage, which was accomplished with the use of 16mm films.

Thanks to Electronic News Gathering and the Minicam, television was able to broadcast live the shoot-out between the Symbionese Liberation Army and the Los Angeles Police Department on May 17, 1974. ENG also made possible the immediate coverage by WNBC–New York of the aftermath of an Eastern Airlines plane crash at Kennedy Airport on June 24, 1975.

BIBLIOGRAPHY

Medoff, Norman J., and Tom Tanquary. *Portable Video: ENG and EFP*. White Plains, N.Y.: Knowledge Industry Publications, 1986.
Sadashige, Ernie. *ENG One: A Practical Guide to Electronic News Gathering*. Gibbsboro, N.Y.: Highlights, 1985.

Shook, Frederick. *The Process of Electronic News Gathering*. Englewood, Colo.: Morton, 1982.
Yoakam, Richard D., and Charles F. Cremer. *ENG: Television News and the New Technology*. New York: Random House, 1985.

ELECTRONIC VIDEO RECORDING (EVR) was a system, first demonstrated by CBS* in 1967, that permitted prerecorded information electronically coded on black-and-white film to be played back through a television receiver. It became obsolete in 1971 as a result of the growth of videotape recording.

THE EMERSON YORKE STUDIO was a New York–based producer of industrial films and sports filler programming for television, including *This Is Baseball*. It was active in the fifties and sixties, with its last documentary being *Our Heritage* (1968).

EMMY is the glossy, bimonthly publication of the Academy of Television Arts and Sciences, founded in 1979 when the group split from the National Academy, which continued publication of *Television Quarterly* (first published in February 1962). The current issues, edited by Hank Rieger, seem very show business–oriented and lack much of the serious quality apparent under the editorship of Rieger's predecessor, Richard Krafsur.

Address: 5220 Lankershim Boulevard, North Hollywood, CA 91601.

BIBLIOGRAPHY

Slide, Anthony, editor. *International Film, Radio, and Television Journals*. Westport, Conn.: Greenwood Press, 1985.

EMPIRE FILMS, INC., founded by Thomas Handel, was a New York–based distributor to television of eighteen feature films, active in the fifties through the seventies.

EMPIRE PRODUCTION CORP. (Arthur Lubo, president) was a New York–based television packager and producer of television commercials, active in the fifties and sixties. It advertised itself as "The first complete Visual-Audio Service Studio in New York City" (at 480 Lexington Avenue).

ENCORE PROGRAMS was created in 1985 by MCA-TV to distribute older television series in syndication. Among the shows that it handled were *The Deputy* (NBC, 1959–1961) and *The Men from Shiloh* (NBC, 1962–1971). It also repackaged failed television series, such as *O'Hara, U.S. Treasury* (CBS, 1971–1972) and *Delvecchio* (CBS, 1976–1977) under the new title of "Five Star Mystery."

ENDORSEMENTS, INC., founded by Jules Alberti, was a New York–based producer of television commercials, active in the fifties through seventies. In 1968, it changed its name to Endorsements International, Inc.

ENTERTAINMENT PRODUCTIONS, INCORPORATED (EPI) was the new name for Louis G. Cowan Productions, Inc. when it introduced *The $64,000 Question* on CBS* on June 5, 1955. EPI was also responsible for *The $100,000 Big Surprise*, introduced in the fall of 1955, and *The $64,000 Challenge*, introduced in the spring of 1956. The company ceased operations as a result of the TV game show* scandals of 1957 to 1959 (in which it was a major player).

Louis G. Cowan (1909–1976) had left the company to become a vice-president with CBS. By 1959, he was the network president but was forced to resign in the wake of the scandal. Among the quiz shows produced by Louis G. Cowan Productions, Inc. are *Quiz Kids* (NBC, 1949–1951; CBS, 1952; NBC, 1952; CBS, 1952–1953, 1956), *Stop the Music* (ABC, 1949–1956), *What's My Name* (NBC, 1950–1953), *Down You Go* (DuMont, 1951–1955; ABC, 1955–1956; NBC, 1956), *Go Lucky* (CBS, 1951), *Ask Me Another* (NBC, 1952), *Balance Your Budget* (CBS, 1952–1953), and *Superghost* (NBC, 1952–1953).
BIBLIOGRAPHY
Fabe, Maxene. *Game Shows!* Garden City, N.Y.: Doubleday, 1979.

ESPN (ENTERTAINMENT & SPORTS PROGRAMMING NETWORK), with its twenty-four hour a day sports programming, claims to be the largest cable network with over 56 million subscribers. It was first seen on September 7, 1979, and three years later began offering material from ABC Sports. In December 1983, ABC Video Enterprises purchased 15 percent of the company, and in May 1984, it took over completely from Texaco, Inc. (the new owners of ESPN's initial owner, the Getty Oil Company).

Address: ESPN Plaza, Bristol, CT 06010.
BIBLIOGRAPHY
Gunther, Noel, "On a Winning Streak," *Channels of Communications*, vol. VIII, no. 7, July/August 1988, pp. 38–44.
Rasmussen, Bill. *Sports Junkies Rejoice!: The Birth of ESPN*. Hartsdale, N.Y.: QV, 1983.

ETV (EDUCATIONAL TELEVISION). In 1949, the FCC* considered the need to provide channels for non-commercial, educational television, and on March 22, 1951, announced recognition of such a need. A year later, it reserved 242 channels (UHF* and VHF) for non-commercial, educational use. The first ETV station was KUHT,* which began broadcasting on May 23, 1953, and was operated by the University of Houston. While many ETV stations are operated as community television, and part of the public broadcasting system, a considerable number are utilized by colleges, universities, or local education systems to bring television to the classroom.

From 1932 to 1939, an educational television station, W9XK, operated in Iowa, broadcasting programs to schools, using mechanical television.*
BIBLIOGRAPHY
Bates, Anthony W. *Broadcasting in Education: An Evaluation*. London: Constable, 1984.
Costello, Lawrence F., and George N. Gordon. *Teach with Television*. New York: Hastings House, 1961.

Hawkridge, David, and Joan Robinson. *Organizing Educational Broadcasting*. Paris: UNESCO, 1982.

Hilliard, Robert L., editor. *Television and Adult Education*. Cambridge, Mass.: Schenkman Books, 1985.

Kaye, Anthony, and Keith Harry, editors. *Using the Media for Adult Basic Education*. London: Croom Helm, 1982.

Kurtz, Edwin B. *Pioneering in Educational Television: 1932–1939*. Ames: State University of Iowa Press, 1959.

Lewis, Philip. *Educational Television Guidebook*. New York: McGraw-Hill, 1961.

Lusted, David, and Philip Drummond, editors. *TV and Schooling*. London: British Film Institute, 1985.

Powell, John Walker. *Channels of Learning: The Story of Educational Television*. Washington, D.C.: Public Affairs Press, 1962.

Robinson, John. *Learning over the Air: 60 Years of Partnership in Adult Learning*. London: British Broadcasting Corporation, 1982.

Schramm, Wilbur, editor. *The Impact of Educational Television*. Urbana: University of Illinois Press, 1960.

THE EUROPEAN BROADCASTING UNION/UNION EUROPÉENNE DE RADIODIFFUSION is an association of national broadcasting companies from sixty-two European countries. It was founded in Torquay, England, in 1950, but has its origins in the International Broadcasting Union, founded in 1925.

Address: Case Postale 67, CH–1218 Grand-Saconnex, Switzerland.

EUROPEAN BUSINESS CHANNEL is a satellite television service, providing business news and information, which began broadcasting in Europe on November 3, 1988. It is seen for a little over two hours each day, and transmits in English and German.

Address: Wagistrasse 4, CH–8952 Schliesen/Zurich, Switzerland.

THE EUROPEAN FOOTBALL COMMENTATORS ASSOCIATION was founded in 1973 as the European Association of Televised Football Commentators to represent the interests of those handling play-by-play reporting of televised soccer games.

Address: 9 Lakelands Lawn, Upper Kilmacud Road, Stillorgan, Dublin, Eire.

THE EUROPEAN GROUP OF TELEVISION ADVERTISING was founded in 1971 to represent the interests of European commercial television companies at the Council of Europe, the European Economic Community (EEC), and elsewhere.

Address: c/o ITVA, Knighton House, 56 Mortimer Street, London W1N 8AN, United Kingdom.

THE EUROVISION SONG CONTEST is an annual event at which each European country submits a song and the winner is selected by votes from participating countries. First broadcast in 1955, the contest is notorious for the banality of the entries and the obvious bias by certain national juries (the French do not vote for the English, and vice versa).

EUSTIS ELIAS PRODUCTIONS, headed by Richard Eustis and Michael Elias, produces *Head of the Class* (ABC, 1986-1991), in association with Warner Bros.

Address: 4000 Warner Boulevard, Burbank, CA 91522.

EUSTON FILMS LIMITED was formed in March 1971 as a subsidiary of Thames Television plc,* for the production of filmed television programs and series. Its first production was the 1973 series *Special Branch*. Other Euston Films series, seen in the United States on public television, include *Danger UXB* (1979), *The Flame Trees of Thika* (1981), and *Reilly—Ace of Spies* (1983).

Address: 365 Euston Road, London NW1 3AR, United Kingdom.

BIBLIOGRAPHY

Alvarado, Manuel, and John Stewart, editors. *Made for Television: Euston Films Limited*. London: British Film Institute, 1985.

EUTELSTAT is the European Satellite Organization, founded in 1977 to co-ordinate all aspects of the European telecommunications satellite program.

Address: 33 avenue du Maine, F–75755 Paris, Cedex 15, France.

EVAN J. ANTON PRODUCTIONS, LTD. was a New York–based producer of television commercials, active in the fifties and early sixties.

EVERGREEN PROGRAMS was a New York–based subsidiary of Worldvision Enterprises,* founded in 1981 to handle distribution of television series to the nostalgia market. Among the programs that it handled were *Ben Casey* (ABC, 1961–1966), *Combat* (ABC, 1962–1967), *The Fugitive* (ABC, 1963–1967), *Dark Shadows* (ABC, 1966–1971), and *The Jackson Five* (Syndicated, 1973).

EWTN (ETERNAL WORD TELEVISION NETWORK) is a basic cable network, offering twenty-four hour a day religious programming to 14 million subscribers (as of 1990). It was launched in August 1981.

Address: 5817 Old Leeds Road, Birmingham, AL 35210.

F

FAIRNESS IN MEDIA. Spearheaded by Senator Jesse Helms, Fairness in Media was founded in 1985 to encourage conservative Americans to purchase stock in CBS* and thus influence its news coverage, which was perceived as liberal-biased.

Address: P.O. Box 25099, Raleigh, NC 27611.

BIBLIOGRAPHY

Buckley, William F., "Jesse v. CBS," *National Review*, March 8, 1985, p. 54.
"Eyeing CBS," *Fortune*, March 18, 1985, pp. 8–9.
Gans, H.J., "Channeling Ideology," *Commonweal*, April 19, 1985, pp. 229–230.
Kilpatrick, Jack J., "Tilting at Newsmills," *Nation's Business*, March 1985, p. 5.
"The Right Takes Aim at CBS," *Newsweek*, January 21, 1985, p. 73.

THE FAMILY CHANNEL is a basic cable network, offering twenty-four hour a day programming intended for family viewing, and including classic television programs, films and documentaries, and inspirational shows. Probably the majority of the 50 million subscribers (as of 1990) are unaware they are watching a religious channel, formerly known as the Christian Broadcast Network. The latter has its origins in the purchase in 1960 by Marion Gordon (Pat) Robertson of WYAH in Portsmouth, Virginia. (Later, Robertson acquired WANX-Atlanta, WXNE-Boston, and KXTX-Dallas.) In 1964, Robertson began broadcasting his popular religious program *The 700 Club*, so named because it was founded with donations of ten dollars a month from 700 partners in the religious network. Color television was introduced in 1967 after Jim Bakker, who was then associated with the Christian Broadcast Network, proclaimed, "I felt the Lord urging me to raise money for CBN to purchase color cameras."

The CBN Family Channel began as a cable network in April 1977, but the "CBN" was dropped, and management has maintained that it is now a secular channel. Pat Robertson is not a voting member of The Family Channel's board, but his son Tim is president. Tim Robertson emphasizes the channel's policy of providing programming "that the family can watch together and [that will] embarrass no one in the group."

In October 1977, Pat Robertson dedicated a new $20 million complex in Colonial Williamsburg style in Virginia Beach, Virginia, which is the world's largest production center for Christian television programming. It has been dubbed "The Video Vatican." On June 1, 1981, the network began producing its own soap opera, *Another Life*. A subsidiary company, CBN Producers Group, is responsible for the production of both theatrical and made-for-television features, including *Rin Tin Tin: K-9 Cop* (1989).

Address: 1000 Centerville Turnpike, Virginia Beach, VA 23463.

BIBLIOGRAPHY

Beale, Lewis, "The Apostles of Christian Film Making," *Los Angeles Times*, April 7, 1985, pp. 17–18.

Dabney, Dick, "God's Own Network," *Harper's*, August 1980, pp. 33–52.

Harrell, David Edwin, Jr. *Pat Robertson: A Personal, Religious, and Political Portrait.* San Francisco: Harper & Row, 1987.

Kerr, Peter, "Carving Out a Niche for Religion," *New York Times*, January 22, 1984, section 2, p. 25.

Ostling, Richard N., "Power, Glory and Politics," *Time*, February 17, 1986, pp. 62–69.

Rosofsky, Ira, "Some of My Best Friends Are Evangelists," *Village Voice,* December 30, 1986, pp. 49–50.

Talbot, Frederick, "A Family Resemblance," *Channels of Communications*, vol. X, no. 7, May 21, 1990, pp. 49–54.

Traub, James, "CBN Counts Its Blessings," *Channels of Communications*, vol. V, no. 1, May/June 1985, pp. 28–34.

THE FAMILY GUIDE NETWORK is an audience-response cable service, specializing in self-improvement and business opportunities. First broadcast in June 1986, it is seen from 3:00 A.M. through 9:00 A.M., and has an audience (as of 1990) of 1.5 million subscribers.

Address: Suite 926, Fox Pavilion, Jenkintown, PA 19046.

FAMILYNET is a basic cable network, providing twenty-four hour a day family entertainment programming to more than 3 million subscribers (as of 1990). It was launched in April 1988.

Address: P.O. Box 196, Forest, VA 24551.

FAN CLUBS. The following is a listing of television-oriented fan clubs. The year of formation is given after the address:

Another World Viewer Alliance, 71 Berry Street, Pittsburgh, PA 15205 (1984)

As the World Turns Fan Club, c/o 212 Oriole Drive, Montgomery, NY 12549 (1984)

We Love Lucy/The International Lucille Ball Fan Club, P.O. Box 480216, Los Angeles, CA 90048 (1977)

Colonial Warriors United, c/o Figurehead Lane, Number 4, Quincy, MA 02169 (*Battlestar Galactica*) (1986)

Pierce Brosnan Fan Club, P.O. Box 9851, Glendale, CA 91206 (1983)

World Federation of *Dark Shadows* Clubs, P.O. Box 92, Maplewood, NJ 07040 (1982)

The World of *Dark Shadows*, P.O. Box 1766, Temple City, CA 91780 (1975)

National Days Fan Club, 380 Sausalito Boulevard, Sausalito, CA 94965 (*Days of Our Lives*) (1983)

A Touch of Days, 116 Boston Avenue, North Arlington, NJ 07032 (*Days of Our Lives*) (1984)

Companions of *Doctor Who* Fan Club, P.O. Box 724002, Atlanta, GA 30339 (1981)

Fans of *General Hospital*, 7623 Thames Court, West Chester, OH 45069 (1980)

Andy Griffith Show Appreciation Society, P.O. Box 330, Clemmons, NC 27012 (1983)

The Andy Griffith Show Rerun Watchers Club, 27 Music Square East, Number 146, Nashville, TN 37203 (1979)

Guiding Light Fan Club, 17 Baltistan Court, Baltimore, MD 21237 (1979)

Official Gumby Fan Club, P.O. Box 447, Schaumburg, IL 60168 (1985)

Royal Association for the Longevity and Preservation of *The Honeymooners* (RALPH), c/o C.W. Post University, Greenvale, NY 11548 (1982)

Joan Lunden Fan Club, P.O. Box 447, Seaford, NY 11783 (1980)

U.N.C.L.E. HQ, c/o 234 Washo Drive, Lake Zurich, IL 60047 (*The Man from U.N.C.L.E.*) (1976)

Mister Ed Fan Club, P.O. Box 1009, Cedar Hill, TX 75104 (1974)

1334 North Beechwood Drive Irregulars, c/o 14873 Heathergreen, Number 301, Riverview, MI 48192 (*The Monkees*) (1985)

National Association for the Advancement of Perry Mason, 2735 Benvenue, Number 2, Berkeley, CA 94705 (1985)

Once upon a Time, 515 Ravenel Circle, Seneca, SC 29678 (*The Prisoner*) (1979)

Six of One Club: *The Prisoner* Appreciation Society, P.O. Box 172, Hatfield, PA 19440 (1977)

Federation Council, 23871 Neuman Road, Corvallis, OR 97333 (*Star Trek*) (1976)

Star Trek: The Official Fan Club, P.O. Box 111000, Aurora, CO 80011 (1980)

Betty White Fan Club, c/o 3552 Federal Avenue, Los Angeles, CA 90066 (1971)

The Young and the Restless Fan Club, 8033 Sunset Boulevard, Number 950, Hollywood, CA 90046 (1985)

FARNSWORTH TELEVISION AND RADIO CORPORATION was founded in February 1939 to combine the research facilities of Farnsworth Television, Inc. and the manufacturing companies of Capehart, Inc. and General Household Utilities Company. It was primarily involved in the manufacture of radio receivers and phonographs, which helped to cover the cost of television research, and was relocated from Philadelphia to Fort Wayne, Indiana, the home of Capehart. Jesse McCarger was chairman of the board, George Everson was secretary-treasurer, Edward A. Nicholson was president, and Philo T. Farnsworth (1906–1971), the man for whom the company was named, was vice-president and director of research.

By 1926, Farnsworth had created a workable, all-electronic television system in Salt Lake City. In search of funding, he moved to Los Angeles and then to San Francisco. On September 7, 1927, at his 202 Green Street, San Francisco, laboratory, he transmitted his first image by wire. On September 2, 1928, he gave the first public demonstration anywhere of a completely all-electric television system. In May 1932, David Sarnoff visited the laboratory, now named Television Laboratories, Ltd., and offered Farnsworth $100,000 for the company. The offer was refused, and led to a long rivalry between Farnsworth and RCA.* In June 1931, a contract with Philco Corporation* allowed Farnsworth to relocate to Chestnut Hill, Philadelphia, and continue his research there. He opened W3XPF in 1937, and also entered into an arrangement to provide pickup equipment for CBS.* In 1935, the company name had been changed to Farnsworth Television, Inc. With the 1939 reorganization as Farnsworth Television and Radio Corporation, W3XPF was sold, but a new station, W9XFT, was created in Fort Wayne.

Following a 1932 filing by Farnsworth, the Patent Office's Board of Appeals ruled, in 1939, that Farnsworth had a prior patent claim to Vladimir Zworykin's iconoscope. As a result, RCA and Farnsworth Television and Radio Corporation filed a non-exclusive, cross-licensing agreement in September 1939. Farnsworth Television and Radio Corporation was liquidated in 1950.

BIBLIOGRAPHY

Abramson, Albert. *The History of Television, 1880 to 1941*. Jefferson, N.C.: McFarland, 1987.

Everson, George. *The Story of Television: The Life of Philo T. Farnsworth*. New York: W.W. Norton, 1949.

Hofer, Stephen F., "Philo Farnsworth, TV's Pioneer," *Journal of Broadcasting*, vol. III, no. 2, Spring 1979, pp. 153–165.

Udelson, Joseph H. *The Great Television Race: A History of the American Television Industry 1925–1941*. University: University of Alabama Press, 1982.

THE FCC (THE FEDERAL COMMUNICATIONS COMMISSION) was created pursuant to the Communications Act of 1934 "to regulate interstate and foreign communications by wire and radio in the public interest." The Communications Satellite Act of 1962 further expanded its regulatory scope, and its area of authority now includes radio, television, telephone, telegraph, cable television operation, two-way radio operation, and satellite communication. Its initial function was primarily to handle technical problems that might arise in the area of radio broadcasting, which was a continuation of the work of the Federal Radio Commission, established by Congress in 1927 to grant exclusive licenses to broadcasters for their frequencies. The Federal Radio Commission came under the secretary of commerce. The Communications Act of 1934 required that the commission comprise seven members appointed by the president with the advice and consent of the Senate. One of the members is designated as chairman by the president. In June 1973, the number of commission members was dropped to five, in part as a cost-cutting move but also to bring the FCC into line with most other federal regulatory bodies.

The actions of the FCC are often perceived as political in nature, and the politicization of the commission is generally dated from 1940, when James Lawrence Fly was appointed its chairman by Franklin D. Roosevelt with specific presidential instructions as to how to handle license applications and renewals; President Roosevelt was opposed to newspaper owners also being permitted to own broadcast outlets.

The FCC's work is divided into the following: The Mass Media Bureau administers the regulatory program for direct broadcast satellite, standards, frequency modulation, television, low power television, translators, instructional TV fixed, related broadcast auxiliary services, cable TV microwave radio relay, and registration of new cable television systems. The Common Carrier Bureau administers the regulatory program for interstate and international common carrier communications by telephone, telegraph, radio, and satellite. The Private Radio Bureau regulates the use of the radio spectrum for the communications needs of businesses, state and local governments, ships, aircraft, and individuals. The Office of Engineering and Technology administers the Experimental Radio Service and Equipment Authorization programs. The Field Operations Bureau carries out investigative and enforcement activities, and also administers the Radio Operator Program.

The FCC maintains regional offices in Atlanta; Bellevue, Washington; Kansas City, Missouri; Park Ridge, Illinois; Quincy, Massachusetts; and San Francisco. It also maintains a Common Carrier Bureau in New York, and field offices throughout the country.

In June 1968, the Supreme Court ruled that the FCC had the legal authority to regulate the cable television industry. In 1975, the FCC determined that there was no objective way of judging "how loud is loud" in response to continued complaints for viewers about the high level of sound on television commercials. In December 1983, the commission refused to set a minimum weekly quota for the number of children's shows on commercial television. In August 1987, under the leadership of a new chairman, Dennis R. Patrick (who served as chairman from 1987 to 1989), the FCC abolished the thirty-eight-year-old Fairness Doctrine, which required broadcasters to present all sides of major public issues, on the grounds that it unconstitutionally restricted the free-speech rights of broadcast journalists. In June 1988, KZKC–Kansas City became the first television station to be fined ($2,000) for indecency, for the presentation in 1987 during prime time of the feature film *Private Lessons*. The fine was lifted following a decision by the U.S. Court of Appeals, Washington, D.C.

ITS, Inc. (2100 M Street, N.W., Washington, DC 20037) is the official FCC contractor for search, replacement, and duplication of FCC file materials. Anyone requiring copies of FCC rulings must contact ITS, which charges an hourly search fee and a per-page reproduction fee.

Address: 1919 M Street, N.W., Washington, DC 20554.

BIBLIOGRAPHY

Baughman, James L. *Television's Guardian: The FCC and the Politics of Programming, 1958–1967*. Knoxville: University of Tennessee Press, 1985.

Besen, Stanley M., and Leland J. Johnson. *An Analysis of the Federal Communications Commission's Group Ownership Rules*. Santa Monica, Calif.: Rand Corporation, 1984.

————. *Regulations of Media Ownership by the Federal Communications Commission: An Assessment*. Santa Monica, Calif.: Rand Corporation, 1984.

Besen, Stanley M., Thomas G. Krattenmaker, A. Richard Metzger, Jr., and John R. Woodbury. *Misregulating Television: Network Dominance and the FCC*. Chicago: University of Chicago Press, 1984.

Bruce, Richard. *Television in the Corporate Interest*. New York: Praeger, 1976.

Cole, Barry, and Mal Oettinger, "Can an Angry Viewer Get Any Action Out of the FCC?" *TV Guide*, April 1, 1978, pp. 4–8.

————. *Reluctant Regulators: The FCC and the Broadcast Audience*. Reading, Mass.: Addison-Wesley, 1978.

Emery, Walter B. *Broadcasting and Government: Responsibilities and Regulations*. East Lansing: Michigan State University Press, 1961.

Geller, Henry. *A Modest Proposal To Reform the Federal Communications Commission*. Santa Monica, Calif.: Rand Corporation, 1974.

Havick, John J., editor. *Communications Policy and the Political Process*. Westport, Conn: Greenwood Press, 1983.

Johnson, Nicholas, and John Dystal, "A Day in the Life: The Federal Communications Commission," *Yale Law Journal*, July 1973, pp. 1575–1634.

Jones, William K. *Cases and Materials on Electronic Mass Media: Radio, Television and Cable*. Mineola, N.Y.: Foundation Press, 1976.

Krasnow, Edwin G., Lawrence D. Longley, and Herbert A. Terry. *The Politics of Broadcast Regulation*. New York: St. Martin's Press, 1982.

LeDuc, Don R. *Cable Television and the FCC: A Crisis in Media Control*. Philadelphia: Temple University Press, 1973.

Minow, Newton N. *Equal Time: The Private Broadcaster and the Public Interest*. New York: Atheneum, 1964.

Patrick, Dennis R., "Should the Government Decide What's Best for Viewers?" *TV Guide*, December 12, 1987, pp. 34–38.

Schmeckebier, Lawrence F. *The Federal Radio Commission: Its History, Activities and Organization*. Washington, D.C.: Brookings Institute, 1932.

Seiden, Martin H. *Cable Television U.S.A.: An Analysis of Government Policy*. New York: Praeger, 1972.

Sperry, Robert, "A Selected Bibliography of Works on the Federal Communications Commission," *Journal of Broadcasting*, vol. XIX, no. 1, Winter 1975, pp. 55–113.

Stern, Robert H. *The Federal Communications Commission and Television*. New York: Arno Press, 1979.

When Citizens Complain: UCC vs. FCC a Decade Later. New York: New York Law School Communications Media Center, 1978.

THE FEDERAL COMMUNICATIONS COMMISSION. See THE FCC

FEDERAL TELEFILMS, INC. Founded in 1953 by former actor William "Buster" Collier (1902–1987), Federal Telefilms, Inc. was located on the Samuel Goldwyn studio lot and operational through 1964. Its best-known productions were *Adventures of the Falcon* (Syndicated, 1954) and *Cross Roads* (ABC, 1955–1957).

FEMALE IMPERSONATION. Milton Berle was television's primary utilizer of female impersonation for comic effect on his NBC show from 1948 to 1956. The first American television situation comedy to feature "drag" as part of its plot was *The Ugliest Girl in Town* (ABC, 1968–1969); the only other series based on the premise of female impersonation was *Bosom Buddies* (ABC, 1980–1982). Memorable female impersonations on television have included Flip Wilson's character of Geraldine Jones; Jamie Farr as Corporal Maxwell Klinger wearing a dress on *M*A*S*H*; and Lori Shannon as the "woman" whose life Archie Bunker saves in a 1976 episode of *All in the Family*. On British television, female impersonation has been featured on *Monty Python's Flying Circus*, *The Benny Hill Show*, and in the BBC* series *Those Dear Ladies*, featuring Dr. Evadne Hinge and Dame Hilda Bracket (played by George Logan and Patrick Fyffe).
BIBLIOGRAPHY
Slide, Anthony. *Great Pretenders*. Lombard, Ill.: Wallace-Homestead, 1986.

THE FENADY ASSOCIATES was an independent production unit formed in 1962 by Andrew J. Fenady, Bernard McEveety, George Fenady, Richard Caffey, and Richard Markowitz, and located on the Screen Gems*/Columbia lot. The following year, it moved to 20th Century–Fox. Among its made-for-television movies, some of which were co-produced, are *Black Noon* (CBS, 1971), *The Voyage of the Yes* (CBS, 1973), *The Hanged Man* (ABC, 1974), *Sky Heist* (NBC, 1975), *Mayday at 40,000 Feet* (CBS, 1976), and *The Hostage Heart* (CBS, 1977).

FILMACK STUDIOS was founded in Chicago in 1919 by Irving Mack as Filmack Trailer Co. From the fifties onward it has been active in the production of television commercials.
    Address: 1327 South Wabash Avenue, Chicago, IL 60605.

FILMASTER PRODUCTIONS, INC. After an earlier involvement with William Boyd Productions,* Robert Stabler (1918–1970) formed Filmaster Productions in 1952 for the production of *Death Valley Days* (Syndicated, 1952–1970). The company was also responsible for *Have Gun Will Travel* (CBS, 1957–1963), *Troubleshooters* (NBC, 1959–1960), and *The Beachcomber* (Syndicated, 1961), together with eight theatrical features.

In 1964, Stabler formed Madison Pacific Films, Ltd., and continued the production of *Death Valley Days* with the new company. In 1978, he moved Madison Pacific to Vancouver, and he continued in production in both Canada and the United States until 1986. While in Vancouver, he was responsible for the 1979 syndicated series *Huckleberry Finn and His Friends*.

BIBLIOGRAPHY
Wedman, Les, "Tom Sawyer, Huck Finn on a Raft of Nations," *Los Angeles Times*, December 28, 1979, part IV, p. 24.

FILMATION ASSOCIATES was a major supplier of Saturday-morning animated programming for children. Until 1987, when it laid off more than 400 employees, it was the only studio to continue to complete the animation process for television in the United States, with its series including *BraveStarr*, *He-Man*, *Star Trek*, *Fat Albert and the Cosby Kids, Shazam!*, *Archie*, and *Ghostbusters*.

The company was created in 1962 by Lou Scheimer, Hal Sutherland, and Norm Prescott, but did not achieve success until 1965, when it produced the *Superman* cartoon series for CBS.* Prescott retired in 1982. Sutherland had retired in 1974, but he returned to Filmation in 1982. Initially located on the Paramount lot, the company opened a major studio complex of its own in Woodland Hills, California, in October 1986.

Filmation's first feature film, *Journey Back to Oz*, was released theatrically in 1974. The company began an active feature film production schedule in 1985, and immediately ran into opposition from Disney because of its use of characters perceived as being part of the Disney legacy in *The New Adventures of Pinocchio* and *Snow White and the Seven Dwarfelles*.

In 1969, the company was acquired by the TelePrompTer Corporation,* becoming a subsidiary of Group W in 1981. The latter offered Filmation for sale in December 1988, and in the spring of 1989 the company was acquired for $25 million by Paravision International, the entertainment arm of L'Oreal, which promptly closed the Woodland Hills facility and shut down American production.

BIBLIOGRAPHY
Bates, Hal, "New Filmation Projects To Boost Payroll to Over 500," *The Hollywood Reporter*, May 19, 1972, pp. 1, 3.
Bates, James, "Color Cartoon Maker Blue over Westinghouse Order To Cut Costs," *Los Angeles Times*, August 25, 1987, Business Section, pp. 1, 2.
————, "Filmation Shuts Plant, Beats Closing Law Deadline by 1 Day," *Los Angeles Times*, February 8, 1989, part IV, p. 2.
Burns, James, "Filmation Produces Feature Length 'Flash Gordon' for NBC," *Millimeter*, July 1979, pp. 134–139.
Kaminsky, Ralph, "Filmation Moving to New Plateau in Animation Field," *The Hollywood Reporter*, March 12, 1973, pp. 1, 22.
Mankin, Eric, "The Wonderful World of Filmation," *Los Angeles Herald Examiner*, March 5, 1985, section B, pp. 1, 6.
Scheimer, Lou, "Animation: Vanishing American Art Form," *Daily Variety*, October 27, 1987, pp. 5, 18.

Silverman, Marie Saxon, "Filmation Boasts Animation That's Homegrown, Meaty," *Variety*, February 19, 1986, p. 111.
Solomon, Charles, "Production Is Less Animated at Filmation Studio," *Los Angeles Times*, January 1, 1988, part VI, p. 8.

FILMCRAFT PRODUCTIONS, headed by Isidore Lindenbaum and, later, his daughter Regina, operated a small studio on Melrose Avenue in Los Angeles, and served as the facilitating producer for *You Bet Your Life* (NBC, 1950–1961), some episodes of *Beulah* (ABC, 1950–1953), and many pilots. Under the former name of Filmtone, the company produced *The Life of Riley* (NBC, 1949–1958).

FILM CREATIONS, INC. was a New York–based producer of television commercials, operated by Joseph Barnett, and active in the fifties.

FILM MAKERS, INC. was a New York–based producer of television commercials, operated by J.H. Lenauer, and active in the early fifties.

FILMNET is a satellite television service, seen in Belgium, the Netherlands, and the Scandinavian countries. It broadcasts feature films twenty-four hours a day, with subtitles where appropriate. FilmNet began in 1986, and is owned by the Swedish company Esselte AB.
	Address: 97 Tollaan, B-1940 St. Stevens Wolvne, Brussels, Belgium.

FILMS FOR TELEVISION OF HOLLYWOOD, INC. was one of the production companies of former rabbi Jack H. Skirball (1896–1985). Active from the early fifties through the seventies, it was an offshoot of Jack H. Skirball Productions, Inc. (formed in 1942).

FILMVIDEO RELEASING CORPORATION was a New York–based company, founded by Maurice H. Zouary, and active in the fifties. It owned 7 million feet of stock footage (the former Miles, Progress, and Advance Television libraries), which it licensed for television use, and also offered the 1959 syndicated series from Maurice H. Zouary TV-Film Productions *Poem for a Day*, consisting of 365 two-minute shorts.

FILMWAYS, INC. In 1952, with an investment of $200, Martin Ransohoff (born 1927) founded Filmways, Inc. as a producer of television commercials and industrial films. He developed the company into a major producer of popular television programming, including *Mr. Ed* (CBS, 1961–1965), *The Beverly Hillbillies* (CBS, 1962–1971), *Petticoat Junction* (CBS, 1963–1970), *The Addams Family* (ABC, 1964–1966), and *Green Acres* (CBS, 1965–1971). Ransohoff also entered theatrical production in 1960, with his first feature being *Boys Night Out*.
	Ransohoff resigned from Filmways in September 1972, but the company continued to expand, acquiring a number of additional companies in 1967 and

1968, including Broadcast Electronics, Inc.; Sigma III Corporation; Cinefx, Inc.; Yorkshire Productions; and Heatter-Quigley, Inc. In July 1979, it merged with American International Pictures (AIP).

Meanwhile, in February 1978, Arthur Krim, Eric Pleskow, William Bernstein, Robert Benjamin, and Mike Medavoy, who had resigned from United Artists where they had been the production and management heads, formed an independent production company, Orion, associated with Warner Communications. In 1982, the group took over an overextended Filmways, which they renamed Orion Pictures Corporation. The latter includes as wholly owned subsidiaries Orion Television, Inc. (which has yet to enjoy any lasting success in television programming) and Century Tower Productions, Inc.*

Address: Orion Pictures Corporation, 1888 Century Park East, Los Angeles, CA 90067.

FILMWRIGHT PRODUCTIONS, INC. (Max Glandbard, president) was a New York–based producer of television commercials, active in the fifties.

THE FINNEGAN-PINCHUK COMPANY was founded in 1976 as Finnegan Associates by the husband-and-wife producing team of Bill and Pat Finnegan. It changed its name in 1987, when independent producer Sheldon Pinchuk became a full partner. Initially a producer of television movies, the company entered theatrical film production in 1983, with its most successful film being *The Fabulous Baker Boys* (1989). Among its made-for-television movies are *Stranger in Our House* (NBC, 1978), *The Ordeal of Patty Hearst* (ABC, 1979), *A Vacation in Hell* (NBC, 1979), *World War III* (NBC, 1982), *Dangerous Company* (CBS, 1982), *Your Place or Mine* (CBS, 1983), and *The Dollmaker* (ABC, 1984). A related company is Pipeline Productions.

Address: 4225 Coldwater Canyon Avenue, Studio City, CA 91604.
BIBLIOGRAPHY
Kleiman, Rena, "Finnegans Go from TV to Feature Films," *The Hollywood Reporter*, August 22, 1983, pp. 1, 13.

FIRST NATIONAL TELEVISION, INC. was a minor television broadcaster, located in Kansas City, Missouri, and operating W9XAL from 1932 to 1941.
BIBLIOGRAPHY
Udelson, Joseph H. *The Great Television Race: A History of the American Television Industry 1925–1941*. University: University of Alabama Press, 1982.

FIVE STAR PRODUCTIONS, INC. was a Los Angeles–based company, specializing in advertising films for television and theatrical markets. It was founded in 1938 by Harry Wayne McMahon and active through the fifties. McMahon was the author of *The Television Commercial* (New York: Hastings House, 1957).

FLAMINGO FILMS, INC., whose name was later changed to Flamingo Telefilm Sales, Inc., was a relatively important television distributor/producer, founded in 1948 by Joseph Harris (who served as the company's president) and David L. Wolper. Among the series that Flamingo distributed are *Beulah* (ABC, 1950–1953), *Wild Bill Hickok* (Syndicated, 1951–1958), *The Adventures of Superman* (Syndicated, 1952–1957), *Cowboy G-Men* (Syndicated, 1952), *Soldier of Fortune* (Syndicated, 1957), and *Deadline* (Syndicated, 1959). Physical distribution of its product was handled in the early fifties by NTA,* but Flamingo later took the series back and became involved in active syndication. As well as distribution, Flamingo did produce a number of syndicated programs in the mid-fifties, notably *TV's Baseball Hall of Fame* and *TV's Football Hall of Fame*. The company went out of business in the sixties.

FLYING A PICTURES, INC. In 1950, Gene Autry (born 1907) became the first major screen star to enter television, with the establishment of Flying A Pictures, Inc. and the production of *The Gene Autry Show* (CBS, 1950–1956). Flying A was also responsible for *Annie Oakley* (Syndicated, 1952–1956), *Buffalo Bill, Jr.* (Syndicated, 1954), and *The Adventures of Champion* (CBS, 1955–1956). A separate company, Range Rider Productions, Inc., was established for the production of *The Range Rider* (Syndicated, 1951–1952). Additionally, the Flying A facilities were utilized for the filming of early episodes of *Death Valley Days*.

The company's president was Armand L. Schaefer (1898–1967), who was also president of Gene Autry Productions from its inception in 1947, and served as producer of the company's thirty-two theatrical features produced between 1947 and 1953. Flying A Pictures ceased operations in 1964, when its assets were sold to ABC.*

BIBLIOGRAPHY

Autry, Gene, with Mickey Herskowitz. *Back in the Saddle Again*. Garden City, N.Y.: Doubleday, 1978.
Rothel, David. *The Gene Autry Book*. Waynesville, N.C.: The World of Yesterday, 1986.

FNN (FINANCIAL NEWS NETWORK) is a twenty-four hour a day (Monday through Friday) basic cable network, providing business news, analysis, stock market reports, and personal money management advice. First seen in November 1981, it provides continuous ticker coverage from the major exchanges for its more than 33 million subscribers. FNN was founded by Glen Taylor (who resigned as chairman and president in July 1982), who earlier had created the FNN Business News on radio, first heard on October 3, 1988. Among the network's regular programming is *FNN Money Talk* and *The Insiders* with Jack Anderson; it is also responsible for FNN/SPORTS, which provides sports highlights, interviews, and so forth on Saturdays and Sundays only between 2:00 P.M. and 6:00 P.M., and was first seen in April 1985 (the same month that FNN began twenty-four hour a day broadcasting). On April 3, 1991, a federal bankruptcy judge approved a bid by NBC* to acquire the financially troubled Financial News Network.

Address: 320 Park Avenue, 3rd Floor, New York, NY 10022.

BIBLIOGRAPHY
Colker, David, "FNN Fans Would Rather Fight Than Switch to New Network," *Los Angeles Times*, June 23, 1989, part IV, pp. 1, 18.
Duffy, Susan, "FNN Takes the Old Ticker into Brave New Worlds," *Business Week*, September 17, 1990, pp. 106, 111.
Schneider, Steve, "Stock Returns Plus Batting Averages," *New York Times*, May 26, 1985, section 2, p. 16.

THE FORD FOUNDATION has been a major financing sponsor of public television in the United States. In 1952, it made an organizing grant of $1.35 million to help establish the Educational Television and Radio Center (NET,* or National Educational Television). A grant from the Ford Foundation created the cultural television series *Omnibus* (CBS, 1953–1956; ABC, 1956–1957). The foundation closed its Communications Office on December 3, 1980, with the retirement of Fred Friendly, former president of CBS News, who had been the office's director since 1966. In all, the Ford Foundation gave more than $45 million to public television, with its last major grant in 1976 being $2 million, which helped start *The MacNeil/Lehrer Report* and *Bill Moyers' Journal*.

FORMONT FILM CORPORATION, headed by Art Ford, was a minor New York–based production company of the fifties and sixties.

FORTUNE MERCHANDISING CORP./FORTUNE ASSOCIATES (Leonard Shane, president) was a Los Angeles–based producer of television commercials, active in the fifties and sixties.

4-D PRODUCTIONS, headed by Danny Arnold (born 1925) was responsible for the popular series *Barney Miller* (ABC, 1975–1982).

BIBLIOGRAPHY
Adler, Dick, "Q&A: Danny Arnold and Hal Linden," *Panorama*, vol. I, no. 10, November 1980, pp. 22–28.

FOUR STAR TELEVISION was created for the production of *Four Star Playhouse* (CBS, 1952–1956). The four stars of the "Playhouse" were originally to be Dick Powell, Charles Boyer, Rosalind Russell, and Joel McCrea. The last two actors dropped out prior to production and were replaced by Ida Lupino and David Niven. There were never four stars in Four Star Television; it was limited to a partnership of three, Powell, Boyer, and Niven, of which Powell (1904–1963) was the dominant partner. William Cruickshank handled the company's administration and served as its president. Niven and Boyer were featured in Four Star's *The Rogues* (NBC, 1964–1965), and Powell starred in *Dick Powell's Zane Grey Theater* (CBS, 1956–1962) and *The Dick Powell Show* (NBC, 1962–

1963). Other Four Star shows include *The Rifleman* (ABC, 1958–1963), *The Detectives* (ABC, 1959–1961; NBC, 1961–1962), *Ensign O'Toole* (NBC, 1962–1963; ABC, 1964), *Burke's Law* (ABC, 1963–1966), *The Big Valley* (ABC, 1965–1969), and *Honey West* (ABC, 1965–1966).

Four Star International, replacing the divisions of Four Star Distribution Corp. and Four Star Television International, was formed in 1965 to distribute theatrical features, to acquire features for television, to produce Broadway shows, and to produce and distribute syndicated television series. In August 1967, a controlling interest in the company was acquired by a group of investors headed by David B. Charnay. In November of the same year, the name was formally changed to Four Star International, Inc., and at the same time the distribution subsidiary was renamed Four Star Entertainment Corp. The latter ceased to exist in 1976 when Avco Embassy Pictures Corp. took over all television distribution. The company announced plans to reactivate production (which had ceased in the late sixties) in 1983, renting space at the Warner Hollywood Studios. A year later, Joseph A. Fisher became chief executive officer and chairman of the board.

Address: 2813 Alameda Avenue, Burbank, CA 91505–4455.

FOX BROADCASTING CO. At first self-proclaimed as, but now generally recognized to be, the fourth network, Fox has slowly built an audience with its programming of innovative and/or outrageous series, such as *The Tracey Ullman Show* (1987–1990), *Married with Children* (1987-   ), *Alien Nation* (1989–1990), *The Simpsons* (1990-   ), and *In Living Color* (1990-   ). From one evening of programming (Sunday) for its affiliated stations in 1987, Fox had expanded to five nights of network programming by the fall of 1990, reaching more than 90 percent of the population. From a $95 million loss in 1988, Fox has moved forward to $550 million in advertising revenues in 1990 and an estimated profit of $70 million in 1991.

The two men behind Fox's success are Barry Diller (born 1942) and Rupert Murdoch (born 1931). In 1977, Diller had attempted unsuccessfully to create a fourth network at Paramount, and after he left the studio to become chief executive officer at 20th Century–Fox in 1984, he determined to try again. He received the full support of Rupert Murdoch, whose company, News Corp., had gained a controlling interest in the studio in 1985. As the backbone of the new broadcasting company, Fox acquired the six stations of Metromedia, Inc.* in 1986, and that same year lined up a further ninety-six independent affiliated stations* across the country. In acquiring the Metromedia stations, Fox de facto became a successor to the old fourth network, DuMont.*

Initially, Fox's programming was criticized as being little more than a copy of what was offered by the three networks. However, the 1988 writers' strike in Hollywood, which paralyzed network programming, helped gain Fox a television audience as viewers switched over from the reruns that the networks were forced to air and discovered the first of Fox's new type of programming, the police drama series *21 Jump Street* (1987-1990); *Married with Children*; and two semi-documentary series, *America's Most Wanted* (1988-) and *Cops* (1988-).

In 1988 Fox initiated a policy of introducing its new shows in the summer months, in advance of the networks, which were still airing reruns during that period. Fox is thus able to gain an audience for its programming, which will, hopefully, stay with Fox after the new network shows begin. It has also proved itself to be a network with an audience from a younger age group, and has thus appealed to advertisers anxious to reach those considered to be "free-spending." Since 1970, FCC* regulations have prevented the networks from owning and syndicating their own shows. Fox has, however, been permitted to produce and syndicate up to fifteen hours of programming each week from its own studio, and in May 1990, the FCC expanded that permission for up to eighteen hours of shows.

On July 11, 1987, Fox introduced its first night of Saturday programming with a two-hour, made-for-television movie, *Werewolf*, the precursor of a short-lived series of the same name. The network's one major failure was a late-night talk show, *The Late Show Starring Joan Rivers* (1986–1987). In 1988, Fox pulled off a major coup in signing with the Academy of Television Arts and Sciences* to produce the annual Emmy Awards shows.

Address: P.O. Box 900, Beverly Hills, CA 90213.

BIBLIOGRAPHY

Block, Alex Ben, "Hey Gang, Let's Put on a Show," *Forbes*, April 6, 1987, pp. 140, 144.

———. *Outfoxed*. New York: St. Martin's Press, 1990.

———, "Twenty First Century Fox," *Channels of Communications*, vol. X, no. 1, January 1990, pp. 36–39.

Fanning, D., "A Different Brand of Entertainment," *Forbes*, November 30, 1987, pp. 49–52.

"Fox Has Big Plans for Prime Time," *Fortune*, May 26, 1986, p. 8.

"The Fox Trots Faster," *Time*, August 27, 1990, pp. 64–67.

Grover, Ronald, "Fox's New Network Goes after the Baby Boomers," *Business Week*, April 6, 1987, pp. 41–43.

Grover, Ronald, and Susan Duffy, "The Fourth Network," *Business Week*, September 17, 1990, pp. 114–120.

Kaplan, Peter W., "Plan for a Fox Network Intrigues TV Industry," *New York Times*, October 11, 1985, p. 29.

"A New Wave Programmer," *Newsweek*, September 1, 1986, p. 62.

"Ready for Prime Time," *Newsweek*, December 25, 1989, pp. 68–70.

Stauth, C., "Fox in the Network Henhouse," *New York Times Magazine*, July 15, 1990, pp. 28–36.

Zoglin, Richard, "Room for One More?" *Time*, April 6, 1987, p. 74.

———, "The Little Network That Might," *Time*, March 28, 1988, p. 86.

FOX/LORBER ASSOCIATES, INC. is a prominent worldwide distributor in the theatrical, television, and home video markets. Formed in May 1981 by David M. Fox and Richard Lorber, the company merged with Prism Entertainment, a major home video distributor, in March 1986. Two years later, the company formed a joint venture with Commtron, the largest videocassette wholesaler in the United States, for direct home video distribution under the Monarch label. In 1989, the company expanded into international film sales through acquisition of the rights to the Atlantic Entertainment and Kings Road libraries. Fox/Lorber Home Video was launched in April 1989. In March 1990, in partnership with GaGa Communications of Japan, Fox and Lorber engineered a management buy-back of the company from Prism.

Address: 432 Park Avenue South, New York, NY 10016.

FRANK COOPER ASSOCIATES was a New York–based producer and distributor, active in the fifties and early sixties.

[JOHN JAY] FRANKLIN TELEVISION PRODUCTIONS was active from the mid-fifties through the mid-sixties as a Los Angeles–based producer of minor programming. It appears to have specialized in Hawaiian-themed syndicated series, such as the fifteen-minute *Hawaiian Paradise* and the thirty-minute *Hula Follies* shows (the latter featuring Alfred Apaka, Ben Palama, and Miss Ventura) from the mid-fifties.

THE FRED SILVERMAN COMPANY was an outgrowth of InterMedia Entertainment, founded by Silverman (born 1937) in 1982 for the production of television pilots. Silverman is notable in television for having been production head of both CBS* and ABC,* as well as president, from 1978 to 1981, of NBC.* His initial independent productions, *The World of Entertainment* (Syndicated, 1982) and *Thicke of the Night* (Syndicated, 1983), were not particularly successful, but in recent years his company has flourished with the production of the Perry Mason television movies and such series as *Matlock* (NBC, 1986-), *Jake and the Fatman* (CBS, 1987-), and *In the Heat of the Night* (NBC, 1988-), often co-produced with Dean Hargrove Productions.

Address: 12400 Wilshire Boulevard, Los Angeles, CA 90025.

BIBLIOGRAPHY

Kaufman, Dave, "Silverman Cranks Up New Company," *Daily Variety*, February 3, 1982, p. 1.

Mann, Arnold, "Innerviews: Fred Silverman—One More Time," *Emmy*, vol. IX, no. 5, September/October 1987, pp. 12–15.

"Return of a Network Reject," *Newsweek*, June 6, 1988, pp. 60–61.

"FREE-TV" is a phrase coined by network executives in reference to non-cable programming, which does not require a payment from the viewer. Because even the basic cable networks can only be seen by most viewers through payment of monthly service charges to the cable television service companies, cable television is dubbed, usually by its network critics, "Pay-TV."

THE FREMANTLE CORPORATION has been active since the early fifties as a major distributor of American television programming abroad. Initially known as Fremantle Overseas Radio & Television, Inc., it handled international distribution for Sterling Television Co., Inc.,* Atlantic TV Films, and others. Its British subsidiary is Talbot Television Ltd., and in Australia, the subsidiary is Fremantle International Productions, Pty. Ltd.

Address: 660 Madison Avenue, New York, NY 10021.

FRIES ENTERTAINMENT, INC. Independent producer Charles W. Fries (born 1928) was the former head of production at Metromedia, Inc.,* and in 1974 he formed his own company, Charles Fries Productions. Fries Entertainment, Inc. was created in 1979 as an umbrella company for both the latter firm and Fries Distribution Co. Five years later, in January 1984, the company became public.

Fries Entertainment, Inc. is one of the most prolific of television production companies, specializing in made-for-television movies and mini-series such as *The Trial of Lee Harvey Oswald* (ABC, 1971), *The House on Garibaldi Street* (ABC, 1979), *The Martian Chronicles* (NBC, 1980), *Rosie: The Rosemary Clooney Story* (CBS, 1982), and *The Burning Bed* (NBC, 1984). It launched a theatrical film division in 1984, having already produced one major feature film, *Cat People*, in 1981. By 1988, the company consisted of six divisions: Fries Television, Fries Distribution, Fries Theatrical, Fries Theatrical Distribution, Fries International, and Fries Home Video. "Chuck" Fries has proven to be an exceptional self-publicist, and the neon sign for his company on the roof of his office building dominates Hollywood Boulevard.

Address: 6922 Hollywood Boulevard, 12th Floor, Hollywood, CA 90028.
BIBLIOGRAPHY
"The Hollywood Reporter Salutes Fries Entertainment, Inc.," *The Hollywood Reporter*, June 19, 1984, pp. S1–S28.
"The Hollywood Reporter Salutes Fries Entertainment on Its 15th Anniversary," *The Hollywood Reporter*, October 17, 1989, pp. S1–S28.
Mann, Arnold, "Innerviews: The Hands-On Man," *Emmy*, vol. IX, no. 2, March/April 1987, pp. 16–25.

FULTON J. SHEEN COMMUNICATIONS LTD. distributes the Bishop Fulton J. Sheen series *Life Is Worth Living*, for all uses. One hundred black-and-white and forty-nine color episodes are available of the program, which was first seen on DuMont* on February 12, 1952, and later seen on ABC* from 1955 to 1957.

Address: 19355 Business Center Drive, Northridge, CA 91324.

G

GAINSBOROUGH ASSOCIATES, INC. was a New York–based producer, primarily of television commercials, operated by Mitchell Jablons, and active in the fifties.

GALAVISION/ECO, INC. began in October 1979 as a pay-cable television network, offering Spanish-language programming for the Hispanic community. In September 1988, it joined forces with ECO, a weekday Mexican news service, and became an advertiser-supported basic cable network. As of 1990, it had 2 million subscribers for its twenty-four hour a day service, which includes news and live entertainment from Mexico City. A satellite service to Europe was announced in December 1988.

Address: 2121 Avenue of the Stars, Suite 2300, Los Angeles, CA 90067.

BIBLIOGRAPHY

Du Brow, Rick, "Galavision Speaks to Hispanics," *Los Angeles Herald Examiner*, June 27, 1982, p. E5.

"Hispanic Cabler Hangs Tough as Subscriber Base Builds," *Daily Variety*, November 12, 1984, p. 9.

GAME SHOWS, also known as quiz shows, first gained popularity on radio, with two of the earliest being *Professor Quiz* and *Uncle Jim's Question Bee*, first heard in 1936. The first game show to be seen on network television was *It's a Gift*, first seen on CBS* on January 29, 1946, and last seen on July 6 of the same year.

The most popular game shows on American television, in terms of duration, are *What's My Line?* (CBS, 1950–1967; Syndicated, 1968–1974), *The Price Is Right* (NBC, 1956–1963; ABC, 1963–1965; Syndicated, 1972–1974, 1985), *I've Got a Secret* (CBS, 1952–1967; Syndicated, 1972–1973; CBS, 1976), *You Bet Your Life* (NBC, 1950–1961; Syndicated, 1980), *The Hollywood Squares* (NBC, 1966–1968; Syndicated, 1971–1980, 1986–1989), *Wheel of Fortune* (NBC,

1975-   ; Syndicated, 1987-   ), *Let's Make a Deal* (NBC, 1963–1968; ABC, 1968–1976; Syndicated, 1971–1976, 1980, 1984), and *Jeopardy!* (NBC, 1964–1975, 1978–1979; Syndicated, 1984-   ).

Among the names most associated with television as hosts or announcers of game shows are Bob Barker, Jack Barry, Dick Clark, Jack Clark, Bert Convy, Bill Cullen, Richard Dawson, Geoff Edwards, Bob Eubanks, George Fenneman, Art Fleming, Joe Garagiola, Johnny Gilbert, Monty Hall, Art James, Dennis James, Tom Kennedy, Jim Lange, Robert Q. Lewis, Allen Ludden, Ed McMahon, Wink Martindale, Jan Murray, Jack Narz, Johnny Olson, Bert Parks, Gene Rayburn, Jay Stewart, Alex Trebek, Bill Wendell, and Gene Wood.

Big-money quiz shows fell into disrepute in the late fifties as a result of a scandal that began developing in 1957. In that year, Herbert Stempel, a contestant on *Twenty-One*, claimed that he was told to lose to Charles Van Doren, who went on to win $129,000, and became a popular personality as a result of his appearances on the show. The producers of *Twenty-One* denied the accusation, and initially it had no impact. However, in August 1957, both *Look* and *Time* published stories indicating that the results of quiz shows were "controlled."

In May 1958, a contestant on *Dotto* saw the current champion receive the answers in advance from the producers. He telephoned the *New York Post*, which informed the District Attorney's Office, and, as a result, *Dotto* was cancelled, and rumors abounded with regard to other quiz shows. In August 1958, the New York district attorney opened a grand jury investigation, and Albert Freedman, producer of *Twenty-One*, was indicted on perjury charges. Congress became interested in the scandal in October 1959, and the House Legislative Oversight Committee began an investigation. On November 2, 1959, when Charles Van Doren appeared before the committee, he revealed that he was provided not only with the answers but also with ad-libs.

Such major proportions did the quiz show scandal reach that even President Dwight Eisenhower commented that this was "a terrible thing to do to the American public." All remaining quiz shows offering large sums of money were immediately cancelled by the networks; Louis G. Cowan, president of CBS, was fired, and two producers of quiz shows, Barry & Enright Productions, Inc.* and Entertainment Productions, Incorporated,* ceased operations.

BIBLIOGRAPHY

Anderson, Kent. *Television Fraud: The History and Implications of the Quiz Show Scandals.* Westport, Conn.: Greenwood Press, 1978.

Blumenthal, Norman. *The TV Game Shows.* New York: Pyramid, 1975.

Fates, Gil. *What's My Line.* Englewood Cliffs, N.J.: Prentice-Hall, 1978.

Fishman, Ed. *How To Strike It Rich on TV Game Shows.* Los Angeles: Price, Stern, Sloan, 1972.

Munteau, Greg. *How To Become a Game Show Contestant: An Insider's Guide.* New York: Fawcett Columbine, 1987.

Sackett, Susan, and Cheryl Blythe. *You Can Be a Game Show Contestant and Win.* New York: Dell, 1982.

Schwartz, David, Steve Ryan, and Fred Worstbrock. *The Encyclopedia of TV Game Shows.* New York: New York Zoetrope, 1987.

Schwartz, Marla Schram. *Be a TV Game Show Winner!* New York: Harmony Books, 1988.

G. & W. TELEVISION PRODUCTIONS, INC. was a New York–based producer of minor television programming, founded by Felix Greenfield and Robert Whiteman, and active in the early fifties.

GANNETT BROADCASTING SERVICES is a division of Gannett Co., Inc., which was founded in 1906 by Frank E. Gannett. The parent company was incorporated in 1923 and listed on the New York stock exchange in 1969. Gannett controls eighty-eight daily newspapers (including *USA Today*), thirty-five non-daily newspapers, and, through Gannett Broadcasting Services, sixteen radio stations and the following television stations: KPNX-Mesa, Arizona; KUSA-Denver; WUSA-Washington, D.C.; WTLV-Jacksonville, Florida; WXIA-Atlanta; WLVA-Cambridge, Massachusetts; KARE-Minneapolis; WFMY-Greensboro, North Carolina; KOCO–Oklahoma City; and KVUE-Austin, Texas. In 1980, Gannett acquired Gateway Productions, Inc., a producer of industrial films and television documentaries. Gannett News Service (founded in 1942) added a television news bureau in 1982.
   Address: 1100 Wilson Boulevard, Arlington, VA 22234.
BIBLIOGRAPHY
Gold, Daniel M., "Mister Fix-It," *Inside Media*, May 2, 1990, pp. 29–31.
Jones, Alex S., "Will Profits Still Grow?" *New York Times*, August 27, 1989, section 3, pp. 1, 6.

GATEWAY COMMUNICATIONS, INC. was founded in 1970 by George A. Koehler from the former television stations of Triangle Publications. It controls WBNG-Binghamton, New York; WTAJ-Altoona, Pennsylvania; WLYH-Lancaster, Pennsylvania; and WOWK-Huntington, West Virginia.
   Address: One Bala Plaza, Suite 237, Bala Cynwd, PA 19004.

THE GAYLORD BROADCASTING CO. dates back to 1928, and it was known at one time as WKY Television Systems, Inc. It is a wholly owned subsidiary of Oklahoma Publishing Co., and owns Opryland USA (acquired in 1983), two radio stations, and the following television stations: WUAB-Lorain, Ohio; KTVT–Fort Worth; KHTV-Houston; KSTW-Tacoma, Washington; and WVTV-Milwaukee. It also operates the television production and syndication subsidiaries Gaylord Production Company and Gaylord Syndication (66 Music Square West, Nashville, TN 37203). Among its television productions is *Stone Pillow* (CBS, 1985), in which Lucille Ball starred as a New York bag lady.
   Address: Box 25125, Oklahoma City, OK 73125.

GENERAL ENTERTAINMENT CORP. (Howard G. Barnes, president) was a New York–based producer, primarily of television commercials, active in the early fifties.

GENERAL TELERADIO, INC. was a subsidiary of the General Tire and Rubber Company, and controlled a number of radio and television stations (including WOR–New York, KHJ–Los Angeles, and WNAC-Boston) in the fifties. Headed by president Thomas F. O'Neill, General Teleradio, Inc. purchased RKO Radio Pictures, Inc. in July 1955, and renamed it RKO Teleradio Pictures, Inc. Prior to the purchase, in 1950, General Teleradio, Inc. had acquired the Don Lee Broadcasting System.*

GENERAL TELEVISION ENTERPRISES, INC., founded in 1949 by Gordon W. Levoy, produced some of the earliest episodes for ABC's* *Fireside Theatre* in the 1949–1950 season. These were later released in syndication by General Television Enterprises under the series title *Strange Adventure*.

GEORGE BAGNALL AND ASSOCIATES was a Beverly Hills–based distributor of television programming, founded in 1952 by Bagnall (1897–1978), who had been a major figure in the administration of the Motion Picture and Television Fund from 1932 until his death. Aside from its distribution activities, the company produced *Westinghouse Adventure* (Syndicated, 1965–1968), which was budgeted at $2.3 million for its first year and was claimed to be one of the biggest multimarket syndicated deals up to that time. An associated company was Cartoon Distributors Corporation.

THE GEORGE FOSTER PEABODY AWARDS, named in memory of the Southern banker and philanthropist (1852–1938), were established in 1940 to recognize achievements in broadcasting. They are administered by the Henry W. Grady School of Journalism at the University of Georgia, and first honored television in 1948 with an award to the Actor's Studio (for "Outstanding Contribution to the Art of Television"). Prior to 1974, awards were presented in designated categories, but they are now given to television stations, networks, and individuals in recognition of specific contributions.

THE GEORGE POLK MEMORIAL AWARDS IN JOURNALISM have been sponsored by the Department of Journalism at Long Island University since 1948. Judged by the university's journalism faculty, the annual spring awards honor journalism in radio, television, magazines, newspapers, and books.
    Address: Long Island University, University Plaza, Brooklyn, NY 11201.

GERRY GROSS–NORMAN BAER PRODUCTIONS was a New York–based production company, founded in 1952. In 1958, it became Gerry Gross–Madison Productions, Inc., and the company continued in existence through the mid-sixties.

[SID] GLENAR PRODUCTIONS/GLENAR STUDIOS is a Los Angeles–based producer of television commercials and educational films, active from the fifties through the present.

Address: 211 South Rose, Burbank, CA 91505.

GLOBAL TELEFILMS, INC., founded by William L. Snyder, was a New York–based producer of television commercials, active in the fifties and sixties.

GLOBE RELEASING CORP. was a Los Angeles–based distributor of films to television, operated in the fifties by Theodore J. Ticktin. In 1957, Sam Nathanson became president, and the name was changed to Globe International Releasing Corp. The company remained active through the mid-sixties.

GLOBE TV CORPORATION was a Los Angeles–based television distributor of forty-three British feature films, founded in 1952 by Edward Sherman and active through 1967. An earlier Sherman-owned company was MPM Corp., founded in 1947 to distribute films to television.

"THE GOLDEN AGE OF TELEVISION" is an expression used to refer to the era of live television production in the United States, basically from 1948 to 1955, although television critic Les Brown has suggested that "the Golden Age" opened with *Kraft Television Theatre* on May 7, 1947, and ended with the last live show in the *Playhouse 90* series ten years later. Interestingly, the majority of the drama shows from "the Golden Age" were anthology series, such as *Kraft Television Theatre* (NBC, 1949–1958), *Philco TV Playhouse* (NBC, 1948–1955), *Studio One* (CBS, 1948–1958), and *Playhouse 90* (CBS, 1956–1961).
BIBLIOGRAPHY
Sturcken, Frank. *Live Television: The Golden Age of 1946–1958 in New York.* Jefferson, N.C.: McFarland, 1990.

THE GOLDEN ROSE OF MONTREUX TELEVISION FESTIVAL was founded in 1960. Specializing in light entertainment television programming, the festival is held in late spring and attracts television executives from around the world.

Address: Direction du Concours de la Rose D'Or de Montreux, Case Postale 97, 1820 Montreux, Switzerland.

GOLDEN WEST BROADCASTERS was founded in 1952 by cowboy star Gene Autry (born 1907) with the acquisition of radio station KMPC–Los Angeles. Autry paid $800,000 for the station, and founded Golden West with paid in capital stock of $300,000. The organization grew in size to include a number of radio and television stations (notably KTLA–Los Angeles,* which Autry purchased from Paramount in 1964), Golden West TV Productions, Golden West Subscription TV, and Golden West Video Tape.

In October 1982, Autry disposed of the television division to Kohlberg, Kravis, Roberts & Co. He retained the California Angels baseball team, the radio division, and KAUT-TV (Oklahoma City).

Address: 5858 Sunset Boulevard, Los Angeles, CA 90078.

GOLD KEY ENTERTAINMENT was a distributor of features and series to television, formed in October 1970 by Harold Goldman following his departure from Commonwealth International, and by Samuel Firks. The company was named after Goldman's Gold Key Industries and was later merged with the Technicolor subsidiary Vidtronics. Gold Key Entertainment became inactive in 1983.

GOMALCO ENTERPRISES/GOMALCO PRODUCTIONS, INC., founded by George Gobel and David P. O'Malley, was responsible for the production of *The George Gobel Show* (NBC, 1954–1959; CBS, 1959–1960) and *Leave It to Beaver* (CBS, 1957–1958; ABC, 1958–1963).

GOODSON-TODMAN PRODUCTIONS was a company whose name was synonymous with television quiz and game shows, and which continues in the present as Mark Goodson Productions. The company was formed in 1946 by radio announcer Mark Goodson and radio writer William (Bill) Todman (1916–1979), with its first production being the radio program *Winner Take All* (which was later seen on CBS* television in 1948).

The company's best known series were *Beat the Clock* (CBS, 1950–1958), *What's My Line* (CBS, 1950–1967), and *I've Got a Secret* (CBS, 1952–1976). As evidence of the popularity of the last two series, the rights to *I've Got a Secret* were sold for $5 million, and CBS paid $2.5 million for the rights to *What's My Line* in 1958. Other Goodson-Todman shows were *The Name's the Same* (ABC, 1951–1954), *It's News to Me* (CBS, 1951–1955), *Two for the Money* (NBC, 1952–1953; CBS, 1953–1956), *To Tell the Truth* (CBS, 1956–1967; Syndicated, 1969–1977, 1980), *The Price Is Right* (NBC, 1957–1963; ABC, 1963–1964), *Play Your Hunch* (CBS, 1958–1962; NBC, 1962–1963), *Split Personality* (NBC, 1959), *Password* (CBS, 1961–1967; ABC, 1971–1975), *Match Game* (NBC, 1962–1969), *Call My Bluff* (NBC, 1965), *Snap Judgment* (Syndicated, 1967–1969), *The New Price Is Right* (Syndicated, 1972–1974, 1985), *Tattletales* (CBS, 1974–1978), *Now You See It* (CBS, 1974–1975), *Show-Offs* (Syndicated, 1975), *Double Dare* (CBS, 1976–1977), *Family Feud* (Syndicated, 1977–1984, 1989-   ), *The Better Sex* (ABC, 1977), and *Card Sharks* (NBC, 1978-   ).

Goodson-Todman Productions was also active in dramatic television programming in the late fifties and sixties, and in 1966 announced plans for theatrical production.

Address: Mark Goodson Productions, 375 Park Avenue, New York, NY 10152.

BIBLIOGRAPHY
Keller, David, "The Game-Show Game: A Goodson-Todman Production," *Emmy*, vol.
    I, no. 4, Fall 1979, pp. 28–31.

GORDON M. DAY PRODUCTIONS was a New York–based producer of television commercials and other programming, founded in 1946 and active through 1982.

GOSTELRADIO (the USSR State Committee for Television and Radio Broadcasting) controls all television broadcasting in the Soviet Union. With a staff of more than 80,000, Gostelradio is the world's largest television satellite broadcasting system, with almost 300 radio and television centers and 270 million viewers. It provides two national channels and various regional channels. An edict of the Presidium of the Supreme Soviet on July 12, 1971, made the chairman of the State Committee for Radio and Television a member of the government of the USSR.

Television broadcasting in the Soviet Union dates back to 1931. Regular television broadcasts began in Moscow and Leningrad in 1939, and television reached Kiev in 1951. Soviet television has 625 lines. Color broadcasts began in October 1967, using the SECAM* system. There were 90 million television sets in the Soviet Union as of 1990.

Gostelradio publishes the weekly *Govorit i Pokazyvayet Moskva/Moscow Calling and Television*, and two monthly periodicals, *Televideniye i Radiovesthtschaniye/Television and Radio Broadcasting* and *Krugozor/Outlook*.

Addresses: Tsentralnaja studija Televidenija, ul. Koroljova 12, Moscow 12700, USSR; Leningradskaya studio Televidenija, ul. Malaja Sadovaja 2, Leningrad, USSR.

BIBLIOGRAPHY
Redmont, Bernard S., "Soviet Television's New Look," *Television Quarterly*, vol.
    XXIV, no. 1, 1989, pp. 31–43.
Sanders, Jonathan, "A Very Mass Media: Soviet Television," *Television Quarterly*, vol.
    XXII, no. 3, 1986, pp. 7–24.

GOULDING-ELLIOTT-GREYBAR PRODUCTIONS, INC. was created in 1955 by "Bob and Ray" (Bob Elliott and Ray Goulding) to produce radio and television commercials.

Address: 420 Lexington Avenue, New York, NY 10017.

THE GOVERNORS AWARD is the highest honor presented by the Academy of Television Arts and Sciences, and is given for a lifetime of outstanding achievement in the television industry. The following is a complete list of winners, with the years in which the awards were presented: William S. Paley (1978), Walter Cronkite (1979), Johnny Carson (1980), Elton H. Rule (1981), Hallmark Greetings Cards for the *Hallmark Hall of Fame* (1982), Sylvester "Pat" Weaver (1983), Bob Hope (1984), Alistair Cooke (1985), Red Skelton

(1986), Grant Tinker (1987), William Hanna and Joseph Barbera (1988), Lucille Ball (1989), and Leonard Goldenson (1990).

GOVERNOR TV ATTRACTIONS (Arthur Kerman, president) was a New York–based distributor of more than 100 feature films and 200 short subjects to television. It was founded in 1951 and remained active through 1965.

GRACIE FILMS was formed in 1984 by producer James L. Brooks (born 1940), who had earlier been responsible for many "hit" films and television shows, including *Room 222* (ABC, 1968–1969), *The Mary Tyler Moore Show* (CBS, 1970–1977), and *Rhoda* (CBS, 1974–1975). Gracie Films produced the two most popular shows on the Fox Network*: *The Tracey Ullman Show* (1987– 1990) and *The Simpsons* (1990-   ), and was also active in theatrical film production. In May 1990, the company signed an exclusive contract with Columbia Pictures Corporation.

Address: 10202 West Washington Boulevard, Culver City, CA 90232.

GRAMPIAN TELEVISION plc is the British independent ("commercial") television network for the north of Scotland (from Fife and Tayside to Shetland and the Western Isles). It began broadcasting on September 30, 1961, and in June 1977, the company diversified into property development with the formation of Glenburnie Properties, Ltd.

Address: Queen's Cross, Aberdeen AB9 2XJ, United Kingdom.

GRANADA TELEVISION LIMITED is one of the better known of the British independent ("commercial") television networks providing service to northern England (from north Staffordshire and the northeast Wales border in the south, west of the Pennines to parts of south Cumbria). It is the longest-serving independent television contractor and the only network program contractor from the mid-fifties that is still operating.

Granada Television was launched on May 3, 1956, as a result of a 1954 decision by the Granada Group, headed by Sidney and Cecil Bernstein, to diversify its cinema and theatre business. Granada Television remains a wholly owned subsidiary of the Granada Group.

American viewers are familiar with Granada's productions of *Brideshead Revisited*, *The Jewel in the Crown*, and *Sherlock Holmes*. In the United Kingdom, it is best known for three long-running series, *What the Papers Say* (1956-   ), *Coronation Street* (1960-   ), and *World in Action* (1963-   ).

Address: Granada TV Centre, Manchester M60 9EA, United Kingdom.

BIBLIOGRAPHY
Granada: The First 25 Years. London: British Film Institute, 1981.
Moorehead, Caroline. *Sidney Bernstein: A Biography*. London: Jonathan Cape, 1984.
Nadelson, Regina, "The Best Television Company in the World," *Channels of Communications*, vol. IV, no. 3, September/October 1984, pp. 26–28.

Year One: An Account of the First Year of Operation of an Independent Television Company in England. Manchester, U.K.: Granada Television, 1958.

[JAMES E.] GRAY–[JOHN F.] O'REILLY STUDIOS was a New York–based producer of television commercials, active in the fifties and early sixties.

GREAT AMERICAN COMMUNICATIONS CO. is the successor company to the Taft Broadcasting Co., which was acquired in the summer of 1986 by a group of investors led by Carl Lindner. The company is also involved in amusement parks, but its most profitable division is Great American Broadcasting, which controls Hanna-Barbera Productions, Inc. (acquired by Taft in 1966), Ruby-Spears Productions, Inc.,* Hamilton Projects, Titus Productions,* Sunn Classic Pictures, Inc. (which Taft acquired in 1980 and renamed Taft International Pictures, Inc.), and QM Productions.* The company also owns five television stations.

Address: 3400 Cahuenga Boulevard, Los Angeles, CA 90068.

GREATEST FIGHTS OF THE CENTURY, INC./TURN OF THE CENTURY FIGHTS, INC./THE BIG FIGHTS, INC. are the New York companies founded by boxing entrepreneur Jimmy Jacobs. Since the fifties, they have produced and distributed a variety of syndicated fight films, including 500 *Big Fights of the Decades* shows and 600 *Knock-Out* shows.

Address: 9 East 40 Street, New York, NY 10016.

GRIFFIN, MERV ENTERPRISES. See MERV GRIFFIN ENTERPRISES

GROSS-KRASNE, INC. was one of the most prominent producers of syndicated television programming in the fifties. It was founded in 1951 by Jack Jerome Gross (1902–1964), who had entered the film industry as a producer in 1939, and Philip N. Krasne (born 1905), who had commenced his career as vice-president in charge of production at Grand National in 1936. Among the series for which Gross-Krasne was responsible were *Mayor of the Town* (1954), *The Lone Wolf* (1954), *Dr. Hudson's Secret Journal* (1955–1956), *The O. Henry Playhouse* (1956), *Adventures of a Jungle Boy* (1957), *African Patrol* (1957), and *The Flying Doctor* (1959).

The partnership was dissolved in 1959, but Gross-Krasne was later reactivated as a producer of theatrical films. Its distribution arm was United Television Programs, Inc.,* which was later acquired by MCA/Universal.

GROUP W. See WESTINGHOUSE

GROVERTON PRODUCTIONS, LTD. was owned by David Victor, and located at Universal Studios, with whom it co-produced all its series. Very active in the seventies, Groverton was responsible for *Marcus Welby, M.D.* (ABC,

1969–1976), *The Man and the City* (ABC, 1971–1972), *Owen Marshall, Counselor at Law* (ABC, 1971–1974), *Griff* (ABC, 1973–1974), *Lucas Tanner* (NBC, 1974–1975), *McNaughton's Daughter* (NBC, 1976), and *Little Women* (NBC, 1979).

GTG ENTERTAINMENT (the initials stand for Grant Tinker Gannett) was founded in 1986, with Tinker as its creative head and the Gannett* newspaper group providing the funding. The company acquired the Culver Studios, which proved a continuing source of revenue as a rental lot, but GTG's productions failed to garner much of an audience. *USA Today on TV* was a short-lived news program in the fall of 1988. *Baywatch* lasted for one season on NBC* during 1989–1990.

Address: 9336 West Washington Boulevard, Culver City, CA 90230.
BIBLIOGRAPHY
Baker, Jeri, "Grant's Back & Gannett's Got Him," *Channels of Communications*, vol. VII, no. 7, July 1987, pp. 40–43.
Lippman, John, "Grant Tinker Tries Again," *Los Angeles Times,* May 7, 1990, section D, pp. 1–2.

GUILD FILMS CO., INC. was a New York–based television producer/distributor, organized early in 1952 by Reub Kaufman, the former president of Snader Telescriptions, Inc.* Its first production, and arguably its most successful, in January 1953, was the *Liberace Show* (Syndicated, 1953–1955). Other syndicated series from Guild were *Jungle Macabre* (1953), *The Joe Palooka Story* (1953), *Life with Elizabeth* (1953–1954), *Conrad Nagel Theatre* (1954), *I Spy* (1955), *The Frankie Laine Show* (1955), and *Captain David Grief* (1956). The company also offered the *Guild Sports Library* (consisting of 400 thirty-second action films), *Call the Play* (a sports quiz with the Brooklyn Dodgers), and a television stock-shot library. Guild Films eventually merged with Official Films, Inc.,* following its bankruptcy in December 1960.

THE GUILD OF TELEVISION CAMERAMEN is a professional organization of British television cameramen, founded in 1972.

Address: 21 Diamond Road, South Ruislip, Middlesex, HA4 0PF, United Kingdom.

H

HA! is MTV's* response to the Comedy Channel,* and it first began broadcasting on April 1, 1990. Ha!'s twenty-four hour a day programming includes both new productions and such classic comedy series as *Your Show of Shows*, *You Bet Your Life/The Best of Groucho*, *The Phil Silvers Show*, and *The Mary Tyler Moore Show*. In April 1991, Ha! merged with The Comedy Channel to form CTV: The Comedy Network.

Address: 1775 Broadway, New York, NY 10019.

BIBLIOGRAPHY

Rubin, Rosina, "Take My Channel, Please!" *Emmy*, vol. XII, no. 4, July/August 1990, pp. 90–94.

HALLMARK GREETINGS CARDS first became involved in broadcast sponsorship in 1938 with a popular radio series on which Tony Wons read poetry. In 1951, Hallmark entered television sponsorship, with *Hallmark Presents Sarah Churchill*, and, in January 1952, it began sponsorship of *The Hallmark Television Playhouse*. When NBC aired Gian-Carlo Menotti's *Amahl and the Night Visitors* on December 24, 1951, the advertising agency of Foote, Cone & Belding was able to persuade its client, Hallmark, to sponsor the production. From this presentation, *The Hallmark Hall of Fame* came into existence, and in 1971, Hallmark created its own in-house production company to create the shows. (An additional sponsored series, *Hallmark Summer Theatre*, was seen on ABC* in the summer of 1952.)

Major productions in the *Hallmark Hall of Fame* include *Hamlet*, with Maurice Evans (NBC, 1953); *Born Yesterday*, with Paul Douglas (NBC, 1956); *All Quiet on the Western Front*, with Richard Thomas (CBS, 1979); and *Gideon's Trumpet*, with Henry Fonda (CBS, 1980). Other *Hallmark Hall of Fame* productions are *The Corn Is Green* (NBC, 1956), *Dial M for Murder* (NBC, 1958), *Winterset* (NBC, 1959), *Macbeth* (NBC, 1960), *Pygmalion* (NBC, 1963), *The Fantasticks* (NBC, 1964), *The Admirable Crichton* (NBC, 1968), *The Snow Goose* (NBC,

1971), *Harvey* (NBC, 1972), *Brief Encounter* (NBC, 1974), *The Hunchback of Notre Dame* (CBS, 1982), *Camille* (CBS, 1984), *The Secret Garden* (CBS, 1987), and *Stones for Ibarra* (CBS, 1988).

BIBLIOGRAPHY

Rinker, Buck, "Hallmark Hall of Fame," *Channels of Communications*, vol. VII, no. 9, October 1987, pp. 47–48.
Wilson, Melissa Moore, "The Hallmark Hall of Fame," *Emmy*, vol. II, no. 4, Fall 1980, pp. 43–45.

HAL ROACH ENTERTAINMENT, INC. With the purchase of his father's Culver City studio in 1955, Hal Roach, Jr., formed Hal Roach Entertainment, Inc., a wholly owned corporation, into which he consolidated his various television production companies: Lincoln Productions (formed in 1953); Showcase Productions, Inc.;* Rovan; H.R. Productions; Rabco; and Hal Roach, Jr. Enterprises. Rovan was responsible for the production of *My Little Margie* (CBS, 1952; NBC, 1952; CBS, 1953; NBC, 1953–1955). H.R. Productions handled *The Public Defender* (CBS, 1954–1955). Rabco produced *Passport to Danger* (Syndicated, 1954–1956) and *Racket Squad* (CBS, 1951–1953).

Hal Roach, Jr., was a pioneer in filmed television programming. In 1950, it was reported that he was producing 80 percent of all television being filmed in Hollywood. Unfortunately, he became overambitious. In 1958, he announced expansion plans and, in association with the F.L. Jacobs Company of Detroit, he purchased the Mutual Broadcasting System, Inc. A year later, he and two of Mutual's officials (president Alexander L. Guterma and Garland L. Culpepper, Jr.) were indicted by a federal grand jury, accused (and later found guilty) of accepting $750,000 to broadcast propaganda favorable to the Dominican Republic and its dictator Rafael Trujillo, in violation of the Foreign Agents Registration Act. Roach lost control of the studio in 1959, and filed for personal bankruptcy in 1962. His last production venture was in 1967 in Canada, where, with six other individuals, he formed VI Productions.

HANDEL FILM CORPORATION was formed in 1953 as a producer of documentary films for both television and industrial use. Among the subjects covered by films from Leo A. Handel's company are nuclear energy, art, American history, science, safety, and the environment.
Address: 8730 Sunset Boulevard, West Hollywood, CA 90069.

[FREDERICK L.] HANKINSON STUDIO, INC. was a New York–based producer of television commercials, active in the fifties and sixties.

HARDIE FRIEBERG TELEVISION ENTERPRISES, INC. was a New York–based producer of live and filmed television shows, active in the early fifties.

"**HARD ROCK**" is the slang expression coined by *Variety* to describe ABC's* corporate headquarters in New York; the NBC* headquarters is called "Thirty Rock," while CBS* headquarters is "Black Rock."

HARMONY GOLD is a major producer of television movies and mini-series, founded in 1984 as a privately held company by Frank Agrama. Its first success was with the 1985 syndicated animated series *Robotech*, and its major television productions have included *The Secret Identity of Jack the Ripper* (Syndicated, 1988), *The Man Who Lived at the Ritz* (Syndicated, 1988), *Around the World in 80 Days* (NBC, 1989), and *Confessional* (1990). In 1988, the company formed the Harmony Premiere Network of independent stations to air its mini-series, beginning with *King of the Olympics: The Lives and Loves of Avery Brundage* (1988). A year later, in February 1989, it moved to new headquarters at the former Preview House in Hollywood.

Subsidiary companies are Intersound, Inc. (a postproduction facility founded in 1980, which Harmony Gold acquired in 1986) and America 5 Entertainment (a production company of which Harmony Gold is co-owner). In 1989, the company formed Crossbow Entertainment Group to undertake theatrical production.

Address: 7655 Sunset Boulevard, Los Angeles, CA 90046.

HARRISCOPE CORPORATION was founded in 1953 by Burt I. Harris to produce and distribute sports films for television. Between 1954 and 1955, it produced 26 thirty-minute episodes of *Jalopy Races from Hollywood* (Syndicated), 52 thirty-minute episodes of *Main Event Wrestling from Hollywood* (NBC), and 13 thirty-minute episodes of *All Girl Wrestling* (Syndicated). It also re-edited a group of "Christie" comedies into 104 fifteen-minute episodes. Later, the company became involved in television station ownership, controlling in whole or part KTWO-Casper, Wyoming; KFBB–Great Falls, Montana; KBAK-Bakersfield, California; KULR-Billings, Montana; WSNS-Chicago; and KGGM-Albuquerque, as well as various cable systems. As of 1990, it controls KWHY–Los Angeles and WSNS-Chicago.

Address: 10920 Wilshire Boulevard, Suite 1420, Los Angeles, CA 90024.

[FRAN] HARRIS–[RALPH G.] TUCHMAN PRODUCTIONS, with offices in Chicago and Los Angeles, has been active as a producer of television commercials since the early fifties.

Address: 4293 Sarah Street, Burbank, CA 91505.

HARRY S. GOODMAN PRODUCTIONS was a New York–based producer and distributor, active in the fifties and sixties. In the mid-fifties, it was responsible for a number of minor syndicated series including: *A Word from the Stars* (fifteen- and thirty-minute programs), *Streamlined Fairy Tales* (fifteen-minute programs) and *Cyclone Malone* (fifteen-minute programs).

HARVEY FILMS, INC./HARVEY CARTOON STUDIOS, INC. was created by Alfred Harvey, who had started Harvey Famous Name Comics and Informational Booklets in 1940. The company took over rights to the cartoon characters created by Famous Studios (notably Casper the Friendly Ghost) in 1957 and retitled the cartoons for television "Harveytoons." The company remained active through the mid-seventies.

HATOS-HALL PRODUCTIONS is the production company of Stephen Hatos and Monty Hall, responsible for one of the most popular daytime game shows on American television: *Let's Make a Deal* (NBC, 1963–1968; ABC, 1968–1976; Syndicated, 1977-   ), which was hosted by Hall. Other Hatos-Hall game shows are *Chain Letter* (Syndicated, 1966), *Split Second* (ABC, 1972–1975), *It Pays To Be Ignorant* (Syndicated, 1973), *High Rollers* (ABC, 1973–1975), *Masquerade Party* (Syndicated, 1974), *Three for the Money* (NBC, 1975), and *It's Anybody's Guess* (Syndicated, 1977).

Address: 7633 West Sunset Boulevard, Los Angeles, CA 90046.
BIBLIOGRAPHY
Hall, Monty, with Bill Libby. *Emcee Monty Hall*. New York: Grosset and Dunlap, 1973.

HAWAII has served as the location for a number of television series: *Hawaiian Eye* (ABC, 1959–1963), *Hawaii Five-O* (CBS, 1968–1980), *Big Hawaii* (NBC, 1977), *The Mackenzies of Paradise Cove* (ABC, 1979), *Magnum, P.I.* (CBS, 1980–1988), *Aloha Paradise* (ABC, 1981), and *Island Son* (CBS, 1989–1990). *Hawaii Calls* was a 1966 syndicated series promoting the islands, and *Diamond Head* (NBC, 1975) was a game show, produced by Columbia Pictures Television and taped on the island of Oahu.

See also THE DIAMOND HEAD STUDIO.

HBO (HOME BOX OFFICE, INC.) is America's largest pay-cable television service. A division of Time Warner, it provides twenty-four hour a day programming for more than 17 million subscribers, offering recent theatrical features, sports events, and special programming, and is also the parent company of The Comedy Channel* and Cinemax.* HBO was created by Chuck Dolan and his company, Sterling Communications, and began as a local pay-television outlet in Wilkes-Barre, Pennsylvania, on November 8, 1972, with its first program being the feature film *Sometimes a Great Notion.*

Time Inc. acquired a majority interest in Sterling Communications, renamed the company Manhattan Cable, and brought in a new president, Jerry Levin, to oversee HBO's expansion. (Levin was replaced in 1976 by N.J. "Nick" Nicholas, who was, in turn, succeeded by Jim Heyworth and Michael Fuchs.) Major expansion took place in 1974, when HBO was able to utilize the newly launched *Satcom 1* satellite, and in December 1975, HBO began national service. That same year, the company began original programming, and it is the only cable network noted for the quality and quantity of its made-for-television movies. Additionally, HBO was involved in the creation of Orion Pictures, Tri-Star Pictures, and Silver Screen Partners.

Address: 1100 Avenue of the Americas, New York, NY 10036.

BIBLIOGRAPHY

"At Age 15, HBO Chases the Networks," *Channels of Communications*, vol. VII, no. 9, October 1987, pp. 78–79.

Mair, George. *Inside HBO: The Billion Dollar War between HBO, Hollywood and the Home Video Revolution.* New York: Dodd, Mead, 1988.

THE HEALTH SERVICES COMMUNICATIONS ASSOCIATION, founded in 1959 as the Council on Medical Television, serves as a clearinghouse for information in the field. The Association of Medical Television Broadcasters is now part of the organization.

Address: 6105 Lindell Boulevard, St. Louis, MO 63112.

HEATTER-QUIGLEY PRODUCTIONS was a prolific producer and packager of game shows, formed by producer Merrill Heatter and writer Roger Quigley, with its first effort being *Video Village* (CBS, 1960–1962). Other Heatter-Quigley series were *People Will Talk* (NBC, 1963), *The Celebrity Game* (CBS, 1964–1965), *PDQ* (NBC, 1965), *Hollywood Squares* (NBC, 1966–1981), *Show Down* (NBC, 1966), *Baffle* (NBC, 1970), *Amateur's Guide to Love* (CBS, 1972), *Gambit* (CBS, 1972–1977), *The Magnificent Marble Machine* (NBC, 1975), *Hot Seat* (Syndicated, 1976), and *To Say the Least* (NBC, 1977).

BIBLIOGRAPHY

Fabe, Maxene. *Game Shows!* Garden City, N.Y.: Doubleday, 1979.

HENSON ASSOCIATES, INC. is the production company of Muppets creator Jim Henson (1937–1990), responsible for the production, in association with ITC,* of the popular television series *The Muppet Show* (Syndicated, 1976–1981), which was shot in England and helped identify the Muppets as entertainment as much for adults as for children.

Address: 117 East 69 Street, New York, NY 10021.

BIBLIOGRAPHY

Loevy, Diana, "Inside the House That Henson Built," *Channels of Communications*, vol. VIII, no. 3, March 1988, pp. 52–61.

HERTZ, named after the German physicist Heinrich Hertz (1857–1894), is a unit of frequency equal to one cycle per second. Electrical current in the U.S. is sixty hertz. American VHF television stations are allocated on a band from 54 to 216 megahertz, and UHF* stations from 470 to 890 megahertz. A megahertz equals 1 million cycles per second.

HIGH DEFINITION TELEVISION (HDTV). The clarity of color television is determined by the number of lines.* In the United States, there are 525 lines. Throughout most of the world, where the PAL* system is in use, there are 625 lines. High Definition Television would use 1,125 lines, making it comparable to viewing 35mm film projected on a movie screen. In addition, High Definition Television would offer stereophonic sound and a picture screen closer to that of a standard movie screen (giving it a wide viewing angle of thirty degrees and making it conform more naturally to the human field of vision).

High Definition Television has been tested in Japan for more than twenty years, and in 1981 and 1982, CBS* sponsored demonstrations in the United States. So successful were these demonstrations that there were predictions that feature films for theatrical release would in future be produced on HDTV. The FCC* has appointed an Advisory Committee on Advanced Television Service, chaired by Richard E. Wiley (FCC chairman from 1974 to 1977), to examine the potential of High Definition Television, and it is scheduled to present its final report by September 30, 1992. The only problem with the system is that it is not compatible with current American television technology, and would require the scrapping of all contemporary television receivers.

BIBLIOGRAPHY

Freeman, John, "A Cross-Referenced Bibliography on High Definition and Advanced Television Systems, 1971–1988," *SMPTE Journal*, vol. LXXXXIX, no. 11, November 1990, pp. 909–935.

Johnson, Tim. *Strategies for Higher-Definition Television*. London: Ovum, 1983.

"May the Best HDTV System Win," *Channels of Communications*, vol. X, no. 11, August 13, 1990, pp. 54–55.

Wiley, Richard E., "HDTV: The New Video Frontier," *Television Quarterly*, vol. XXIII, no. 4, 1988, pp. 7–11.

HILL-EUBANKS PRODUCTIONS is an inactive company, formed in 1976 by Mike Hill and game show personality Bob Eubanks. It produced *All Star Secrets* (NBC, 1978), *The Guinness Game* (Syndicated, 1979), and *You Bet Your Life* (Syndicated, 1980).

HIT VIDEO USA is a basic cable network, broadcasting contemporary hit music videos from midnight through 10:00 A.M. It was launched in December 1985.
Address: 1000 Louisiana Street, Suite 3500, Houston, TX 77002.

HOBART PRODUCTIONS was the Sinatra-owned company responsible for *The Frank Sinatra Show* (ABC, 1957–1958).

HOFFBERG PRODUCTIONS, INC. was a New York–based distributor to television of "B" features from the thirties and forties. It was founded in 1924 by Jack H. Hoffberg upon his resignation as export manager for Goldwyn Pictures Corporation; its assets were acquired in the early seventies by Raymond Rohauer.

HOGAN'S RADIO PICTURES, INC. was the licensee of W2XR–New York, beginning in March 1929. The company, founded by John V.L. Hogan, began regular transmission from Long Island City in 1930, but by 1934, the television station, now called W2XDR, was operated only for research purposes. W2XR continued as a radio station and became WQXR in 1936.

BIBLIOGRAPHY

Udelson, Joseph H. *The Great Television Race: A History of the American Television Industry 1925–1941*. University: University of Alabama Press, 1982.

HOLLYWOOD FILM COMMERCIALS, founded by David Commons, was a Los Angeles–based producer of television commercials, active in the fifties and sixties.

THE HOLLYWOOD RADIO & TV SOCIETY, founded in 1947, has a membership comprised of individuals active in radio, television, and advertising. It sponsors monthly luncheons and presents the annual International Broadcasting Award for best radio and television commercials.

Address: 5315 Laurel Canyon Boulevard, Suite 202, North Hollywood, CA 91607.

HOLLYWOOD TELEVISION PRODUCTIONS (Jack McGowan, president) was a New York–based (despite its name) producer and distributor, primarily of television commercials, active in the early fifties.

HOLLYWOOD TELEVISION SERVICE, INC., headed by Earl R. Collins, was a Los Angeles–based subsidiary of Republic Pictures Corporation. Founded in 1951, it distributed a number of syndicated series, including *Stories of the Century* (1954), *Stryker of Scotland Yard* (1955), and *Frontier Doctor* (1956). When Republic ceased operations in 1959, the company became a division of NTA.*

THE HOLLYWOOD TELEVISION SOCIETY was created in 1938 by enthusiasts interested in experimental television. It published a newsletter, *Televisor*, edited by George Stewart, dealing primarily with technical aspects of television.

HOME BOX OFFICE. See HBO

THE HOME SHOPPING NETWORK. First seen in July 1985, and with almost 20 million subscribers, the Home Shopping Network is the best known of the cable networks offering viewers at home the opportunity to purchase an ever-changing assortment of products at discount prices. Other cable home shopping networks are: America's Value Network (Route 2, Eau Claire, WI 54703), America's Shopping Channel (1919-A Friendship Drive, El Cajon, CA 92020), QVC Network (Goshen Corporate Park, West Chester, PA 19380), Shop Television Network (5842 Sunset Boulevard, Los Angeles, CA 90028), Shoppers Advantage (707 Summer Street, Stamford, CT 06901), Sky Merchant (9697

East Mineral Avenue, Englewood, CO 80112), The Country Store (Box 82, Bernalillo, NM 87004), and Video Shopping Mall (929 Fox Pavilion, Suite 930, Jenkintown, PA 19046).

Address: P.O. Box 9090, Clearwater, FL 34618–9090.

HOMOSEXUALITY. While the subject remains one with which American television feels awkward, homosexuality has been dealt with more openly in recent years, largely because of the acquired immune deficiency syndrome (AIDS) epidemic.

Perhaps the earliest television program to deal with the subject was the British *Homosexuality and the Law: A Prologue to the Wolfenden Report*, aired on Granada Television Limited* in 1957. In 1980, London Weekend Television* produced *Gay Life*, the first European program openly sympathetic to homosexuality, which was followed the same year by the BBC's* *Coming Out*, a frank and friendly look at five homosexuals in the United Kingdom.

In the United States, ABC* is the only network to broadcast programs with gay characters on a regular basis. In 1975, the short-lived *Hot L Baltimore* had a number of gay characters. On *Soap* (ABC, 1977–1981), Billy Crystal played the ongoing gay character, Jodie Dallas, in a sympathetic and humorous manner. Less sympathetic, and far more confused sexually, was the character of Steven Carrington, played by Jack Coleman, on *Dynasty* (ABC, 1982–1989). Producer and writer Danny Arnold introduced the gay character of Marty for occasional appearances on *Barney Miller*, and, with Chris Haywood, developed a gay series for ABC in 1980 titled *Adam and Yves*, which was eventually shelved.

In 1977, the writers of the soap opera *Another World* attempted to introduce a gay character, but the idea was vetoed by Procter & Gamble Productions.* However, in 1984, again on ABC, Donna Pescow played the first openly lesbian woman on a soap opera, in *All My Children*. Ten years earlier, lesbians had been portrayed as psychopathic killers on the "Flowers of Evil" episode of *Police Woman*.

In 1973, "The Other Martin Loring," an episode of *Marcus Welby, M.D.*, considered the question of a married man trying to come to terms with his homosexuality. As the central character in *Love, Sidney* (NBC, 1981–1983), Tony Randall was homosexual, but the character was never adequately developed to make this obvious to most viewers. Far more evident was the sexual preference of the character of Clifford Waters, first seen on the Showtime* series *Brothers*, on July 13, 1984. The first episode of *Golden Girls*, airing on NBC* in September 1985, featured a gay housekeeper, played by Charles Levin, but the character was dropped after the initial episode.

The first major breakthrough for a sympathetic portrayal of a homosexual on American television came with *That Certain Summer* (seen on ABC on November 1, 1972), in which Hal Holbrook played a divorced man explaining his homosexuality to his son, played by Scott Jacoby. *An Early Frost* (first seen on NBC on November 11, 1985) presented a moving study of AIDS as it affected the

central gay character, played by Aidan Quinn, and his family. In *Welcome Home, Bobby* (CBS, 1986), a teenager came to grips with his gayness, and in *Consenting Adult* (ABC, 1985), an American family dealt with their son's homosexuality.
BIBLIOGRAPHY

Deiter, Newton E., "The Last Minority: Television and Gay People," *Television Quarterly*, vol. XIII, no. 3, Fall 1976, pp. 69–72.

Henry, William A., "That Certain Subject," *Channels of Communications*, vol. VII, no. 4, April 1987, pp. 43–45.

Russo, Vito, "AIDS in 'Sweeps' Time," *Channels of Communications*, vol. V, no. 3, September/October 1985, pp. 6–7.

Toogood, Alex, "The Gay Life in Television," *Television Quarterly*, vol. XI, no. 3, Spring 1974, pp. 22–26.

HOPE ENTERPRISES, INC. was created by comedian Bob Hope (born 1903) to handle various of his business activities, including the production of his many NBC* television specials. The company also produced a short-lived series titled *Joe & Valerie* (NBC, 1978–1979).

Address: 3808 Riverside Drive, Suite 100, Burbank, CA 91505.

HOTELVISION, which provides pay-cable movies to hotel guests on an individual, room-by-room basis, was introduced in 1972. It is provided by a number of different companies.

HOUR GLASS PRODUCTIONS was created by screenwriter (and occasional director) Wanda Tuchock (1899–1985), and was responsible for the fifteen-minute, 1955 syndicated series *Man of Tomorrow*.

THE HOUSE OF COMMONS BROADCASTING UNIT is a private, limited company, jointly owned by the Independent Broadcasting Authority (IBA*) and the BBC,* which began experimental transmission of the proceedings of the House of Commons after the State Opening of Parliament in November 1989.
BIBLIOGRAPHY

Clarke, Tom, "Lights! Camera! Action?" in *British Film Institute Film and Television Handbook 1990*, editor David Leafe. London: British Film Institute, 1989, pp. 34–38.

HTV GROUP plc. Originally known as Harlech Television, HTV is the British independent ("commercial") television network for Wales and Avon and parts of Gloucestershire, Somerset, and Wiltshire. It began broadcasting on March 4, 1968, and took over from TWW (Television Wales and West), which had commenced broadcasting in the same region on January 14, 1958. While it has produced many dramas and sponsors a playwriting contest in cooperation with the Bristol Old Vic, HTV productions have failed to find an audience in the United States. The company maintains studios in Cardiff and Bristol.

Addresses: The Television Centre, Culverhouse Cross, Cardiff CF5 6XJ,

United Kingdom; The Television Centre, Bath Road, Bristol BS4 3HG, United Kingdom.

HURRELL PRODUCTIONS, INC., owned by the well-known photographer George E. Hurrell, was active in the early and mid-fifties as a Beverly Hills–based television producer/distributor. The company listed itself as a subsidiary of Walt Disney Productions, probably as a result of Hurrell's marriage to Mrs. Lillian Disney's niece.

HUT is a television industry abbreviation for "homes using television" and is often cited in television audience rating reports.
      See also PUT.

[MICHAEL] HYAMS T.V. FILMS, INC. was a New York–based distributor to television of 200 feature films, active in the fifties and sixties.

HYGO TV FILMS, INC. was a minor producer of syndicated programs. Founded by Jerome Hyams in 1950, it merged with Screen Gems* in 1956.

HYTRON RADIO AND ELECTRONICS was a manufacturer of television receivers, acquired by CBS* in 1951 for a reported $17.5 million. The venture was not successful because of the outdated nature of Hytron's "Air King" receivers; CBS renamed the company CBS Electronics in 1959, and two years later it ceased operations.

I

THE IBA. In basic terms, the IBA (Independent Broadcasting Authority) is required by the British Parliament to provide quality public television (and, since 1973, radio) services additional to those of the BBC.* Such services are provided by the fifteen ITV* companies, together with TV-am,* which are contracted to the IBA. Each company pays a rental to meet IBA's administrative and transmission costs. They also pay a subscription to the IBA for the cost of Channel 4,* which is a wholly owned subsidiary of the IBA. The latter publishes various pamphlets on its activities, including the annual *Factfile* and *This Is Independent Broadcasting* (1988), together with the quarterly journal *Airwaves*.

IBA has its origins in the Independent Television Authority (ITA), which was formed in August 1954, under the Independent Television Act, to oversee the introduction of commercial television in the United Kingdom, and to grant franchises for the operation of regional television companies. The first four such franchises granted were to Granada Television Limited* (broadcasting weekdays in the north of England), Associated Rediffusion (broadcasting weekdays in London), Association British Cinemas Television (broadcasting weekends in the north of England and the Midlands), and Associated Broadcasting Development Company (broadcasting weekends in London and weekdays in the Midlands). The first independent transmitter opened in Croydon, Surrey, on September 22, 1955, serving Associated Broadcasting Development Company and Associated Rediffusion.

The Independent Television Authority was renamed the Independent Broadcasting Authority under the provisions of the Sound Broadcasting Act of 1972, at which time it also accepted responsibility for independent radio broadcasting. The IBA's board is appointed by the Home Secretary, and the IBA also maintains five advisory groups: the Independent Broadcasting Authority General Advisory Council, the Independent Broadcasting Authority Advisory Committee, the Independent Broadcasting Authority Scottish Committee, the Independent Broadcasting Authority Northern Ireland Committee, and the Independent Broadcasting Authority Welsh Committee.

The Broadcasting Bill, passed in December 1989, sets out legislation to establish two new public bodies, the Independent Television Commission and the Radio Authority, which will replace the IBA. The new Independent Television Commission (ITC) will be responsible for licensing and regulating all commercially funded British television services (cable, satellite, or terrestrial), and it will also oversee the creation of the new Channel 3.

Address: 70 Brompton Road, London SW3 1EY, United Kingdom.

BIBLIOGRAPHY

Potter, Jeremy. *Independent Television in Britain. Vol. 3: Politics and Control, 1968–1980.* London: Macmillan, 1990.

Sendall, Bernard. *Independent Television in Britain. Vol. 1: Origin and Foundation, 1946–1962.* London: Macmillan, 1982.

————. *Independent Television in Britain. Vol. 2: Expansion and Change, 1958–1968.* London: Macmillan, 1983.

ICELAND BROADCAST SERVICE-TELEVISION/RÍKISÚTVARPID SJÓNVARP began operations in September 1966. It introduced color television, using the PAL* system, in 1978.

Address: Krókhálsi 6, 110 Reykjavik, Iceland.

IDÉES GRANDES, INC. is the cute name used for a company co-owned by Jackie Gleason, but if it is remembered at all, it is as the producer of the game show *You're in the Picture*, seen only once, on CBS,* on January 21, 1961. The company was formed in New York by Gleason and Jack Philbin, who was executive producer of *The Honeymooners* (CBS, 1955–1956) and Gleason's personal manager.

IFA-TV CORP. (International Film Associates) was a New York–based producer, primarily of television commercials, headed from 1949 through the mid-fifties by B. Bernard Kreisler.

IMPRO PRODUCTIONS, INC. (the letters stand for Independent Motion Picture Producers and Releasing Organization) was owned by Herbert L. Strock. It appears to have produced only one series for television, thirteen episodes of *Cases of Eddie Drake*, starring Dan Haggerty, and was purchased by CBS* in 1948.

INDEPENDENT NETWORK NEWS (INN) was created by the Tribune Broadcasting Co. to provide a news service for independent television stations. It began as a thirty-minute program of national and international news on June 9, 1980, and was available Mondays through Fridays. INN was headed by John R. Corporon, vice-president of news at WPIX–New York,* the city where the programming originated. With an annual budget of $6 million, INN had 30 stations signed up when it went on the air, and had advanced to 144 stations by 1985.

BIBLIOGRAPHY

Bergmann, David, " 'Independent News' Moves to Upgrade Indies' 2d-Class Image," *Daily Variety*, April 27, 1984, p. 18.

Goldman, Kevin, "INN Fights for Entry into Prestigious Washington News Pool," *Daily Variety*, January 7, 1985, p. 14.

Schwartz, Tony, "New TV Network To Offer News Show," *New York Times*, May 2, 1980, p. C28.

INDEPENDENT PRODUCERS FILM LIBRARY was operated by Jack A. Eisenbach (who also had Jack Eisenbach Productions) as a distributor of features to television and as a stock-footage library, in the fifties and sixties. It distributed the 1956 syndicated series *Chummy's Animal Theatre*, consisting of filler shows of three-and-a-half minutes in length. It was taken over by Allan Sandler and renamed Independent Producers Film Exchange, Inc.

THE INDEPENDENT PROGRAMME PRODUCERS ASSOCIATION, founded in 1981, is the negotiating body for independent television production companies in the United Kingdom.

Address: 50–51 Berwick Street, London W1V 3RA, United Kingdom.

THE INDEPENDENT TELEVISION ASSOCIATION, incorporated as a company limited by guarantee, represents the sixteen ITV* companies, providing a central secretariat and determining joint policy. It was founded in 1955 as the Television Programme Contractors' Association; the name was changed in 1958 to the Independent Television Companies Association, and the new name took effect in 1987.

Address: Knighton House, 56 Mortimer Street, London W1N 8AN, United Kingdom.

THE INDEPENDENT TELEVISION LABORATORY AT WNET was created in 1972 with a grant from the Rockefeller Foundation, and was headed from the time of its inception by producer David Loxton. Similar laboratories were also established at WGBH* and WQED,* and all sponsored the production of experimental videos. Among the programs created through the Independent Television Laboratory at WNET were San Francisco–based Top Value Television's *Lord of the Universe* (1974), Alan and Susan Raymond's *The Police Tapes* (1977), Jon Alpert and Keiko Tsuno's *Vietnam: Picking Up the Pieces* (1978), and Skip Blumberg's *Pick Up Your Feet: The Double-Dutch Show* (1981). The laboratory ran into severe financial problems in 1984 and ceased operations shortly thereafter.

BIBLIOGRAPHY

Davis, Ben, "The Right Fail," *Emmy*, vol. VI, no. 5, September/October 1984, pp. 46–49.

Loxton, David, "Uncharted Territory—The TV Lab at WNET/13," *Television Quarterly*, vol. XV, no. 4, Winter 1978–79, pp. 73–77.

INDEPENDENT TELEVISION NEWS (ITN), which began broadcasting in September 1955, is a non-profit company jointly owned by all the independent British television companies. It provides the national news programs for independent television, and since February 1987 has also produced the daily *World News* program for various cable and satellite channels in Europe. When Independent Television News began broadcasting, it was the first time that viewers in the United Kingdom were able to see their television newscasters—up to then the BBC* had not permitted its news readers to appear on camera—and ITN's first newscaster was the former athlete Chris Chataway.

Address: ITN House, 48 Wells Street, London W1P 4DE, United Kingdom.
BIBLIOGRAPHY
Bosanquet, Reginald. *Let's Get Through Wednesday: My Twenty-Five Years with ITN.* London: Michael Joseph, 1980.
Cox, Geoffrey. *See It Happen: The Making of ITN.* London: The Bodley Head, 1983.
Hunter, Pat, "ITN Makes News—Television House to Wells Street," *Television*, March/April 1990, pp. 95–98.

INDEPENDENT TELEVISION PUBLICATIONS LIMITED is responsible for the publication of *TV Times*, first published on September 22, 1955, which serves as a weekly guide to all "commercial" television programming in the United Kingdom (in exactly the same manner that *Radio Times** handles BBC* programming). The company was jointly owned by the fifteen independent television companies until June 9, 1989, when it was sold to Reed International plc.

Address: 247 Tottenham Court Road, London W1P 0AU, United Kingdom.

INDIAN TRIBES are believed to have successfully opposed the televising of only one series, *Daniel Boone* (NBC, 1964–1970). When it was shown, in syndication, by WTEV, various New England tribes objected to episodes that unfavorably depicted Native Americans. As a result, WTEV agreed not to air 37 of the 165 episodes.
BIBLIOGRAPHY
Efron, Edith, "This Time the Indians Won," *TV Guide*, January 22, 1972, pp. 44–45.

INDRA DHNUSH is a British cable channel, owned by Ealing Cabletel, which provides films and other programming in the Indian language. It is seen daily from 9:00 A.M. to midnight.

Address: Unit K1/K2, Fieldway, Bristol Road, Greenford, Middlesex UB8 8UM, United Kingdom.

INFORMATION PRODUCTIONS, INC. (Thomas H. Wolf, president) was a New York–based producer, primarily of television commercials, active in the fifties and early sixties.

THE INSPIRATIONAL NETWORK is the current name, as of May 1987, of the PTL Television Network, which was founded by Jim and Tammy Faye Bakker (pronounced Baker). The couple had begun their ministry on the Christian Broadcast Network in 1961. They left the network in 1974 to form PTL, which variously stands for "Praise the Lord" or "People That Love." Bakker, an Assembly of God evangelist, hosted the best-known program on the network, *The PTL Club*, which is also seen on non-cable television stations. All other programming on the network, which was seen on as many as 213 stations in 1980, had religious overtones.

In 1987, the PTL was hit by a number of scandalous accusations affecting both Jim and Tammy Faye Bakker. Bakker resigned from the PTL in 1987 and turned over the ministry, which was $66 million in debt, to the Reverend Jerry Falwell. The ministry included not only the television satellite network of 178 stations (as of 1987), but also the Christian Vacation Park in Fort Fell, South Carolina (opened in 1978). In October 1989, Bakker was convicted on twenty-four fraud and conspiracy charges. The newly named Inspirational Network provides twenty-four hour a day multidenominational programming for the entire family, and has 6.5 million subscribers. It is a basic cable service, funded by contributions from viewers.

Address: Charlotte, NC 28241–0325.

BIBLIOGRAPHY

Barnhart, Joe E., and Steven Winzenburg. *Jim and Tammy: Charismatic Intrigue inside PTL*. Buffalo, N.Y.: Prometheus Books, 1988.
"Heaven Can Wait," *Newsweek*, June 8, 1987, pp. 58–65.

"INSTANT ANALYSIS" was a term introduced by Vice-President Spiro T. Agnew in his Des Moines, Iowa, speech attacking television news, in November 1969. It refers to the media's immediate analysis of a political speech, permitting television commentators to influence the public perception of what was said.

THE INSTRUCTIONAL TELEVISION FIXED SERVICE (ITFS) was established by the Federal Communications Commission (FCC*) on July 25, 1963, for the transmission to schools of materials of an instructional or cultural nature. The Plainview–Old Bethpage Schools system on Long Island, New York, was the first to utilize the service, beginning on March 2, 1964.

INTELSAT (The International Telecommunications Satellite Consortium) was founded in 1964 by nineteen nations, including the United States. It oversees global satellite communications, providing international cooperation in the development and operation of telecommunications satellites. In 1965, it launched its first commercial communications satellite, *Early Bird*. More than one hundred countries are currently members of Intelstat, with the notable exception of the Soviet Union, which created its own organization, Intersputnik, in 1971.

BIBLIOGRAPHY
Alper, Joel, and Joseph N. Pelton, editors. *The Intelsat Global Satellite System*. New York: American Institute of Aeronautics and Astronautics, 1984.
Galloway, Jonathan F. *The Politics and Technology of Satellite Communications*. Lexington, Mass.: Lexington/Heath, 1972.

INTER-CONTINENTAL TELEVISION CORP. was a New York–based (with an office also in Paris) producer of television programming, founded by Edward Gruskin and Martin H. Poll. Active in the fifties, it produced the 1952 syndicated series *Flash Gordon*.

INTERCONTINENTAL TELEVISION, INC. was a New York–based distributor of foreign films to television, founded in 1961. It was a subsidiary of Continental Distributing, Inc., which was, in turn, an affiliate of the Walter Reade Organization. It ceased operations in 1977, when the parent company filed for reorganization under Chapter XI of the Federal Bankruptcy Act.

THE INTERNATIONAL ASSOCIATION OF BROADCASTING/ASSOCIACIÓN INTERNACIONAL DE RADIODIFFUSIÓN is a professional organization of commercial radio and television broadcasters in North, South, and Central America, founded in 1946 as the Inter-American Association of Broadcasters.
    Address: Calle Yi 1264, Montevideo, Uruguay.

THE INTERNATIONAL ASSOCIATION OF FRENCH-SPEAKING RADIO AND TELEVISION/CONSEIL INTERNATIONAL DES RADIO-TÉLÉVISION D'EXPRESSION FRANÇAISE or CIRTEF, is a professional association of radio and television stations broadcasting in whole or part in French, and founded in 1975. It presents the annual Prix CIRTEF Award.
    Address: 23 rue Gourgas, CH–1205 Geneva, Switzerland.

THE INTERNATIONAL RADIO AND TELEVISION SOCIETY, INC. was founded in 1952 as the Radio and Television Executives Society, with the merger of the Radio Executives Club (formed 1939) and the American Television Society (founded 1940). An organization for individuals involved in broadcast management, it sponsors seminars, luncheon meetings, internship programs for college students, and an annual award.
    Address: 420 Lexington Avenue, New York, NY 10170.

THE INTERNATIONAL TELECOMMUNICATIONS UNION (ITU) was created in 1865 as the International Telegraph Union. An intergovernmental organization, to which 164 countries belong, it develops regulations and voluntary recommendations, provides coordination of telcommunications development, and fosters technical assistance to developing countries.

BIBLIOGRAPHY
Codding, George. *The International Telecommunications Union: An Experiment in International Cooperation.* New York: Arno Press, 1972.

INTERNATIONAL TELE-FILM PRODUCTIONS, INC. (Paul F. Moss, president) was a New York–based producer of television commercials, active in the early fifties.

THE INTERNATIONAL TELEVISION AND VIDEO ALMANAC. The major reference source for contemporary information on the American television industry, *The International Television and Video Almanac* has its origins in *The International Motion Picture Almanac*, first published in 1929. The latter first included television data in 1952, and four years later the first volume of *The International Television Almanac* appeared. In 1987, the title was changed to *The International Television and Video Almanac*, and it now includes considerable information also on cable television and home video, but continues, as the *Television Almanac* has always done, to reprint the "Who's Who" section from *The International Motion Picture Almanac*.

Address: Quigley Publishing Company, 159 West 53 Street, New York, NY 10019.

THE INTERNATIONAL TELEVISION ASSOCIATION (ITVA) was formed in 1973 with the merger of the Industrial Television Society (ITS) and the National Industrial Television Association (NITA). Until 1978, it was known as the International Industrial Television Association. It is dedicated to serving the needs of non-broadcast professional video communicators; namely, those working in the corporate, government, educational, and other "non-entertainment" fields. ITVA has more than 9,000 U.S. members in more than ninety-five chapters, and an additional 3,000 foreign members from fourteen countries. Ten times a year it publishes *International Television News*.

Address: 6311 North O'Connor Road, LB51, Irving, TX 75039.

INTERNATIONAL TV & VIDEO GUIDE was an annual publication of the London-based Tantivy Press, intended as a companion volume to the popular *International Film Guide*. Its *International TV & Video Guide* was published from 1983 to 1987. The first two volumes were edited by Olli Tuomol and the last three by Richard Patterson.

INTERSTATE TELEVISION CORP. was the television subsidiary of Allied Artists. Primarily a distributor, it did produce the thirteen-episode 1953 syndicated series *The Ethel Barrymore Theatre*. Among the series that it distributed were *Hans Christian Andersen Tales* (1954), *Snip Snap* (1961), *Foo Foo* (1961), and, in syndication, *I Married Joan* (NBC, 1952–1955) and *The Public Defender* (CBS, 1954–1955).

INTER-TV FILMS, LTD., was a Montréal, Canada–based company, responsible for the production of the 1956 syndicated series *Errol Flynn Theatre*, which was more notable for its leading ladies (including June Havoc, Mai Zetterling, and Paulette Goddard) than its aging star.

THE ISLAMIC STATES BROADCASTING SERVICES ORGANIZATION was founded in 1975 as an affiliate of the Organization of the Islamic Conference. It produces and exchanges radio and television programming propagating the teachings and heritage of Islam.
Address: P.O. Box 6351, Jeddah 21442, Saudi Arabia.

THE ISRAEL BROADCASTING AUTHORITY introduced television to Israel in 1968 with a live broadcast of the Independence Day Parade. It was initially on the air only three nights a week, and seven-day service did not start until 1969. Color broadcasting utilizes the PAL* system. Daytime television had been seen in Israel since 1966 on Israel Educational Television, organized by the Ministry of Education and Culture. The authority continues to provide daytime programming except on Saturday.
Address: P.O. Box 7139, Jerusalem, Israel.

ITC. In 1955, ITP (Incorporated Television Program Company, Ltd.) was formed in England to package programming from ATV (Associated Television), with its first effort being *The Adventures of Robin Hood* (CBS, 1955–1958). Three years later, ATV merged ITP into a new international distribution arm, ITC (Incorporated Television Company, Ltd.), with Lew Grade as its first managing director (until 1981). In the United States, ITC operated as a partnership with Jack Wrather (1918–1984), and William Kingsley was named its president.

In its first two years, ITC became the largest grossing television distributor in the international market, selling twenty-four series in fifty-three countries. Its television library was one of the largest in the world, and among its syndicated series were *Ivanhoe* (1958), *The Four Just Men* (1959), *Interpol Calling* (1959), *Ding Dong School* (1959), *Seven League Boots* (1959), *The Beachcomber* (1961), *Whiplash* (1961), *The Ghost Squad* (1962), *Mister Piper* (1962), *The Saint* (1963–1966), *Man of the World* (1964), *Seaway* (1966), *Gideon C.I.D.* (1966), *Captain Scarlet and the Mysterions* (1968), *U.F.O.* (1972), *The Adventurer* (1972), *The Protectors* (1972–1973), *Department S* (1973), *My Partner the Ghost* (1974), *Space 1999* (1975–1976), *Crimes of Passion* (1976), and *Bonkers* (1978).

In 1978, ITC created a Hollywood production entity, Marble Arch Productions,* which became ITC Productions in 1982, with Jerry Leider as its president. The company had already diversified into theatrical production in the early seventies, and in 1980 created ITC Films International, Ltd. In 1981, the company was acquired by Australian entrepreneur Robert Holmes a Court. He sold the company in 1988 to the Australian conglomerate Bell Group International, Ltd., headed by Alan Bell. A management buy-out of ITC by Jerry Leider and

Chris Gorog (the company's chief executive officer) took place in November 1988.

Address: 12711 Ventura Boulevard, Studio City, CA 91604.

BIBLIOGRAPHY

"The Hollywood Reporter Salutes ITC on Its 30th Anniversary," *The Hollywood Reporter*, August 3, 1988, pp. S1-S40.

ITV (Independent Television) is the umbrella title by which the fourteen British independent television networks and Channel 4* are known. ITV, which in turn controls Independent Television News,* comes under the IBA* (Independent Broadcasting Authority). The original ITV companies began broadcasting on September 22, 1955, with a live transmission of the inaugural banquet of ITV at London's Guildhall. Because they are financed entirely by advertising revenues, the ITV companies are often referred to by the name "commercial television," and the first television commercial to be seen in the United Kingdom was for Gibbs SR toothpaste.

BIBLIOGRAPHY

Fulton, Roger. *The Encyclopedia of TV Science Fiction*. London: TV Times/Boxtree, 1990.

Guide to Independent Television. London: ITV, 1973.

Rogers, Dave. *The ITV Encyclopedia of Adventure*. London: TV Times, 1988.

25 Years on ITV. London: ITV Books/Michael Joseph, 1980.

Wilson, H.H. *Pressure Groups: The Campaign for Commercial Television*. London: Secker & Warburg, 1961.

J

JACK CHERTOK PRODUCTIONS, INC./JACK CHERTOK TELEVISION, INC./CHERTOK TELEVISION, INC. was a prominent producer of television programming and commercials in the fifties. It produced the early episodes of *The Lone Ranger* (ABC, 1949–1957), prior to its being taken over by Jack Wrather; the first nineteen episodes of *Sky King* (ABC, 1953–1954); *Private Secretary* (CBS, 1953–1957); and *Johnny Midnight* (Syndicated, 1960), among other shows.

JACK DENOVE PRODUCTIONS, INC. was a Los Angeles–based producer of television programming and commercials, active in the fifties and sixties. It produced some episodes of *Dupont Cavalcade Theatre* (ABC, 1955), but Denove (1911–1968) is best remembered for the production of Father James Keller's *The Christopher Program* (Syndicated, 1952–1969).

JACK DOUGLAS PRODUCTIONS was a major supplier of documentary television programming in the fifties and sixties, often in association with Col. John D. Craig in the latter decade. Among the series produced by Jack Douglas are *I Search for Adventure* (1954), *Kingdom of the Sea* (1956), *Bold Journey* (ABC, 1956–1959; Syndicated, 1959), *Danger Is My Business* (Syndicated, 1958), *Sweet Success* (Syndicated, 1960), *Keyhole* (Syndicated, 1962), and *Across the Seven Seas* (Syndicated, 1962).

J & M PRODUCTIONS, INC. was owned by Jack Benny (1894–1974) and his manager, Irving Fein. With offices in Beverly Hills, its most important production was *The Jack Benny Show* (CBS, 1950–1964; NBC, 1964–1965), but it was also responsible for *The Gisele Mackenzie Show* (NBC, 1957–1958), *Checkmate* (CBS, 1960–1962), and *Holiday Lodge* (CBS, 1961).

JAN PRODUCTIONS, INC. was a Los Angeles–based producer of the fifties, headed by Ann Fairleigh and Jack Denove, and responsible for the mid-fifties, thirty-minute syndicated series *This Is Your Music*.

JANTONE was the production company of Jan Murray, and was responsible for *Meet Your Match* (NBC, 1952), *Treasure Hunt* (ABC, 1956–1957; NBC, 1957–1959), *Wingo* (CBS, 1958), and *The Jan Murray Show* (NBC, 1960–1962).

JAPAN SATELLITE TELEVISION is a Japanese-language television cable channel, serving Japanese nationals in Europe, and transmitted on the *Astra* satellite two hours daily. It began broadcasting in March 1990.
    Address: Marubeni UK plc, New London Bridge House, London Bridge Street, London SE1 9SW, United Kingdom.

JAYARK FILMS CORPORATION was a New York–based producer/distributor of television programming, founded in May 1958 by Reub Kaufman, and active through the seventies.

JAY-KAY PRODUCTIONS was an Australian-based company, responsible for the 1955 syndicated television series *Long John Silver*, starring Robert Newton.

JENKINS TELEVISION CORPORATION. Charles Francis Jenkins (1867–1934) is one of the forgotten pioneers of television, and yet his researches into both that medium and the motion picture date back to 1890. In July 1916, he helped found the Society of Motion Picture Engineers. In March 1922, Jenkins applied for his first patent for transmitting motion pictures by wireless, and a year later claimed to have successfully transmitted a television picture. On July 2, 1928, Jenkins began television broadcasting on a regular basis. Two years earlier, in December 1926, he had formed the Jenkins Television Corporation to provide ready-built receivers and also build-it-yourself receivers, "Radio-Movies," which could receive broadcasts from his two transmitters, W3XK in Washington, D.C., and W2CXR in Jersey City, New Jersey. Unfortunately, Jenkins' television system was mechanical* and basically crude. His laboratory in Washington, D.C., ceased operations with his death, and on April 1, 1934, Jenkins Television Corporation ceased to exist for failure to pay taxes.
BIBLIOGRAPHY
Cooke, Bob, "The First Story Ever Written about Television," *TV Guide*, September 29, 1973, pp. 25–28.
Jenkins, Charles Francis, "Recent Progress in the Transmission of Motion Pictures by Radio," *Transactions of the Society of Motion Picture Engineers*, no. 17, October 1923, pp. 81–85.
————, "Radio Movies," *Journal of the Society of Motion Picture Engineers*, no. 21, May 18–21, 1925, pp. 7–11.

————. *Vision by Radio, Radio Photographs, Radio Photograms*. Washington, D.C.: Jenkins Laboratories, 1925.

————. *Radiomovies, Radiovision, Television*. Washington, D.C.: Jenkins Laboratories, 1929.

Lachenbruch, David, "They Called It RadioMovies," *TV Guide*, July 3, 1971, pp. 5–10.

JERRY COURNEYA PRODUCTIONS was a Los Angeles–based producer, active in the fifties, whose syndicated series included *The Chimps* (1951) and *Noah Beery, Jr.* (1952).

JERRY FAIRBANKS PRODUCTIONS/JERRY FAIRBANKS, INC. Jerry Fairbanks (born 1904) is a major figure in early television history. He had entered the film industry in 1919 as a projectionist, and produced many prominent series of short subjects for theatrical release in the thirties and forties. In 1948, he began providing film footage for NBC* news broadcasts, setting up a film division for the network, and the following year, he created *NBC Newsreel*. Also in the late forties, Fairbanks began filming filler programming for NBC, but the network did not air the shows, and instead they became the first syndicated television programming. Television historians generally agree that the first syndicated program on television was *Public Prosecutor*, a series of seventeen-and-a-half minute shows produced by Fairbanks in 1948. The following year, Fairbanks produced the first syndicated sitcom, *Jackson and Jill*, a series of twenty-six-minute shows starring Todd Karns and Helen Chapman. Fairbanks was also responsible for *Crusader Rabbit* (1950), produced in association with Jay Ward, the rights to which were eventually acquired by 20th Century–Fox. Other Fairbanks productions are *Front Page Detective* (DuMont, 1951–1953), early episodes of *Family Theatre* (Syndicated, 1951–1958), and *Hollywood Off-Beat* (Syndicated, 1952). While the company continued operations in other areas of production, it became disassociated with television in 1953.

Many of the Fairbanks productions are preserved at the UCLA Film and Television Archive.*

Address: P.O. Box 50553, Santa Barbara, CA 93150.

THE JEWISH TELEVISION NETWORK is a non-profit corporation, headed by UCLA law professor Monroe E. Price. A basic cable television network, with few subscribers, it was first seen on the Los Angeles Theta Cable on May 4, 1981. Its first program was *The Jewish Wife*, a one-act play starring Viveca Lindfors. It should not be confused with the other Jewish basic cable network, NJT (National Jewish Television; P.O. Box 480, Wilton, CT 06897), which also began broadcasting in May 1981, claims more than 7 million subscribers, and is seen on Sundays only from 1:00 P.M. to 4:00 P.M.

Address: 9021 Melrose Avenue, Suite 309, Los Angeles, CA 90069.

BIBLIOGRAPHY
Gelman, Morrie, "Jewish Network Struggles for Survival on Cable TV," *Daily Variety*, November 10, 1988, p. 8.
Graham, Nancy, "Jewish Network on Cable TV Airs Music, Movies, Talk Shows," *Los Angeles Times*, July 19, 1981, p. 2.
"Jewish TV Network Kicks Off on Theta Cable," *Daily Variety*, May 5, 1981, p. 7.

JIM HENSON PRODUCTIONS is the U.K.–based film and television production company, founded by Henson (1937–1990), headed by Duncan Kenworthy and Martin Baker, and responsible for the Channel 4* series *The Jim Henson Hour*, and various other programming for British television. A related company is Jim Henson's Creature Show (1b Devonshire Hill, Hampstead, London NW3).

Address: 2 Old Brewery Mews, Hampstead High Street, London NW3 1P2, United Kingdom.

JIM VICTORY TELEVISION, INC. was a New York–based distributor of major programming for syndication, including *Concentration*, *Rhoda*, *Match Game P.M.*, and *The Streets of San Francisco*. It dates from the mid-seventies to the present and is currently known as Victory Television.

Address: One Hollow Lane, Lake Success, New York, NY 11042.

JOE HAMILTON PRODUCTIONS, INC. was formed in 1977, shortly before the demise of *The Carol Burnett Show* (CBS, 1967–1979), starring Hamilton's former wife, which had been executive-produced by Hamilton (born 1929) through his and Burnett's companies, Punkin Productions, Inc. (through 1977) and Whacko, Inc. (post-1977). Joe Hamilton Productions was responsible for a number of pilots and one reasonably successful series, *The Tim Conway Show* (CBS, 1980–1981). Taking a character played by Vicki Lawrence from *The Carol Burnett Show*, it also produced *Mama's Family* (Syndicated, 1986–1990). Hamilton and Burnett also had another company, Jocar Productions, which was formed to produce Carol Burnett specials for CBS in 1977 and 1978.

Address: 5746 Sunset Boulevard, Hollywood, CA 90028.

THE JOHN AND MARY MARKLE FOUNDATION (created in 1927) has funded a considerable amount of programming on PBS.* In 1980, it helped launch the magazine *Channels of Communications*,* and also provided the funding for the creation of the Boston-based ratings company Television Audience Assessment.

Address: 75 Rockefeller Plaza, Suite 1800, New York, NY 10019–6908.

BIBLIOGRAPHY
Daviss, Ben, "The $3 Million Giveaway," *Emmy*, vol. VIII, no. 2, March/April 1986, pp. 53–55.

JOHN BLAIR COMMUNICATIONS, INC. dates back to 1936, when broad-cast pioneer John Blair created one of the earliest national sales organizations for radio stations. Blair Television was formed in 1948 to provide a similar service for independent television stations, and, as of 1990, John Blair Communications represents 140 stations. A subsidiary company, Blair Entertainment, produces and distributes syndicated television programming, including *Divorce Court* (1984-   ). Another subsidiary company, Blair Interactive, was formed in October 1989 to produce and market informational mini-programs utilizing interactive technology for advertisers and broadcasters. In April 1987, John Blair Communications, Inc. was acquired by an investment group led by James H. Rosenfield, formerly a senior executive vice-president with the CBS/Broadcast Group.

Address: 1290 Avenue of the Americas, New York, NY 10104.

JOHN GUEDEL PRODUCTIONS (which its principals proudly pointed out was not incorporated) was formed by John Guedel and Art Linkletter (born 1912) for the production of the radio version of *People Are Funny*, first heard on NBC* on April 3, 1942. The company had no president; everyone from Guedel and Linkletter down to the secretaries was titled vice-president. For television, John Guedel Productions was responsible for many popular audience participation programs, including *You Bet Your Life* (NBC, 1950–1961), *Life with Linkletter* (ABC, 1950–1952), and *People Are Funny* (NBC, 1954–1961).
BIBLIOGRAPHY
"Everyone a Vice President," *TV Guide*, September 3, 1960, pp. 24–27.

THE JOINT COMMITTEE OF INTERSOCIETY COORDINATION was founded in 1982 by the Electronic Industries Association, the Institute of Electrical and Electronic Engineers, the National Association of Broadcasters,* the National Cable Television Association,* and the Society of Motion Picture and Television Engineers, to coordinate broadcast standards.

Address: 1771 N Street, N.W., Washington, DC 20036.

THE JOINT COUNCIL ON EDUCATIONAL BROADCASTING or JCEB, was a Washington, D.C.–based organization, active in the fifties and sixties. According to contemporary publicity, "The primary role of the JCEB is to maintain leadership in the formation and enunciation of important educational policy decisions having a bearing upon educational radio and television broadcasting. The JCEB will provide the chief forum for discussion and policy formation on national issues affecting all aspects of educational broadcasting."

THE JOZAK COMPANY, founded in 1973 by Gerald Isenberg, was a prolific producer of television movies, including: *James Dean* (NBC, 1976), *Secrets* (ABC, 1977), *Ski Lift to Death* (CBS, 1978), *Murder at the Mardi Gras* (CBS, 1978), *Letters from Frank* (CBS, 1979), and *The Gift* (CBS, 1979).

K

KAGRAN CORP. was a New York–based production company, owned by Martin Stone and formerly titled Martin Stone Associates. In the fifties, it produced a number of series for young people: *Howdy Doody* (NBC, 1947–1960), *The Gabby Hayes Show* (NBC, 1950–1954; ABC, 1956), *Johnny Jupiter* (DuMont, 1953; Syndicated, 1953–1954), and *Circus Time* (ABC, 1956–1957). It was also responsible for *The Author Meets the Critics* (NBC, 1947–1949; ABC, 1949–1950; DuMont, 1952–1954).

THE KAKNÄS TOWER/KAKNÄSTORNET is 508 feet high and Stockholm's tallest building. The majority of the tower's thirty-four floors are occupied by the Swedish State Telecommunications Administration/Televerket, which utilizes the tower as its main distribution center for radio and television broadcasts. Designed by Hans Borgström and Bengt Lindroos, the tower was officially opened on May 12, 1967.

Address: Mörkakroken, 115 27 Stockholm, Sweden.

KANIN-GALLO PRODUCTIONS was formed in September 1978 by Fay Kanin and Lillian Gallo. It produced only one made-for-television movie, *Fun and Games* (ABC, 1980), from which the director asked that his name be removed, and ceased operations in the summer of 1980.

BIBLIOGRAPHY

Kaufman, Dave, "Kanin-Gallo Tackle on-the-Job Chauvinism via ABC Vidpic," *Daily Variety*, May 19, 1980, p. 10.

Smith, Cecil, "Fun and Games with Rhoda on the Job," *Los Angeles Times Calendar*, May 26, 1980, pp. 1, 9.

KCET. The Los Angeles–based public television station, KCET (Channel 28) began broadcasting on September 28, 1964. It was incorporated as Community Television of Southern California, a non-profit organization, in April 1962,

KCET's first major production, in association with WGBH, was *The Advocates*, first seen in October 1969. A year later, KCET began production of its "Hollywood Television Theatre" series, under the guidance of Lewis Freedman and Norman Lloyd, with the first production being *The Andersonville Trial*. The series ran for eight years and included the controversial and critically acclaimed *Steambath*, written by Bruce Jay Friedman. Other KCET-originated programming for PBS* are *Meeting of the Minds* (1977), *Sylvia Fine Kaye's Musical Comedy Tonight* (1979), *Cosmos* (1980), and *California Stories* (1987).

KCET was a successor to KTHE (Channel 28), operated by the University of Southern California, which began broadcasting on August 3, 1953, and went off the air on September 10, 1954.

Address: 4401 Sunset Boulevard, Los Angeles, CA 90027.

BIBLIOGRAPHY

"KCET's 25th Anniversary Special Section," *Daily Variety*, July 26, 1989, pp. K1–
    K20.

THE KEFAUVER CRIME HEARINGS is the name by which the 1950–1951 televised hearings of the Senate Crime Investigation Committee, headed by Estes Kefauver (1903–1963), are commonly known. The hearings revealed ties between national crime syndicates and the political establishment, and their televising created a sensation.

KESTREL FILMS is a British television production company noted for the quality of its programming, thanks to writers such as Colin Welland and Alan Bennett. Formed in 1968, Kestrel was responsible for two Dennis Potter–scripted programs, *Moonlight on the Highway* (1968) and *Cream in My Coffee* (1982).

Address: 45 Walham Grove, London SW6 1QR, United Kingdom.

KEY PRODUCTIONS, INC. was a New York–based producer and packager of television programming, headed by Morton Schindel, and active in the fifties and sixties.

KILLIAM SHOWS, INC. was founded in 1950 by Paul Killiam (born 1916) to handle the latter's live presentations at New York's Old Knick Music Hall. Within a few years, it had become the name most associated with the presentation of silent films on television with the series *The Paul Killiam Show* (CBS, 1952); *Movie Museum* (Syndicated, 1954–1955), produced by an associated company, Biograph Television Co. Inc.;* *Silents Please* (ABC, 1960–1961), which was released in 16mm and on videotape as *The History of the Motion Picture*; and *The Silent Years* (PBS, 1978–1979). The company, which was at one time closely associated with Saul J. Turell and known as the Killiam-Sterling Collection, is also active in other areas of production and operates a stock footage library.

Address: 6 East 39 Street, New York, NY 10016.

BIBLIOGRAPHY
Manilla, James, "More Tips on the 'Stock' Market," *Industrial Photography*, June 1982,
    pp. 18–20.
Slide, Anthony. *Films on Film History*. Metuchen, N.J.: Scarecrow Press, 1979.
"Television Turns to Silents," *TV Guide*, September 17, 1960, pp. 20–22.

KINESCOPE is a method of making a film copy directly from a cathode ray tube with the use of a motion picture camera. This method can also be called a telerecording or a teletranscription. Kinescope is also the name of a television receiver developed in 1926 by Vladimir Zworykin (1889–1982).

THE KING BROADCASTING COMPANY began in 1946 with the acquisition by Dorothy Stimson Bullitt of Seattle AM radio station KEVR, which she renamed KING. Two years later, Mrs. Bullitt acquired KING-FM. That same year, she acquired the first television station in the Pacific Northwest, KRSC-Seattle, which had been on the air only eight months, and which she renamed KING-TV. Additional purchases of television stations began in 1956, and as of 1990, King owns six radio stations and six television stations: KING-Seattle; KGW-Portland, Oregon; Washington; KREM-Spokane; KTVB-Boise, Idaho; K38AS–Twin Falls, Idaho; and KHNL-Honolulu.

Dorothy Stimson Bullitt was succeeded as president of the company in 1961 by her son, Stimson Bullitt. She continued as chairman of the board until 1967 and remained an active member of the board until her death in 1989. In 1972, Ancil Payne succeeded Stimson Bullitt as president.

Aside from its television and radio stations, King Broadcasting also owns thirteen cable television systems, and operates Northwest Mobile Television, the largest mobile production company in the country, whose origins date back to the late sixties.

Address: 333 Dexter Avenue North, Seattle, WA 98109.

KING BROS. PRODUCTIONS, INC. was founded in 1949 by Maurice and Frank King, former vending machine operators who had entered the film industry in 1941. The company formed a television production department, headed by Hyman King, in 1951, but it appears to have been largely inactive. In the seventies, the company name was changed to King International Corporation.

Address: 124 Lasky Drive, Beverly Hills, CA 90212.

KING-SHORE FILMS, LTD. was a New York–based distributor of primarily foreign-language feature films to television. It was formed by Sy Sig Steven Shore and Stephen Markelson, and was active in the fifties.

KING WORLD PRODUCTIONS, INC. A major distributor of first-run syndicated shows, King World was incorporated on December 16, 1964, founded by Charlie King with the acquisition of the rights to *The Little Rascals* series. Following King's death in 1972, his two sons, Michael and Roger, expanded the company. Between 1978 and 1982, they handled the sale of game shows such as *Tic Tac Dough* and *The Joker's Wild* for Colbert Television Sales.

Major growth took place in the eighties as King World became the syndicated distributor for *Jeopardy!* (from 1983), *Wheel of Fortune* (from 1983), and *The Oprah Winfrey Show* (from 1987). In December 1988, King World acquired WIVB-Buffalo. In July 1990, the company announced the creation of Merlin Capital Corp. to fund new programming. Wholly owned subsidiaries of King World are Camelot Entertainment Sales, Inc. and Inside Edition, Inc.

Addresses: 12400 Wilshire Boulevard, Suite 1200, Los Angeles, CA 90025–1006; 830 Morris Turnpike, Short Hills, NJ 07078.

BIBLIOGRAPHY

Capuzzi, Cecilia, "Now and Future Kings?" *Channels of Communications*, vol. VIII, no. 3, March 1988, pp. 80–86.

Lippman, John, "King World To Take New Firm Public," *Los Angeles Times*, July 17, 1990, Business Section, p. 3.

THE KNOWLEDGE NETWORK was founded in 1980 as an educational television service for British Columbia.

Address: P.O. Box 3200, Victoria, British Columbia V8W 3H4, Canada.

THE KOMACK CO. was created by James Komack (born 1930), and responsible for the production of *Chico and the Man* (NBC, 1974–1978), *Welcome Back Kotter* (ABC, 1975–1979), *Me and Maxx* (NBC, 1980), and *9 to 5* (ABC, 1982–1983).

KQED (Channel 9) is the public television station for the San Francisco area. It began broadcasting in June 1954, but fared so badly with its very limited scheduling (one hour a day for two days a week) that its trustees proposed to dissolve the station early the following year. However, community support and an on-the-air auction (which became an annual event) helped KQED to survive.

In 1969, Metromedia, Inc.* gave Channel 32 to KQED; the new station became KQEC and broadcasts a complementary program schedule to KQED. In 1968, KQED purchased an FM radio station and in September 1990 began a twenty-four hour a day broadcast schedule.

Address: 500 8 Street, San Francisco, CA 94103.

BIBLIOGRAPHY

Kiester, Edwin, Jr., "The Battle for Control of Public TV," *TV Guide*, December 11, 1976, pp. 4–8.

KTLA–LOS ANGELES became the first commercially licensed television station in the western United States on January 22, 1947, when it changed its call letter from W6XYZ. Because the station was owned by Paramount, its opening night program relied heavily on studio contractees. The opening speech was made by director Cecil B. DeMille, and the opening night variety program was hosted by Bob Hope. W6XYZ was created for Paramount by Klaus Landsberg (born 1916) and went on the air in September 1942. One of its earliest broadcasts was the first remote telecast, from the Paramount set, of *This Gun for Hire*. On April 22, 1952, KTLA presented the first television coverage of an atomic explosion, at Yucca Flats, Nevada.

The station was sold in 1956 to Golden West Broadcasters.* It changed hands again in 1982.

Address: P.O. Box 500, Los Angeles, CA 90078.

KUHT (Channel 8) was the first educational television station in the United States. It began broadcasting on May 25, 1953. The station became involved in controversy in 1980, when it scheduled *Death of a Princess*, a BBC* docudrama on the 1977 public execution of a Saudi Arabian princess and her lover. The president of the University of Houston, which operates KUHT, overruled the station's management and cancelled the presentation, supposedly because of the university's involvement with oil interests and the Saudi Arabian royal family. A district court judge agreed with viewers that the cancellation was a violation of the First Amendment rights to freedom of speech in that KUHT was a public forum, but the decision was overturned on appeal by the university.

Address: 4513 Cullen Boulevard, Houston, TX 77004.

THE KUSHNER-LOCKE CO. was founded in July 1988 with the dissolution of Atlantic/Kushner-Locke, Inc. The latter was formed in January 1987 and included all the assets of the partnership of producers Donald Kushner and Peter Locke and all the television-related activities of Atlantic Entertainment Group. In August 1987, the company considered and rejected a proposed merger with All-American TV, which was founded in 1982 by George Back as a major barter syndicator. Eventually, Kushner and Locke made a buy-out payment to Atlantic and relaunched their production company. In 1990, Kushner-Locke began production on a series of thirteen one-hour fairy tale specials for The Disney Channel,* directed by former Monkee Mickey Dolenz.

Address: 10850 Wilshire Boulevard, 9th Floor, Los Angeles, CA 90024.

BIBLIOGRAPHY

Daniels, Bill, "AEG, K-LC Team To Make Bigger TV Impression," *Daily Variety*, January 16, 1987, pp. 1, 96.

L

LAKESIDE TELEVISION CO., INC. (Richard Stevens, president) was a New York–based producer and distributor of the fifties and early sixties. It was responsible for a number of very minor syndicated programs in the mid-fifties: *Wild Life in Action* (fifteen minutes each), *Where in the World* (fifteen minutes each), *On the Spot* (fifteen minutes each), *Adventure Is My Job* (fifteen minutes each), and *Out of the Past* (thirty minutes each).

LALLEY & LOVE, INC. was a New York–based production company, founded by James A. Love and responsible for the 1955 syndicated series *Professor Yes 'n' No*. It was active in the early to mid-fifties.

THE LANDSCAPE CHANNEL was perhaps the strangest or most original concept for cable programming. It presented footage of natural landscapes with no voice-over commentary, the only sound being orchestral music. Intended to provide viewers with stress-free viewing, the cable service was financed by direct-mail sales of the recordings that it used. The Landscape Channel was first seen in the United Kingdom in November 1988 and ceased operations the following year.

LATIMER PRODUCTIONS was owned by actor Lee Marvin (1924–1987), and was responsible for his 1963 syndicated series *Lee Marvin's Lawbreakers*.

LATIN-AMERICAN RADIO & TV CORPORATION (Joseph Novas, president) was a New York–based distributor of the fifties and early sixties, handling the release of U.S. television product in South America, and Latin American films in the United States. It also produced and distributed sports films for the Latin American market.

LAUGH TRACKS (sometimes called "sweetening") is a subject about which television producers are unwilling to talk. Laugh tracks can be used to enhance the comedic value of a program filmed or taped before a live audience, and can also be added to the soundtrack of a program that had no audience. Originally, laugh tracks were added "live" for the benefit of the performers working without an audience, and one of the earliest examples of the use of a laugh track is on *The George Burns and Gracie Allen Show* (CBS, 1950–1958). It has also been claimed, but cannot be substantiated, that a laugh track was used in whole or in part on *I Love Lucy* (CBS, 1951–1961). In 1959, CBS* announced that it would identify its use of a laugh track or "canned laughter" as such, but quickly abandoned the suggestion. One of the earliest providers of a mechanical laugh track, "the Laff Box," was developed by Charley and Bob Douglass while working at CBS in the mid-fifties.

BIBLIOGRAPHY

Shindler, Merrill, "Those Devilish Machines Get the Last Laugh," *Panorama*, vol. I, no. 6, July 1980, pp. 75–77.

LBS COMMUNICATIONS, INC., formerly known as Lexington Broadcast Services Co., is a major television syndicator. In October 1987, it announced the creation of four separate divisions: LBS Entertainment, LBS Marketing and Distribution, TV Horizons, and LBS Telecommunications.

Address: 875 Third Avenue, New York, NY 10022.

THE LEARNING CHANNEL is a basic cable channel with some 20 million subscribers. It began in 1972 under the sponsorship of the Department of Health and Welfare and the National Aeronautics and Space Administration (NASA), using a NASA satellite. In 1980, it became a private channel, known as the Appalachian Community Service Network, but later that same year it was renamed the Learning Channel. Totally devoted to education, the Learning Channel provides foreign language instruction, college credit courses, Scholastic Aptitude Test (SAT) preparation, and career information; it also sponsors the series *Independents*, featuring works from independent film and videomakers. In February 1991, the Learning Channel was purchased by the Discovery Channel.*

Address: 1525 Wilson Boulevard, Rosslyn, VA 22209.

BIBLIOGRAPHY

Salmans, Sandra, "TLC's Learning Cure," *Channels of Communications*, vol. VIII, no. 5, May 1988, pp. 69–71.

LEE ENTERPRISES, INC. has its origins in the 1890 purchase of the *Ottumwa* [Iowa] *Courier*. Incorporated in August 1950, it controls eighteen daily newspapers, the film buff publication *Classic Images*, and the following television stations: KGUN-Tucson; KGMD-Hilo, Hawaii; KGMV-Wailuku, Hawaii; KGMB-Honolulu; KMTV-Omaha; KGGM-Albuquerque; KOIN-Portland, Oregon; and WSAZ-Huntington, West Virginia.

Address: 130 East Second Street, Davenport, IA 52801.

THE LEGAL PROFESSION. The following is a listing of the more popular television series that have dealt with the legal profession: *On Trial* (ABC, 1948–1952), *The Black Robe* (NBC, 1949–1950), *They Stand Accused* (CBS, 1949; DuMont, 1950–1954), *Your Witness* (ABC, 1949–1950), *I Married Joan* (NBC, 1952–1955), *Justice* (NBC, 1954–1956), *The Public Defender* (CBS, 1954–1955), *Mister District Attorney* (Syndicated, 1954), *His Honor, Homer Bell* (Syndicated, 1955), *Perry Mason* (CBS, 1957–1966, 1973–1974), *Accused* (ABC, 1958–1959), *Night Court USA* (Syndicated, 1958), *The People's Court of Small Claims* (Syndicated, 1958), *Grand Jury* (Syndicated, 1959), *The D.A.'s Man* (ABC, 1959), *Lock Up* (Syndicated, 1959–1961), *The Law and Mr. Jones* (ABC, 1960–1962), *The Witness* (CBS, 1960–1961), *The Defenders* (CBS, 1961–1965), *The Trials of O'Brien* (CBS, 1965–1966), *The Lawyers* (NBC, 1969–1972), *The Young Lawyers* (ABC, 1970–1971), *Storefront Lawyers* (CBS, 1970–1971), *The D.A.* (NBC, 1971–1972), *Owen Marshall, Counselor at Law* (ABC, 1971–1974), *Hawkins* (CBS, 1973–1974), *Petrocelli* (NBC, 1974–1976), *Kate McShane* (CBS, 1975), *The Tony Randall Show* (ABC, 1976–1977; CBS, 1977–1978), *Rosetti and Ryan* (NBC, 1977), *The Paper Chase* (CBS, 1978–1979, *Park Place* (CBS, 1981), *People's Court* (Syndicated, 1981-), *Guilty or Innocent* (Syndicated, 1984), *Night Court* (NBC, 1984-), *L.A. Law* (NBC, 1986-), *Superior Court* (Syndicated, 1986-), *Equal Justice* (ABC, 1990-), and *Trials of Rosie O'Neill* (CBS, 1990-).

LEO A. GUTMAN, INC. was a New York–based television distributor from the mid-seventies through the mid-eighties, handling the "Sherlock Holmes" features, starring Basil Rathbone and Nigel Bruce; the "Mr. Moto" features; the "Charlie Chan" series from Monogram; and the "East Side Kids" features. Its product was sold to Goodson-Todman Productions,* which later sold it to King World Productions, Inc.* Leo Gutman continues in television distribution with a new company, Gutman & Gutman.

Address: 230 Park Avenue, New York, NY 10022.

THE LEONARD GOLDBERG CO. was founded by the producer (born 1934) in 1978, and became inoperative when Goldberg became president and chief executive officer of 20th Century–Fox on December 1, 1986. Among its productions were the series *The Cavanaughs* (CBS, 1986), and the made-for-television movies *Fantasies* (ABC, 1982) and *Something about Amelia* (ABC, 1984).

LEONARD HILL FILMS is a production company founded in August 1980 as Hill-Mandelker Films by Leonard Hill, a former ABC* vice-president, and Philip Mandelker. The name was changed following the 1984 death of Mandelker. The company was responsible for two short-lived series, *Tucker's Witch* (CBS, 1983) and *The Insiders* (ABC, 1985); among the television movies that it has made are *Mae West* (ABC, 1982), *The Long Hot Summer* (NBC, 1985), and *Nitti: The Story of Frank Nitti, the Enforcer* (ABC, 1988). In 1985, Leonard Hill Films announced plans to expand into theatrical production.

Address: 10202 West Washington Boulevard, Culver City, CA 90232.

BIBLIOGRAPHY

Kaufman, Dave, "Len Hill, Philip Mandelker Join Forces To Form Their Own Indie Prod'n Company," *Daily Variety*, August 14, 1980, pp. 1, 15.

————, "Hill Films Skeds Expansion into Theatrical Pix," *Daily Variety*, February 22, 1985, pp. 1, 35.

LEWISLOR ENTERPRISES, INC. was a Beverly Hills–based company, formed by Thomas H. Lewis and Loretta Young to produce *The Loretta Young Show* (NBC, 1953–1961).

[VERNON] LEWIS SOUND FILMS/VERNON LEWIS PRODUCTIONS, INC. was a New York–based producer of television commercials and industrial films, active in the fifties and early sixties.

LEWMAN LIMITED was a production company owned by Edward Lewis and Jane Wyman, which produced, in association with Universal, *Fireside Theatre* (NBC, 1955–1957), *Schlitz Playhouse of Stars* (CBS, 1956–1959), *The Jane Wyman Theatre* (NBC, 1957–1958), and *Lux Playhouse* (CBS, 1958–1959).

LIBRA FILM DISTRIBUTORS & PRODUCERS was a Los Angeles–based producer, primarily of television commercials, active in the fifties through the mid-seventies.

LIFESTYLE TELEVISION LTD. is a British and Dutch cable channel, aimed primarily at a female audience. Owned in the majority by the WH Smith Group plc, TV South, and Yorkshire Television Limited,* Lifestyle began broadcasting on October 20, 1985.

Address: The Quadrangle, 180 Wardour Street, London W1V 3AA, United Kingdom.

LIFETIME is a basic cable channel, providing twenty-four hour a day programming for some 47 million subscribers. First seen on February 1, 1984, Lifetime is noted for its Monday-through-Friday programming of shows of special interest to women such as *The Days and Nights of Molly Dodd* and *Cagney and Lacey*. Each Sunday it becomes Lifetime Medical Television, with programming for physicians and others in the health care community. It is the only cable channel to have created a major television personality, Dr. Ruth Westheimer, with her show *Good Sex*. Lifetime began airing feature films in August 1985, and in 1989, it paid $43 million for a package of forty-two Orion features. The network began broadcasting *The Days and Nights of Molly Dodd* in January 1989, following that show's cancellation in the summer of 1988 by NBC.*

Lifetime came into existence in 1982 as two separate cable channels, Daytime and The Cable Health Network, owned, respectively, by ABC* and Hearst, and Viacom, Inc.* The merger took place in 1984, but the three joint owners remain the same, operating as Hearst/ABC-Viacom Entertainment Services. In January 1985, the network shifted its prime time focus to concentrate on entertainment programming.

Address: 36–12 35 Avenue, Astoria, NY 11106.

BIBLIOGRAPHY

Ainslee, Peter, "Chances of a Lifetime," *Channels of Communications*, vol. V, no. 6, March 1986, pp. 53–54.

Gerber, Cheryl, "New Lease on Lifetime: Its Latest Metamorphosis May Be the Best," *Channels of Communications*, vol. VII, no. 9, October 1987, p. 13.

McManus, Neil, "Tuning into Today's Women," *Cable Choice*, December 1987, pp. 22–23.

Taubin, Amy, "Cable's Babel," *Village Voice*, August 6, 1985, p. 32.

THE LIN BROADCASTING CORP. was founded in 1961. It owns seven television stations: WAND-Decatur, Illinois; WANE–Fort Wayne, Indiana; WISH-Indianapolis; WOTV-Grand Rapids, Michigan; KXAN-Austin; KXAS–Fort Worth; and WAVY-Portsmouth, Virginia. In March 1990, the company was acquired by McCaw Cellular Communications, Inc.

Address: 1370 Avenue of the Americas, New York, NY 10019.

BIBLIOGRAPHY

Jaffe, Al, "LIN's True Believers," *Channels of Communications*, vol. X, no. 11, August 13, 1990, p. 16.

LINES. The television picture is made up of elements arranged in lines, which determine the vertical resolution. The U.S. standard is 525 lines, which is also true for Japan, Canada, and South and Central America. Europe, the USSR, and China use 625 lines, with the only exception being France with 819 lines. The higher the number of lines, the higher the quality of the image.

THE LISTENER was for sixty years a weekly publication of the BBC,* first published on January 16, 1929, and intended to provide a printed record of the more interesting items from BBC radio and television productions. In 1989, publication was taken over by Listener Publications, Inc., a company jointly owned by the BBC and Independent Television Publications.* *The Listener* is available on microfilm from Chadwyck-Healey Inc. (623 Martense Avenue, Teaneck, NJ 07666).

Address: 199 Old Marylebone Road, London NW1 5QS, United Kingdom.

LONDON WEEKEND TELEVISION (LWT) is the independent ("commercial") television network that broadcasts from 5:15 P.M. on Friday evenings through early Monday mornings in London and the Home Counties area of the United Kingdom. It is the only broadcasting authority in the world whose hours of transmission are confined to the weekend. LWT is the major subsidiary of the publicly owned LWT (Holdings) plc, and began broadcasting on August 2, 1968. The original shareholders included *The Daily Telegraph*, *The Observer*, *Economist*, *New Statesman*, and *The Spectator*. A substantial holding was acquired by News International Limited in 1970, and *The Observer*, *New Statesman* and *The Spectator* are no longer shareholders.

Among LWT's best-known productions, a number of which have been seen on American television, are *On the Buses* (1969–1975), *Upstairs, Downstairs* (1970–1975), *The Stanley Baxter Show* (1973–1982), *Love for Lydia* (1977), *The South Bank Show* (1978-   ), *Cannon and Ball* (1979–1988), *Agony* (1979), *Dempsey and Makepiece* (1985), and *The Charmer* (1987).

Address: South Bank Television Centre, London SE1 9LT, United Kingdom.
BIBLIOGRAPHY
Taylor, Edward Durham. *The Great TV Book: 21 Years of LWT*. London: Sidgwick & Jackson, 1989.

LONE RANGER, INC. was the company created by Jack Wrather (1918–1984) to produce the television series *The Lone Ranger* (ABC, 1949–1957), when he acquired the rights to the character in 1954.
BIBLIOGRAPHY
Harris, Sherman, "Filming Lone Ranger in Color," *Television Daily Program Buyers Guide*, 1956, p. 88.

LONGACRE PROGRAMS, LTD., a subsidiary of Times Square Productions, Inc.,* was a New York–based producer, primarily of television commercials, active in the fifties.

LOOK MAGAZINE presented annual television awards of excellence from 1950 to 1959. Initially, members of the industry were polled, but from 1955 onward, selections were made by television critics and editors. A complete listing of the Look Awards can be found in *TV Facts* by Cobbett S. Steinberg (New York: Facts on File, 1980, pp. 414–417).

LORIMAR TELEVISION was founded in 1968 by Lee Rich and Merv Adelson as Lorimar Productions, and is noted for its long-running television series *The Waltons* (CBS, 1972–1981), *Dallas* (CBS, 1978-1991), *Knots Landing* (CBS, 1979-   ), and *Falcon Crest* (CBS, 1981–1990). Between 1977 and 1983, it was also heavily involved in feature film production. A private company owned by Rich, Adelson, and Irwin Molasky, the company went public in 1981, and two years later merged with the New York advertising agency of Kenyon & Eckhardt. Following heavy financial losses, Lorimar was acquired by Warner Bros. in 1988, and in 1990 was relocated to that studio's lot in Burbank. (Lorimar had initially been at the same lot, then known as the Burbank Studios, and had moved to the former M-G-M lot in Culver City in 1978.)

In January 1980, Lorimar acquired the assets of Allied Artists for $7 million. In May 1985, it acquired Syndivision Corp., a major syndication distributor, and in October of the same year merged with Telepictures (founded in 1978 by Michael Garin and Michael Jay Solomon) to become Lorimar-Telepictures. Despite its involvement in film production, Lorimar is, in the words of Lee Rich (in the *New York Times*, May 2, 1983), "basically a television company."

Address: 4000 Warner Boulevard, Burbank, CA 91522.

BIBLIOGRAPHY

Dempsey, John, "Lorimar, Telepictures To Merge," *Daily Variety*, October 8, 1985, pp. 1, 19.

Fabrikant, Geraldine, "Lorimar in Accord to Merger," *New York Times*, October 8, 1985, pp. 29, 33.

———, "Warner in Deal To Acquire Lorimar," *New York Times*, May 11, 1988, pp. 27, 30.

Harmetz, Aljean, "Small Film Companies Gamble for 'Big Hit,' " *New York Times*, March 21, 1981, p. 11.

"The Hollywood Reporter Salutes Lorimar," *The Hollywood Reporter*, March 8, 1983, special supplement.

Lippman, John, "LT Restructuring in the Works," *Daily Variety*, June 23, 1987, pp. 1, 15.

Richter, Paul, "Who Shot Lorimar?" *Los Angeles Times*, April 10, 1988, part IV, pp. 1, 4–5.

———, "Troubled Lorimar Agrees To Merge with Warner," *Los Angeles Times*, May 11, 1988, part IV, pp. 1, 6.

Waters, Harry F., and Janet Huck, "Rich Man, Pitch Man," *Newsweek*, February 9, 1981, pp. 94–95.

LOUCKS & NORLING STUDIOS, INC., a New York–based company, was active in the fifties as a producer of television commercials. The company had been founded in 1923 by John A. Norling and Arthur H. Loucks as a producer of educational and industrial films, and is best known for its handling of the three-dimensional effects in the Pete Smith/M-G-M shorts *Audioscopiks* (1935), *New Audioscopiks* (1938), and *Third-Dimensional Murder* (1941).

LOUIS G. COWAN, INC. was a New York–based producer and packager of quiz shows, including *Stop the Music* (ABC, 1949–1956), *Quiz Kids* (NBC, 1949–1952; CBS, 1953–1956), and *$64,000 Question* (CBS, 1955–1958). Active from 1946 to 1955, it ceased operations when owner Cowan became vice-president in charge of creative services at CBS-TV.

LOVETON-SCHUBERT PRODUCTIONS, INC. was founded by John W. Loveton and Bernard L. Schubert to produce *Topper* (CBS, 1953–1955; ABC, 1955–1956; NBC, 1956). The series was later syndicated by Bernard L. Schubert, Inc. and other related companies.

LOW POWER TELEVISION (LPTV). In 1980, the FCC* introduced a new type of broadcast service, Low Power Television, licenses for which would be granted on a demand basis. There were no limitations as to where these new broadcast outlets could be located except that they must not interfere with existing broadcast stations. The new stations would have low power and resulting short-range signals. Rules for licensing the new stations were adopted in 1982, and almost 200 stations had been granted licenses by 1983. Interest in obtaining such licenses continues to be considerable, and as a result, *The LPTV Report* is published by Kompas/Biel & Associates, Inc., a major consultant to the low power television industry (Box 25510, Milwaukee, WI 53225–0510).

BIBLIOGRAPHY

Biel, Jacquelyn. *Low Power Television: Developments and Current Status of the LPTV Industry*. Washington, D.C.: National Association of Broadcasters, 1985.

Carey, John. *An Assessment of Low-Power Television for the Nonprofit Community*. Washington, D.C.: Corporation for Public Broadcasting, 1983.

Nadel, Mark, and Eli Noam, editors. *The Economics of Low Power Television (LPTV): An Anthology*. New York: Columbia University Graduate School of Business, 1983.

Schmuckler, Eric, "Low-Power Brokers," *Emmy*, vol. IV, no. 6, November-December 1982, pp. 14, 54.

LUTHERAN TELEVISION is responsible for the longest running dramatic series on television, *This Is the Life*, which airs weekly, as a public service, on 200 television stations, 100 cable systems, 22 foreign television stations, and Armed Forces Television. The concept for the series dates from 1951 when the Lutheran Church–Missouri Synod formed a Television Productions Board with a $750,000 budget. *This Is the Life* began airing the following year on the DuMont* network. In 1965, the series began re-issues under the title *Pattern for Living*, and in 1976 the International Lutheran Laymen's League accepted financial and administrative responsibility for Lutheran Television. In 1974, *This Is the Life* received an Emmy for technical direction and camera work for the episode "A Gift of Tears"—it was the first Emmy ever awarded to a religious series. Aside from *This is the Life*, Lutheran Television has also produced a number of television specials: *Christmas Is* (1970), *Amazing Grace* (1973), *Easter Is* (1974), *The City That Forgot about Christmas* (1974), *Freedom Is* (1976), *Miles To Go* (1978), *The Stableboy's Christmas* (1979), and *The Dream That Wouldn't Die* (1980).

M

MCCADDEN PRODUCTIONS was formed by George Burns (born 1896) for the production of *The George Burns and Gracie Allen Show* (CBS, 1950–1958). It was named McCadden after McCadden Place in Hollywood, where Burns' brother Willie lived, but the company was located on the General Service Studios lot on Las Palmas Avenue in Hollywood. McCadden also produced two additional popular situation comedies, *The Bob Cummings Show* (NBC, 1955; CBS, 1955–1957; NBC, 1957–1959) and *The People's Choice* (NBC, 1955–1958), starring Jackie Cooper. The company ceased operations after completion of filming on *The Bob Cummings Show*, and the rights to *The George Burns and Gracie Allen Show* were sold to Screen Gems.*

BIBLIOGRAPHY

Blythe, Cheryl, and Susan Sackett. *Say Goodnight, Gracie*. New York: E.P. Dutton, 1986.

MACE NEUFELD PRODUCTIONS was formed in 1952 by Mace Neufeld (born 1928) as a television production company; it was also active in personal management (of Don Knotts, Gabe Kaplan, Don Adams, and others). It branched out into theatrical production in the mid-seventies, and among its television productions are the 1981 ABC mini-series *East of Eden*; the made-for-television movies *Angel on My Shoulder* (ABC, 1980) and *The American Dream* (ABC, 1981); and the series *Cagney and Lacey* (CBS, 1982–1989).

Address: 5555 Melrose Avenue, Hollywood, CA 90038.

MCGRAW-HILL BROADCASTING CO. was founded in 1972 by the publishing conglomerate McGraw-Hill, Inc., with the purchase of the majority of the Time-Life owned television stations. (Incorporated in 1925, McGraw-Hill's predecessor company dates back to 1899.) McGraw-Hill Broadcasting controls

KERO-Bakersfield, California; KGTV–San Diego; KMGH-Denver; and KRTV-Indianapolis.
   Address: 1221 Avenue of the Americas, New York, NY 10020.

MAGNAVOX CO. was one of the best-known names in the manufacture of television receivers, noted for its low prices, which were made possible by the company's sale of its product directly to dealers rather than through distributors. Magnavox became a public company in 1942, and showed a continuous profit into the late sixties. According to *Newsweek*, it was "consistently one of the most profitable companies in the business and one of the most profitable corporations in the country." Unfortunately, Maganvox's profits declined in the early seventies, and on July 24, 1975, it was merged into American Philips Development Corp.
BIBLIOGRAPHY
"Minivox," *Newsweek,* September 16, 1974, p. 74.

MAJOR TELEVISION PRODUCTIONS, INC. was a New York/Los Angeles distributor to television of fifty-one feature films and various short subjects and series. Active in the fifties, Major was founded by Irving Lesser, and was a subsidiary of Producers Representatives, Inc.

M. & A. ALEXANDER PRODUCTIONS, INC., founded by Max and Arthur Alexander, was a Los Angeles–based company, active in the fifties. In 1952, it was responsible for the NBC situation comedy *Boss Lady*, starring Lynn Bari, but most of its productions were more unusual. It re-edited one group of features to half-hour episodes for a series titled *Renfrew of the Royal Mounted.* Another series titled *Chico and Pablo* was, in reality, one-hour re-edited versions of "Cisco Kid" features. Because the company did not have the right to use the names "Cisco Kid" or "Pancho," the television series was re-dubbed, with the leading characters given new names. M. & A. Alexander Productions was also a distributor, and prior to its entry into television had been active in the forties as a producer of "B" features. The distribution of its product was taken over by NTA* in the sixties.

MARATHON INTERNATIONAL PRODUCTIONS, INC. was founded in 1954 as Marathon TV Newsreel, Inc., an international news service, by Konstantin Kaiser. The name was changed in 1963.
   Address: Box BJ, Armagansett, NY 11930.

MARBLE ARCH PRODUCTIONS was formed in 1978 by ITC* as its Hollywood production entity. Headed by Martin Starger, the company produced a number of made-for-television movies, including *Friendly Fire* (ABC, 1979), *Sanctuary of Fear* (NBC, 1979), *Rodeo Girl* (CBS, 1980), and *Red Flag: The Ultimate Game* (CBS, 1981). It was also responsible for the game show *Whodunnit?* (NBC, 1979).

MARCH OF TIME. Aside from the production of the popular theatrical series of the same name, the March of Time division of Time, Inc. was also involved in television production with two early series, *Crusade in Europe* (ABC, 1949) and *Crusade in the Pacific* (Syndicated, 1951). Simultaneous with the television presentation of its first episode, on October 30, 1951, the latter program also opened theatrically at New York's Guild Newsreel Theatre.

MARCONI-EMI TELEVISION LTD. was a jointly owned subsidiary of the British companies EMI and Marconi, formed in 1936 to exploit an all-electronic, 405-line television system, utilizing EMI's "Emitron" camera tube. One of two systems utilized by the BBC* when it began regular television transmissions on November 2, 1936, it was the one that was ultimately adopted early in 1937.
BIBLIOGRAPHY
Geddes, Keith, and Gordon Bussey. *Television: The First Fifty Years*. Bradford, U.K.: National Museum of Photography, Film & Television, 1986.

MARK VII LTD. was founded in 1951 by actor Jack Webb (1920–1982) for the production of the television version of *Dragnet* (NBC, 1952–1970). The name was chosen by Webb because he thought it had a feeling of quality; associated with him in the venture were Stanley Meyer and Michael Mershekoff. For most of its life, the company was located on the Republic Studios lot; Webb had an apartment on the top floor of his office, and lived close by in North Hollywood. Other productions by Mark VII are *General Electric True* (CBS, 1962–1963), *Adam 12* (NBC, 1968–1975), *The D.A.* (NBC, 1971–1972), *Emergency* (NBC, 1972–1977), and *Mobile One* (ABC, 1975), plus many theatrical features and made-for-television movies.
BIBLIOGRAPHY
Buck, Jerry, "Just the Facts: The Secret of Dragnet's—and Webb's—Success," *Emmy*, vol. IX, no. 1, January/February 1987, pp. 38–47, 79.
"Jack, Be Nimble!" *Time*, March 15, 1954, pp. 47–56.
Webb, Jack, as told to Dean Jennings, "The Facts about Me," *Saturday Evening Post*, September 5, 1959, pp. 51–53.
———, "The Facts about Me," *Saturday Evening Post*, [part 2], September 12, 1959, pp. 36, 84–86.
———, "The Facts about Me," *Saturday Evening Post*, [part 3], September 19, 1959, pp. 144–148.

MARTERTO PRODUCTIONS, INC. was a Beverly Hills–based company, formed by Danny Thomas for the production of his star vehicle, *Make Room for Daddy* (ABC, 1953–1956). It also produced *It's Always Jan* (ABC, 1955–1956), starring Janice Paige, and was active as a producer of television commercials.

"MASTERPIECE THEATRE" the best-known series on public television, is presented by WGBH-Boston and sponsored by Mobil Oil. Since its inception, the series has been hosted by Alistair Cooke. "Masterpiece Theatre" came about as a result of the 1970 success on PBS* of the BBC* series *The Forsyte Saga*, which proved to be tremendously popular despite its being shot in black-and-white. WGHB producer Christopher Sarson conceived of the new series and approached Mobil Oil, requesting that it sponsor a series of BBC productions. Mobil's response was an initial grant of $400,000. The first presentation on "Masterpiece Theatre" was *The First Churchills*, seen between January 10 and March 28, 1971.

Sarson regarded "Masterpiece Theatre" as a "literary series," and when *Upstairs, Downstairs* was acquired for the series in 1973, he resigned. Sarson's replacement was Joan Wilson (1929–1985), whose name has become most associated with the program. Upon her death, she was replaced by Rebecca Eaton. *Upstairs, Downstairs* was produced by John Hawkesworth for London Weekend Television* and was created by Eileen Atkins and Joan Marsh. It was first seen on PBS from January 6 through March 31, 1974. It was not the first non-BBC production to be seen on "Masterpiece"; that honor goes to *The Little Farm*, produced by Granada Television Limited,* and seen immediately before *Upstairs, Downstairs* on December 30, 1973.

Some of the more memorable productions presented by "Masterpiece Theatre" are *Elizabeth R* (1972), *The Edwardians* (1974), *Poldark* (1977), *I, Claudius* (1977), *The Duchess of Duke Street* (1978–1979), *Danger UXB* (1981), and *The Jewel in the Crown* (1984–1985).

BIBLIOGRAPHY

Cooke, Alistair. *Masterpieces: A Decade of Masterpiece Theatre*. New York: Alfred A. Knopf, 1981.

Ellis, Robin. *Making Poldark*. Bodmin, U.K.: Bossiney Books, 1978.

Gill, Brendan, "Masterpiece Theatre's Most Memorable Moments," *Panorama*, vol. II, no. 2, March 1981, pp. 38–43.

Henry, William A., III, "Remembering Joan Wilson," *Channels of Communications*, vol. V, no. 5, January/February 1986, pp. 72–73.

The Making of The Jewel in the Crown. New York: St. Martin's Press, 1983.

Morgenroth, Lynda, "The Best Job in Television: Joan Wilson May Have It," *Emmy*, vol. VI, no. 5, September/October 1984, pp. 30–33.

O'Connor, John, "Masterpiece Theatre: A Retrospective," *Television Quarterly*, vol. XXII, no. 3, 1986, pp. 31–37.

Trewin, J.C., editor. *Six Wives of Henry VIII*. New York: Frederick Ungar, 1972.

MAVRO TELEVISION COMPANY (Arthur Rosenblum, president) was a New York–based distributor of educational films and a producer of television commercials, active in the fifties.

MDS (Multipoint Distribution Service) is the name given to an authorized common carrier for a short-distance line of sight transmission of a single channel of television programming. MDS provides specialized "programming," such as text and data information to business subscribers, using a special antenna and converter combination to receive the signal, which can be scrambled if necessary. Many companies are licensed by the FCC* to offer MDS.

BIBLIOGRAPHY

Frank, Peter. *Multichannel MDS: New Allocations, New Systems and New Market Opportunities*. Washington, D.C.: National Association of Broadcasters, 1984.

Frank, Peter, and John Shackleford. *Business Opportunities for Broadcasters in MDS Pay Television*. Washington, D.C.: National Association of Broadcasters, 1982.

Nadel, Mark, and Eli Noam, editors. *The Economics of Multipoint Distribution Service (MDS): An Anthology*. New York: Columbia University School of Business, 1983.

MEADOWLANE ENTERPRISES, INC. is the production company of television personality/writer/composer Steve Allen (born 1921). It produced *Meeting of the Minds* (PBS, 1977–1981) in association with KCET.*

Address: 15201 Burbank Boulevard, Van Nuys, CA 91411.

MECHANICAL TELEVISION is the name given to the pioneering television systems that used mechanical parts to dissect an image. One of the earliest known proposals for mechanical television was by the Englishman William Lucas in April 1882. The two most prominent names in the development of mechanical television are Charles Francis Jenkins (1867–1934) in the United States and John Logie Baird (1888–1946) in the United Kingdom. Mechanical scanning devices are incapable of producing pictures of more than 240 lines, and most mechanical television experiments produced blurry and flickering images with 90 lines.

Because it was less expensive, mechanical television encouraged a great deal of experimentation, while its successor, electronic television, pioneered by Philo T. Farnsworth (1906–1971) and Vladimir Zworykin (1889–1982), was the domain of the major corporations. The failure of mechanical television, whose era ended in the early thirties, can be attributed in part to the inability of its pioneers to obtain adequate programming.

BIBLIOGRAPHY

Abramson, Albert. *The History of Television, 1880 to 1941*. Jefferson, N.C.: McFarland, 1987.

Sweeney, Daniel, "The Age of Mechanical Television," *The Perfect Vision*, no. 3, Indian Summer 1987, pp. 26–39.

Udelson, Joseph H. *The Great Television Race: A History of the American Television Industry 1925–1941*. University: University of Alabama Press, 1982.

MEDALLION TV ENTERPRISES, INC., operated by John A. Ettlinger, has been active as a distributor, primarily of independent features films to television, since the fifties (when it was named Medallion Productions & TV Sales Corp.). In the mid-fifties, it was responsible for two syndicated series, *View the Clue* (thirty-minute programs) and *Sew Easy* (fifteen-minute programs), and in 1960 it produced the syndicated series *Danger Zone*, narrated by "Pappy" Boyington.

Address: 8831 Sunset Boulevard, West Hollywood, CA 90069.

THE MEDIA ACTION RESEARCH CENTER, founded in 1974, is concerned with television's influence on consumers, and seeks to heighten awareness of such influence through workshops and publications.

Address: 475 Riverside Drive, Suite 1370, New York, NY 10115.

MEDICAL THEMES. The following is a listing of the most popular television series with medical themes: *The Doctor* (NBC, 1952–1953), *Janet Dean, Registered Nurse* (Syndicated, 1953–1955), *Medic* (NBC, 1954–1956), *Dr. Hudson's Secret Journal* (Syndicated, 1955–1957), *Kings Row* (ABC, 1955–1956), *Medical Horizons* (ABC, 1955–1956), *Dr. Christian* (Syndicated, 1956), *Diagnosis Unknown* (CBS, 1960), *The Eleventh Hour* (NBC, 1962–1964), *The Nurses* (CBS, 1962–1965), *Breaking Point* (ABC, 1963–1964), *The New Doctors* (NBC, 1969–1973), *The Interns* (CBS, 1970–1971), *The Psychiatrist* (NBC, 1971), *Dr. Simon Locke* (Syndicated, 1971–1974), *Emergency* (NBC, 1972–1977), *Temperatures Rising* (ABC, 1972–1974), *Police Surgeon* (Syndicated, 1972–1973), *Paul Bernard, Psychiatrist* (Syndicated, 1972), *Young Dr. Kildare* (Syndicated, 1972), *M*A*S*H* (CBS, 1972–1983), *Medical Center* (CBS, 1973–1976), *Doc Elliott* (ABC, 1974), *Doc* (CBS, 1975–1976), *Doctors' Hospital* (NBC, 1975–1976), *Medical Story* (NBC, 1975–1976), *The Practice* (NBC, 1976–1977), *Quincy, M.E.* (NBC, 1976–1983), *Rafferty* (CBS, 1977), *A.E.S. Hudson Street* (ABC, 1978), *Doctors' Private Lives* (ABC, 1979), *House Calls* (CBS, 1979–1982), *Trapper John, M.D.* (CBS, 1979–1986), *Nurse* (CBS, 1981), *St. Elsewhere* (NBC, 1982–1988), and *Doogie Howser, M.D.* (ABC, 1989–   ).

The three most famous television doctors are Richard Chamberlain as Dr. James Kildare, supported by Raymond Massey as Dr. Leonard Gillespie, on *Dr. Kildare* (NBC, 1961–1966); Vince Edwards as Dr. Ben Casey, supported by Sam Jaffe as Dr. David Zorba, on *Ben Casey* (ABC, 1961–1966); and Robert Young as Dr. Marcus Welby, supported by James Brolin as Dr. Steven Kiley, on *Marcus Welby, M.D.* (ABC, 1969–1976).

See also DENTISTS.

"THE MEDIUM IS THE MESSAGE" is a well-known quote by English professor Marshall McLuhan (1911–1980), who argued that the electronic media (particularly television) would replace the published book. The full quote, which implies that the type of medium used to convey a message is far more important than the actual message, is, "It is the medium which is the message because the medium creates an environment that is indelible and lethal." The quote is utilized as the first chapter heading in McLuhan's *Understanding Media: The Extensions of Man* (New York: McGraw-Hill, 1964) and is also the title of a recording by McLuhan, released in September 1967 by Columbia Records.

MELODY RANCH ENTERPRISES, INC. was one of Gene Autry's companies, active in the sixties in the production of filmed television commercials.

MERIDIAN PICTURES was located at the Samuel Goldwyn Studios in West Hollywood (now the Warner-Hollywood lot), and was owned by William Self. For CBS,* it produced the first four seasons, 1951 to 1955, of *Schlitz Playhouse of Stars*, and was also involved in the production of *Hudson's Bay* (Syndicated, 1958).

MERIT PRODUCTIONS, INC., founded by Emanuel E. Spioi, was a New York–based producer of television commercials, active in the fifties and sixties.

MERV GRIFFIN ENTERPRISES was created, as Merv Griffin Productions, in 1963 by the popular entertainer of the same name. After *The Merv Griffin Show* was no longer seen on network television, Merv Griffin Enterprises produced the syndicated version, from 1965 to 1969 and from 1972 to 1986. It also produces three series created by Griffin: *Jeopardy!* (NBC, 1969–1975; Syndicated, 1984-), *Dance Fever* (Syndicated, 1979-), and *Wheel of Fortune* (Syndicated, 1983-). In the summer of 1986, Merv Griffin Enterprises was acquired by the Coca-Cola Company, and came under the umbrella of Columbia Pictures Corporation, which was owned at that time by Coca-Cola. Merv Griffin Enterprises also owns the extensive postproduction facility TAV (Trans-American Video), which it acquired in 1977.

Address: 9860 Wilshire Boulevard, Beverly Hills, CA 90212.

BIBLIOGRAPHY

Griffin, Merv, with Peter Barsocchini. *Merv: An Autobiography*. New York: Simon and Schuster, 1980.

METROMEDIA, INC. A company that seemed at one time to be poised to become the fourth network, Metromedia's broadcasting activities can be dated from 1958, when Metropolitan Broadcasting was founded from what was left of DuMont.* John Kluge (born 1914) acquired the company from Paramount the following year and integrated it within his Metromedia organization. In October 1968, Wolper Productions, Inc. was also acquired, and was renamed Metromedia Producers Corporation. In addition to the latter, Metromedia's entertainment interests also included the Ice Capades, the Harlem Globetrotters, and Ice Capade Chalets.

Metromedia Producers Corporation continued limited production until 1974, and then was inactive for the next two years. It expanded production in 1981, when Robert Wood (former CBS-TV president) was appointed its president. In 1983, it began first-run television production through involvement in the co-production of the unsuccessful late-night talk show *Thicke of the Night* (Syndicated, 1983–1984), starring Alan Thicke, and continued the production of *Fame* and *Too Close for Comfort* after they were cancelled by the networks. Production ceased in the summer of 1985.

The company was taken private by John Kluge in 1984, and the following year he sold its seven television stations to 20th Century–Fox for $2 billion. The stations were to form the basis for Fox Broadcasting Co.*: WNEW–New York; KTTV–Los Angeles; WFLD-Chicago; WTTG-Washington, D.C.; WNBN-Dallas; KRIV-Houston; and WCVB-Boston. In 1986, Metromedia's nine radio stations and the Texas State Networks were sold to a group of investors, headed by Carl C. Brazell, Jr., for $285 million. Kluge abandoned his interest in television, and decided to concentrate the company in other areas.

Metromedia was last in the public eye in 1986, when Paul Winchell was awarded $17.8 million in damages, resulting from Metromedia's erasing the videotapes of his show, *Winchell Mahoney Time*, in 1972, and thus preventing him from profiting from their potential syndication.

Address: 1 Harmon Plaza, Secaucus, NJ 07094.

BIBLIOGRAPHY

Sharbutt, Jay, "Metromedia Pursues Its Quest for First-Run Shows," *Los Angeles Times Calendar*, March 11, 1984, p. 4.
Sherman, Strat, "Why Metromedia's Stock Went from $4.25 to $175," *Fortune*, April 5, 1982, pp. 96–103.

MIDWEST TELEVISION, INC. was founded in 1952 by August C. Meyer. It controls KFMB–San Diego; WCIA-Champaign, Illinois; WMBD-Peoria, Illinois; and WCFN-Springfield, Illinois.

Address: Box 777/509 South Neil Street, Champaign, IL 61820.

MILLER-MILKIS-BOYETT PRODUCTIONS, INC. In 1972, former Paramount executives Thomas L. Miller and Edward K. Milkis formed Miller-Milkis Productions, Inc., and in association with Paramount Television* produced three of the most popular comedy series on television: *Happy Days* (ABC, 1974–1984), *Laverne & Shirley* (ABC, 1976–1983), and *Mork & Mindy* (ABC, 1978–1982). Not so successful was their 1979 NBC series *$weepstakes*. In 1979, Paramount production executive Robert Lee Boyett joined the company, and the name was changed to Miller-Milkis-Boyett. The first production of the new company was *Bosom Buddies* (ABC, 1980–1984). It was followed by three highly successful comedy programs, produced in association with Lorimar Television*: *Valerie/Valerie's Family/The Hogan Family* (NBC, 1986-1990), *Perfect Strangers* (ABC, 1986-   ), and *Full House* (ABC, 1987-   ).

Address: 4000 Warner Boulevard, Burbank, CA 91522.

MILVERNE PRODUCTIONS, INC., operated by Milton E. Stanson and Vernon P. Becker, was a New York–based producer, primarily of television commercials, active in the early fifties.

MIND EXTENSION UNIVERSITY/THE EDUCATION NETWORK is a cable network, offering self-help programming; college-level courses for credits, including MBA degree programs; and English as a second language, as well as other subjects. It also provides The Global Library Program, offering library-related information, in association with the Library of Congress. Launched in

November 1987, Mind Extension University is available twenty-four hours a day for its 8 million subscribers (as of 1990).

Address: 9697 East Mineral Avenue, Englewood, CO 80112.

MINOT FILMS, INC. was founded in New Orleans by Charles M. Amory for the production of industrial films. In 1954, it became part of U.M. & M., Inc.,* and was renamed Minot TV, Inc. The company was later reformed by Amory for the production of two series filmed in New Orleans, *New Orleans Police Department* and *The Tracer*, both released in syndication in 1956. The company ceased operations in 1958.

MIPCON, held annually each fall in Cannes, France, is a festival and market-place devoted to the sale of all types of television programming from throughout the world.

Address: Marché International des Films et des Programmes pour la TV, la Video, le Cable et le Satellite, 179 avenue Victor Hugo, 75116 Paris, France.

MIP/TV is the international television program market, attended by buyers and sellers from all over the world, and held each April in Cannes, France. It was first organized in 1964.

Address: 179 avenue Victor Hugo, 75116 Paris, France.

THE MR. PEEPERS CO., owned by David Swift and Joyce Coe, controls rights to the Wally Cox series *Mr. Peepers* (NBC, 1952–1955).

Address: 12831 Hanover Street, Los Angeles, CA 90049.

"THE MOBIL SHOWCASE NETWORK." The Mobil Oil Company has long been known for its sponsorship of "Masterpiece Theatre"* and "Mystery" on Public Television. In 1977, it decided to create its own, occasional network on commercial television, with the release of the ten-week series *Ten Who Dared*, a dramatization of the lives of famous explorers, first seen on the BBC under the title *The Explorers*. Because network television would not run the Mobil series over concern at the oil company's editorializing commercials, Mobil was forced to sign up individual stations, including network affiliates, for the presentation of the British-produced series *Edward the King* (1979), which was followed a year later by *Edward and Mrs. Simpson*. In 1980, Mobil brought the British variety program *The Kenny Everett Video Show* to American television, and in 1983 it sponsored the three-part Royal Shakespeare Company production of *Nicholas Nickleby*, starring Roger Rees in the title role.

THE MONTBELIARD INTERNATIONAL VIDEO AND TELEVISION FESTIVAL was founded in 1984 to recognize serious documentary work in television. It takes place each fall.

Address: Centre d'Action Culturelle de Montbeliard, PB 236, 25204 Montbeliard Cedex, France.

THE MONTE CARLO INTERNATIONAL TELEVISION FESTIVAL is both a competitive festival and a television marketplace. Held each February, the festival was first organized in 1961.

Address: Palais des Congres, Av. d'Ostende, Monte Carlo, Monaco.

MOON LANDING. Neil Armstrong, commander of Apollo XI, was the first person to set foot on the moon, at 10:56 EDST on July 20, 1969. That moon landing was watched by 723 million television viewers, of which 125 million were in the United States.

MORNING SHOWS are a blend of informational programming and talk shows, and the first of the genre to be seen on network television was *The Today Show* on NBC.* Hosted by Dave Garroway, the program was first seen on January 14, 1952. Its popularity, particularly among children, was increased considerably the following year with the introduction of a chimpanzee named J. Fred Muggs. Garroway left the program in 1961, succeeded briefly by John Chancellor and then by Hugh Downs (who was its host from 1962 to 1971). Jane Pauley joined *The Today Show* in 1976, working first, until 1981, with Tom Brokaw, and then, from 1982, with Bryant Gumbel. Pauley's departure from the show in January 1990, and her replacement by Deborah Norville, created considerable controversy.

ABC's* morning program is titled *Good Morning America*, and it was introduced in 1975 and originally hosted by David Hartman and Nancy Dussault. It replaced an earlier morning show from 1975, *A.M. America*. Joan Lunden joined the program in 1980. On CBS,* *The Morning Show*, hosted by Walter Cronkite, was seen from 1954 to 1957. In 1979, CBS introduced *Morning*, with Charles Kuralt as the host (until 1982). It underwent a variety of changes to become *This Morning*, co-anchored by Kathleen Sullivan and Harry Smith in 1987. *The Dick Cavett Show* had earlier used the series title *Morning* on ABC in 1968.

BIBLIOGRAPHY

Evans, T. Bentley, "The Wake-Up Wars," *Emmy*, vol. VIII, no. 3, May/June 1986, pp. 33–36, 74–75, 82.

Lunden, Joan, with Andy Friedberg. *Good Morning, I'm Joan Lunden*. New York: G.P. Putnam's Sons, 1986.

Metz, Robert. *The Today Show*. Chicago: Playboy Press, 1977.

MOTION PICTURES FOR TELEVISION, INC. (MPTV) was an important distributor of the early fifties, owned by Matthew Fox (1911–1964). Among its releases (all syndicated) were *Flash Gordon* (1952), *Junior Science* (1954), *Drew Pearson's Washington Merry-Go-Round* (1954–1957), and *Duffy's Tavern* (1954). It is often credited as co-producer of the 1952 syndicated series *The Adventures of Superman*, but despite its name appearing on the filmed series, this appears to be a spurious claim. In the late fifties, the company was absorbed by Guild Films Co., Inc.

MOTOROLA, INC. was a manufacturer of popular television receivers, incorporated in Illinois on September 25, 1928, as the Galvin Manufacturing Corporation. The name was changed to Motorola, Inc. on May 15, 1947. The company was acquired by Four-Phase Systems, Inc. on March 2, 1982.

Address: 1303 East Algonquin Road, Schaumburg, IL 60196.

THE MOVIE ADVERTISING BUREAU was a New York–based producer of television commercials, active in the fifties.

MPO VIDEOTRONICS was founded as MPO Productions, Inc. in 1947 by Larry Madison, Judd Pollock, and Paul O'Hare. Initially a producer of industrial and sponsored films, with its first effort being *Wings to Hawaii* for Pan American Airlines, the company became a major producer of television commercials in the fifties. Among the classic advertising characters introduced in MPO commercials are Little Speedy Alka Seltzer and the Ajax White Knight. The company maintained the largest production studio in New York, with nine stages and twenty editing rooms, which it sold to Screen Gems* in 1974. MPO Videotronics remains active in many fields (for example, in 1975, it acquired the Miller Harness Company, Inc., the largest supplier of English riding saddlery).

Address: 2580 Turquoise Circle, Newbury Park, CA 91320.

MSO are the initials used to identify "Multiple System Operators" or distributors in the cable television industry. According to the National Cable Television Association,* the top ten MSOs are Tele-Communications, Inc.* (P.O. Box 5630 Terminal Annex, Denver, CO 80217); Time Warner Cable Group (300 First Stamford Place, Stamford, CT 06902–6732); United Artists Cablesystems (4700 South Syracuse Parkway, Denver, CO 80237); Continental Cablevision, Inc. (The Pilot House, Lewis Wharf, Boston, MA 02110); Comcast Cable Communications, Inc. (1414 South Penn Square, Philadelphia, PA 19102); Cox Cable Communications (1400 Lake Hearn Drive, Atlanta, GA 30319); Storer Communications Cable Division (P.O. Box 61–8000, North Miami, FL 33261–8000); Cablevision Systems Corporation (One Media Crossways, Woodbury, NY 11797); Jones Spacelink (9697 East Mineral Avenue, Englewood, CO 80112); and Newhouse Broadcasting/New Channels Corporation (P.O. Box 4872, Syracuse, NY 13221).

MTM ENTERPRISES was formed in 1970 by Grant Tinker (born 1926), his then-wife Mary Tyler Moore (born 1936), and agent Arthur Price. Taking its initials from Ms. Moore's name, the company's original purpose was the production of *The Mary Tyler Moore Show* (CBS, 1970–1977). However, it quickly became synonymous with some of the best programming on television; among the series that the company produced on its Studio City lot (formerly Republic Studios) are:

The Bob Newhart Show (CBS, 1972–1978), *Rhoda* (CBS, 1974–1978), *The*

Texas Wheelers (ABC, 1974–1975), *Friends and Lovers* (CBS, 1974–1975), *Doc* (CBS, 1975–1976), *Phyllis* (CBS, 1975–1977), *Three for the Road* (CBS, 1975), *The Tony Randall Show* (ABC, 1976–1978), *The Betty White Show* (CBS, 1977–1978), *Lou Grant* (CBS, 1977–1982), *We've Got Each Other* (CBS, 1977–1978), *WKRP in Cincinnati* (CBS, 1978–1982), *The White Shadow* (CBS, 1978–1981), *The Last Resort* (CBS, 1979–1980), *Paris* (CBS, 1979–1980), *Hill Street Blues* (CBS, 1981–1987), *St. Elsewhere* (NBC, 1982–1988), *Newhart* (CBS, 1982–1990), *Remington Steele* (NBC, 1982–1987), and *The Bay City Blues* (NBC, 1983).

Grant Tinker sold his interest in MTM to his partner in the summer of 1981, at which time he left the company to become chief executive officer of NBC. In 1988, the company was purchased by the British commercial broadcasting conglomerate TVS Entertainment plc, controlled by James Gatwood, for $320 million.

Address: 4024 Radford Avenue, Studio City, CA 91604.

BIBLIOGRAPHY

Feuer, Jane, Paul Kerr, and Tise Vahimagi. *MTM: Quality Television*. London: British Film Institute, 1984.

Melcher, Richard A., and Ronald Grover, "No Longer the Cat's Meow," *Business Week*, September 25, 1989, p. 49.

Rosenberg, Howard, "Above the Crowd," *Emmy*, vol. III, no. 2, Spring 1981, pp. 23–29.

MTV: MUSIC TELEVISION is a basic cable network, with twenty-four hour a day programming, the best-known items in which are its all-stereo music videos.* MTV was founded by Robert W. Pittman, with financial backing from Warner Amex Satellite Entertainment Company, and began broadcasting on August 1, 1981. The first music video played on the network was "Video Killed the Radio Star," performed by the Buggles. The network did not pay for any of the music videos it aired until December 1984, when it paid a reported $250,000 for the one-hour documentary *Making Michael Jackson's Thriller*, which included the fourteen-minute video "Thriller." The following year, MTV began paying major record companies for exclusive use of their music videos. The first annual MTV Video Music Awards was staged in October 1984.

In 1985, Warner Communications, Inc. bought out the share in MTV owned by American Express (Warner Amex was a joint venture between the two companies). Later that year, Warner tried unsuccessfully to sell the two-thirds of MTV that it now owned to Forstmann Little & Company. However, still later in the year, it did sell its share in MTV and Showtime/The Movie Channel* to Viacom, Inc.* for a reported $667.5 million. Pittman continued to run the company, being named president and chief executive officer, but on January 1, 1986, he quit, and was replaced by Thomas E. Freston, as president, and Robert A. Roganti, as chief executive officer. In 1989, Freston was named chairman and chief executive officer.

MTV expanded in 1988, opening networks throughout the world: MTV Europe, MTV Australia, MTV Internacionale (serving Latin America), and MTV Japan. It gained a potential audience of 90 million in thirty countries. As of 1990, it had more than 50 million subscribers in the United States. In the late eighties, the network moved increasingly away from the music video format and began presenting more and more regular-type programming. The MTV Network also includes VH–1* and Nickelodeon.*

Address: 1775 Broadway, New York, NY 10019.

BIBLIOGRAPHY

Dalton, Joseph, "The Televisionary," *Esquire*, December 1985, pp. 380–387.

Dannen, Frederic, "MTV's Great Leap Backward," *Channels of Communications*, vol. VII, no. 7, July 1987, pp. 45–47.

Denisoff, R. Serge. *Inside MTV*. New Brunswick, N.J.: Transaction Books, 1988.

Duffy, Susan, "Will a Little Less Rock Get MTV Rolling Faster?" *Business Week*, April 30, 1990, pp. 62, 66.

Goldstein, Patrick, "In Rock, To Be or Not To Be May Depend on MTV," *Los Angeles Times Calendar*, August 22, 1983, pp. 1, 6.

———, "MTV: Can It Handle a Competitor?" *Los Angeles Times Calendar*, August 19, 1984, pp. 70–71, 80.

———, "The Rise and Stall of MTV," *Los Angeles Times Calendar*, July 27, 1986, p. 64.

Hall, Peter, "MTV Wants It All," *Village Voice*, February 21, 1984, pp. 48, 49.

Hilburn, Robert, "Flashrock—MTV's Brave New World," *Los Angeles Times Calendar*, August 21, 1983, pp. 66–69.

Kaplan, Peter W., "MTV: 21st Century–Box," *Esquire*, March 1983, p. 222.

Knoedelseder, William K., Jr., "MTV Turning Video Rock into Gold," *Los Angeles Times*, August 26, 1984, part V, pp. 1, 4.

———, "MTV Goes Global," *Los Angeles Times*, December 18, 1986, part IV, pp. 1, 4.

Lansky, Karen, "Psyching Out MTV," *Los Angeles Times Calendar*, July 8, 1984, pp. 4–5.

Levine, Ed, "TV Rocks with Music," *New York Times Magazine*, May 8, 1983, pp. 42, 55–61.

Levy, Steven, "Ad Nauseum: How MTV Sells Out Rock & Roll," *Rolling Stone*, December 8, 1983, pp. 30–38, 76, 78–79.

McFadden, Cyra, "MTV," *TV Guide*, June 8, 1985, p. 47.

Maslin, Janet, "A Song Is No Longer Strictly a Song, Now It's a Video," *New York Times*, January 23, 1983, section 2, pp. 25–26.

"MTV Special Report," *The Hollywood Reporter*, February 23, 1984, pp. S1-S16.

O'Connor, John J., "MTV—A Success Story with a Curious Shortcoming," *New York Times*, July 24, 1983, section 2, p. H23.

Pareles, Joe, "After Music Videos, All the World Has Become a Screen," *New York Times*, December 10, 1989, p. E6.

Polskin, Howard, "MTV Rocks and Rolls Over Its Rivals," *TV Guide*, September 22, 1984, pp. 40–44.

Smucker, Tom, "MTV Plays the Same Old Song," *Village Voice*, March 29, 1983, p. 60.

Stokes, Geoffrey, "The Sound and Fury of MTV," *Channels of Communications*, vol. II, no. 3, September/October 1982, p. 64.

Walters, Barry, "MTV Lives!" *Village Voice*, June 2, 1987, pp. 39–40.
Zoglin, Richard, "MTV Faces a Mid-Life Crisis," *Time*, June 29, 1987, p. 67.

MULTIMEDIA BROADCASTING CO. was founded in 1968 with the merger of the Greenville News-Piedmont Co., the Asheville Citizen-Times Publishing Co. and Southeastern Broadcasting Corp., although the parent company, Multimedia, Inc., dates back to 1888. The company owns fifty-four newspapers, seven radio stations, and the following television stations: WMAZ-Macon, Georgia; KSDK–St. Louis; WLWT-Cincinnati; and WBIR-Knoxville.

Address: 140 West 9 Street, Cincinnati, OH 45202.

MULTI MOTION PICTURE CAMERA FILMING of television shows was introduced in 1951 by Desilu, when it asked Karl Freund (1890–1969) to film episodes of *I Love Lucy* (CBS, 1951–1961) using three Mitchell cameras. The new system provided more flexibility in editing and better picture quality than had been possible through the use of a kinescope,* the only previous method of recording live television shows before an audience. Four days were required to line up each weekly show, with the last two days occupied by camera rehearsals. The same setup was subsequently used by Freund for *Our Miss Brooks* (CBS, 1952–1956).

BIBLIOGRAPHY
Freund, Karl, "Shooting Live Television Shows on Film," *Journal of the Society of Motion Picture and Television Engineers*, vol. LX, no. 1, January 1953, pp. 9–19.

MUNIMOVIES was an experimental presentation of television to passengers traveling on the San Francisco Municipal Railway. Financed through grants from the National Endowment for the Arts and the San Francisco Arts Commission, an experimental forty-minute video presentation by Armin Ganz was seen on five San Francisco commuter lines in the winter of 1979–1980.

BIBLIOGRAPHY
"Moving Picture," *Panorama*, vol. I, no. 3, April 1980, p. 3.

MUNTZ TV INC. Earl William "Madman" Muntz was a used car salesman in Los Angeles who introduced cheap television receivers in Chicago in 1949. The receivers proved popular with consumers, who also enjoyed "Madman" Muntz's outrageous advertising slogans. Muntz TV survived at least two bankruptcies. However, on January 1, 1967, the name was changed to Television Manufacturers of America Co., and on July 28, 1972, that company declared a final bankruptcy.

BIBLIOGRAPHY
"Dig That Crazy Man," *Time*, July 13, 1953, pp. 84, 86.
"Muntz Keeps Branching Out," *Business Week*, July 25, 1953, pp. 99–100.
"Muntz Makes It Back," *Business Week*, November 9, 1963, p. 70.
"Where Are They Now?" *Newsweek*, December 2, 1957, p. 18.

MURAKAMI-WOLF-SWENSON is an animation production house headed by Jimmy Murakami, Fred Wolf, and Charles Swenson. It has been responsible for a number of television "firsts." It produced the first animated special to air in prime time, *The Point*, seen on ABC* on February 2, 1971. It produced the first "Strawberry Shortcake" special, *The World of Strawberry Shortcake* (Syndicated, 1980), and was also responsible for the "Puff the Magic Dragon" specials, beginning with *Puff and the Magic Dragon* (CBS, 1978). In addition, the company made the adult animation special *Carlton Your Doorman* (CBS, 1980).

Address: 1463 Tamarind Avenue, Hollywood, CA 90028.

THE MUSEUM OF BROADCAST COMMUNICATIONS is primarily concerned with the preservation of the history of broadcasting in the Chicago area. The concept was formulated in 1982 by founder/president Bruce DuMont, and the museum opened in the spring of 1987. It includes the ninety-nine-seat Kraft Television Theatre, the result of a $400,000 donation by Kraft, Inc. Among the museum's holdings are the David Susskind Collection, *Kraft Music Hall*, *Texaco Star Theatre*, *Kukla Fran and Ollie* shows, the *NBC Tomorrow Show with Tom Snyder*, and more than 7,000 television commercials. It has tapes of local Chicago nightly newscasts from January 4, 1987, to the present.

Address: 800 South Wells Street, Chicago, IL 60607.

THE MUSEUM OF BROADCASTING was opened to the public on November 9, 1976. It was created as a result of a March 1971 meeting in New York to discuss a library and history center for radio and television, sponsored by the William S. Paley Foundation, and was established with a personal grant from Paley. The museum holds more than 10,000 videotapes from 1939 to the present, and the nucleus of its radio holdings is the NBC Radio Archive, consisting of 175,000 discs dating from 1927 to 1969. In March 1991, the name was changed to the Museum of Radio & Television, and on September 12, 1991, the museum moved from its original building at 1 East 53 Street to new headquarters (built at a cost of $45 million).

Address: 25 West 52 Street, New York, NY 10022.

BIBLIOGRAPHY

Catalog of the Museum of Broadcasting: The History of American Broadcasting as Documented by the Programs in the Radio and Television Collection. New York: Arno Press, 1981.

Gibbons, Douglas F., "The Museum of Broadcasting, New York," *Historical Journal of Film, Radio and Television*, vol. I, no. 1, 1981, pp. 67–70.

Henderson, Mary C., editor. *Performing Arts Resources*. New York: Theatre Library Association, 1980 (contains "What the Dumbwaiter Saw," by Mary V. Ahern, pp. 84–88; "Using the Museum of Broadcasting's Catalogue," by Douglas Gibbons, pp. 89–90; and "Creating an Exhibition at the Museum of Broadcasting," by Judith E. Schwartz, pp. 91–93).

MUSHI PRODUCTIONS. Founded in 1961 by Osamu Tezuka, Mushi Productions specialized in the production of animated television series for children, beginning with *Astro Boy* (Syndicated, 1963), featuring the popular comic strip character Tetsuwan-Atom/Mighty Atom, created by Tezuka. Other Mushi series are *Kimba the White Lion* (Syndicated, 1966), *The Amazing 3* (Syndicated, 1967), and the live-action *Space Giants* (Syndicated, 969).

MUSICAL FEATURES, INC. (Guy Haenshen, president) was a New York–based producer of television commercials, active in the fifties and early sixties.

MUSIC BOX is an all-pop-music cable channel, which was created by Thorn EMI, the Virgin Group, and Yorkshire Television Limited,* and began broadcasting in the United Kingdom on July 12, 1984. It was originally intended as a British version of MTV* (which subsequently began European broadcasting on August 1, 1987). Seen on the Super Channel* for three or four hours each day, Music Box is currently owned by Yorkshire Television Holdings plc and the Granada Group plc.
    Address: 19–22 Rathbone Place, London W1P 1DS, United Kingdom.

MUSIC VIDEOS are short (usually three-minute) videotapes of music entertainers performing their latest recordings. They came into vogue with the opening of MTV* in 1981, but have their origins in Soundies, filmed musical numbers played on film jukeboxes in the forties. Two of the earliest music videos predate video and were produced in 1966: the Kinks performing "Dead End Street" and The Who singing "Happy Jack." Music videos began by featuring rock music stars only, but by the mid-eighties had broadened to include country-and-western, rhythm and blues, and even stars from the musical establishment (Bob Hope has starred in at least one music video). Many companies specialize in the production of music videos, under contract to various recording companies, and as early as 1977, Warner Bros. Records started its own video department. The television series *The Monkees* (NBC, 1966–1968) produced two major names in music video history, director Bob Rafaelson, and actor Mike Nesmith, whose Pacific Arts company was a pioneer in the field.
    A very relevant point with regard to music videos has been made by critic Pat Aufderheide, "As commercials in themselves, they have erased the very distinction between the commercial and the program."

BIBLIOGRAPHY

Aufderheide, Pat, "The Look of the Sound," in *Watching Television*, editor Todd Gitlin. New York: Pantheon, 1986, pp. 111–135.
Kinder, Marsha, "Music Video and the Spectator: Television, Ideology and Dream," *Film Quarterly,* Fall 1984, pp. 2–15.
Shore, Michael. *The Rolling Stone Book of Rock Video*. New York: Quill, 1984.
———. *Music Video: A Consumer's Guide*. New York: Ballantine Books, 1987.

MUTUAL OF OMAHA is the sponsor of the popular nature series *Wild Kingdom*, seen on NBC* from 1963 to 1971, and syndicated since 1971. It was hosted by Marlin Perkins until his death in 1986. Mutual of Omaha is also the syndicator of the program through its advertising agency, Bozell & Jacobs, Kenyon & Eckhardt.

Address: Dodge at 33rd, Omaha, NE 68131.

MUTUAL TELEVISION PRODUCTIONS, INC. was a Los Angeles–based producer and distributor of television programming, founded in 1950 by Edward M. Gray. It provided material for the 1951 DuMont* film series *International Playhouse*. The company ceased operations in 1954, when Gray joined National Telefilm Associates (NTA*). A related company was Monter-Gray, Inc., founded in 1954.

N

NABET (THE NATIONAL ASSOCIATION OF BROADCAST EMPLOY-EES AND TECHNICIANS) is the primary negotiating union serving the radio and television industries. It was founded in 1933 as the Association of Technical Employees, with its initial support coming from employees at NBC.* The name was changed in 1940. In recent years, NABET has been seen as a viable alternative to IATSE (the International Alliance of Stage and Theatrical Employes), more willing to grant membership to younger film and television craftspersons with a more reasonable initiation fee, and boasting a membership more willing to work on low-budget, independent productions at a lesser scale than required by IATSE.

Address: 7101 Wisconsin Avenue, Suite 800, Bethesda, MD 20814.

NAME CHANGES to feature films being aired on television take place when a network feels a new title will help the ratings for a box-office failure. Among such name changes are *Sometimes A Great Notion* (1971), which became *Never Give an Inch*; *September 30, 1955* (1978), which became *24 Hours of the Rebel*; *Bloodbrothers* (1978), which became *A Father's Love*; and *Hurricane* (1979), which became *Forbidden Paradise*. NBC* changed the title of *Honeysuckle Rose* (1980) to *On the Road Again* in recognition of the popularity of the Willie Nelson song of the same name featured in the film.

NASSOUR PICTURES, INC. was a subsidiary of Nassour Studios, founded in 1945 as Consolidated Studios by brothers Edward and William Nassour. The name was changed in 1946, and in May 1950, the studios (located in Hollywood at Sunset Boulevard and Van Ness Avenue) were purchased by KTTV. The brothers continued to maintain offices there, and for Nassour Pictures produced the 1955 syndicated series *Sheena, Queen of the Jungle*. (Edward Nassour committed suicide in 1962 at the age of forty-five.)

THE NATIONAL ASIAN AMERICAN TELECOMMUNICATIONS AS-SOCIATION, founded in 1980, promotes the interests of Asian-Americans in film, radio, and television.
Address: 346 Ninth Street, 2nd Floor, San Francisco, CA 94103.

THE NATIONAL ASSOCIATION FOR BETTER BROADCASTING was founded in 1949 as the Southern California Association for Better Radio and Television. For much of its life it was known as the National Association for Better Radio and Television, led by Mrs. Clara S. Logan, and boasting the support of pioneer inventor Lee De Forest. According to contemporary publicity, it was formed "to co-ordinate the interest of civic, religious, educational, business and labor organizations and individuals for the purpose of encouraging the presentation of radio and television programs of high standards." Today, it serves as a watchdog agency for children's programming, television commercials, and consumer interests in broadcasting regulations.
Address: 7918 Naylor Avenue, Los Angeles, CA 90045.

THE NATIONAL ASSOCIATION OF BLACK OWNED BROAD-CASTERS was founded in 1976 to represent the interests of current or potential black-owned radio and television stations.
Address: 1730 M Street, N.W., Room 412, Washington, DC 20036.

THE NATIONAL ASSOCIATION OF BROADCASTERS is America's leading fraternal organization for members of the radio and television industries. Founded in 1922, it represents the interests of its members in governmental and other matters, opposes censorship of the media, presents various awards, and also maintains a library. In 1951, it absorbed the Television Broadcasters Association, Inc., which had been founded in January 1944. Other organizations that it has absorbed are the Daytime Broadcasters Association (in 1985) and the National Radio Broadcasters Association (in 1986).
Address: 1771 N Street, N.W., Washington, DC 20036.

THE NATIONAL ASSOCIATION OF COLLEGE BROADCASTERS was founded in 1988 to bring together students, faculty members, and representatives of the radio and television industries for meetings, seminars, and workshops. It also publishes the only trade magazine for the college broadcasting and communications market, *College Broadcaster*, and operates U-NET. The latter, whose full name is University Network, is a non-profit satellite network, broadcasting five hours a week during the academic year (excluding winter break). U-NET television began airing on May 1, 1989, and U-NET radio was first heard on February 2, 1990.
Address: Box 1955, Brown University, Providence, RI 02912.

THE NATIONAL ASSOCIATION OF EDUCATIONAL BROAD-CASTERS. According to contemporary publicity, the National Association of Educational Broadcasters represented "non-commercial, educational AM, FM and TV Stations, workshops and production centers and closed circuit TV installations, owned and operated by colleges, universities, school systems, state systems, community organizations, and public service agencies." Based sometimes in Washington, D.C., and sometimes in Urbana, Illinois, the association was active in the fifties and sixties.

THE NATIONAL ASSOCIATION OF FARM BROADCASTERS was founded in 1944 as the National Association of Radio Farm Directors, and represents the interests of stations broadcasting farm news and information; it also works to improve the quality of such broadcasting.
    Address: P.O. Box 119, Topeka, KS 66601.

THE NATIONAL ASSOCIATION OF PUBLIC TELEVISION STATIONS was formed in 1979 to represent the interests of member stations, and works in close cooperation with the Corporation for Public Broadcasting (CPB*).
    Address: 1350 Connecticut Avenue, N.W., Washington, DC 20036.

THE NATIONAL ASSOCIATION OF STATE CABLE AGENCIES (NASCA) was founded in 1978 as the Conference of State Cable Agencies. It was created, by the nine U.S. states possessing cable regulatory bodies, to meet once a year and discuss topics of major regulatory importance.
    Address: c/o New York Cable Commission, Empire State Plaza, Town Building, Albany, NY 12223.

THE NATIONAL ASSOCIATION OF TELECOMMUNICATIONS OF-FICERS AND ADVISORS is an affiliate of the National League of Cities, concerned with the development, regulation, and administration of cable television and other telecommunications systems.
    Address: 1301 Pennsylvania Avenue, N.W., Washington, DC 20004.

THE NATIONAL AUDIENCE BOARD, INC. was a New York–based organization, with chapters in Los Angeles and San Francisco, active in the fifties. According to contemporary publicity, it was created "to represent the public to the broadcasting industry; to crystallize public opinion in radio and television programming and to act as a liaison group between the public and the broadcasting industry."

THE NATIONAL BLACK MEDIA COALITION was founded in 1973 to promote access to the communications industry for blacks and other minorities.
    Address: 38 New York Avenue, N.E., Washington, DC 20002.

THE NATIONAL BROADCAST EDITORIAL ASSOCIATION (NBEA) was organized in December 1972 at a meeting of the Radio-Television News Directors Association (RTNDA).* Its primary purpose is to encourage editorializing by radio and television stations, and to help write, produce, and present effective editorials. The association presents the annual Madison Award to an individual or group that has distinguished itself in working to preserve and protect freedom of expression.

Address: 6223 Executive Boulevard, Rockville, MD 20852.

THE NATIONAL CABLE TELEVISION ASSOCIATION. Founded in 1951, the National Cable Television Association is the principal trade organization for the cable television industry in the United States. It is an active lobbyist at all levels of government, with the media, and, particularly, with the Federal Communications Commission (FCC*). It recognizes excellence in the cable industry through its annual Vanguard and President's awards. There are five membership classifications: System (for all cable system operators regardless of size), Programmer (for suppliers of cable programming), Associate (for suppliers of cable equipment), Affiliate (for companies providing a service to the cable industry), and Patron (for individuals with an interest in the industry).

Address: 1724 Massachusetts Avenue, N.W., Washington, DC 20036.

THE NATIONAL CABLE TELEVISION CENTER AND MUSEUM was established at the Pennsylvania State University in 1985 under the original title of the National Cable Television Museum. The new name was adopted in 1988. Its board of directors is made up of representatives of the National Cable Television Association,* the Community Antenna Television Association, the Cable Television Pioneers, state and regional cable associations, the cable industry in general, and faculty members from Penn State. The center sponsors a chair in telecommunications at Penn State, administers an oral history program and a library and information service, and maintains exhibits and publications programs.

Address: 211 Mitchell Building, The Pennsylvania State University, University Park, PA 16802.

THE NATIONAL CABLE TELEVISION INSTITUTE is a technical training institute, producing home-study technical training programs for all phases of the cable industry.

Address: P.O. Box 27277, Denver, CO 80227.

THE NATIONAL CITIZENS COMMITTEE FOR PUBLIC TELEVISION was a short-lived organization, founded in 1967 to promote an independent public television system in the United States. Headed by Thomas P. Hoving, director of the Metropolitan Museum, the name was changed in October 1968 to the National Citizens Committee for Broadcasting.

BIBLIOGRAPHY
Coe, Brian L., "The National Citizens Committee for Broadcasting: What Is It?" *Television Quarterly*, vol. VIII, no. 3, Summer 1969, pp. 48–55.

THE NATIONAL COALITION ON TELEVISION VIOLENCE was founded on February 1, 1980, with the primary objective of reducing the depiction of violence on television. A non-profit organization, it monitors television programs, documenting the amount of violence depicted and its contextual usage. It publishes listings of the best and worst programs for the guidance of its 3,000 members, and in the cases of shows that it considers excessively violent, such as the syndicated series *Friday the 13th* and *Freddy's Nightmares*, it advocates boycotts and advises sponsors and television stations of its concerns.

Address: P.O. Box 2157, Champaign, IL 61820.

THE NATIONAL COMMUNITY TELEVISION ASSOCIATION, INC. was a Washington-based, non-profit trade organization, assisting the growth and development of community antenna television systems. In 1969, it was absorbed by the National Cable Television Association.*

THE NATIONAL COUNCIL FOR FAMILIES & TELEVISION was founded in 1978 as a non-profit, non-adversarial educational organization bringing together members of the television industry and other groups concerned with family life. It publishes the quarterly magazine *Television & Families*, edited by Richard Krafsur.

Address: 3801 Barham Boulevard, Suite 300, Los Angeles, CA 90068.

THE NATIONAL FEDERATION FOR DECENCY, founded in 1977 as the American Family Association by the Rev. Donald E. Wildmon, promotes "the Biblical ethic of decency in American society with a primary emphasis on television." The organization compiles listings of programs that it feels advocate violence, immorality, alcohol abuse, and sexual promiscuity. In an often abrasive and shrill manner, it encourages its members to boycott networks and sponsors of programs that do not meet its ultra-conservative standards of morality. Wildmon also founded the Coalition for Better Television in February 1981, whose chief aim is the removal of all morally offensive programming from American television, primarily through a boycott of products advertised on such shows. In addition, he is one of the most prominent members of a similar group, CLear-TV (Christian Leaders for Responsible Television).

Address: P.O. Drawer 2440, Tupelo, MS 38803.

BIBLIOGRAPHY
"Boycott Pro—Donald Wildmon," *Emmy*, vol. III, no. 3, Summer 1981, pp. 39–40.
Doudna, Christine, "The Rev. Donald Wildmon," *Channels of Communications*, vol. I, no. 2, June/July 1981, pp. 19–21.

THE NATIONAL FEDERATION OF LOCAL CABLE PROGRAMMERS (NFLCP), founded in 1976, is a non-profit association promoting the development of local programming on cable television and providing information on national cable policy issues. It publishes *Community Television Review* and operates the consulting service Cable Utilization Service.

Address: P.O. Box 27290, Washington, DC 20038.

THE NATIONAL GEOGRAPHIC SOCIETY formed a television division, under the direction of Robert Doyle, in 1962, but it was not until 1965 that its documentaries began to air on CBS,* beginning with *Americans on Everest*. In 1972, Doyle resigned, and was replaced by Dennis Kane, who took the series to ABC* in 1973 for a one-year period. In 1975, the National Geographic specials began their now-permanent relationship with PBS,* produced in association with WQED* (which replaced David L. Wolper as co-producer). In 1985, the *National Geographic Explorer* series began airing on the Turner Broadcasting System,* and shows from that series were later syndicated under the title *National Geographic on Assignment*. (The PBS series is syndicated as *The Best of National Geographic*.) According to *Emmy* magazine, the society's television division is its fastest growing operation, with gross revenues having risen from $1.95 million in 1985 to $30 million in 1990.

Address: 17 and M Streets, N.W., Washington, DC 20036.

BIBLIOGRAPHY

Krampner, Jon, "Around the World in Twenty-Five Years," *Emmy*, vol. XII, no. 2, March/April 1990, pp. 37–41.

THE NATIONAL JEWISH ARCHIVE OF BROADCASTING was created in 1981 as part of the Jewish Museum, with a grant from the Charles H. Revson Foundation (which had funded a 1979 commission to study the feasibility of such an archive). It collects, catalogs, preserves, and exhibits radio and television programming of Jewish interest and Jewish culture, both American and foreign.

Address: 1109 Fifth Avenue, New York, NY 10128.

BIBLIOGRAPHY

Hartley, Arnold, "The First Ethnic Broadcasting Museum in the United States (And a Few Thoughts About It)," *Television Quarterly*, vol. XXII, no. 2, 1986, pp. 45–53.

THE NATIONAL NEWS COUNCIL was created as an independent agency by the Twentieth Century Fund in 1973, with three-year funding from various foundations. The purpose of the council was to consider complaints from the public about inaccuracy in the print and broadcast media.

Address: 41 East 70 Street, New York, NY 10021.

THE NATIONAL PUBLIC AFFAIRS CENTER FOR TELEVISION was created in July 1971 as the Washington, D.C., production arm for public television, responsible for *Washington Week in Review*, *Washington Straight Talk*, and other programming. The center was merged with the Washington, D.C.–based public television station WETA in 1976.

NATIONAL RELIGIOUS BROADCASTERS was founded in 1944 to represent the interests of religious radio and television producers; it presents awards, sponsors workshops and seminars, and maintains a publications program.

Address: P.O. Box 1926, Morristown, NJ 07960.

THE NATIONAL TELEMEDIA COUNCIL was founded in 1953 as the American Council for Better Broadcasts. Concerned with improving the quality of television, it submits reports on its evaluations of television programming to sponsors, networks, and government agencies. In 1965, it absorbed the Television Action Committee for Today and Tomorrow.

Address: 120 East Wilson Street, Madison, WI 53703.

NATIONAL TELEPIX. Active in the sixties, and founded by Edward N. White, National Telepix specialized in the editing of silent comedies and Westerns for release to television in series such as *The Mischief Makers* (Syndicated, 1961–1962), which utilized "Our Gang" comedies, and *Wally Western* (Syndicated, 1962).

THE NATIONAL VIEWERS' AND LISTENERS' ASSOCIATION was founded in 1966 by Mrs. Mary Whitehouse (born 1910) to fight "permissiveness" in the British broadcast media. It has its origins in the 1963 "Clean Up TV" movement, launched in Birmingham, England.

Address: Ardleigh, Colchester, Essex CO7 7RH, United Kingdom.

BIBLIOGRAPHY
Caulfield, Max. *Mary Whitehouse*. London: Mowbrays, 1975.
Tracy, Michael, and David Morrison. *Whitehouse*. London: Macmillan, 1979.
Whitehouse, Mary. *Cleaning Up TV: From Protest to Participation*. London: Blandford Press, 1967.
———. *Who Does She Think She Is?* London: New English Library, 1971.

NATIONWIDE TELEVISION CORP. was a New York–based television distributor of classic comedy shorts (featuring Laurel and Hardy, Charlie Chase, and others), founded by Irwin Shapiro and active from 1957 to 1961.

NATPE (NATIONAL ASSOCIATION OF TELEVISION PROGRAM EXECUTIVES) sponsors the world's largest television marketplace, an annual, week-long programming conference held at various locations throughout the United States. An association of television program directors and others involved in television programming, NATPE was founded as a non-profit organization in New York in 1963 by five program managers, Stan Cohen, Roy Smith, Lew Klein, Pete Kizer, and Tom Jones. It held its first conference in New York in May 1964, but it was not until the Los Angeles conference in 1969 that syndicators, such as Viacom, Inc.* and MCA, rented hotel suites from which to "sell" their wares. As of 1990, it had 1,700 members.

Address: 10100 Santa Monica Boulevard, Suite 300, Los Angeles, CA 90067.

BIBLIOGRAPHY

Link, Tom, "What's a NATPE?" *Emmy*, vol. IX, no. 1, January/February 1987, pp. 30–36.

NBC (NATIONAL BROADCASTING COMPANY). The corporate histories of NBC and RCA* are interlinked in that the latter is NBC's parent company. In 1926, RCA purchased its first radio station, WEAF–New York (later, the call letters were changed to WNBC), and, with 25 affiliates, launched the National Broadcasting Company (NBC) network on November 15, 1926. A year later, NBC split its network into two, the Red and the Blue (the latter was sold in 1941 and became ABC*). Also in 1927, NBC introduced its familiar sound logo of three musical tones (G, E, C).

NBC entered television on April 4, 1928, when it received permission from the Federal Radio Commission to operate experimental television station W2XBS, which began transmitting from the Empire State Building on October 30, 1931. NBC began broadcasting on a regular basis on April 30, 1939, beginning with President Franklin D. Roosevelt's opening speech from the New York World's Fair.* The NBC network is generally dated from January 12, 1940, when two stations, WNBC–New York and WRGB-Schenectady, New York, began broadcasting NBC programming. In the summer of 1941, NBC television signed up its first sponsors, Procter & Gamble,* Lever Brothers, Sun Oil, and Bulova. On June 19, 1946, Gillette became the first advertiser to sponsor a television program, the Joe Louis–Billy Conn title fight on NBC, and on October 27, 1946, Bristol-Myers became the first sponsor of a network television series, *Geographically Speaking*. The network introduced coast-to-coast television coverage in 1951, and three years later launched color* television.

The most famous name on NBC television in the forties and fifties—indeed "Mr. Television" himself—was Milton Berle (born 1908), who first hosted *Texaco Star Theater* on June 8, 1948. Berle remained a fixture on NBC on Tuesday nights until 1956, with his show changing its name to the *Buick-Berle Show* in 1953 and *The Milton Berle Show* in 1954. In 1951, NBC signed a thirty-year, $200,000 a year contract with Berle, which was to continue regardless of whether the comedian's program remained on the air.

In 1949, Sylvester L. "Pat" Weaver (born 1908) joined NBC as head of its television division. In December 1953, David Sarnoff appointed him president. Weaver introduced a new style of programming to television, created the "spectacular,"* and enthusiastically dictated lengthy memoranda to his staff. In 1955, he was named chairman of the board, and Sarnoff's son, Robert W. Sarnoff (born 1918), was appointed president. Weaver quit later that year; Robert W. Sarnoff was named chairman and Robert Kintner (former ABC president) became president.

NBC pioneered early-morning programming with *The Today Show*, first seen in 1952. It also introduced the most famous show on late-night television, *The Tonight Show Starring Johnny Carson*, which began in 1962 and succeeded *The Jack Paar Show*, seen at the same time from 1957 to 1962.

The peacock logo, demonstrative of the network's predominance in color television, was introduced in 1956. It was replaced in 1976 with an abstract letter "N," but was reinstituted in 1980.

After successful programming ventures at ABC and CBS,* Fred Silverman (born 1937) took over as president and chief executive officer in June 1978, replacing Herbert S. Schlosser (born 1926), who had been associated with NBC since the mid-fifties. Silverman hired Brandon Tartikoff (born 1949) as president of the Entertainment Division. With the appointment of Thornton F. Bradshaw (born 1917) as chairman of NBC's parent company, RCA, Silverman resigned in June 1981. (He had been hired by Bradshaw's predecessor, Edgar Griffiths.) Bradshaw named Grant A. Tinker (born 1947) as chairman and chief executive officer, and Robert E. Mulholland (born 1934) as president and chief operating officer. (Mulholland resigned in March 1984.)

Tinker took over a network that had been in third place in the ratings since 1976, a position it was to retain until 1984. Thanks to the efforts of Tinker and Tartikoff, NBC eventually moved up to first place in the 1985–1986 season. Among the popular shows that Tinker and Tartikoff brought to NBC were *St. Elsewhere* (NBC, 1982–1988), *Family Ties* (NBC, 1982–1989), *Cheers* (NBC, 1982-   ), and *The Cosby Show* (NBC, 1984-   ). The popularity of programming such as this ended a four-year profits decline in 1982.

That same year, the Rev. Donald E. Wildmon launched a well-publicized but unsuccessful boycott of NBC and RCA because the network "excluded Christian characters, Christian values and Christian culture from their programming."

Tinker voluntarily resigned from NBC in September 1986, and was replaced by Robert C. Wright (born 1943). In July 1990, Tartikoff was promoted to chairman of the NBC Entertainment Group. He was succeeded by Warren Littlefield, who, at thirty-eight, was seven years older than Tartikoff when he first took the job.

To celebrate its sixtieth anniversary, on April 29, 1986, NBC presented its entire collection of early television shows from 1948 to 1977—more than 20,000 programs—to the Library of Congress. In July 1987, it sold its radio network to Westwood One, Inc. for $50 million. The network suffered its longest strike—by NABET*—from June to October 1987. NBC entered the cable television industry in May 1988, with the purchase of the Tempo cable system from Tele-Communications, Inc.* for $21 million. In November of the same year, it acquired a 38 percent share in the international news organization Visnews.

NBC owns the following television stations: WNBC–New York, WMAQ-Chicago, WKYC-Cleveland, KCNC-Denver, KNBC–Los Angeles, WTVJ-Miami, and WRC-Washington, D.C.

Addresses: 30 Rockefeller Plaza, New York, NY 10112; 3000 West Alameda Avenue, Burbank, CA 91523.

BIBLIOGRAPHY

"As We See it," *TV Guide*, December 15, 1956, p. 2.

Bedell, Sally, "Will NBC Be Proud as a Peacock by April?" *TV Guide*, January 19, 1980, pp. 6–8.

———, "Aiming for a Late Rally To Turn the Tide," *TV Guide*, January 26, 1980, pp. 28–31.

"Bye Bye Birdie," *Newsweek*, January 26, 1976, pp. 62–63.

Campbell, Robert. *The Golden Years of Broadcasting: A Celebration of the First 50 Years of Radio and Television on NBC*. New York: Scribners, 1976.

Connections: Reflections on Sixty Years of Broadcasting. New York: NBC, 1986.

Corliss, Richard, "Fred Finally Comes A-Cropper," *Time*, July 13, 1981, pp. 61–62.

———, "Coming Up from Nowhere," *Time*, September 16, 1985, pp. 64–67.

Diamond, Edwin, "The 'World's Richest TV Station' Goes for Broke," *New York*, September 16, 1974, pp. 97–107.

Farley, Ellen, "After Years of Ruffled Feathers NBC Peacock Has Reason To Strut," *Los Angeles Times*, September 9, 1984, Part v, pp. 1, 2, 9.

Kleinfield, N.R., "Fred Silverman's NBC: It's Still Out of Focus," *New York Times*, July 13, 1980, section 3, pp. 1, 4.

"NBC: Heady for Freddie," *Time*, January 30, 1978, p. 74.

"NBC's Farewell to Fred," *Newsweek*, July 13, 1981, pp. 69–70.

Oney, Steve, "That Championship Season," *California*, February 1984, pp. 42–48, 155–160.

"Proud as a Peacock," *Newsweek*, May 28, 1979, p. 62.

Radatz, Leslie, "A Few Things NBC Forgot on Its 50th Anniversary—And Maybe It's Just as Well," *TV Guide*, February 12, 1977, pp. 39–40.

Schwartz, Tony, "Our Newest Columnist Delivers a Grim Prognosis for the Once-Proud Peacock," *Playboy*, vol. XXX, no. 5, May 1983, pp. 42–43.

"60 Years of Broadcast Excellence," *The Hollywood Reporter*, June 6, 1986, pp. S7–S22.

"Slaughter on Sixth Avenue," *Time*, December 11, 1978, p. 103.

Stahl, Bob, "Five Who Are Taking a Giant Step at NBC," *TV Guide*, October 10, 1959, pp. 8–11.

Turner, Richard, "Watch the Master Strategist Plot To Stay No. 1," *TV Guide*, October 8, 1988, pp. 4–10.

———, "Countdown to the Final Choices," *TV Guide*, October 15, 1988, pp. 26–34.

Waters, Harry F., "The Peacock Lays an Egg," *Newsweek*, January 12, 1981, p. 58.

———, "Can Tinker Save NBC?" *Newsweek*, June 14, 1982, pp. 97–98.

Wilson, Earl. *The NBC Book of Stars*. New York: Pocket Books, 1957.

Woodstone, Arthur, "Has God Chosen Jane Pfeiffer To Run NBC?" *New York*, October 23, 1978, pp. 61–64.

Zoglin, Richard, "A Giant Leap to No. 2," *Time*, December 3, 1984, p. 74.

NBC FILMS, INC. was the network's syndication arm, which began as NBC Television Films, Inc. in the fifties. During that decade and the next, it was active in distributing dozens of series, including *The Life of Riley* (NBC, 1949–1958), *You Bet Your Life/The Best of Groucho* (NBC, 1950–1961), *Foreign Intrigue* (Syndicated, 1951–1955), *The Lili Palmer Theatre* (Syndicated, 1952), *Hopalong Cassidy* (Syndicated, 1952), *Medic* (NBC, 1954–1956), *The Great*

Gildersleeve (Syndicated, 1955), *The Silent Service* (Syndicated, 1957–1958), and *Laramie* (NBC, 1959–1963). For some years it was a division of California National Productions, Inc.* Morris Rittenberg was the company's president for many years, succeeded in 1970 by Jim Victory. Following the FCC* ruling that networks must refrain from program syndication by June 1, 1973, NBC disposed of the subsidiary to NTA.*

NCTV (NATIONAL COLLEGE TELEVISION) is a cable network providing programming for college students, including reviews, game shows, soap operas, cartoons, and music videos. Launched in January 1984, it is seen from between midnight and 6:00 A.M., seven days a week, by 5.5 million subscribers (as of 1990).

Address: 1 Madison Avenue, New York, NY 10010.

THE NEBRASKA EDUCATIONAL TELEVISION COMMISSION was founded in 1963 to create a statewide network of stations in partnership with University of Nebraska Television (which had opened KUON-Lincoln in 1954). In 1972, the commission opened the Nebraska Educational Telecommunications Center, which also houses the Great Plains National Instructional Television Library and Nebraskans for Public Television, Inc. The following Nebraskan stations are members of the commission: KLNE-Lexington, KPNE–North Platte, KTNE-Alliance, KMNE-Bassett, KXNE-Norfolk, KRNE-Merrimon, KHNE-Hastings, KYNE-Omaha, and KUON–Lincoln and Omaha.

Address: P.O. Box 83111/1800 North 33 Street, Lincoln, NE 68501.

NEPTUNE PRODUCTIONS CO., founded by John Gibbs and Robert Montgomery, was a New York–based producer of live television programming, active in the early fifties.

NET (NATIONAL EDUCATIONAL TELEVISION) was the first attempt to create a central source of programming for public television, and was a precursor of both the CPB* and PBS.* The organization was established in 1952 as a non-profit Illinois corporation, the Educational Television and Radio Center. A year later, it opened its headquarters in Ann Arbor, Michigan, and on May 16, 1954, it began a program exchange service. Primary funding for the project came from the Fund for Adult Education, a division of the Ford Foundation. In 1958, the Ford Foundation took over direct funding of NET, and its headquarters were moved to New York, with a branch office in Washington, D.C., and its technical center remaining in Ann Arbor.

NET produced or acquired five hours of programming a week, half of it in the area of public affairs. The organization possessed no production facilities, but had a staff of executive producers who would supervise outside production, often at local public broadcasting stations. Funding from the Ford Foundation averaged $6 million a year. Public television stations paid an average of $100 a year for affiliation, which gave them access to 260 hours of new programming and unlimited use of the NET program library at a rate of $5 per half-hour show. As of January 1966, 104 stations were affiliated with NET, with an average weekly viewing audience of between 10 and 15 million.

Many public television stations felt uneasy with the perceived left-wing bias in NET programming, and as a result, the Ford Foundation decided to throw its support behind the establishment of the Public Broadcasting Service (PBS). In 1970, the foundation arranged the assimilation of NET into the New York public television station, WNDT, which was renamed WNET,* and which continued some of the production activities of NET.

NEWS broadcasting on American television dates from May 3, 1939, when *Tele-Topics* was first seen on NBC. The first regular news broadcast in the United States began on WCBS–New York and WNBT–New York on July 1, 1941. ABC* began its regular nightly news broadcasts on August 11, 1948, with H.R. Baughage and Jim Gibbons. Later ABC news anchormen were John Daly, Ron Cochran, Peter Jennings, Frank Reynolds, and Max Robinson. In 1976, Barbara Walters joined ABC and became the first network anchorwoman, at a reported salary of $1 million a year, a salary that created considerable irritation on the part of her co-anchor Harry Reasoner (who had joined with Howard K. Smith to co-anchor the *ABC Evening News* in December 1970). Other prominent names associated with *ABC News* are Sylvia Chase, Sam Donaldson, Brit Hume, Tom Jarriel, Ted Koppel, Diane Sawyer, and Kathleen Sullivan.

Smith and Reasoner were not the first two anchorpersons to make a major impact on television news. On October 15, 1956, Chet Huntley and David Brinkley were first seen on NBC,* forming *The Huntley-Brinkley Report*. It ceased in 1970 with Huntley's retirement, and thereafter, the *NBC Nightly News* was hosted by Brinkley, John Chancellor, and Frank McGee until 1971, when Chancellor became the sole anchorman. He was succeeded in 1982 by Tom Brokaw. NBC was the earliest network to introduce a regular news service, which began on April 10, 1944, as the weekly program *The War as It Happens*. Other prominent names associated with *NBC News* are Connie Chung, Lloyd Dobyns, Linda Ellerbee, John Hart, Floyd Kalber, John Palmer, Jessica Savitch, Garrick Utley, and Chris Wallace.

CBS* began regular news broadcasts on May 3, 1948, hosted by Douglas Edwards, who was succeeded in 1962 by Walter Cronkite. Cronkite retired in 1981, succeeded on a regular basis later that same year by Dan Rather. Other names associated with CBS News are Ed Bradley, Morton Dean, Bruce Morton, Charles Osgood, Forrest Sawyer, Bob Schieffer, and Susan Spencer.

Aside from the nightly network news broadcasts, other major news-oriented programs are *60 Minutes* (CBS, 1968-   ), *20/20* (ABC, 1978-   ), and *Nightline* (ABC, 1980-   ).

See also CNN (CABLE NEWS NETWORK).

BIBLIOGRAPHY

Adams, William C., editor. *Television Coverage of International Affairs*. Norwood, N.J.: Ablex, 1982.

Adams, William, and Fay Schreibman, editors. *Television Network News*. Washington, D.C.: George Washington University, School of Public and International Affairs, 1978.

Batscha, Robert M. *Foreign Affairs News and the Broadcast Journalist*. New York: Praeger, 1975.

Benjamin, Burton. *The CBS Benjamin Report: CBS Reports "The Uncounted Enemy: A Vietnam Deception": An Examination*. Washington, D.C.: Media Institute, 1984.

Blair, Gwenda. *Almost Golden: Jessica Savitch and the Selling of Television News*. New York: Simon and Schuster, 1988.

Calmer, Ned. *The Anchorman*. Garden City, N.Y.: Doubleday, 1970.

CBS News. *Television News Reporting*. New York: McGraw-Hill, 1958.

CNN vs. The Networks: Is More News Better News? Washington, D.C.: Media Institute, 1983.

Cohler, David Keith. *Broadcast Journalism: A Guide for the Presentation of Radio and Television News*. Englewood Cliffs, N.J.: Prentice-Hall, 1985.

Diamond, Edwin. *The Tin Kazoo—Television, Politics, and the News*. Cambridge, Mass.: MIT Press, 1975.

Dickerson, Nancy. *Among Those Present*. New York: Ballantine Books, 1976.

Dudek, Lee J. *Professional Broadcast Announcing*. Boston: Allyn and Bacon, 1982.

Epstein, Edward J. *News from Nowhere: Television and the News*. New York: Random House, 1973.

Face the Nation 1975: The Collected Transcripts from the CBS Radio and Television Broadcasts. Metuchen, N.J.: Scarecrow Press, 1976.

Fang, I.E. *Television News*. New York: Hastings House, 1972.

Field, Stanley. *The Mini-Documentary—Serializing TV News*. Blue Ridge Summit, Pa.: TAB Books, 1975.

Frank, Robert Shelby. *Message Dimensions of Television News*. Lexington, Mass.: Lexington/Heath, 1973.

Gans, Herbert J. *Deciding What's News: A Study of CBS Evening News, NBC Nightly News and Time*. New York: Pantheon, 1979.

Gates, Gary Paul. *Air Time: The Inside Story of CBS News*. New York: Harper & Row, 1978.

Gelfman, Judith S. *Women in Television News*. New York: Columbia University Press, 1976.

Gordon, George N., and Irving A. Falk. *TV Covers the Action*. New York: Julian Messner, 1968.

Green, Maury. *Television News: Anatomy and Process*. Belmont, Calif.: Wadsworth, 1969.

Hallin, Daniel C. *The "Uncensored" War: The Media and Vietnam*. New York: Oxford University Press, 1986.

Harrison, Martin. *Television News: Whose Bias? A Casebook Analysis of Strikes, Television and Media Studies*. Hermitage, U.K.: Policy Journals, 1985.

Hazlett, Thomas W. *TV Coverage of the Oil Crises: How Well Was the Public Served?* Washington, D.C.: Media Institute, 1982.

Herschensohn, Bruce. *The Gods of Antenna*. New Rochelle, N.Y.: Arlington House, 1975.

Hetherington, Alastair. *News, Newspapers and Television*. London: Macmillan, 1985.

Hewitt, Don. *Minute by Minute. . . .* New York: Random House, 1985.

Jasperjohn, William. *A Day in the Life of a Television News Reporter*. Boston: Little, Brown, 1981.

King, Norman. *Dan Rather*. New York: Leisure Books, 1981.

Kowet, Don. *A Matter of Honor: General William C. Westmoreland versus CBS*. New York: Macmillan, 1984.

Kurtis, Bill. *Bill Kurtis on Assignment*. Chicago: Rand McNally, 1983.

Larson, James F. *Television's Window on the World: International Affairs Coverage on the U.S. Networks*. Norwood, N.J.: Ablex, 1984.

Lashner, Marilyn A. *The Chilling Effect in TV News: Intimidation by the Nixon White House*. New York: Praeger, 1984.

Lawler, Philip F. *The Alternative Influence: The Impact of Investigative Reporting Groups on America's Media*. Washington, D.C.: Media Institute, 1984.

Lefever, Ernest W. *TV and National Defense: An Analysis of CBS News, 1972–1973*. Boston, Va.: Institute for American Strategy Press, 1974.

LeRoy, David J., and Christopher H. Sterling, editors. *Mass News: Practices, Controversies, and Alternatives*. Englewood Cliffs, N.J.: Prentice-Hall, 1973.

Lesher, Stephen. *Media Unbound: The Impact of Television Journalism on the Public*. Boston: Houghton Mifflin, 1982.

Lewis, Carolyn Diana. *Reporting for Television*. New York: Columbia University Press, 1984.

Lyons, Louis M., editor. *Reporting the News*. Cambridge, Mass.: Belknap Press of Harvard University, 1965.

MacDonald, J. Fred. *Television and the Red Menace: The Video Road to Vietnam*. New York: Praeger, 1985.

Madsen, Axel. *60 Minutes: The Power and the Politics of America's Most Popular TV News Show*. New York: Dodd, Mead, 1984.

Matusow, Barbara. *The Evening News: The Making of the Network News Anchor*. Boston, Mass.: Houghton Mifflin, 1983.

Nash, Alanna. *Golden Girl: The Story of Jessica Savitch*. New York: E.P. Dutton, 1988.

Nimmo, Dan, and James E. Combs. *Nightly Horrors: Crisis Coverage by Television Network News*. Knoxville, Tenn.: University of Tennessee Press, 1985.

Paisner, Daniel. *The Imperfect Mirror: Inside Stories of Television Newswomen*. New York: William Morrow, 1989.

Peterson, Sheldon, editor. *Television Newsfilm: Content*. New York: Time-Life, 1965.

———, editor. *The Newsroom and the Newscast*. New York: Time-Life, 1966.

Powers, Ron. *The News-Casters: The News Business as Show Business*. New York: St. Martin's Press, 1978.

Rather, Dan. *The Camera Never Blinks*. New York: Ballantine Books, 1977.

Reasoner, Harry. *Before the Colors Fade*. New York: Alfred A. Knopf, 1981.

Robinson, John P., and Mark R. Levy, with Dennis K. Davis. *The Main Source: Learning from Television News*. Beverly Hills, Calif.: Sage, 1986.

Robinson, Michael J., and Margaret A. Sheehan. *Over the Wire and on TV: CBS and UPI in Campaign '80*. New York: Russell Sage Foundation, 1983.

Rollin, Betty. *Am I Getting Paid for This?* Boston: Little, Brown, 1982.

Savitch, Jessica. *Anchorwoman*. New York: G.P. Putnam's Sons, 1982.

Schoenbrun, David. *On and Off the Air: An Informal History of TV News*. New York: E.P. Dutton, 1989.

Sevareid, Eric. *This Is Eric Sevareid*. New York: McGraw-Hill, 1964.

Shook, Frederick, and Don Lattimore. *The Broadcast News Process*. Englewood, Colo.: Morton, 1982.

Siller, Bob, Ted White, and Hal Terkel. *Television and Radio News*. New York: Macmillan, 1960.

Skornia, Harry J. *Television and the News: A Critical Appraisal*. Palo Alto, Calif.: Pacific Books, 1966.

Small, William. *To Kill a Messenger: Television News and the Real World*. New York: Hastings House, 1970.

Smith, Myron J., Jr., editor. *U.S. Television Network News: A Guide to Sources in English*. Jefferson, N.C.: McFarland, 1984.

Stephens, Mitchell. *Broadcast News*. New York: Holt, Rinehart and Winston, 1986.

Teague, Bob. *Live and Off-Color: News Biz*. New York: A and W, 1982.

Television Newsgathering. New York: SMPTE, 1976.

Wallace, Mike, and Gary Paul Gates. *Close Encounters*. New York: William Morrow, 1984.

Weaver, J. Clark. *Broadcast Newswriting as Process*. New York: Longman, 1984.

Westin, Av. *Newswatch: How TV Decides the News*. New York: Simon and Schuster, 1982.

Wolf, Frank. *Television Programming for News and Public Affairs: A Quantitative Analysis of Networks and Stations*. New York: Praeger, 1972.

Woodruff, Judy, with Kathleen Maxa. *This Is Judy Woodruff at the White House*. Reading, Mass.: Addison-Wesley, 1982.

Yorke, Ivor. *The Technique of Television News*. New York: Focal Press, 1978.

THE NEW YORK FESTIVALS, not to be confused with the New York Film festival, were founded in 1957 to honor achievements in industrial and educational filmmaking. In the seventies, the festivals began recognizing television programming and advertising, and later added music videos. Awards are now presented in the following categories: Promotion Spots/Openings and IDs; Television News: Programs; Television News: Inserts; Television Documentary & Information Programs; Technical; Television Entertainment Programs; Television Entertainment Specials; Children's Programming; and Music Videos.

Address: 5 West 37 Street, New York, NY 10018.

THE NEW YORK TIMES CO. (publisher of the *New York Times*) owns two New York radio stations and five television stations: WHNT-Huntsville, Alabama; KFSM–Fort Smith, Arkansas; WQAD-Moline, Illinois; WNEP-Scranton; and WREG-Memphis. In August 1989, it sold its cable television system, NYT Cable TV, for $422 million.

Address: 229 West 43 Street, New York, NY 10036.

THE NEW YORK WORLD'S FAIR OF 1939 was the site of what is generally considered to be the introduction of television broadcasting to the United States. President Franklin D. Roosevelt's two-minute speech opening the fair on April 30, 1939, was televised by NBC,* an event that was also the first outside television broadcast in the United States, and one that made Roosevelt the first American President to appear on television.

NHK (Nippon Hoso Kyokai) is Japan's official television network, financed through licenses purchased by owners of television receivers. It began broadcasting, in Tokyo, on February 1, 1953.

Address: 2–2–1 Jinnan, Shibuya-ku, Tokyo 150, Japan.

BIBLIOGRAPHY

50 Years of Japanese Broadcasting. Tokyo: NHK, 1977.

NICHOLSON-MUIR PRODUCTIONS, founded by Nick Nicholson and E. Roger Muir (born 1916) has specialized in the production of children's programming and game shows. In the latter category are *Howdy Doody* (NBC, 1947–1960) and its later incarnations, and *The Funny Manns* (Syndicated, 1960). Game shows created by Nicholson-Muir include *Matches 'n' Mates* (Syndicated, 1967) and *Pay Cards* (Syndicated, 1968).

Address: 1465 East Putnam Avenue, Old Greenwich, CT 06870.

NICKELODEON. Part of the MTV* network, Nickelodeon is a basic cable network with more than 50 million subscribers as of 1990. It began as "Nick Flicks," a local, experimental program in Columbus, Ohio, in 1977, and became a national network in April 1979. Until the summer of 1985, Nickelodeon was exclusively a channel for children (and it remains the most popular cable network for children), presenting programs with no advertising support until 1983. Children's programming had been scheduled from 7:00 A.M. until 8:00 P.M. As of 1985, the additional hours were taken up by "Nick at Nite," which billed itself as programming for "people who grew up with television," and specializes in black-and-white series such as *The Donna Reed Show* and *Route 66*. In August 1989, Nickelodeon announced plans for a home video label, in association with Elektra Entertainment.

Address: 1775 Broadway, New York, NY 10019.

BIBLIOGRAPHY

Hennessee, Judith Adler, "Cable's Nickelodeon Wrestles with the Lure of Commercials," *New York Times*, January 2, 1983, pp. H19, H22.

Townley, Rod, "Room Noodles—and Livewire—to the Rescue," *TV Guide*, September 24, 1983, pp. 20–23.

Zoglin, Richard, "Letting Kids Just Be Kids," *Time*, December 26, 1988, p. 78.

NIELSEN RATINGS. See THE A.C. NIELSEN COMPANY

THE NIPKOW DISC was a mechanical screening device invented by a German, Paul Nipkow, in 1884. It was the first workable means of breaking down an image and converting it into electrical impulses, and as such is the precursor of mechanical television.*

NJT. See THE JEWISH TELEVISION NETWORK

**THE NORTH AMERICAN NATIONAL BROADCASTERS ASSOCIA-
TION** was founded in 1972 and formalized in 1978. It is an international or-
ganization representing the interests of Canadian and U.S. broadcasters.
   Address: 1500 Bronson Avenue, Ottawa, Ontario, Canada K1G 3J5.

NORTH AMERICAN TELEVISION PRODUCTIONS, INC. (E.M. Glucks-
man, president) was a New York–based producer of filmed programming, active
in the fifties and early sixties.

NORTHSTAR PICTURES, LTD., based in Ontario, Canada, was responsible
for the production of the 1958 syndicated (and basically unsuccessful) series
Hudson's Bay.

THE NOSTALGIA NETWORK, INC. is a basic cable channel, broadcasting
twenty-four hours a day, with 8.5 million subscribers as of 1990. Financed by
a group of private investors headed by Sergio Bosco, Ken Nimmer, and Raymond
Horn, Nostalgia began broadcasting on February 1, 1984. Nostalgia lives up to
its name, claiming to provide programming for the over-forty-five age group,
and its first spokesman was George "Spanky" McFarland of "Our Gang" fame.
   Address: 71 West 23 Street, New York, NY 10010.
BIBLIOGRAPHY
Hawn, Jack, "The Old Is New on Nostalgia Channel," *Los Angeles Times*, January 23,
   1984, part VI, p. 9.

NTA (National Telefilm Associates) was formed in 1954 by Ely Landau (born
1920) in association with Oliver A. Unger and Harold Goldman. It had developed
from the earlier Ely Landau, Inc., formed in 1951, and became a major distributor
to television of feature films from producers J. Arthur Rank and David O.
Selznick, as well as many series. Among the syndicated series in distribution
from NTA were *Sheriff of Cochise* (1956–1957), *Official Detective* (1957), *The
Adventures of William Tell* (1958), *Danger Is My Business* (1958), *Man without
a Gun* (1958–1959), *Grand Jury* (1959), *Mantovani* (1959), *George Jessel's
Show Business* (1959), *Henry Morgan and Company* (1959), *The Mike Wallace
Interview* (1959–1961), and *Assignment: Underwater* (1960).
   In 1956, the company formed the NTA Film Network, after the acquisition
of television rights to 390 20th Century–Fox features, in return for a 50 percent
interest in the network. Despite the participation of 104 television stations, the
NTA Film Network was not successful.
   In 1959, Landau sold the company to National Theatres for $4 million, but
continued to operate WNTA–New York (Channel 13) until 1961, when the station
was sold to the National Educational Group. In 1984, NTA, which had purchased

the library of Republic Pictures Corporation in 1967, voted to change its name to Republic and to utilize the Republic logo of the American eagle as its own.
    Address: 12636 Beatrice Street, Los Angeles, CA 90066.

NTSC are the initials of the National Television System Committee, formed by the Radio Manufacturers Association in cooperation with the FCC* in 1940. Comprised of technicians from all branches of the industry, the NTSC drew up standards for television regarding the number of channels (later amended), and the use of 525 horizontal lines of resolution and thirty frames of picture per second. Such standards were adopted by the FCC in April 1941. Somewhat jokingly, NTSC is also claimed to stand for "Never the Same Color Twice," a reference to the easy distortion of color–phase relationships.

NUCLEAR WAR. While *The Day After* (ABC, 1983) is the best-known television fictional drama to deal with a nuclear holocaust and its aftermath, it is not the best. In a very restrained manner, the *Medic* series, starring Richard Boone, aired an episode on the same subject, "Flash of Darkness," on CBS* on February 14, 1955. In the same year that *The Day After* was shown in the United States, the BBC* produced a similar drama set in the north of England and titled *Threads*. It was first seen in the United States on WTBS on January 13, 1985. In 1984, the BBC produced a documentary on the scientific aspects of nuclear war, titled *On the Eighth Day*. Some eighteen years earlier, in 1966, the BBC had commissioned Peter Watkins to direct a film titled *The War Game*, dealing with the buildup to and consequences of a nuclear attack on the United Kingdom. The BBC refused to air the finished production, claiming it "too horrifying," but the general feeling was that the film would have turned public opinion away from the stockpiling of nuclear weapons, which was increasing at that time, and was thus banned.

NUDITY. Male and female nudity, both frontal and rear, is unknown on American network television, except in the presentation of British-produced series on PBS.* Nudity has been acceptable on British television, after 9:00 P.M., from the mid-seventies. One of the earliest examples of male nudity took place, by accident, on April 20, 1974, when the BBC* was broadcasting a live rugby match from Twickenham: A male streaker ran across the field and was picked up by the television cameras. On August 24, 1975, opera singer Annabel Hunt faced the camera nude in the opening aria of *Ulysses* (broadcast on Southern Television).
    Probably the first and only example of rear male nudity on American network television occurred in some episodes of the 1983 NBC* series *The Bay City Blues,* the story of a minor-league baseball team, with a considerable amount of footage shot in the locker room. For the record, no one actually goes to bed nude for a love-making scene on television—actresses wear bodystockings and actors wear shorts.

BIBLIOGRAPHY
Miller, Annetta, "Television: And Now, the Naked Truth," *Newsweek*, May 11, 1987,
    p. 54.

NUNS might not seem to be a popular subject for television sitcoms* but they were featured, with great success, in *The Flying Nun* (ABC, 1967–1970), which made a star of Sally Fields. The only other sitcom about nuns is the short-lived *In the Beginning* (CBS, 1978). Nuns have appeared in peripheral roles in a number of dramatic series, notably *The Father Dowling Mysteries* (NBC, 1989-).

NUSTAR TELEVISION NETWORK was a twenty-four hour a day, nation-wide satellite broadcasting system, which offered diverse low-budget programming such as *Garage Sale for the Rich and Eccentric* and *This Week in Real Estate*. Located in Tujunga, California, and founded by Peter A. O'Neil, Nustar began broadcasting on June 13, 1986, with the main attraction on its opening night being the 1961 feature *El Cid*. The system filed for Chapter XI protection under the U.S. Bankruptcy Code on September 11, 1987, and ceased broadcasting. Shortly before, it had been fined by the FCC* for broadcasting without a license.

BIBLIOGRAPHY
Akst, Daniel, "TV Network Debuts on Low Funds, High Hopes," *Los Angeles Times*,
    June 17, 1986, part IV, pp. 1, 5.
Bates, James, "Nustar TV Goes Black: Firm Turns to Chapter 11," *Los Angeles Times*,
    October 13, 1987, part IV, p. 1.

O

O&O is the acronym for owned and operated, and is used in the television industry to refer to stations that are both owned and operated by the networks, as opposed to "network affiliates," which are independent stations affiliated to individual networks and agreeing to show that network's schedule of programming.

The ABC* O&O stations are WABC–New York, WPVI-Philadelphia, WTVD-Raleigh/Durham, WLS-Chicago, KABC–Los Angeles, KGO–San Francisco, KFSN-Fresno, and KTRK-Houston. The CBS* O&O stations are WCBS–New York, WBBM-Chicago, KCBS–Los Angeles, WCAU-Philadelphia, and WCIX-Miami. The NBC* O&O stations are WNBC–New York; WMAQ Chicago; WTVJ-Miami; WKYC-Cleveland; WRC-Washington, D.C.; KCNC-Denver; and KNBC–Los Angeles.

ODYSSEY PRODUCTIONS, INC. was owned by Lowell Thomas (1892–1981), who had been seen and heard on local New York television as early as 1940. It was responsible for the 1964 CBS* series *High Adventure*. Thomas served as president for a number of years, but the company was presided over by Milton A. Fruchtman for some of the earlier years.

Address: 24 East 51 Street, New York, NY 10022.

THE OFFICE OF TELECOMMUNICATIONS POLICY (THE OTP) was created in 1970 by the presidential administration of Richard M. Nixon. Under the leadership of Clay Whitehead, it was intended to advise the president on communications policy questions, but was generally considered to be more concerned with obtaining sympathetic news coverage for the president. In 1972, Torbert H. Macdonald, chairman of the House Communications and Power Subcommittee, called the OTP "the most serious, continuous threat to free broadcasting in this country." The OTP was superseded in 1978 by the National

Telecommunications and Information Administration (NTIA), which was established in response to executive order No. 12046 (March 27, 1978).

Address: National Telecommunications and Information Administration, Department of Commerce, Washington, DC 20230.

OFFICIAL FILMS, INC., which was organized in 1939 as a 16mm producer and distributor, became active in television distribution in the fifties. Among the series that it handled, all syndicated, were *Colonel March of Scotland Yard* (1953), *Secret File USA* (1954), *The Scarlet Pimpernel* (1956), *The Errol Flynn Theatre* (1956), *The Big Story* (1957), *Sword of Freedom* (1957), *The Veil* (1958), *International Detective* (1959), *Greatest Headlines of the Century* (1960–1963), *Biography* (1962–1963), and *Battle Line* (1963). In May 1951, the company merged with Jerry Fairbanks Productions,* but the merger was dissolved in August of the same year. However, Official continued to distribute Jerry Fairbanks Productions through the beginning of 1952. The company name was changed to Official Industries, Inc. in November 1969, and shortly thereafter, Official Films ceased operations.

"OFF-NETWORK SERIES" is the term given to a program formerly seen on network television but now in syndication.

OHLMEYER COMMUNICATIONS CO. was founded by Donald W. Ohlmeyer, Jr. (born 1945), a leading figure in ABC Sports, in 1982, with financial backing from RJR Nabisco Co. Among the made-for-television movies that it has produced are *Special Bulletin* (NBC, 1983), *Crime of Innocence* (NBC, 1985), and *Under Siege* (NBC, 1986). It has also been responsible for such series as *People Are Funny* (NBC, 1984) and *Fast Copy* (NBC, 1986). Related companies are OCC Productions and OCC/The Management Company.

Address: 962 North La Cienega Boulevard, Los Angeles, CA 90069.
BIBLIOGRAPHY
Mann, Arnold, "Innerviews: From Pool Hustler to Empire Builder," *Emmy*, vol. IX, no. 1, January/February 1987, pp. 18–25.

OLIO VIDEO TELEVISION PRODUCTIONS, INC., formed by Harvey Cort, was active in the fifties as a distributor of "B" features and Westerns to television.

OLYMPUS is the European Space Agency's direct-broadcast satellite, placed in orbit by the *Ariane* rocket on July 11, 1989.

"ONE DAY IN THE LIFE OF TELEVISION" was a project initiated by the British Film Institute, under the guidance of Geoffrey Nowell-Smith. On November 1, 1988, all television programming in the United Kingdom was videotaped, and voluntary observers were asked to keep diaries commenting on what they viewed. The results were published in a book of the same title, edited by Sean Day-Lewis (London: Grafton Books, 1989).

ON FILM, INC., founded by Robert Bell, was a New York–based producer of television commercials, active in the fifties and sixties.

ON-LINE and OFF-LINE are two of the most common terms used in videotape editing. Off-Line is the editing process used to produce a videotape workprint with a visible time code. On-Line is the master editing system for the creation of master release tapes, which conform to the edited off-line cassettes. Off-Line tapes are off the air, and On-Line tapes are on the air.

ON-TV was a Los Angeles–based over-the-air pay-television service, started in April 1977 by Jerry Perenchio and San Diego–based Oak Industries, Inc. (Perenchio's 49 percent share was sold to Oak in September 1981.) It offered movies, sports events, concerts, and old television series, and boasted its highest number of subscribers (380,000) in 1981. On-TV was acquired by SelecTV* in August 1984.

ONYX PICTURES CORP. (Sam Lake, president) was a New York–based distributor to television, active in the fifties handling the "Our Gang" comedies and various minor features.

OPERA. Gian-Carlo Menotti's *Amahl and the Night Visitors* was the first opera commissioned for television, and it was first seen on NBC* on December 24, 1951. NBC was the only network to present operas on a regular basis with its *NBC Opera of the Air*, the first presentation of which, in 1950, was Kurt Weill's *Down in the Valley*. Other operas in the occasional series were *Die Fledermaus* (1950), *Billy Budd* (1952), *Carmen* (1953), *The Magic Flute* (1956), and *Cosi Fan Tutte* (1958). Excerpts from operas were frequently heard on anthology programs such as *The Voice of Firestone* (NBC, 1949–1954), which was simultaneously heard on radio, and Maria Callas made her television debut on *The Ed Sullivan Show* on November 25, 1956.

Opera has not been a staple of network television since the fifties, but in that decade a number of programs were devoted to the subject: *Metropolitan Opera Auditions of the Air* (ABC, 1952), with Milton J. Cross; *Opera vs. Jazz* (ABC, 1953); *Opera Cameos* (DuMont, 1954), with Giovanni Martinelli; and *The Patrice Munsel Show* (ABC, 1957–1958).

OPERATION PRIME TIME was created by MCA Television Limited in 1976 to provide "prime time" (in other words, top quality) programming to independent television stations. Ninety-five independent stations were involved in the project, including WPIX–New York and KCOP–Los Angeles. The first program provided by MCA was the mini-series *Testimony of Two Men* (aired in

May 1977), based on the novel by Taylor Caldwell. Interest from independent television stations in Operation Prime Time grew, and by 1979, some 188 stations were involved. A year later, the project was being handled by Television Program Entertainment, and included programming from other studios. Operation Prime Time's most successful presentation was *The Dream Merchants* (1980), based on the Harold Robbins novel; it was followed by *A Woman Called Golda* (1982), *Sadat* (1983), *Blood Feud* (1983), *A Woman of Substance* (1985), and *Hold the Dream* (1986), among many others.

ORF (Österreichischer Rundfunk Gesellschaft m.b.h.) is the state-owned Austrian corporation for both radio and television. It is supervised by the Kuratorium, a thirty-five-member board of trustees, and financed by license fees and advertising revenues. Regular television broadcasts began in Austria in 1956; the PAL* color system is used, and there are two channels.

Address: Wurzburggasse 30, A–1136 Vienna, Austria.

ORIGINAL FILMVIDEO LIBRARY is one of the largest private archives of original television programming, with more than 10,000 16mm and 35mm film episodes available on site. It was founded by Ronnie James in 1976 as Encore Entertainment; the name was changed in 1990. Original FilmVideo Library holds many public-domain television shows from the forties, fifties, and sixties, available in their entirety or for clip or stock-footage use. Film-to-tape transfer and research services are also available.

Address: P.O. Box 3457, Anaheim, CA 92803.

ORION TELEVISION, INC. See FILMWAYS, INC.

ORTF (Office de la Radiodiffusion-Télévision Française) was created in 1964 as the governing body for French radio and television, replacing RTF (Radiodiffusion Télévision Française), which had been created in 1945 under the Minister of Information. ORTF administered two television channels, on which collective advertising had been permitted since 1949, and on which brand advertising was introduced in October 1968. Color television, utilizing the SECAM* system, was introduced in 1967.

Following a strike by ORTF journalists in 1968, the Ministry of Information was abolished in 1969, and ORTF was placed under the direct control of the prime minister. In 1972, the government announced that the director general of ORTF would be appointed for a three-year period and would not be subject to government removal. Eventually, in January 1975, ORTF was disbanded. L'Institut National de l'Audiovisuel was created out of the remnants of ORTF, and it became known for its experimental television work, including films by Jean-Luc Godard and Jacques Rivette. Two separate television channels, TF1 and Antenne 2, were created, and a third channel, FR3, was added later.

Addresses: TF1 (Télévision Française), 15 rue Cognacq Jay, F–75330 Paris,

France; Antenne 2, 22 Ave Montaigne, F–75008 Paris, France; FR3 (France Région 3), 5 Ave du Recteur-Poincaré, F–75782, France.
BIBLIOGRAPHY
Taylor, Peggy, and Bernard Redmont, "French Television: A Changing Image," *Television Quarterly*, vol. VIII, no. 4, Fall 1969, pp. 39–48.

THE OVERMYER NETWORK, also known as the United Network, was created in the fall of 1966 by Ohio entrepreneur Daniel H. Overmyer with an initial investment of $15 million. Overmyer's intention was to distribute productions from independent stations and thus allow them to make more from advertising than could be achieved as network affiliates. To head the network, Overmyer hired former ABC*-TV president Oliver E. "Ollie" Treyz. One of the network's programs was *The Las Vegas Show* (1967), but it was terminated when the network went off the air, heavily in debt and involved in legal problems, in June 1967. As a result, as television historian Hal Erickson has pointed out, *The Las Vegas Show* is the first series in history to leave the air because its network was cancelled.
BIBLIOGRAPHY
Efron, Edith, "This Man is Betting $15,000,000," *TV Guide*, January 21, 1967, pp. 27–31.

P

PACE was a proposed national pay-cable network for culture and the performing arts, which was to be developed in 1980 by public television.
BIBLIOGRAPHY

Mahoney, Sheila, Nick Demartino, and Roger Stengel. *Keeping PACE with the New Television: Public Television and Changing Technology.* New York: Carnegie Corporation of New York/VNU Books International, 1980.

O'Connor, John J., "Would Viewers Be Willing To Pay for Culture?" *New York Times*, June 8, 1980, section 2, pp. 1, 31.

PACIFIC COAST NETWORK (PCN) was a short-lived satellite/cable company (September 1984-February 1985), created by Peter A. O'Neil. Located in a converted chapel in Burbank, California, it went off the air after its equipment was repossessed.
BIBLIOGRAPHY

Wharton, David, "Cable Network off Air as Equipment Is Taken," *Los Angeles Times*, February 2, 1985, part II, p. 8.

PAISANO PRODUCTIONS was formed by actress Gail Patrick Jackson, her husband Cornwall Jackson (of the J. Walter Thompson Agency), and writer Erle Stanley Gardner, for the production of *Perry Mason* (CBS, 1957–1974).

PAL (Phase Alternation Line) is the color television system in use throughout most of Western Europe. It was introduced by Dr. W. Bruch of Telefunken in West Germany in 1963, and came into use in the United Kingdom in 1967. It is not compatible with the American NTSC* color system.
BIBLIOGRAPHY

"PAL Colour System," in *The Focal Encyclopedia of Film & Television*, editor Raymond Spottiswoode. New York: Hastings House, 1969, pp. 533–537.

PALISADE TELEVISION PRODUCTIONS, INC. was a New York–based producer and television packager, founded in 1954 by George F. Foley, and active for only a few years. An associated company was Gothic Films, Inc.

PAN-AMERICAN TELEFILMS, INC., active in the fifties and sixties, was a Los Angeles–based distributor of Spanish-language features to the Latin American and U.S. television markets. Another company involved in a similar operation was the New York–based Latin American Radio-Television Corporation (LARDIOTEL).

"PANEL PROGRAMS" is a term used to describe game shows, apparently based on the concept of "Twenty Questions." Obvious examples are *What's My Line?* (CBS, 1950–1967), *Masquerade Party* (NBC, 1952; CBS, 1953–1954; ABC, 1954–1956; NBC, 1957; CBS, 1958; NBC, 1958–1959; CBS, 1959–1960; NBC, 1960), *I've Got a Secret* (CBS, 1952–1976), and *To Tell the Truth* (Syndicated, 1969–1977, 1980).
BIBLIOGRAPHY
"Television," *Fortnight*, August 18, 1951, p. 8.

PANNING-AND-SCANNING. Because the television screen has an aspect ratio of 1.33:1, films shot in other aspect ratios, such as CinemaScope or any other widescreen process commonly in use since 1953, can only be seen in their entirety on television through use of the so-called "letterbox" method with a black strip of empty picture at the top and bottom of the screen. The letterbox method is generally disliked by television networks and stations, and in order to avoid its use, a panning-and-scanning process has been adopted. This involves the rephotographing and recomposition of films, with the result that the television viewer never sees the entire image as it was originally intended to be seen in theatres. Almost half the original image is lost when films shot in 70mm, CinemaScope, or Panavision are shown on television by the pan-and-scan process.
BIBLIOGRAPHY
Belton, John, "Pan & Scan Scandals," *The Perfect Vision*, no. 3, Summer 1987, pp. 40–49.

PAPAZIAN-HIRSCH ENTERTAINMENT was formed in 1988 by producer Robert A. Papazian and writer-producer James G. Hirsch. It was responsible for the dramatic series *The Outsiders* (Fox, 1989), and has also produced a number of made-for-television movies, including *Guts and Glory: The Rise and Fall of Oliver North* (CBS, 1989).
Address: 500 South Sepulveda, Suite 600, Los Angeles, CA 90049.

PARAMOUNT TELEVISION. The earliest involvement of Paramount in television dates from 1938, when the studio purchased a half-interest in the Allen B. DuMont Laboratories, Inc.; later, it linked up some of the television stations that it owned to help form the DuMont* network. In 1940, through a subsidiary company, Television Productions, Inc., Paramount opened two television stations, WBKB-Chicago and W6XYZ-Hollywood, California. The latter began broadcasting two nights a week on a regular basis on February 1, 1943, from Paramount Studios under the direction of Klaus Landsberg. In 1949, Paramount formed a network of five television stations to play kinescopes* produced by W6XYZ, which was now renamed KTLA, and had plans to extend the network to twenty-five outlets. KTLA was sold to Golden West Broadcasters* in 1965.

In 1957, Paramount announced plans to make its feature films available to television, and also to enter television production on a steady basis. In the seventies, Paramount produced or co-produced some of the most popular sitcoms* on television: *Happy Days* (ABC, 1974–1984), *Laverne & Shirley* (ABC, 1976–1983), *Taxi* (ABC, 1978–1982; NBC, 1982–1983), and *Mork & Mindy* (ABC, 1978–1982). The Paramount Television Group was created in 1983, succeeding Paramount Television and Paramount Television Distribution. Richard H. Frank, who had been with Paramount Television since 1977, headed the new division until 1985, when he was succeeded by Mel Harris.

In 1987, Paramount announced plans for a "fourth network" of syndicated television stations, to begin in spring 1988, but the idea was permanently postponed. The centerpiece of the new network's programming was to be *Star Trek: The Next Generation* (Syndicated, 1987-   ). In 1990, Paramount announced a new comedy production unit, Triangle Entertainment, headed by Glen and Les Charles, James Burrows, and Fran McConnell.

Address: 5555 Melrose Avenue, Hollywood, CA 90038.

PARK COMMUNICATIONS, INC. was formed in 1962 by Roy H. Park. It was incorporated in October 1971 as Park Broadcasting, Inc., and adopted the present name in August 1983. It controls forty daily newspapers, nineteen Sunday newspapers, eighty-nine non-daily newspapers, seventeen radio stations, and the following television stations: WBMG-Birmingham, Alabama; WNCT-Greenville, North Carolina; WDEF-Chattanooga; WJHL–Johnson City, Tennessee; WTVR-Richmond, Virginia; WSLS-Roanoke, Virginia; and WJKA-Wilmington, North Carolina.

Address: Box 500, Ithaca, NY 14851.

PAUL ALLEY PRODUCTIONS was a New York–based producer of television shows, commercials, and industrial films, founded in 1949 and active through 1958.

PBS (THE PUBLIC BROADCASTING SERVICE) was founded in 1969, as a successor to NET,* and answerable directly to the CPB.* An independent public television interconnection system, PBS was headed initially by James Loper of KCET–Los Angeles* as the chairman of its board. Loper resigned in 1973, and was succeeded by Ralph Rogers. A year earlier, PBS ceased to be subservient to the CPB, and was revamped in 1973 as a private membership organization of licensees of public television stations, responsible for the distribution and scheduling of programming but not its production. *Sesame Street* was the first program to be broadcast over the PBS network, followed in 1970 by *World Press, The Advocates, Mister Rogers' Neighborhood, Washington Week in Review*, and *The Great American Dream Machine*.

Aside from the PBS network, various PBS stations have formed their own regional networks, such as SECA (the Southern Educational Communications Association).* All public television stations must carry the PBS schedule of eight prime time hours of programming, Sundays through Wednesdays.

Addresses: 1320 Braddock Place, Alexandria, VA 22314–1698; 1790 Broadway, New York, NY 10019–1412; 4401 Sunset Boulevard, Suite 335, Los Angeles, CA 90027.

BIBLIOGRAPHY

Avery, Robert K., and Robert Pepper. *The Politics of Interconnection: A History of Public Television at the National Level*. Washington, D.C.: National Association of Educational Broadcasters, 1979.

Blakely, Robert J. *The People's Instrument: A Philosophy of Programming for Public Television*. Washington, D.C.: Public Affairs Press, 1971.

————. *To Serve the Public Interest: Educational Broadcasting in the United States*. Syracuse, N.Y.: Syracuse University Press, 1979.

Carey, John. *Telecommunications Technologies and Public Broadcasting*. Washington, D.C.: Corporation for Public Broadcasting, 1986.

Cater, Douglass, and Michael J. Nyhan, editors. *Public Television: Towards Higher Ground*. Palo Alto, Calif.: Aspen Institute Program on Communications and Society, 1975.

————, editors. *The Future of Public Broadcasting*. New York: Praeger, 1976.

Frank, Ronald E., and Marshall G. Greenberg. *Audiences for Public Television*. Beverly Hills, Calif.: Sage Publications, 1982.

Gibson, George H. *Public Broadcasting: The Role of the Federal Government, 1912–1976*. New York: Praeger, 1977.

Koughan, Martin, "The Fall and Rise of Public Television," *Channels of Communications*, vol. III, no. 1, May/June 1983, pp. 23–29, 40.

Macy, John, Jr. *To Irrigate a Wasteland: The Struggle To Shape a Public Television System in the United States*. Berkeley, Calif.: University of California Press, 1974.

Margulies, Lee, "PBS—What Price?" *Emmy*, vol. IV, no. 3, May/June 1982, pp. 17–19, 46.

Weber, Kathleen. *Public Television and Radio and State Governments*. Washington, D.C.: National Association of Public Television Stations, 1984.

THE PBS CHILDREN'S AND FAMILY CONSORTIUM is headed by WQED-Pittsburgh,* and includes KCET–Los Angeles,* KTCA–Minneapolis/ St. Paul, the South Carolina ETV Network, and WETA-Washington, D.C. It is responsible for the series *WonderWorks* (PBS, 1984–1990), and in December 1986 announced that it would co-produce films in association with The Disney Channel* for both the latter and PBS.*

PBS ENTERPRISES is a for-profit subsidiary, created in 1985 to search out sources of commercial income, and headed by Neil B. Mahrer. Its first venture was to join with IBM and Merrill Lynch in February 1985 in broadcasting stock quotations and financial news to subscribers with personal computers under the project title IMNET (International MarketNet).

PENNIES FROM HEAVEN LTD. is a company formed by producer Kenith Trodd and writer Dennis Potter (born 1935), and named after the highly popular 1978 BBC* television series written by the latter. The company produces programs and mini-series written by Potter, including *The Singing Detective* (1986) and *Cristabel* (1989).

Address: 82 Eastbourne Mews, London W2, United Kingdom.

PEOPLE METERS are similar in appearance to cable television boxes with remote control devices, and provide information not only as to what a viewer is watching, but also the type of viewers. They were introduced by the A.C. Nielsen Company* for the 1987–1988 television season, and were immediately popular with advertisers because they provided data as to what was being watched by whom; in other words, audience composition and demographics. They were not popular with the networks, and in July 1987, CBS* cancelled its use of Nielsen audience research data for the fall season. As of September 1, 1987, people meters became the sole source of national ratings data for A.C. Nielsen, replacing audimeters. Arbitron introduced its version of people meters for the 1988–1989 television season.

BIBLIOGRAPHY

Behrens, Steve, "People Meters' Upside," *Channels of Communications*, vol. VII, no. 5, May 1987, p. 19.

Boyer, Peter J., "TV Turning to People Meters To Find Who Watches What," *New York Times*, June 1, 1987, pp. 1, 16.

"Brother Nielsen Is Watching," *Time*, June 12, 1989, p. 61.

Carter, Bill, "TV Viewers Beware: Nielsen May Be Looking," *New York Times*, June 1, 1989, pp. A1, B3.

Gelman, Morrie, "Coming of People Meters Heralds Uneasy Autumn for TV Industry," *Daily Variety*, April 28, 1987, pp. 8, 15.

Hickey, Neil, "The Verdict—So Far—on People Meters," *TV Guide*, August 5, 1989, pp. 6–7.

Kanner, Bernice, "Now, People Meters," *New York*, May 19, 1986, pp. 16, 19, 20.

Richter, Paul, "Eyes Focus on 'People Meter' as It Gauges TV Viewing," *Los Angeles Times*, May 10, 1987, part IV, pp. 1, 6.

Sharbutt, Jay, "People Meters: Start of Something Big," *Los Angeles Times*, September 14, 1987, part VI, pp. 1, 7.

THE PEOPLE'S CHOICE was a New York–based pay-per-view cable channel, offering a variety of feature films to its 150,000 subscribers. It was launched on January 3, 1986, financed by MarketCorp Venture Associated, and headed by president Lee Eden.

PETER ARNELL PRODUCTIONS was a New York–based producer of game shows, active in the fifties. Among the series that the company created and produced were *The Name's the Same* (ABC, 1951–1955), *Wheel of Fortune* (CBS, 1952–1953), *Take a Guess* (CBS, 1953), *I'll Buy That* (CBS, 1953–1954), *What's in a Word* (CBS, 1954), *High Finance* (CBS, 1956), and *Chance for Romance* (ABC, 1958). A related company was IMPA Productions Ltd. (co-owned by Peter Arnell and Irving Mansfield).

PETER ELGAR PRODUCTIONS, INC., founded in 1953, was a New York–based producer, primarily of television commercials, active through the sixties.

PHILCO CORPORATION was a well-known manufacturer of television receivers, originally incorporated in 1892 in Pennsylvania as the Helios Electric Company. In 1959, it introduced the first battery-operated portable television receiver, the Philco Safari H–2010. In addition to the manufacture of television sets, Philco also operated W3XE-WPTZ in Philadelphia, one of nine active television stations in 1945. The company was acquired by the Ford Motor Co. on December 11, 1961.

PHONOVISION was a primitive system for recording television programs on discs (one for sound and one for the picture), developed in 1928 by John Logie Baird (1888–1946). The discs were intended for sale to viewers who could then play them back on Baird's Televisor. The system proved impractical.

PICTURE MUSIC INTERNATIONAL was founded in 1980 as EMI Music Video, with the name being changed in 1983 when the company became the music film and video division of EMI Music. It claimed to be the largest producer of music video programming in the world.

Address: 20 Manchester Square, London W1A 1ES, United Kingdom.

PIERRE COSSETTE PRODUCTIONS is best known for *The Grammy Awards*, the live telecasts of which it has produced since its inception in 1971. The company has also been responsible for the popular syndicated series *Sha Na Na* (1977–1981), as well as producing several syndicated series with well-known musical entertainers: *Sammy & Company*, with Sammy Davis, Jr. (1975–1976); *Andy*, with Andy Williams (1976); and *The Glen Campbell Music Show* (1982). A motion picture division, Pierre Cossette Films, was formed in 1987.

Address: 8899 Beverly Boulevard, Los Angeles, CA 90048.

BIBLIOGRAPHY

Mann, Arnold, "Innerviews: Flamboyant Pierre Cossette," *Emmy*, vol. VIII, no. 3, May/June 1986, pp. 13–17.

PINTOFF PRODUCTIONS was a New York–based company, specializing in animated television commercials, founded by Ernest Pintoff, and active in the sixties. In 1963, it became involved in the production of television programs and theatrical short subjects.

PLAUTUS PRODUCTIONS was a New York–based company, headed by Herbert Brodkin (1912–1990), which was acquired by Paramount in June 1963. Among the series for which it was responsible are *The Defenders* (CBS, 1961–1965), *The Doctors and the Nurses* (CBS, 1962–1965), *For the People* (CBS, 1965), and *Coronet Blue* (CBS, 1967).

THE PLAYBOY CHANNEL began in November 1982 as a joint venture of Playboy Enterprises, Cablevision, Daniels & Associates, and Cox Cable Communications. Initially headed by Paul Klein, it was a successor to the Escapade Channel, which Playboy had organized in association with Rainbow Programming Services Corp.* Broadcasting from 8:00 P.M. through 6:00 A.M., the Playboy Channel offered no hard-core pornography, but did claim, "We take the staples out of the centerfold." With only a half-million subscribers, it ceased to be a cable network as of December 1, 1989, and began offering programming on a pay-per-view basis.

Address: 8560 Sunset Boulevard, West Hollywood, CA 90069.

BIBLIOGRAPHY

Frankel, Mark, "Can Playboy Save Its Skin?" *Channels of Communications*, vol. VI, no. 7, November 1986, pp. 37–40.
Graham, Jefferson, "Playboy, Disney Pay Channels Most Likely To Survive Shake-Out," *The Hollywood Reporter*, May 16, 1983, p. 54.
Handler, David, "Now the Playmates Move—But Will America Pay To Watch?" *TV Guide*, June 25, 1983, pp. 45–48.
Stengel, Richard, "A Tale of a Bunny and a Mouse," *Time*, September 12, 1983, pp. 60, 62.

THE PLEASURE CHANNEL was the first adult film service offering X-rated films through satellite distribution to its subscribers, who needed to rent decoders to unscramble the signals. Launched on June 1, 1984, the Pleasure Channel was a Los Angeles–based company operated jointly by Norman Smith (who served as the channel's president) and Video Company of America (a distributor of adult videos).

BIBLIOGRAPHY

Bierbaum, Tom, "Pleasure Channel Takes to the Skies," *Daily Variety*, May 11, 1984, p. 6.

"PLUGOLA" was a word introduced in the fifties to describe on-camera use of a product on a television program. Such use "plugged" or advertised the item without the viewer being aware that this was taking place. Companies would usually offer payments to writers or directors for the promotion, unbeknown to the producers or the networks. A related term in the record industry is "payola."

POLARIS PICTURES, INC. (Juan C. Hutchinson, president) was a producer of television commercials, active in the early fifties, with offices in both New York and Los Angeles.

POLICE DRAMAS. The following is a listing of the more popular police dramas on American television: *Rocky King, Inside Detective* (DuMont, 1950–1954), *Racket Squad* (CBS, 1951–1953), *City Detective* (Syndicated, 1953–1954), *The Lineup* (CBS, 1954–1960), *Highway Patrol* (Syndicated, 1955–1959), *Sergeant Preston of the Yukon* (CBS, 1955–1958), *The Sheriff of Cochise* (Syndicated, 1956–1960), *State Trooper* (Syndicated, 1956–1959), *M Squad* (NBC, 1957–1960), *Policewoman Decoy* (Syndicated, 1957), *Naked City* (ABC, 1958–1963), *Manhunt* (Syndicated, 1959–1960), *The Untouchables* (ABC, 1959–1963), *Brenner* (CBS, 1959–1964), *The Lawless Years* (NBC, 1959–1961), *Burke's Law* (ABC, 1963–1966), *The F.B.I.* (ABC, 1965–1974), *Felony Squad* (ABC, 1966–1969), *Ironside* (NBC, 1967–1975), *Adam 12* (NBC, 1968–1975), *Hawaii Five-O* (CBS, 1968–1980), *The Mod Squad* (ABC, 1968–1973), *McCloud* (NBC, 1970–1977), *Columbo* (NBC, 1971–1977), *McMillan and Wife* (NBC, 1971–1977), *The Rookies* (ABC, 1972–1976), *The Streets of San Francisco* (ABC, 1972–1977), *Kojak* (CBS, 1973–1978), *Police Story* (NBC, 1973–1977), *Police Woman* (NBC, 1974–1978), *Baretta* (ABC, 1975–1978), *Starsky and Hutch* (ABC, 1975–1979), *Quincy, M.E.* (NBC, 1976–1987), *CHIPS* (NBC, 1977–1983), *240-Robert* (ABC, 1979–1981), *Hill Street Blues* (NBC, 1981–1987), *T.J. Hooker* (ABC, 1982–1985; CBS, 1985–1987), *Cagney & Lacey* (CBS, 1982–1989), *Hunter* (NBC, 1984-   ), *Downtown* (CBS, 1986–1987), *Crime Story* (NBC, 1986–1988), *21 Jump Street* (Fox, 1987-1990), *Hooperman* (ABC, 1987–1988), and *Jake and the Fatman* (CBS, 1987-   ).

POLICE WOMEN SERIES first came to prominence with the 1974 made-for-television movie *Get Christie Love!*, which introduced the series of the same name (ABC, 1974–1975), starring Teresa Graves. Also in 1974, Angie Dickinson began her series *Police Woman* (NBC, 1974–1978). A less serious view of women officers was provided by Suzanne Somers in *She's the Sheriff* (Syndicated, 1987).

The most widely publicized of all police women series was *Cagney & Lacey* (CBS, 1982–1989), starring Sharon Gless as Det. Chris Cagney and Tyne Daley as Det. Mary Beth Lacey, and created by Barney Rosenzweig in collaboration with Barbara Corday and Barbara Avedon. The role of Cagney was played initially, in 1982, by Meg Foster, but she was replaced after CBS network executives complained that the two leading actresses seemed too masculine and the characters might be perceived as "dykes" (a comment which, understandably, resulted in a storm of protests).

POLITICS AND TELEVISION. The political power of television was first demonstrated in 1952, when Dwight D. Eisenhower became the first presidential candidate to use television advertising, which was created by Rosser Reeves of the Ted Bates Agency, as part of his campaign. That same year, on September 23, 1952, Richard Nixon made his famous "Checkers" speech, in which he claimed that the only gift he had received and kept from his supporters was a small dog named Checkers. During September and October 1952, ABC* broadcast *Politics on Trial*, a courtroom-style debate, in which prominent members of the Republican or Democratic party would present their party's position on a major issue and defend it from attack.

On September 26, 1960, the first of the Richard Nixon–John F. Kennedy debates was televised; this was the first time that television had broadcast a presidential debate. Kennedy was the first president to permit live television coverage of his press conferences on a regular basis, but it was Eisenhower who had first allowed television cameras to cover a presidential press conference— on January 19, 1955.

The Nixon White House was openly hostile to the television media, and in November 1969, Vice President Spiro Agnew delivered a highly critical attack on broadcasters' attitudes toward the Nixon administration, which was written by Patrick Buchanan. Much of former president Nixon's feelings toward the media were reiterated in the 1977 syndicated series *The Nixon Interviews*, conducted by David Frost. Conservatives have long protested a left-wing balance in news reporting, which led in 1985 to Senator Jesse Helms' Fairness in Media* campaign.

All presidential inaugurations have been televised beginning with that of Harry S. Truman on January 20, 1949. Legislature granting all parties in an election equal time in broadcasting was enacted in 1927, and confirmed and amended with the Federal Election Campaign Act of 1971.

BIBLIOGRAPHY

Bishop, George F., editor. *The Presidential Debates: Media, Electoral, and Policy Perspectives.* New York: Praeger, 1979.

Blumler, Jay G., and Denis McQuail. *Television in Politics: Its Uses and Influences.* Chicago: University of Chicago Press, 1969.

Chester, Edward. *Radio, Television and American Politics.* New York: Sheed & Ward, 1969.

Gilbert, Robert E. *Television and Presidential Politics.* North Quincy, Mass.: Christopher, 1972.

Hofstetter, C. Richard. *Bias in the News: Network Television Coverage of the 1972 Election Campaign.* Columbus: Ohio State University Press, n.d.

Kraus, Sidney, editor. *The Great Debates: Background—Perspectives—Effects.* Bloomington: Indiana University Press, 1962.

Kraus, Sidney, and Dennis Davis. *The Effects of Mass Communication on Political Behavior.* University Park: Penn State University Press, 1976.

Lang, Kurt, and Gladys Engel Long. *Politics and Television.* Chicago: Quadrangle, 1968.

MacNeil, Robert. *The People Machine: The Influence of Television on American Politics.* New York: Harper & Row, 1968.

Mendelsohn, Harry, and Irving Crespi. *Polls, Television and the New Politics*. Scranton, Pa.: Chandler, 1970.

Michelson, Sig. *The Electric Mirror: Politics in an Age of Television*. New York: Dodd Mead, 1972.

Minow, Newton N. *Equal Time: The Private Broadcaster and the Public Interest*. New York: Atheneum, 1964.

Minow, Newton N., John Batlow Martin, and Lee M. Mitchell. *Presidential Television: A Twentieth Century Fund Report*. New York: Basic Books, 1973.

Mitchell, Lee M. *With the Nation Watching*. Lexington, Mass.: Lexington Books, 1979.

Patterson, Thomas E. *The Mass Media Election: How Americans Choose Their President*. New York: Praeger, 1980.

Patterson, Thomas E., and Robert D. McClure. *The Unseeing Eye: The Myth of Television Power in National Elections,* New York: Putnam, 1976.

Perry, Larry, and Barry Selvidge. *Perry's Broadcast Regulation Political Primer*. Knoxville, Tenn.: Perry, 1984.

Porter, William E. *Assault on the Media: The Nixon Years*. Ann Arbor: University of Michigan Press, 1976.

Ranney, Austin, editor. *The Past and Future of Presidential Debates*. Washington, D.C.: American Enterprise Institute, 1979.

Rowan, Ford. *Broadcast Fairness: Doctrine, Practice, Prospects: A Reappraisal of the Fairness Doctrine and Equal Time Rule*. New York: Longman, 1984.

Rubin, Bernard. *Political Television*. Belmont, Calif.: Wadsworth, 1967.

Spragens, William C. *The Presidency and the Mass Media in the Age of Television*. Washington, D.C.: University Press of America, 1978.

Thomson, Charles A.H. *Television and Presidential Politics: The Experience in 1952 and the Problems Ahead*. Washington, D.C.: Brookings Institute, 1956.

Tracey, Michael. *The Production of Political Television*. London: Routledge and Kegan Paul, 1978.

Whale, John. *The Half-Shut Eye: Television and Politics in Britain and America*. New York: St. Martin's Press, 1969.

Wilhelmsen, Frederick D., and Jane Bret. *Telepotics: The Politics of Neuronic Man*. Plattsburgh, N.Y.: Tundra Books, 1972.

PORTLAND PRODUCTIONS, INC. was the production company of actor James Mason and his wife Pamela, and was named after their daughter Portland. In the mid-fifties it was responsible for the syndicated series *The James Mason Show* (also known as *The Readers*), on which the Masons, together with Richard Burton, would read selections from the classics. In 1965, Pamela Mason had her own talk show, *The Pamela Mason Show*, syndicated by Spangler Films.

POST PICTURES CORP. Founded in 1936 by Harry A. Post, the New York–based Post Pictures Corp. was typical of the many companies in the fifties that discovered a new market in television for their minor feature films. Post offered thirteen films; six "Lum 'n' Abner" features, six "Scattergood Baines" features, and *Shadows of the Orient* (1937).

PREMIERE (U.K.) is a British all-movie cable channel, founded by Thorn EMI, which began broadcasting in September 1984. When Robert Maxwell acquired a controlling interest in the channel, he merged his MirrorVision film network (which was started in 1985) into Premiere on April 1, 1986.

See also TEN—THE ENTERTAINMENT NETWORK (U.K.)

Address: 7 Arblay Street, London W1V 2AD, United Kingdom.

PREMIERE (U.S.) was an abortive, pay-cable television service, created in 1980 by Columbia, Paramount, Universal, and 20th Century–Fox, with funding from the Getty Oil Company. Premiere was to have first access to productions from the four studios, and the two major competing cable networks, HBO* and Showtime,* would have to wait up to nine months before the films could be licensed for their use. However, the Justice Department conducted an investigation that led to a ruling, on December 31, 1980, that Premiere was in violation of the Sherman Anti-Trust Act.

THE PREVIEW CHANNEL, based in Los Angeles, was launched in April 1987 by nine cable system operators as a "video guide" for its subscribers, providing a sampling of programming available on the various cable networks.
BIBLIOGRAPHY
Ross, Chuck, "PreView Channel To Promote Cable," *The Hollywood Reporter*, November 17, 1986, p. 1.

PREVUE GUIDE CHANNEL is a cable television network, providing a system-specific programming promotion and listings service. First broadcast in January 1988, it is seen by 18.5 million subscribers, twenty-four hours a day.

Address: Prevue Networks, Inc., 3801 South Sheridan, Tulsa, OK 74145.

THE PRIME TIME ACCESS RULE, adopted by the FCC* to take effect in 1972, was intended to lessen network domination in the prime television hours, between 7:00 P.M. and 11:00 P.M. During that period, stations in the top fifty markets are prohibited from carrying more than three hours of network prime time programming. The additional hour was supposed to be used for community access programming and the presentation of new sources of programming by independent producers. Because news programs were excluded from the ruling, it was and is still possible for network news broadcasts to fill thirty minutes, and so, in reality, prime time access is limited to the period from 7:30 P.M. to 8:00 P.M. Unfortunately, instead of opening up a new market for independent creative productions, the Prime Time Access Rule has led to the programming of game shows and syndicated series between 7:00 P.M. and 8:00 P.M. each weeknight. One positive aspect has been the creation of the occasional progressive series, such as *The Muppet Show* (Syndicated, 1976–1981).
BIBLIOGRAPHY
Mandell, Abe, "Problems of Prime Time Access," *Television Quarterly*, vol. XV, no. 2, Summer 1978, pp. 69–70.

PRIME TIME SCHOOL TELEVISION was a Chicago-based non-profit organization, founded in 1971, which prepared and distributed materials on television programming to schools. The selected programming was considered to have educational value, and the project was funded by subscriptions, grants, and, in some cases, by underwriting from the featured programs.

BIBLIOGRAPHY
Margulies, Lee, "A Lesson Plan for the Tube," *Los Angeles Times*, April 7, 1977, part IV, p. 18.

PRIX ITALIA was created in 1948 by RAI* and the European Broadcasting Union to recognize quality television programming.

Address: Viale Mazzini 14, 00195 Rome, Italy.

PRIX JEUNESSE is an international award for children's programming given every two years since 1964 by the Prix Jeunesse Foundation. The latter was created by the state of Bavaria, the city of Munich, and the Bavarian Broadcasting Corporation.

Address: Bayerischer Rundfunk, Rundfunkplatz 1, D-8000 Munich 2, Germany.

PROCTER & GAMBLE PRODUCTIONS. As might be expected, the soap manufacturer Procter & Gamble is also the biggest producer of television soap operas.* Writing in *The Soap Opera Encyclopedia* (New York: Ballantine Books, 1985), Christopher Schemering commented, "Run much like the movie studios of the '30s and '40s, employing a stable of writers working at the peak of their powers and the most talented performers of the New York theater, Procter & Gamble's soap operas were conservative in content, strongly conceived and plotted, and immensely popular."

Among the company's productions are: *The First Hundred Years* (CBS, 1950–1952), *Search for Tomorrow* (CBS, 1951–1982; NBC, 1982-   ), *The Guiding Light* (CBS, 1952-   ), *The Brighter Day* (CBS, 1954–1962), *The Seeking Heart* (CBS, 1954), *Golden Windows* (NBC, 1954–1955), *The Road of Life* (CBS, 1954–1955), *As the World Turns* (CBS, 1956-   ), *The Edge of Night* (CBS, 1956–1975; ABC, 1975-   ), *From These Roots* (NBC, 1958–1961), *Today Is Ours* (NBC, 1958), *Young Dr. Malone* (NBC, 1958–1963), *Another World* (NBC, 1964-   ), *Somerset* (NBC, 1970–1976), *Lovers and Friends* (NBC, 1977), *For Richer, For Poorer* (NBC, 1977–1978), and *Texas* (NBC, 1980–1982).

Address: 9200 Sunset Boulevard, Suite 525, Los Angeles, CA 90069.

THE PRODUCERS & WRITERS, INC. was a New York–based producer of television programs and commercials, active from 1956 to 1957 and owned by actress Elissa Landi's brother, Anthony Z. Landi. In 1956, it produced at least one pilot for television, *Brother Mark* starring Richard Kiley, but a series did not materialize.

"PROJECT 120" was NBC's first involvement with made-for-television movies, a series of films produced by Universal and running 120 minutes including commercial breaks (hence the title). The series began on October 7, 1964, with *See How They Run.*
BIBLIOGRAPHY
Krampner, Jon, "In the Beginning . . . The Genesis of the Telefilm," *Emmy,* vol. XI, no. 6, November/December 1989, pp. 30–35.

"PROJECT PEACOCK" was the title given to NBC's prime time anthology series for children, headed by Edgar J. Scherick, which began broadcasting in February 1981.

A PSA (Public Service Announcement) is a television commercial of a noncommercial nature, usually promoting a charitable cause. PSAs are televised without charge by networks and independent stations, usually at times for which paid advertising has not been obtained.

PUBLIC ACCESS. Many cable systems provide public access to a selected channel on a first-come, first-served basis, either free or at cost. Such access permits individuals or groups to express both their opinions and their creativity. The FCC* made public access a mandatory element of cable franchise agreements in 1972, but the Supreme Court voided this ruling in 1979. The first national public-access satellite network is Deep Dish TV (339 Lafayette Street, New York, NY 10012).
BIBLIOGRAPHY
Beale, Lewis, "The Rights of the Far Right: Has Public Access Gone Too Far?" *Emmy,* vol. VIII, no. 2, March/April 1986, pp. 47–50.
Bretz, Rudy. *Handbook for Producing Educational and Public-Access Programs for Cable Television.* Englewood Cliffs, N.J.: Educational Technology Programs, 1976.
Brown, Ben, "Public Access: The Anybody Channel," *Channels of Communications,* vol. II, no. 4, November/December 1982, pp. 12–13.
Doty, Pamela, "Public Access: Community Blessing or Bloody Show?" *Television Quarterly,* vol. XIII, no. 2, May-July 1976, pp. 23–28.
Gillespie, Gilbert. *Public Access Cable Television in the United States and Canada.* New York: Praeger, 1975.
Kletter, Richard C. *Cable Television: Making Public Access Effective.* Santa Monica: Rand Corporation, 1973.
Othmer, David. *The Wired Island: The First Two Years of Public Access Cable Television in Manhattan.* New York: Fund for the City of New York, 1973.
Tate, Charles, editor. *Cable Television in the Cities: Community Control, Public Access, and Minority Ownership.* Washington, D.C.: Urban Institute, 1971.
Schmidt, Beno C. *Freedom of the Press vs. Public Access.* New York: Aspen/Praeger, 1976.

PUBLIC ARTS PRODUCTIONS was formed by writer/producer Roy Huggins in 1963, and remained active through 1980. During that time it produced a number of important television series, in association with Universal: *The Outsider* (NBC, 1968–1969), *The Lawyers* (NBC, 1969–1972), *The Protectors* (NBC, 1969–1970), *Toma* (ABC, 1973–1974), *The Rockford Files* (NBC, 1974–1980), *Baretta* (ABC, 1975–1978), *City of Angels* (NBC, 1976), and *Aspen* (NBC, 1977).

BIBLIOGRAPHY

Wheelock, Julie, "Roy Huggins: With Over 30 Years in the Business, He Has a Lot To Say," *Television & Families*, vol. XI, no. 4, Spring 1990, pp. 12–17.

THE PUBLIC BROADCAST LABORATORY (PBL) was created by former CBS* News president Fred W. Friendly to provide in-depth coverage of new events for the PBS* network. Headed by Avram (Av) Westin, with initial funding from the Ford Foundation,* PBL's first program, seen live on eighty-nine public television stations on November 5, 1967, dealt with the mayoral races in Boston, Cleveland, and Gary, Indiana. PBL also featured avant-garde plays, cultural events, and interviews; it ceased in 1969.

THE PUBLIC SERVICE SATELLITE CONSORTIUM was founded in 1975 to represent the interests of the various organizations and associations in the telecommunications field.

Address: 600 Maryland Avenue, S.W., Suite 220, Washington, DC 20024.

THE PUBLIC TELECOMMUNICATIONS FINANCIAL MANAGEMENT ASSOCIATION was founded in 1981, and is involved in the development and maintenance of financial management techniques for public television stations.

Address: P.O. Box 50008, Columbia, SC 29250.

PUPPETS. The use of puppets on television has not been limited to children's programming. The BBC* series *Spitting Image* caricatured prominent figures in politics and entertainment. It has been seen in the United States on Cinemax,* and was first seen on network television in a 1986 NBC* special, *Spitting Image: Down and Out at the White House*. The series also served as the basis for Sid and Marty Krofft's *DC Follies* (Syndicated, 1987–   ). Jim Henson's *The Muppet Show* (Syndicated, 1976–1981), while often programmed by local stations for children's viewing, was intended as much for an adult audience. Henson's puppets are also seen on the PBS series *Sesame Street*, and appeared on the first season of *Saturday Night Live* and elsewhere. A short-lived adult puppet series, syndicated in 1982, was *Madame's Place*, starring "Wayland Flowers" and "Madame."

The most popular of children's programming featuring puppets were *Howdy Doody* (NBC, 1947–1960), with Buffalo Bob Smith; *Kukla, Fran and Ollie* (NBC, 1948–1952; ABC, 1954–1957; NBC, 1961–1962; PBS, 1969–1971; Syndicated, 1975–1976), with Burr Tillstrom and Fran Allison; and *Time for Beany* (Syndicated, 1950–1953), with Bob Clampett. Other children's programming featuring puppets includes *Sparring Partners* (ABC, 1949), *The Adventures of Blinky* (Syndicated, 1952), *Johnny Jupiter* (DuMont, 1953), *Bobo the Hobo* (Syndicated, 1955), *Dusty's Treehouse* (Syndicated, 1971–1976), *Hot Fudge* (Syndicated, 1976–1980), *The New Howdy Doody Show* (Syndicated, 1976), *Rainbow Patch* (Syndicated, 1982), *Hugga Bunch* (Syndicated, 1984), *Kids-a-Littles* (Syndicated, 1984), and *Kids Incorporated* (Syndicated, 1985).

PUT is a television industry abbreviation for "persons using television," and is often cited in television audience-ratings reports.
     See also HUT.

PYRAMID PRODUCTIONS, INC. was a successor company to the companies of Bernard J. Prockter, who had been active as a producer of both live and filmed television programs in the early fifties. The new company, operated by Everett Rosenthal and in which Prockter was not associated, often put its name on Prockter's productions, such as *The Man behind the Badge* (Syndicated, 1954). Pyramid took over Prockter's production of *The Big Story* (NBC, 1949–1957) and did produce *Decoy* (Syndicated, 1957).

Q

QM PRODUCTIONS was formed in 1960 by Quinn Martin (1922–1987), and specialized in the production of police drama series for television. As the interest in the genre dwindled, so did the fortunes of the company. QM's best-known productions are *The Fugitive* (ABC, 1963–1967), *The FBI* (ABC, 1965–1974), *Dan August* (ABC, 1970–1971), *Streets of San Francisco* (ABC, 1972–1977), *Barnaby Jones* (CBS, 1973–1980), and *The Runaways* (NBC, 1978–1979).

In 1978, QM Productions was purchased from its founder by the company's president and chief operating officer, Merrill H. Karpf, and its vice-chairman and chief executive officer, Allan D. Yasni. A year later, the pair sold QM Productions to the Taft Broadcasting Co. for a reported $12 million. After Taft's acquisition of the company, QM Productions continued limited production with a made-for-television movie, *Airlift Berlin* (CBS, 1979), and other programming. It ceased operations as an independent unit in 1981. In the meantime, Martin had formed Quinn Martin Films in 1979 as a theatrical production company; he had already produced one major feature film, *The Mephisto Waltz*, in 1971.

BIBLIOGRAPHY

Berges, Marshall, "The Quinn Martins," *Los Angeles Times Home Magazine*, July 27, 1975, pp. 30–32.

Smith, Cecil, "Martin Drills in TV Woodwork," *Los Angeles Times Calendar*, November 6, 1974, pp. 1, 19.

Whitney, Dwight, "Sometimes He Just Sits in the Bathtub," *TV Guide*, October 23, 1965, pp. 24–27.

QUANTUM MEDIA, INC. was a company formed in January 1987, with funding from MCA, by Bob Pittman, who had largely been responsible for the creation of MTV.* The company was responsible for the outrageous talk program *The Morton Downy Jr. Show*.

BIBLIOGRAPHY
Ainslee, Peter, ''Wild Blue Bob,'' *Channels of Communications*, vol. VIII, no. 5, May
      1988, pp. 54–55.

QUBE is an interactive cable service, developed by Warner Cable, and first
tested in Columbus, Ohio, in 1977. The service permits viewers to participate
in games, opinion polls, and various tests, by way of special home terminals,
but it has never been cost-effective.

BIBLIOGRAPHY
Levy, Stephen, ''Speak Up, Columbus,'' *Panorama*, vol. II, no. 2, February 1981,
      pp. 56–59, 90, 98, 100.

QUINTET PRODUCTIONS was a company formed in the mid-fifties by actor
Russell Hayden to co-produce the 1955 syndicated series *Judge Roy Bean*.

QUIZ SHOWS. See GAME SHOWS

R

RADIO AND TELEVISION PACKAGERS, INC. has been involved in television distribution, and to a lesser extent production, since the fifties. It specializes in the distribution of children's programming, including cartoons, with one of its series releases being *Bill Clayton's Cartoon Classics* (Syndicated, 1967).

Address: 9 East 40 Street, New York, NY 10016.

RADIO-NEWSREEL-TELEVISION WORKING PRESS ASSOCIATION, INC. was a New York–based organization, promoting and protecting the professional interests of working newsmen and -women, and active in the sixties.

THE RADIO-TELEVISION CORRESPONDENTS ASSOCIATION was founded in 1938 as the Radio Correspondents Association, and is a professional organization for those assigned to cover Congress for the broadcast media.

Address: c/o Senate Radio-TV Gallery, U.S. Capitol, Room S–325, Washington, DC 20510.

THE RADIO-TELEVISION NEWS DIRECTORS ASSOCIATION (RTNDA) was founded in 1946 through the efforts of John Hogan, a Portland, Maine, news editor. It is a non-profit professional organization of more than 3,500 members, concerned with improving the quality of radio and television news.

Address: 1717 K Street, N.W., Suite 615, Washington, DC 20006.

RADIO TIMES provides information on all the BBC's* programming, both in radio and television, with supplemental articles relating to the week's broadcasting schedule. It was first published on September 28, 1923, to help shape the corporation's public image. *Radio Times* is available on microfilm from

Chadwyck-Healey Inc. (623 Martense Avenue, Teaneck, NJ 07666).
Address: 35 Marylebone High Street, London W1M 4AA, United Kingdom.

RAI (Radiotelevisione Italiana) is the state-run Italian broadcasting authority, administered by a parliamentary commission, which first began television broadcasts on January 1, 1954. Color transmissions commenced on February 1, 1977, and RAI operates three channels. A monopoly until the seventies, it is now in competition with a number of privately owned networks, notable among which are Canale–5, Italia–1, and Rete–4. RAI is also involved in film production through SACIS (Societa' per Axioni Commerciale Iniziative Spettacolo).
Address: Viale Mazzini 14, 00915 Rome, Italy.

RAINBOW PROGRAMMING SERVICES CORP. is a cable distribution network founded in the summer of 1980 as a consortium of four cable companies—Cablevision, Comcast Corp., Cox Cable Communications, and Daniels & Associates—headed by Jerry Maglio. Currently responsible for American Movie Classics,* Bravo! (U.S.),* and SportsChannel America,* Rainbow's original cable networks were Escapade (introduced October 28, 1980), Bravo! (U.S.) (introduced October 26, 1980), and Sneak Preview (introduced October 26, 1980; the first movie offered to viewers was *Being There*). In 1986, Rainbow was split into two divisions, a National Services Division (to run American Movie Classics and Bravo! [U.S.]), headed by John A. Janas, and a Regional Division (to run three regional sports networks and Prism, the Philadelphia-based sports and entertainment service), headed by Jack Williams.
Address: 120 Crossways Park West, Woodbury, NY 11797.
BIBLIOGRAPHY
Gelman, Morrie, "Cox Cable Added Partner in New Rainbow Venture," *Daily Variety*, August 5, 1980, pp. 1, 8, 9.

RALPH EDWARDS PRODUCTIONS is one of the more familiar names in television production. Founded in 1940 by former radio announcer Ralph Edwards (born 1913), the company was operated as a sole proprietorship until February 15, 1957, when it was incorporated as Aquarius Productions, Inc. However, it was still generally known as Ralph Edwards Productions, but usually, from 1952 to 1977, new corporations were formed by Edwards and his wife to serve as production entities for his various television series.

The following series were produced by the company prior to 1977: *Truth or Consequences* (CBS, 1950–1951; NBC, 1954–1965; Syndicated, 1966–1974, 1977–1978, 1987), *This Is Your Life* (NBC, 1952–1961; Syndicated, 1971–1972, 1983), *Place the Face* (NBC, 1953; CBS, 1953; NBC, 1954–1955), *Funnyboners* (NBC, 1954–1955), *It Could Be You* (NBC, 1956–1961), *The End of the Rainbow* (NBC, 1958), *About Faces* (ABC, 1960–1961), *The Wide Country* (NBC, 1962–1963), *Who in the World* (CBS, 1962), *The Woody Woodbury Show* (Syndicated, 1967–1968), *Name That Tune* (NBC, 1974–1975, 1977;

Syndicated, 1974–1981), *The Cross-Wits* (Syndicated, 1975–1981), and *Knock-out* (NBC, 1977–1978).

On July 31, 1978, all the corporations owned or controlled by Ralph Edwards and his wife were merged into Aquarius, and the resultant corporation was officially renamed Ralph Edwards Productions. On July 16, 1979, the company entered into an agreement with Stu Billett Productions,* and developed a new television series, *The People's Court* (Syndicated, 1981-). On January 1, 1987, a new company, Ralph Edwards/Stu Billett Productions was created between Ralph Edwards Productions and Stu Billet's S.C.B. Productions, Inc. It has produced *Superior Court* (Syndicated, 1986-), *The New Truth or Consequences* (Syndicated, 1987), and *Family Medical Center* (Syndicated, 1988–1989).

Address: 1717 North Highland Avenue, Suite 1018, Hollywood, CA 90028.

RANKIN/BASS PRODUCTIONS has been a familiar name in television animation for many years. Headed by Arthur Rankin, Jr., and Jules Bass, the company pioneered stop-motion puppet animation for television, calling it Animagic, and beginning with *The Ballad of Smokey the Bear* (NBC, 1964). Rankin/Bass produced the most popular animated puppet film of all time, *Rudolph, the Red-Nosed Reindeer*, first seen on NBC* on December 6, 1964. Other productions include *The New Adventures of Pinocchio* (Syndicated, 1961), *Tales of the Wizard of Oz* (Syndicated, 1961), *The Hobbit* (NBC, 1977), and *The Wind in the Willows* (NBC, 1983).

Address: 1 East 53 Street, New York, NY 10022.

RCA (Radio Corporation of America), initially headed by Owen D. Young, was created as a subsidiary of General Electric in November 1919, to handle the assets of the American Marconi Company. Additional investors in the company included AT&T and Westinghouse,* which, together with General Electric, sold their stock holdings in 1932, as a result of a government antitrust suit. Two years earlier, David Sarnoff (1891–1971), who had been associated with Marconi as early as 1912, became president of RCA. (He became chairman of the board, succeeding James G. Harbord, in 1947, a position that he held until his death, and was chief executive officer from 1947 to 1966.)

In February 1925, Sarnoff had proposed that a new company be formed to run the radio stations owned by RCA, General Electric, Westinghouse, and AT&T; the outcome was NBC,* formed in September 1926. NBC had two networks, the Red, based on the AT&T chain of stations, and the Blue, based on those of RCA.

In 1927, RCA merged with the Victor Talking Machine Company (which became the RCA Victor Division), and two years later created RKO Radio Pictures. By 1928, it had three experimental television stations, W2XBS–New York, W2XBU–New York, and W2XBW–Bound Brook, New Jersey. In March 1923, the company paid $500,000 for the assets of the De Forest Radio Company.

Following successful testing of the iconoscope and kinescope* picture tubes, RCA announced its intention in May 1935 to invest $1 million in the development of a complete television system. Vladimir Zworykin headed the company's television research division, which had been created as a separate unit in Camden, New Jersey, in 1929.

Because of recognized patents claims by Philo T. Farnsworth, RCA was required to sign a non-exclusive, cross-licensing arrangement with Farnsworth Television and Radio* in 1939. It had already commenced building television receivers, and, in 1940, helped to increase interest in the medium by reducing the cost of its receivers by one-third.

During World War II, Sarnoff served as General Dwight D. Eisenhower's Communications Consultant. On March 18, 1946, RCA was awarded the Medal for Merit in recognition of its services to the nation between October 1942 and March 1944. Following the war, Sarnoff became increasingly interested in his company's potential for aiding the government through communications technology. In 1955, Senator Lyndon B. Johnson called RCA, "a key element in our defense structure."

Nineteen sixty-six was a year of diversification for the company. In March, it acquired the publishing company of Random House, and in October, the Hertz Corporation.

Financial losses by RCA in the seventies resulted in its 1981 profits dropping 83 percent. In December 1985, the company of which RCA had once been a subsidiary, General Electric Co., purchased it (and its subsidiary, NBC) for $6.28 billion. (General Electric had been founded by Thomas Alva Edison in 1878 as Edison Electric Light.) General Electric chairman John F. Welch, Jr. (who had held the position since 1951) negotiated the takeover with RCA chairman Thornton F. Bradshaw. The acquisition was approved by the FCC* in June 1986.

Address: 3135 Easton Turnpike, Fairfield, CT 06431.

BIBLIOGRAPHY

Alexander, Charles P., "A Reunion of Technological Titans," *Time*, December 23, 1985, pp. 48–49.

Bilby, Kenneth. *The General: David Sarnoff and the Rise of the Communications Industry*. New York: Harper and Row, 1986.

Byron, Christopher, "His Master's New Voice," *Time*, January 18, 1982, p. 49.

Dreher, Carl. *Sarnoff: An American Success*. New York: Quadrangle, 1977.

Lyons, Eugene. *David Sarnoff*. New York: Harper and Row, 1966.

Sarnoff, David. *Looking Ahead: The Papers of David Sarnoff*. New York: McGraw-Hill, 1968.

Tebbel, John. *David Sarnoff: Putting Electrons To Work*. New York: Encyclopaedia Press, 1963.

RCA SATCOM was a twenty-four-channel domestic communications satellite (DOMSAT*) launched in December 1975; *SATCOM 2* was launched in 1976 and *SATCOM 3* in 1982.

REDE GLOBO/GLOBO NETWORK is based in Brazil and is the world's fourth largest television network, seen in over ninety countries by satellite. Headed by Roberto Marinho, who publishes *O Globo* newspaper and heads a radio network and a foundation bearing his name, Rede Globo first went on the air in 1965.

Address: Rua Lopes Quintas 303, Jardim Botanico, Rio de Janeiro, Brazil.

BIBLIOGRAPHY

Henstell, Bruce, "Rede Globo," *Emmy*, vol. VI, no. 1, January/February 1984, pp. 41–42.

REEMACK ENTERPRISES, INC. was a New York–based company, owned by Ted Mack and Lou Goldberg, and responsible for the production of *The Original Amateur Hour* (DuMont, 1948–1949; NBC, 1949–1954; ABC, 1955–1957; NBC, 1957–1958; CBS, 1959; ABC, 1960), hosted by Mack.

REEVES COMMUNICATIONS CORP., a major company primarily involved in postproduction work, was founded in 1933 by Hazard E. Reeves (born 1906) as Reeves Sound Studios, Inc. Reeves, who was also the co-founder and the first president of Cinerama, Inc. (in 1947), later created Reeves Industries, Inc., in 1946. The latter became a division of Reeves Broadcasting & Development Corporation, organized in 1960. One of that corporation's divisions was Reeves Production Service, which advertised itself in 1970 as "the largest independent video and sound services facilities in the world." A subsidiary company, Reeves Entertainment Group (REG), was founded in 1985, and it took over responsibility for the production of *Gimme a Break* (NBC, 1981–1987), *Kate & Allie* (CBS, 1984–1990), and *I Married Dora* (ABC, 1987). REG was headed by Merrill T. Grant (born 1932), who was appointed president and chief executive officer of Reeves Communications Corp. in January 1988. (Grant had joined Reeves in 1979 as president of yet another subsidiary, Grant-Reeves Entertainment.)

Initially a New York–based company, Reeves has since opened production facilities in Los Angeles. On January 17, 1990, it was acquired by Thames (USA) Inc., a subsidiary of Thames Television plc.*

Addresses: 708 Third Avenue, 8th Floor, New York, NY 10017; 3500 West Olive Avenue, Suite 500, Burbank, CA 91505.

REGAL TELEVISION PICTURES CORP. was a New York–based distributor of feature films and short subjects to television, active in the fifties, and founded by Moe Kerman, who had entered the film industry in 1915.

RELIGIOUS PROGRAMMING. Billy Graham pioneered the use of television in the packaging of his religious crusades in 1951, a year after he had started regular radio broadcasts. Graham helped pave the way for the "televangelists" who were to follow, among whose number are Oral Roberts, Rex Humbard, Jimmy Lee Swaggart, Robert Schuller, Jerry Falwell, Jim and Tammy Faye

Bakker, Pat Robertson, Kathryn Kuhlman, Ernest Angley, James Robison, Terry Cole-Whittaker, Dr. Gene Scott, and Paul and Jan Crouch.

On February 12, 1952, Bishop Fulton J. Sheen began broadcasting his thirty-minute series *Life Is Worth Living* on the DuMont* network. The program was seen on DuMont, and later ABC,* until 1957, and revived from 1961 to 1968 on ABC as *The Bishop Sheen Program*. With his opening words, "Friends, thank you for allowing me to come into your home," Bishop Sheen became a popular figure on television, providing stiff competition to comedian Milton Berle, whose program aired opposite Sheen on NBC.* "We're both using old material," commented the comedian. On January 21, 1979, CBS* discontinued two of its best-known, establishment-style religious programs, *Look Up* (first broadcast on January 3, 1954) and *Lamp unto My Feet* (first broadcast on November 21, 1948).

Religious broadcasters formed the National Religious Broadcasters Association in Columbus, Ohio, in April 1944. Disturbed by television evangelism, Billy Graham created the Evangelical Council for Financial Accountability in 1979, but none of television's top evangelists are members of the group, and all are in breach of its code of ethics. Jerry Falwell created the Moral Majority in 1979 as an outreach of his television preaching, and in December 1980 announced that the organization would monitor television shows and boycott sponsors of morally offensive programming. In reaction to the Moral Majority, producer Norman Lear, in association with others, formed People for the American Way, with an avowed purpose of opposing the political-religious activities of Falwell and Pat Robertson.

BIBLIOGRAPHY

Armstrong, Ben, and M. Lay Vay Sheldon. *Religious Broadcasting Source Book*. Morristown, N.J.: National Religious Broadcasters, 1976.

Bachman, John W. *Media: Wasteland or Wonderland*. Minneapolis: Augsburg, 1984.

Bleum, A. William. *Religious Television Programs: A Study in Relevance*. New York: Hastings House, 1968.

Diamond, Edwin, "God's Television," *American Film*, vol. V, no. 5, March 1980, pp. 30–35.

Gorfain, Louis, "Pray TV," *New York*, October 6, 1980, pp. 47–57.

Hadden, Jeffrey K., and Anson Shupe. *Televangelism: Power and Politics on God's Frontier*. New York: Henry Holt, 1988.

Hill, George H. *Airwaves to the Soul: The Influence and Growth of Religious Broadcasting in America*. Saratoga, Calif.: R and E, 1983.

Hill, George H., and Lenwood Davis. *Religious Broadcasting, 1920–1983: A Selectively Annotated Bibliography*. New York: Garland, 1984.

Horsfield, Peter G. *Religious Television: The American Experience*. New York: Longman, 1984.

Martz, Larry, with Ginny Carroll. *Ministry of Greed*. New York: Newsweek/Weidenfeld & Nicholson, 1988.

Oberdorfer, Donald N. *Electronic Christianity: Myth or Ministry*. Taylor Falls, Minn.: John L. Brekke and Sons, 1982.

Ostling, Richard N., "Power, Glory and Politics," *Time*, February 17, 1986, pp. 62–69.

————, "Enterprising Evangelism," *Time*, August 3, 1987, pp. 50–53.

"Stars of the Cathode Church," *Time*, February 4, 1980, pp. 64–65.

Van Horne, Harriet, "The Bishop versus Berle," *Theatre Arts*, December 1952, pp. 65, 95.

REQUEST TELEVISION is a pay-per-view cable network, offering an average of ten first-run feature films and special events a month to its 6 million subscribers (as of 1990). Boasting the participation of all the major Hollywood studios, Request was launched in November 1985, and utilizes "impulse ordering," which is available to subscribers by dialing a telephone number just prior to the airing of the desired film. A second network, Request 2, offering fifteen feature films a month, was introduced in July 1988.

Address: 685 Third Avenue, 20th Floor, New York, NY 10017.

BIBLIOGRAPHY

"Request TV Eyes Impulse PPV Rise," *The Hollywood Reporter*, April 2, 1987, pp. 1, 21.

RESIDUALS. Actors receive residual payments for appearances in all television programming made from 1952 onward, and for appearances in all feature films made from 1960 onward and broadcast on television. Sometimes, actors "sell" their potential residuals to a show's producer. For example, in 1961, Milburn Stone and Dennis Weaver sold their residuals interest in all the thirty-minute episodes of *Gunsmoke* for $250,000 and $400,000, respectively.

BIBLIOGRAPHY

Henderson, Bruce, "How Residual Checks Surprise Actors," *TV Guide*, December 22, 1979, p. 3.

Nassif, Fred, "How Do Those Residuals Work?" *Television Quarterly*, vol. XII, no. 1, Fall 1974, pp. 45–49.

Whitney, Dwight, "So Who Counts?" *TV Guide*, April 30, 1966, pp. 23–25.

RETLAW ENTERPRISES, INC. was formed in 1953 by Walt Disney—the company's name is Walter spelled backwards—to provide his family with income from the various activities of the Walt Disney Company. The company was formerly known as WED Enterprises and Walt Disney, Inc. In 1982, the company surrendered most of its assets, including the rights to the Disney name, to the Walt Disney Company. Retlaw continues to hold real estate investments and, through the Retlaw Broadcasting Co., owns six television stations: KJEO-Fresno, California; KMST-Monterey, California; KIDK–Idaho Falls, Idaho; KLEW-Lewiston, Idaho; KEPR-Pasco, Washington; and KIMA-Yakima, Washington.

Address: Box 5455, Fresno, CA 93755.

BIBLIOGRAPHY

Peltz, James F., "Retlaw is Quietest of Disney's Offspring," *Los Angeles Times*, October 2, 1990, pp. D9A, D9C.

REVUE PRODUCTIONS, INC. was the television division of the MCA Talent Agency, formed in 1950, with production facilities on the Republic Studios lot. The revenues from Revue helped MCA in its 1959 acquisition of Universal. In 1964, Revue was renamed Universal Television, but its syndication arm, MCA Television Limited, continued under that name. Universal Television began production of made-for-television movies in 1964, and made its first mini-series, *Rich Man, Poor Man*, in 1976.

Among the series produced by Revue are *General Electric Theatre* (CBS, 1953–1962), *The Ray Milland Show* (CBS, 1954–1955), *Wagon Train* (NBC, 1957–1962; ABC, 1962–1965), *The Deputy* (NBC, 1959–1961), and *Laramie* (NBC, 1959–1963).

BIBLIOGRAPHY

Perry, Jeb H. *Universal Television: The Studio and Its Programs, 1950–1980*. Metuchen, N.J.: Scarecrow Press, 1983.

RICHARD M. FALK ASSOCIATES was a New York–based producer, primarily of television commercials, active from the fifties through the mid-seventies.

"ROADBLOCKING" is the name given to the practice of airing a program or commercial simultaneously on all three networks, with the idea being to eliminate program choice. It was first used to advantage during the 1972 presidential campaign.

THE ROBERT E. SHERWOOD AWARDS, named for the playwright (1896–1955) were presented in the mid- to late fifties by the Fund for the Republic for best network drama, best network documentary, and best production of either type by an independent television station which "increase[s] public understanding of the principles set down in the Constitution and the Bill of Rights." The Fund for the Republic ceased to exist in 1981, when it was merged into what became the Center for Democratic Institutions. In 1953, Sherwood was signed to a three-year, nine-play contract by NBC.* His first play under that contract was *The Backbone of America*, broadcast in December 1953.

ROBERT MAXWELL & ASSOCIATES, utilizing rental space on the Samuel Goldwyn Studios lot, was responsible for the production of *Lassie* (CBS, 1954–1955) and *Cannonball* (Syndicated, 1958).

ROCKET PICTURES, INC., operated by J. Richard Westen, was a Los Angeles–based producer of films and television programming, active from the fifties through the mid-seventies.

ROCKHILL PRODUCTIONS, operated by Stanley J. Wolf, was a New York–based producer and packager of television and radio programming, active from the fifties through the mid-seventies.

ROGO was co-founded by Norman Rosemont (born 1924) and Robert Goulet (born 1933) to produce television versions of Broadway musicals, all starring Goulet and all seen on ABC*: *Brigadoon* (1966), *Carousel* (1967), *Kismet* (1967), and *Kiss Me Kate* (1968).

RONALD DAWSON ASSOCIATES was a New York–based producer, active in the fifties.

RONCOM PRODUCTIONS, INC. was established in 1958 by entertainer Perry Como (born 1912) and named for his son Ronald. It produced the one-hour version of *The Perry Como Show* (NBC, 1959–1963) and the show's two summer replacement series, *Tate* (NBC, 1960) and *Happy* (NBC, 1960–1961), and co-produced *Run for Your Life* (NBC, 1965–1968), in association with Universal.

Address: 305 Northern Boulevard, Great Neck, Long Island, NY 11021.

RORABAUGH TV REPORT was published in the fifties by the N.C. Rorabaugh Co. to provide data on what programs television advertisers were sponsoring and with how much money.

ROSAMOND PRODUCTIONS, INC. was a Los Angeles–based producer of television programming, named by David Chudnow for his wife, Rosamond, and active from the fifties through the mid-seventies.

ROSEMONT PRODUCTIONS, LTD. is a prolific producer of movies made for television, founded in 1972 by Norman Rosemont (born 1924). Its first production was *Man without a Country* (ABC, 1973). Other productions include: *Miracle on 34th Street* (CBS, 1973), *A Tree Grows in Brooklyn* (NBC, 1974), *The Red Badge of Courage* (NBC, 1974), *The Count of Monte Cristo* (NBC, 1975), *All Quiet on the Western Front* (CBS, 1979), *Little Lord Fauntleroy* (CBS, 1980), *Witness for the Prosecution* (CBS, 1982), *The Secret Garden* (CBS, 1987), and *The Tenth Man* (CBS, 1988).

Address: 100 Universal City Plaza, Bungalow 73, Universal City, CA 91608.
BIBLIOGRAPHY
Mann, Arnold, "Norman Rosemont's Classic Struggle for Quality," *Emmy*, vol. XI, no. 5, October 1989, pp. 20–21.

THE ROYAL TELEVISION SOCIETY was formed on September 7, 1927, and was granted its royal title in 1966. The only British society devoted exclusively to television, with members from all areas of the industry, it organizes lectures and training courses, makes awards, and publishes *Television** and *Talkback*.

Address: Tavistock House East, Tavistock Square, London WC1H 9HR, United Kingdom.

ROYALTY. HRH the Duchess of Kent was the first member of the British Royal Family to be seen on television—on the Baird system in 1935. The coronation of King George VI on May 12, 1937, was televised, and he and Queen Elizabeth were televised from the New York World's Fair* on June 10, 1939 (making them the first members of the British royal family to be seen on American television). The annual Christmas event of the Queen's Speech was first televised on December 25, 1957. The largest television audience for a royal event was for the wedding of Prince Charles and Lady Diana Spencer on July 29, 1981, which was seen by some 750 million viewers worldwide.

BIBLIOGRAPHY

"Royalty," in *The Guinness Book of TV Facts and Feats*, editor Kenneth Passingham. Enfield, Middlesex, U.K.: Guinness, 1984, pp. 121–131.

RTBF (Radio Télévision Belge de la Communauté Française) is the French-speaking Belgian television company, which (along with BRT*) began broadcasting in October 1953 as a division of the National Institute of Radio. In 1960, it became an independent public broadcasting service; color was introduced in 1971, and a second channel became operational in 1977. RTBF is administered by a board of directors appointed by the French Cultural Community Council, and it is financed through license fees paid to the Belgian government. It does not carry advertising. The structure of the system is governed by a decree dated December 12, 1979.

Address: Boulevard Reyers 52, 1040 Brussels, Belgium.

RTE (Radio Telefis Eireann) is the national television and radio broadcasting authority for the Republic of Ireland. Radio broadcasting began on a regular basis in the Republic on January 1, 1926, and until 1966, the authority was known simply as Radio Eireann. Television broadcasting began on December 31, 1966, as a result of the passage of the Broadcasting Authority Act in April 1960. A second television channel was introduced by RTE in 1978. Television and radio broadcasting, 10 percent of which is in the Irish language, with the remaining portion in English, is financed through license fees paid for the use of television and radio receivers, and from advertising revenue.

In 1966, RTE founded the Golden Harp TV Festival, which takes place in Dublin each summer.

Address: Donnybrook, Dublin 4, Eire.

BIBLIOGRAPHY

Dowling, Jack, Lelia Doolan, and Bob Quinn. *Sit Down and Be Counted: The Cultural Evolution of a Television Station*. Dublin: Wellington, 1969.

Fisher, Desmond. *Broadcasting in Ireland*. Boston: Routledge and Kegan Paul, 1978.

Gorham, Maurice. *Forty Years of Irish Broadcasting*. Dublin: The Talbot Press, 1967.

McLoone, Martin and John MacMahon, editors. *Television and Irish Society: 21 Years of Irish Television*. Dublin: RTE/IFI, 1984.

Sheehan, Helena. *Irish Television Drama: A Society and Its Stories*. Dublin: RTE, 1987.

RUBY-SPEARS PRODUCTIONS, INC. is a producer of animated television programming formed in 1977 by Joseph Ruby and Kenneth Spears, both of whom had been active with Hanna-Barbera, where they had created the character of "Jabberjaw." A wholly owned subsidiary of Filmways, Inc.,* Ruby-Spears began production in January 1978. It was acquired by Taft Broadcasting in 1981.

Address: 3330 Cahuenga Boulevard, Hollywood, CA 90068.

S

SABAN ENTERTAINMENT was formed in 1980 by Haim Saban, who had commenced his career as a band manager in Israel and later became a record producer in France. The company gained a reputation for the production of various children's programs for television, and in 1989 embarked on plans to produce TV movies and mini-series in association with Edgar J. Scherick.

Address: 4000 West Alameda, 5th Floor, Burbank, CA 91505.

BIBLIOGRAPHY

Lowry, Brian, "Saban Shakes Hands across the Sea," *Daily Variety*, February 2, 1990, pp. 1, 30.

SACK TELEVISION ENTERPRISES was a New York–based producer and distributor to television of 29 features and 150 short subjects, founded in 1948 by the brothers Julius and Alfred N. Sack, and active through 1957. The company was the television arm of Sack Amusement Enterprises, founded in 1919 by Alfred N. Sack (born 1898).

ST. CLARE OF ASSISI was proclaimed Patron Saint of Television by Pope John XXIII in February 1959. A thirteenth-century nun, she claimed to have seen a vision of a church service taking place several miles away, which the Pope likened to the modern miracle of television.

SANDY FRANK ENTERTAINMENT, INC., the umbrella company for Sandy Frank Film Syndication, Inc. and Sandy Frank Productions, Inc., is claimed by its founder to be "the oldest independent distributor in the business and, in fact, perhaps the first truly independent distributor." Sandy Frank (born 1933) entered the television industry in 1951. He formed his own company in 1964, and began distribution of a wide range of black-and-white television programming for syndication. In 1971, the company distributed, in syndication, its first off-network color series, *The Bill Cosby Show* (NBC, 1969–1971). A year later, it embarked on a major syndicated distribution project with *The Parent Game* (1972), *The Dating Game* (1973), and *Treasure Hunt* (1974–1977).

In 1974, it acquired the rights to two former network series, *Stop the Music* and *Name That Tune*, and entered into a co-production arrangement for new series of those titles with Ralph Edwards Productions.* Additional series co-produced and distributed by Sandy Frank include *The Bobby Vinton Show* (1975–1976), *Battle of the Planets* (1978), *Face the Music* (1980), *The Judge* (1986-   ), and *$200,000 Name That Tune* (1989).

Address: 645 Madison Avenue, New York, NY 10022.

BIBLIOGRAPHY

"The Living Legend of Sandy Frank," *Broadcasting,* December 10, 1979, p. 129.

SAPPHIRE FILMS, LTD. was responsible for virtually all the filmed costume dramas seen on American television. Based at the Walton Studios in the English county of Surrey, the company, under the supervision of its executive producer, Hannah Weinstein, produced *The Adventures of Robin Hood* (CBS, 1955–1958), *The Adventures of Sir Lancelot* (NBC, 1956–1957), *The Buccaneers* (CBS, 1956–1957), and *Sword of Freedom* (Syndicated, 1957).

THE SATELLITE BROADCASTING AND COMMUNICATIONS AS-SOCIATION is made up of individuals and companies involved in the satellite earth-stations industry, and promotes public interest in satellite communications. It was formed in 1986 with the merger of the Direct Broadcast Satellite Association (founded 1983), the Satellite Television Industry Association (founded 1980), and the Society for Private and Commercial Earth Stations (founded 1985).

Address: c/o 300 North Washington Street, Suite 208, Alexandria, VA 22314.

THE SATELLITE EDUCATIONAL RESOURCES CONSORTIUM or SERC (pronounced ser-see) was created by SECA (The Southern Educational Communications Association)* with a pilot semester in the spring of 1989. It provides for-credit courses, via satellite television, to high school students for whom such courses would otherwise be unavailable. It is a partnership of state departments of education and state public television networks (with twenty states participating as of 1990).

Address: P.O. Box 50008, Columbia, SC 29250.

SATELLITE MASTER ANTENNA TELEVISION (SMATV) utilizes a central antenna to pick up broadcast or satellite signals for a group of television receivers in an apartment building, hotel, or similar facility. It first gained popularity in the early eighties.

BIBLIOGRAPHY

Howard, Herbert H., and Sidney L. Carroll. *SMATV: Strategic Opportunities in Private Cable*. Washington, D.C.: National Association of Broadcasters, 1982.

————. *SMATV: Changing Environment for Private Cable*. Washington, D.C.: National Association of Broadcasters, 1984.

Nadel, Mark, and Eli Noam, editors. *The Economics of Satellite Master Antenna Television (SMATV): An Anthology*. New York: Columbia University Graduate School of Business, 1983.

THE SATELLITE NEWS CHANNEL (SNC) was a basic cable network, providing twenty-four hour a day news programming for an initial audience of 2.6 million. Headed by S. William Scott, SNC was a joint venture of ABC* and Westinghouse,* and was advertiser-supported. It began broadcasting on June 21, 1982, and the honor of flipping the control panel switch that put SNC on the air went to eighty-six-year-old Leo Rosenberg, who had been the news reader at KDKA-Pittsburgh in 1920. Despite heavy losses—more than $40 million in 1983—SNC announced plans for a second channel to begin in the spring of 1983. However, on October 12, 1983, SNC was acquired by Ted Turner for $25 million in cash. At the end of the month he closed the network down, thus removing competition for his own CNN.*

BIBLIOGRAPHY

Brewin, Bob, "The 18-Minute Hour," *Village Voice*, July 26, 1983, pp. 24–25.

————, "Turner vs. SNC: Still at It," *Village Voice*, October 11, 1983, p. 26.

"Sole Survivor," *Time*, October 24, 1983, p. 70.

Waters, Harry F., and Neal Karlen, "Has CNN Met Its Match?" *Newsweek*, June 28, 1982, p. 53.

SCANDINAVIAN-AMERICAN PRODUCTIONS was responsible for the 1954 syndicated series *The Amazing Tales of Hans Christian Andersen*, hosted by the popular European entertainers George and Gene Bernard.

SCHWERIN RESEARCH CORPORATION was founded in 1946 by Horace S. Schwerin (born 1914). It specialized in pre-testing commercials and new programming ideas for radio and television at a research theatre in New York. As of 1953, the company claimed to have conducted 1,400 tests, each consisting of approximately two hours of programming. The company was sold in 1968 to Research Systems Corporation.

BIBLIOGRAPHY

"They Say It Again and Again," *TV Guide*, November 13, 1953, pp. 18–19.

SCIENCE FICTION. The following is a listing of the more popular science fiction series on American television: *Buck Rogers* (ABC, 1950–1951), *Tom Corbett, Space Cadet* (CBS, 1950; NBC, 1951; ABC, 1951–1952), *Space Patrol* (ABC, 1951–1952), *Tales of Tomorrow* (ABC, 1951–1953), *The Adventures of Superman* (Syndicated, 1952–1957), *Flash Gordon* (Syndicated, 1952), *Science Fiction Theatre* (Syndicated, 1953–1956), *The Twilight Zone* (CBS, 1959–1965), *Lost in Space* (CBS, 1965–1968), *The Outer Limits* (ABC, 1963–1965), *Voyage to the Bottom of the Sea* (ABC, 1964–1968), *Star Trek* (NBC, 1966–1969), *The*

Time Tunnel (ABC, 1966–1967), *UFO* (Syndicated, 1972), *Starlost* (Syndicated, 1973), *The Planet of the Apes* (CBS, 1974), *The Six Million Dollar Man* (ABC, 1974–1978), *Space: 1999* (Syndicated, 1975–1976), *Wonder Woman* (ABC, 1976–1979), *The Bionic Woman* (ABC, 1976–1977; NBC, 1977–1978), *Logan's Run* (CBS, 1977–1978), *The Incredible Hulk* (CBS, 1978–1982), *Battlestar Galactica* (ABC, 1978–1980), *Project U.F.O.* (NBC, 1978–1979), *Buck Rogers in the 25th Century* (NBC, 1979–1981), *Voyagers* (NBC, 1982–1983), *V* (NBC, 1984–1985), *Max Headroom* (ABC, 1987), *Werewolf* (Fox, 1987), and *Star Trek: The Next Generation* (Syndicated, 1987–1988).

Aside from *Star Trek*, the most enduring of televised science fiction series is the BBC's* *Doctor Who*, which was first televised on November 23, 1963. It began its syndicated presentation on American television in 1970, and has been seen for many years on various PBS* stations. Six actors have portrayed Doctor Who—William Hartnell, Patrick Troughton, Jon Pertwee, Tom Baker, Peter Davison, and Colin Baker—and the series has generated more than twenty related books.

"Cult" status was, at one time, accorded to the "Quatermass" series, produced in the United Kingdom, and written by Nigel Kneale: *The Quatermass Experiment* (BBC, 1953), *Quatermass II* (BBC, 1955), *Quatermass and the Pit* (BBC, 1958), and *Quatermass* (Thames, 1979).

BIBLIOGRAPHY

(Only the more important of the books on *Doctor Who* and *Star Trek* are listed here.)

Dicks, Terrance, and Malcolm Hulke. *The Making of Doctor Who*. London: W.H. Allen, 1980.

Gerani, Gary, and Paul H. Schulman. *Fantastic Television*. New York: Harmony Books, 1977.

Haining, Peter. *Twenty Years of Doctor Who*. London: W.H. Allen, 1983.

Neyland, James. *The Official Battlestar Galactica Scrapbook*. New York: Grosset and Dunlap, 1978.

Road, Alan. *Doctor Who—The Making of a Television Series*. London: Andre Deutsch, 1982.

Turnbull, Gerry, editor. *A Star Trek Catalog*. New York: Grosset and Dunlap, 1979.

Tulloch, John, and Manuel Alvarado. *Doctor Who: The Unfolding Text*. New York: St. Martin's Press, 1984.

Whitfield, Stephen E., and Gene Roddenberry. *The Making of Star Trek*. New York: Ballantine Books, 1968.

Wright, Gene. *The Science Fiction Image: The Illustrated Encyclopedia of Science Fiction in Film, Television, Radio and the Theater*. New York: Facts on File, 1983.

Zicree, Marc Scott. *The Twilight Zone Companion*. New York: Bantam Books, 1982.

SCOTTISH TELEVISION plc is the independent ("commercial") television network for central Scotland (including Edinburgh and Glasgow). It began broadcasting on August 31, 1957, and its best-known production is the thriller series *Taggart*. Until 1968, it was a subsidiary of The Thomson Organization, but in that year the latter was required by the IBA* to reduce its holdings to 25 percent, and in 1977 that share was acquired by a number of Scottish investors. In 1972,

Scottish Television began work on a new studio center in Glasgow, which was completed in 1974.

Address: Cowcaddens, Glasgow G2 3PR, United Kingdom.

SCRAMBLING was introduced by the cable television industry to prevent owners of satellite dishes from receiving programming without payment of monthly service fees. As early as 1984, the FCC* had ruled that satellite dish owners had the right to receive programming from satellites, and so the only means that cable networks had to prevent what they considered to be theft of their signals was through scrambling, particularly as the Communications Act of 1984 had stipulated that it was illegal to view scrambled programming without authorization. HBO* became the first cable network to scramble its programming, on January 15, 1986, and it was followed in July of the same year by CNN.* For a variety of reasons, the networks and public television have also taken to scrambling their programming. As a result, many satellite dishes include built-in descramblers, and a variety of such devices are also offered for sale separately.

BIBLIOGRAPHY

Davis, Gary, "Scrambling!" *The Perfect Vision*, vol. I, no. 4, Spring/Summer 1988, pp. 54–69.

SCREENCRAFT PICTURES, INC. was a New York–based distributor to television of some ninety features, seventy-six Westerns, and many short subjects, active in the fifties. Under the direction of Edward Berkson, it co-produced *Judge Roy Bean* (Syndicated, 1955) and was also the syndicator of *The Mickey Rooney Show* (1954–1955).

SCREEN ENTERTAINMENT CO. was a major distributor of independent films to television, active in the sixties, and founded by Henry G. Saperstein and Harold Goldman. It used a fairly well-known logo of an animated curtain rising to reveal the company name.

SCREEN GEMS. Columbia was the first major Hollywood studio to become actively involved in television production and distribution through the creation of its wholly owned subsidiary Screen Gems, in 1951. The company was initially headed by Ralph Cohn (whose father Jack had co-founded Columbia with his brother Harry). John H. Mitchell is the executive most closely associated with Screen Gems, and when the name was dropped in May 1974, he was named president of the new division, Columbia Pictures Television. At the same time, David Gerber was named executive vice-president, but he also continued to run his own company, David Gerber Productions.

Among the series bearing the Screen Gems name are *Jungle Jim* (Syndicated, 1955), *Rescue Flight* (Syndicated, 1958–1959), *Manhunt* (Syndicated, 1959–1960), *Shannon* (Syndicated, 1961), *Tallahassee 7000* (Syndicated, 1961), *Be-*

witched (ABC, 1964–1972), *I Dream of Jeannie* (NBC, 1965–1970), *Adventures of the Sea Spray* (Syndicated, 1968), *The Partridge Family* (ABC, 1970–1974), *Getting Together* (ABC, 1971–1972), and *The Good Life* (NBC, 1971–1972).

Columbia features released to television were also identified as Screen Gems presentations, and at one time Screen Gems also owned KCPX–Salt Lake City, WVUE–New Orleans, and two Puerto Rican television stations.

SCREEN SPORT is a European sports cable network, seen throughout Europe with commentaries in English, French, and German. First seen on March 29, 1984, it is owned by WH Smith Group plc, the Ladbroke Group, and ESPN.*

Address: The Quadrangle, 180 Wardour Street, London W1V 3AA, United Kingdom.

SCREEN-TELEVIDEO PRODUCTIONS, INC. was a Beverly Hills–based producer and distributor, primarily of television commercials, headed by Robert Lord, and active in the fifties.

THE SCRIPPS HOWARD BROADCASTING COMPANY is an 80.4 percent owned subsidiary of The E.W. Scripps Company, a diversified media corporation controlling nineteen daily newspapers. It owns and operates radio stations in Baltimore, Memphis, and Portland, Oregon; cable television systems in California, Colorado, and Florida; and nine television stations: KCPO-Cincinnati; WEWS-Cleveland; WXYZ-Detroit; WMC-Memphis; KJRH-Tulsa; WPTV–West Palm Beach, Florida; KSHB–Kansas City, Missouri; KNXV-Phoenix; and WFTS-Tampa.

The company was incorporated as Scripps-Howard Radio, Inc. on August 24, 1935. The name was changed in 1985, at which time the hyphen was removed from the company name. Jack R. Howard is chairman of the board of the Scripps Howard Broadcasting Company, and has been a director since 1946.

Address: P.O. Box 5380/1100 Central Trust Tower, Cincinnati, OH 45201.

SECA (THE SOUTHERN EDUCATIONAL COMMUNICATIONS ASSOCIATION) was founded in 1967 by Southern public radio and television stations in response to the need for a common voice. Its membership consists of virtually every eligible public radio and television station in Alabama, Arkansas, Florida, Georgia, Kansas, Kentucky, Louisiana, Maryland, Mississippi, Missouri, North Carolina, Oklahoma, Puerto Rico, South Carolina, Tennessee, Texas, Virginia, West Virginia, and the U.S. Virgin Isles. Its purposes are to help develop and encourage the educational, instructional, and cultural resources of its members; to produce, distribute, and/or promote radio and television materials that are useful to the individual and beneficial to the community; to implement the exchange of instructional, educational, and cultural broadcast programming among its members; to further the use of other forms of electronic communications of educational materials; to further the professional growth of the broadcasters of its member stations; and to provide regional and national representation on behalf of its members.

The best-known program produced and distributed by SECA is the weekly public-affairs interview show *Firing Line*, hosted by William F. Buckley, Jr., which SECA has handled, in association with Producers, Inc., since May 1971.

Address: P.O. Box 50008, Columbia, SC 29250; 2628 Millwood Avenue, Columbia, SC 29205.

SECAM (Séquentiel Couleur à Mémoire) is the color system utilized for television in France, the USSR, most of Eastern Europe, and parts of the Middle East. It was introduced by Henri de France in 1958, and first used in France in 1967. It is not compatible with the American NTSC,* system, which has led to the joke among technicians that the letters actually mean "System Evidently Contrary to American Method."

BIBLIOGRAPHY

"SECAM Colour System," in *The Focal Encyclopedia of Film & Television*, editor Raymond Spottiswoode. New York: Hastings House, 1969, pp. 654–659.

THE SECOND CITY comedy group (which was officially formed in Chicago on December 16, 1959) was first seen on television in the United Kingdom in 1963. Following television airings of the comedy troupe's work in Canada in the late 1970s, Second City was introduced to American network television, via NBC,* in May 1981. SCTV, as it is more popularly known, has since been seen on a regular basis on American television, primarily on cable. Among the best-known members of the group were Dan Aykroyd, John Belushi, John Candy, Eugene Levy, Shelley Long, Andrea Martin, Bill Murray, Gilda Radner, Harold Ramis, Joan Rivers, Martin Short, and John Steinberg.

BIBLIOGRAPHY

McCroha, Donna. *The Second City: A Backstage History of Comedy's Hottest Troupe*. New York: Perigree Books, 1987.

"The 30th Anniversary of the Second City," *Daily Variety*, December 14, 1989, pp. S1–S28.

SELECTV was a Los Angeles–based over-the-air pay-television service, founded by Jim Levitus in 1978, whose majority shareholder was Clarion Co. of Japan. In 1984, it acquired On-TV,* and the following year boasted its highest number of subscribers, 200,000. Specializing primarily in the presentation of feature films, SelecTV was acquired by Telstar Corp. in January 1987, and later that same year was sued by Tri-Star, 20th Century–Fox, and Columbia Pictures for failure to pay in full for the films that it aired. In October 1988, the company was acquired by Interlink Transfer Group Ltd., and in March 1989 it filed for Chapter XI bankruptcy protection. It ceased broadcasting on April 4, 1989.

BIBLIOGRAPHY

Gelman, Morrie, "SelecTV Goes off Air after 11 Years," *Daily Variety*, March 21, 1989, pp. 1, 29.

Graham, Jefferson, "SelecTV Satellite-Delivered Programming Hot Growth Area," *The Hollywood Reporter*, October 25, 1982, p. 8.

THE SELSDON REPORT, published on January 31, 1935, is generally considered to be the document responsible for the birth of television in the United Kingdom. It came about as a result of Lord Selsdon being asked to chair a committee, in May 1934, "to consider the development of Television and to advise the Postmaster General on the relative merits of the several systems and on the conditions under which any public service of Television should be provided."

THE 7–7–7 RULE adopted by the FCC* was in force for thirty-two years, and prohibited a corporation or individual from owning more than seven television stations, seven AM radio stations, and seven FM radio stations. In April 1985, the ruling was amended to 12–12–12, and that change permitted Capital Cities Communications, Inc.* (with seven television stations) to acquire ABC* (with five television stations). In cases where the licensee is minority-controlled, the limit is fourteen stations. Efforts to abolish the rule entirely by 1990 have been opposed by Congress and the motion picture industry.

SEXTANT, INCORPORATED was a New York–based production company founded by Robert D. Graff, in creative partnership with Robert Emmet Ginna and Milton Fruchtman. Aside from many other film projects, it produced two memorable documentary series for prime time television: *Winston Churchill: The Valiant Years* (ABC, 1960–1961) and *FDR* (ABC, 1965), together with the CBS* world premiere ballet *The Flood*, composed by Igor Stravinsky and choreographed by George Balanchine. Sextant was incorporated on January 15, 1959, and dissolved in 1984. A related company, Sextant Films Ltd., was formed in 1961 to produce the theatrical feature *Young Cassidy*. It was dissolved in 1968.

S4C—THE WELSH FOURTH CHANNEL was established under the Broadcasting Act of 1981 to provide Welsh and some English-language programming on Channel 4* in Wales. S4C is the abbreviation for Sianel Pedwar Cymru (Channel Four Wales). It programs an average of twenty-five hours per week of Welsh-language shows, produced by HTV Group plc,* the BBC,* and independent contractors, with the idea being that all programs in Welsh are seen on one British television channel; it also transmits regular English-language programming from Channel 4. A wholly owned subsidiary, Mentrau CYF (or Enterprises Ltd.), exploits the commercial potential of S4C's programs.

Address: Sophia Close, Cardiff CF1 9XY, United Kingdom.

BIBLIOGRAPHY

Hill, Doug, "Last Stand of the Welsh," *Channels of Communications,* vol. II, no. 5, January/February 1983, p. 17.

SHAMLEY PRODUCTIONS, INC. was formed by Alfred Hitchcock (1899–1980) for the production of four television series at Universal. It was named for a summer home that Hitchcock had bought in Shamley Green, England, in 1928. The series, which it co-produced with Revue Productions, Inc.,* are *Alfred Hitchcock Presents* (CBS, 1955–1960; NBC, 1960–1962), *Suspicion* (NBC, 1957–1959), *Startime* (NBC, 1959–1960), and *The Alfred Hitchcock Hour* (CBS, 1962–1964; NBC, 1964–1965).
BIBLIOGRAPHY
McCarty, John, and Brian Kelleher. *Alfred Hitchcock Presents*. New York: St. Martin's Press, 1985.

SHAMUS CULHANE PRODUCTIONS, INC./CULHANE FILM STUDIOS, INC. was established in New York in 1947 by veteran animator Shamus Culhane, who had been active since 1924 and had worked on a number of Walt Disney features and short subjects. The company made more than 3,500 television commercials as well as three films in the Bell Telephone science series, *Hemo the Magnificent* (1956), *The Strange Case of the Cosmic Rays* (1957), and *The Unchained Goddess* (1958). The company opened a Los Angeles office, under the direction of William T. Hurtz, in 1954, and remained active through 1958.

Earlier, Culhane had formed Television Art Enterprises with Sobey Martin in Los Angeles, and it had produced an abortive television pilot for an animated series of *Robin Hood*. Culhane was later involved in other television series: *Rocket Robin Hood* (1967), for Steve Krantz Productions; *Professor Kitzel* (1972), *Spirit of '76* (1975), and *Spirit of Independence* (1976) for M.G. Films; and *Noah's Animals* (1975 special), *The King of the Beasts* (1975 special), and *Last of the Red-Hot Dragons* (1977 special), for Westfall Productions.
BIBLIOGRAPHY
Culhane, Shamus. *Talking Animals and Other People*. New York: St. Martin's Press, 1986.

SHELLRIC CORPORATION was formed by comedian Sid Caesar for the production of *Caesar Presents* (NBC, 1955) and *Caesar's Hour* (NBC, 1956–1957). It was named after Caesar's children, Shelly and Rick, and when a third child, Karen, was born, the company was renamed Shellrick Corporation. Caesar was also president of another company, Box Office Television, Inc.
BIBLIOGRAPHY
Caesar, Sid, with Bill Davidson. *Where Have I Been?* New York: Crown, 1982.

SHERMAN H. DRYER PRODUCTIONS was a minor New York–based producer of television programming, active from the fifties through the mid-seventies.

SHORTWAVE AND TELEVISION CORPORATION was founded in Boston in 1929, and the following year went on the air with W1XAV. The latter ceased broadcasting in 1934, and the company, renamed General Television Corporation, continued operations into the forties with W1XG-Boston (which had started broadcasting in October 1931).

BIBLIOGRAPHY

Udelson, Joseph H. *The Great Television Race: A History of the American Television Industry 1925–1941*. University: University of Alabama Press, 1982.

SHOW BIZ, INC. was a Southern-based television distributor, specializing in syndicated country-and-western programs, including *That Good Ole Nashville Music* (1972–1983), *Pop! Goes the Country* (1974–1983), *Nashville on the Road* (1976–1983), and *Marty Robbins' Spotlight* (1978–1979).

SHOWCASE PRODUCTIONS, INC. was responsible for *The Alcoa Hour* (NBC, 1955–1957).

SHOWTIME/THE MOVIE CHANNEL, INC. was formed with the merger of Showtime (originally owned by Viacom, Inc.*) and The Movie Channel (originally owned by Warner Amex Satellite Entertainment Corp.) in September 1983. The company operates two twenty-four hour a day pay-television networks, each with 10 million subscribers. It also operates Showtime Satellite Networks, providing a package of programming services to home satellite dish owners, and SET Pay per View, for pay-per-view event programming.

Showtime began broadcasting in 1976, and was followed three years later by The Movie Channel. Viacom acquired total ownership of the network in August 1985 with its purchase of MTV,* and Showtime/The Movie Channel remains part of the MTV networks.

Address: 1633 Broadway, New York, NY 10019.

BIBLIOGRAPHY

Girard, Tom, "Showtime/TMC Gets Down to Biz," *Daily Variety*, December 12, 1983, pp. 1, 12.

Graham, Jefferson, "An In-Depth Appraisal of the Showtime/Movie Channel Gang," *The Hollywood Reporter*, February 6, 1984, p. 7.

"HBO Vs. Showtime Vs. VCR," *Newsweek,* April 23, 1984, p. 86.

Noglows, Paul, "Showtime Promises To Try Harder," *Channels of Communications*, vol. VIII, no. 6, June 1988, pp. 78–79.

SHUKOVSKY/ENGLISH is a production company owned by Joel Shukovsky and Diane English and responsible for *Murphy Brown* (CBS, 1988-   ).

Address: 4000 Warner Boulevard, Burbank, CA 91522.

SIGN-OFFS. The FCC* requires that stations identify themselves prior to leaving the air. Traditionally, most stations sign off with a film or tape of the national anthem, provided by one of the armed services.

BIBLIOGRAPHY
Cogan, Jesse, "Our Flag is Still There," *TV Guide*, November 22, 1975, pp. 40–41.

THE SILENT NETWORK, INC. was founded in October 1979 by Sheldon Altfeld and Kathleen Gold to produce programming for the deaf and hearing-impaired. SILENT is an acronym for Sign Language Entertainment. The network began cable service on 200 systems on February 2, 1984, and as of 1990, The Silent Network had 14 million subscribers for its basic cable programming from 9:30 A.M. through 11:30 A.M. on Thursday and Saturday. As of 1987, it was completely advertiser-supported, with its first sponsor being Hallmark Greetings Cards.*

Address: 6363 Sunset Boulevard, Suite 930, Los Angeles, CA 90028.

BIBLIOGRAPHY
Rothman, Cliff, "Special Report: The Silent Network," *The Hollywood Reporter*, August 31, 1984, pp. 9–14.
Stilson, Janet, "Silent Net Coming Through Loud, Clear; Expansion Seen," *Daily Variety*, February 26, 1986, pp. 20, 22.
Warfield, Polly, "Sheldon Altfeld Launches Silent Network by Satellite," *Drama-Logue*, October 6, 1983, p. 3.

SILVERMAN, FRED COMPANY. See THE FRED SILVERMAN COMPANY

SIMULCAST is the name given to a program broadcast simultaneously on both radio and television. In the past, simulcasts were often aired to provide stereo sound for the television viewer, via an FM radio station.

THE SINGAPORE BROADCASTING CORPORATION is responsible for radio and television broadcasting on the island of Singapore. The corporation began as Radio-Television Singapore, established by the government, in August 1963. A second television channel and color (using the PAL* system) were introduced in August 1974. The Singapore Broadcasting Corporation is a part of the Ministry of Culture.

Address: P.O. Box 60, Singapore 9128.

SITCOMS. The following is a listing of the more popular Sitcoms (situation comedies) on American television, arranged by decade:

Forties

Mary Kay and Johnny (DuMont, 1947–1948; NBC, 1948–1949; CBS, 1949; NBC, 1949–1950), *Mama* (CBS, 1949–1956), *The Life of Riley* (NBC, 1949–1958), *The Ruggles* (ABC, 1949–1952), *The Goldbergs* (CBS, 1949–1951; NBC, 1952–1953; DuMont, 1954), and *The Aldrich Family* (NBC, 1949–1953).

Fifties

The Stu Erwin Show (ABC, 1950–1955), *The George Burns and Gracie Allen Show* (CBS, 1950–1958), *Beulah* (ABC, 1950–1953), *The Abbott and Costello Show* (Syndicated, 1951–1953), *Amos 'n' Andy* (CBS, 1951–1953), *I Love Lucy* (CBS, 1951–1961), *The Adventures of Ozzie & Harriet* (ABC, 1952–1966), *Meet Millie* (CBS, 1952–1956), *My Friend Irma* (CBS, 1952–1954), *My Little Margie* (CBS, 1952; NBC, 1952; CBS, 1953; NBC, 1953–1955), *I Married Joan* (NBC, 1952–1955), *Topper* (CBS, 1953–1955; ABC, 1955–1956; NBC, 1956), *The Danny Thomas Show* (ABC, 1953–1957; CBS, 1957–1965; ABC, 1970–1971), *Our Miss Brooks* (CBS, 1953–1956), *Private Secretary* (CBS, 1953–1957), *Life with Elizabeth* (Syndicated, 1953–1955), *Life with Father* (CBS, 1953–1955), *That's My Boy* (CBS, 1954–1959), *Father Knows Best* (CBS, 1954–1962; ABC, 1962–1963), *Duffy's Tavern* (Syndicated, 1954), *Meet Corliss Archer* (Syndicated, 1954), *The Phil Silvers Show* (CBS, 1955–1959), *The Honeymooners* (CBS, 1955–1956), *The Great Gildersleeve* (Syndicated, 1955), *The Gale Storm Show* (CBS, 1956–1959; ABC, 1959–1960), *Hey Jeannie* (CBS, 1956–1957; ABC, 1960), *Bachelor Father* (CBS, 1957–1959; NBC, 1959–1961; ABC, 1961–1962), *The Real McCoys* (ABC, 1957–1962; CBS, 1962–1963), *Leave It to Beaver* (CBS, 1957–1958; ABC, 1958–1963), *The Ann Sothern Show* (CBS, 1958–1961), *The Donna Reed Show* (ABC, 1958–1966), and *The Many Loves of Dobie Gillis* (CBS, 1959–1963).

Sixties

The Andy Griffith Show (CBS, 1960–1968), *My Three Sons* (ABC, 1960–1965; CBS, 1965–1972), *The Dick Van Dyke Show* (CBS, 1961–1966), *Mr. Ed* (CBS, 1961–1965), *Hazel* (NBC, 1961–1965; CBS, 1965–1966), *McHale's Navy* (ABC, 1961–1966), *The Beverly Hillbillies* (CBS, 1962–1971), *Petticoat Junction* (CBS, 1963–1970), *The Patty Duke Show* (ABC, 1963–1966), *My Favorite Martian* (CBS, 1963–1966), *Bewitched* (ABC, 1964–1972), *Gilligan's Island* (CBS, 1964–1967), *The Munsters* (CBS, 1964–1966), *F-Troop* (ABC, 1965–1967), *Get Smart* (NBC, 1965–1969; CBS, 1969–1970), *That Girl* (ABC, 1966–1971), *The Monkees* (NBC, 1966–1968), *The Flying Nun* (ABC, 1967–1970), *The Mothers-in-Law* (NBC, 1967–1969), *Blondie* (NBC, 1957; CBS, 1968–1969), *The Doris Day Show* (CBS, 1968–1973), *Mayberry R.F.D.* (CBS, 1968–1971), *Julia* (NBC, 1968–1971), *The Brady Bunch* (ABC, 1969–1974), and *The Courtship of Eddie's Father* (ABC, 1969–1972).

Seventies

The Mary Tyler Moore Show (CBS, 1970–1977), *The Odd Couple* (ABC, 1970–1975), *The Partridge Family* (ABC, 1970–1974), *All in the Family* (CBS, 1971–1983), *M*A*S*H* (CBS, 1972–1983), *Maude* (CBS, 1972–1978), *Sanford and*

Son (NBC, 1972–1976), *The Bob Newhart Show* (CBS, 1972–1978), *Ozzie's Girls* (Syndicated, 1973), *Good Times* (CBS, 1974–1979), *Rhoda* (CBS, 1974–1978), *Chico and the Man* (NBC, 1974–1978), *Welcome Back, Kotter* (ABC, 1975–1979), *Barney Miller* (ABC, 1975–1982), *One Day at a Time* (CBS, 1975–1984), *Phyllis* (CBS, 1975–1977), *The Jeffersons* (CBS, 1975–1985), *Laverne & Shirley* (ABC, 1976–1983), *Alice* (CBS, 1976–1985), *The Tony Randall Show* (ABC, 1976–1977; CBS, 1977–1978), *What's Happening!!* (ABC, 1976–1979), *Fernwood 2-Night* (Syndicated, 1977), *Operation Petticoat* (ABC, 1977–1979), *Taxi* (ABC, 1978–1987), *Diff'rent Strokes* (NBC, 1978–1986), *WKRP in Cincinnati* (CBS, 1978–1982), *America 2-Night* (Syndicated, 1978), *Please Stand By* (Syndicated, 1978), *The Baxters* (Syndicated, 1979–1981), *Benson* (ABC, 1979–1986), and *The Facts of Life* (NBC, 1979–1988).

Eighties

Cheers (NBC, 1982-   ), *Too Close for Comfort* (Syndicated, 1983–1986), *Night Court* (NBC, 1984-   ), *Who's the Boss?* (1984-   ), *The Cosby Show* (NBC, 1984-   ), *It's a Living* (Syndicated, 1985–1989), *The Golden Girls* (NBC, 1985-   ), *Mr. Belvedere* (ABC, 1985–1990), *Mama's Family* (Syndicated, 1986-   ), *Alf* (NBC, 1986-1990), *Perfect Strangers* (ABC, 1986-   ), *Amen* (NBC, 1986-   ), *Designing Women* (CBS, 1986-   ), *Throb* (Syndicated, 1986–1987), *Bustin' Loose* (Syndicated, 1987), *Charles in Charge* (Syndicated, 1987), *Duet/ Open House* (Fox, 1987-   ), *Marblehead Manor* (Syndicated, 1987), *Married with Children* (Fox, 1987-1989), *Mister President* (Fox, 1987), *The New Adventures of Beans Baxter* (Syndicated, 1987), *She's the Sheriff* (Syndicated, 1987), *Silver Spoons* (Syndicated, 1987), *Empty Nest* (NBC, 1988-   ), *Murphy Brown* (CBS, 1988-   ), *The Ten of Us* (ABC, 1988–1990), *Roseanne* (ABC, 1988-   ), *Dear John* (NBC, 1988-   ), *Major Dad* (CBS, 1989-   ), and *Coach* (ABC, 1989-   ).

BIBLIOGRAPHY

Adler, Richard P. *All in the Family: A Critical Appraisal*. New York: Praeger, 1979.
Alda, Alan. *The Last Days of MASH*. Verona, N.J.: Unicorn, 1983.
Alley, Robert S., and Irby B. Brown. *Love Is All Around: The Making of the Mary Tyler Moore Show*. New York: Delta, 1989.
———. *Murphy Brown: Anatomy of a Sitcom*. New York: Dell, 1990.
Andrews, Bart. *Lucy & Ricky & Fred & Ethel*. New York: E.P. Dutton, 1976.
———. *The "I Love Lucy" Book*. Garden City, N.Y.: Doubleday, 1985.
Andrews, Bart, with Cheryl Blythe. *The Official Cheers Scrapbook*. New York: New American Library, 1987.
Andrews, Bart, and Ahrgus Juilliard. *Holy Mackerel: The Amos 'n' Andy Story*. New York: E.P. Dutton, 1986.
Applebaum, Irwin. *The World according to Beaver*. New York: Bantam Books, 1984.
Beck, Ken, and Jim Clark. *The Andy Griffith Book*. New York: St. Martin's Press, 1985.
Blythe, Cheryl, and Susan Sackett. *Say Goodnight, Gracie!: The Story of Burns and Allen*. New York: E.P. Dutton, 1986.
Cox, Stephen. *The Beverly Hillbillies*. Chicago: Contemporary Books, 1988.

Crescenti, Peter, and Bob Columbe. *The Official Honeymooners Treasury: To the Moon and Back with Ralph, Norton, Alice and Trixie*. New York: Putnam, 1985.

Eisner, Joel, and David Krinsky. *Television Comedy Series: An Episode Guide to 153 TV Sitcoms in Syndication*. Jefferson, N.C.: McFarland, 1984.

Green, Jonathon. *The Fonz & Henry Winkler*. New York: Bunch Books, 1978.

Grote, David. *The End of Comedy: The Sit-Com and the Comedic Tradition*. Hamden, Conn.: Archon Books, 1983.

Jacobs, Will, and Gerard Jones. *The Beaver Papers*. New York: Crown, 1983.

Javna, John. *The Best of TV Sitcoms: Burns and Allen to the Cosby Show, the Munsters to Mary Tyler Moore*. New York: Harmony Books, 1988.

Kalter, Suzy. *The Complete Book of M*A*S*H*. New York: Harry N. Abrams, 1984.

Kelly, Richard Michael. *The Andy Griffith Show*. Winston-Salem, N.C.: John F. Blair, 1984.

Lovece, Frank, and Jules Franco. *Hailing Taxi*. New York: Prentice-Hall, 1988.

McCrohan, Donna. *Archie & Edith, Mike & Gloria*. New York: Workman, 1987.

————. *The Life & Times of Maxwell Smart*. New York: St. Martin's Press, 1988.

McCrohan, Donna, and Peter Crescenti. *The Honeymooners Lost Episodes*. New York: Workman, 1986.

Mitz, Rick. *The Great TV Sitcom Book*. New York: Richard Marek, 1980.

Munshower, Suzanne. *Hollywood's Newest Superstar—Henry Winkler*. New York: Berkeley Medallion, 1976.

Pruetzel, Maria, and John A. Barbour. *The Freddie Prinze Story*. Kalamazoo, Mich.: Master's Press, 1978.

Reiss, David S. *M*A*S*H: The Exclusive, Inside Story of TV's Most Popular Show*. Indianapolis, Ind.: Bobbs-Merrill, 1983.

Schwartz, Sherwood. *Inside Gilligan's Island*. Jefferson, N.C.: McFarland, 1988.

Seabrook, Steven. *The Official Mork & Mindy Scrapbook*. New York: Pocket Books, 1979.

Silvers, Phil, and Robert Saffron. *This Laugh Is on Me*. Englewood Cliffs, N.J.: Prentice-Hall, 1973.

Thomas, David and Ian Irvine. *Bilko: The Fort Baxter Story*. London: Vermilion/Hutchinson, 1985.

Waldron, Vince. *Classic Sitcoms: A Celebration of the Best in Prime-Time Comedy*. New York: Macmillan, 1987.

Weissman, Ginny, and Coyne Steven Sanders. *The Dick Van Dyke Show: Anatomy of a Classic*. New York: St. Martin's Press, 1983.

Winkler, Henry. *The Other Side of Henry Winkler*. New York: Warner Books, 1976.

SKIATRON was one of the earliest pay-as-you-view television systems, first tested over WOR–New York in 1951. In March 1954, Matthew Fox (1911–1964) formed Skiatron of America, Inc. (whose name was later changed to Tolvision of America, Inc.) to provide programming for the system (which was, in turn, owned by Skiatron Electronics & Television Corp.).

SKY CABLE is a $1.3 billion, 108-channel satellite-based direct broadcast system, which is scheduled to be launched in the United States, subject to congressional approval, in 1993. Sky Cable is owned by NBC,* Rupert Murdoch's News Corp., Hughes Communications, Inc., and Cablevision Systems Corp. It is opposed by cable system operators, led by Tele-Communications, Inc.,* which perceive Sky Cable as major competition.

SKY CHANNEL is the major European satellite cable channel, providing general entertainment programming throughout Europe, and originating in London and Amsterdam. The service was created in April 1982 by Rupert Murdoch as Satellite Television.

Address: 6 Centaurs Business Park, Grant Way, off Syan Lane, Isleworth, Middlesex, TW7 5QD, United Kingdom.

BIBLIOGRAPHY
Maddox, Brenda, "Sky King," *Channels of Communications*, vol. V, no. 5, January/February 1986, pp. 53–55.
Melcher, Richard A., and Ronald Grover, "Bart Simpson Could Put Murdoch's Sky TV in Orbit," *Business Week*, September 17, 1990, p. 121.

SMART (Stop Marketing Alcohol on Radio and Television) was a 1985 initiative of the Washington, D.C.–based Center for Science in the Public Interest. The initiative was directed by George Hacker, and its aim was to present Congress with 1 million signatures in favor of a ban on the advertising of beer and wine products on radio and television.

SMITH-HEMION PRODUCTIONS has its origins in Yorkshire Productions, which was formed in 1966 by Gary Smith and Dwight Hemion. From 1971 to 1975, the pair was active in London, but they then returned to Los Angeles in the fall of 1975, at which time Smith-Hemion Productions was organized. The company is noted for its production of variety and entertainment specials (including several Emmy shows), among which are *Elvis in Concert* (CBS, 1977), *IBM Presents Barishnikov on Broadway* (ABC, 1980), *Pavarotti and Friends* (ABC, 1982), and *Liberty Weekend* (ABC, 1986).

Address: 1438 North Gower Street, Hollywood, CA 90028.

BIBLIOGRAPHY
Buck, Mason, "Smith and Hemion: Razzle-Dazzle Makers," *Pan-Am Clipper*, January 1980, pp. 61–64.
"The Hollywood Reporter Salutes Smith-Hemion Productions," *The Hollywood Reporter*, April 28, 1986, pp. S1-S40.

SNADER TELESCRIPTIONS, INC. was a Beverly Hills–based company, founded in 1948 by Louis D. Snader (1898–1971), and active through the sixties. It distributed three-minute musical shorts for use as "fillers" on television, called "telescriptions." Such shorts featured numbers by Gale Storm, Cab Calloway, Peggy Lee, Mel Tormé, Nat "King" Cole, Lanny Ross, Red Nichols, and others, and some 800 were available at one time. The company also distributed to television thirteen Alexander Korda–produced feature films, as well as a number of syndicated series.

A related company, founded in 1952, was Snader Productions, Inc., which, in the early fifties, produced the thirty-minute syndicated series *Korla Pandit*, featuring the turban-crowned organist.

SNN (SPORTS NEWS NETWORK) is a twenty-four hour a day cable network, providing sports news and information for 6.25 million subscribers. It was launched in February 1990.

Address: 352 7 Avenue, New York, NY 10001.

SOAP OPERAS. So named because of their sponsorship by soap companies (such as Lever Brothers and Procter & Gamble*), soap operas were originally a radio phenomenon. The first was *Painted Dreams*, created by Irna Phillips, and first heard on WGN-Chicago* in 1930. Ms. Phillips was also involved in soap operas on television, beginning with *The Guiding Light*, which she created for radio in 1937, and which was first seen on television, on CBS,* in 1952; she later created *As the World Turns* (CBS, 1956-   ) and *Another World* (NBC, 1964-   ).

DuMont's* WABD experimented with television versions of radio soap operas as early as May 1944, and DuMont was also responsible for the first network soap opera, *Faraway Hill* (1946). NBC* began telecasting soap operas in 1949 with *These Are My Children* (1949), and CBS started in 1950 with *The First Hundred Years* (1950–1952). Soap operas were limited to daytime entertainment until 1978, when CBS introduced its popular nighttime series *Dallas*, which also led to a spin-off, *Knots Landing* (CBS, 1979-   ).

Television soap operas have been much parodied, notably by Carol Burnett with her ongoing sketch "As the Stomach Turns," and in two series, *Soap* (ABC, 1977–1981) and *Mary Hartman, Mary Hartman* (Syndicated, 1975–1978).

BIBLIOGRAPHY

Ang, Ien, translated by Della Couling. *Watching Dallas: Soap Opera and the Melo-dramatic Image*. London: Methuen, 1985.

Angel, Velma. *Those Sensational Soaps*. Brea, Calif.: Uplift Books, 1983.

Blumenthal, John. *Anthony Geary*. New York: Wallaby Books, 1982.

Buchman, Peter. *All for Love: A Study in Soap Opera*. Salem, N.H.: Salem House, 1985.

Cantor, Muriel G., and Suzanne Pingree. *The Soap Opera*. Beverly Hills, Calif.: Sage Publications, 1983.

Cassata, Mary B., and Thomas Skill. *Life on Daytime Television*. New York: Ablex, 1983.

Denis, Paul, editor. *Daytime TV's Star Directory*. New York: Popular Library, 1976.

Dynasty: The Authorized Biography of the Carringtons. Garden City, N.Y.: Doubleday, 1984.

Edmondson, Madeleine, and David Rounds. *The Soaps: Daytime Serials of Radio and Television*. New York: Stein and Day, 1973.

Gilbert, Annie. *All My Afternoons*. New York: A & W, 1979.

Groves, Seli, and the editors of the Associated Press. *Soaps: A Pictorial History of America's Daytime Dramas*. Chicago: Contemporary Books, 1983.

Inintoli, Michael James. *Taking Soaps Seriously: The World of Guiding Light*. New York: Praeger, 1984.

Kalter, Suzy. *The Complete Book of Dallas: Behind the Scenes at the World's Favorite Television Program*. New York: Harry N. Abrams, 1986.

Kutler, Jane, and Patricia Kearney. *Super Soaps*. New York: Grosset and Dunlap, 1977.

LaGuardia, Robert. *The Wonderful World of TV Soap Operas*. New York: Ballantine Books, 1974.

————. *From Ma Perkins to Mary Hartman: The Illustrated History of Soap Operas*. New York: Ballantine Books, 1977.

Matelski, Marilyn J. *The Soap Opera Evolution: America's Enduring Romance with Daytime Drama*. Jefferson, N.C.: McFarland, 1988.

Meyers, Richard. *The Illustrated Soap Opera Companion*. New York: Drake, 1977.

————. *Super TV Stars*. New York: Drake, 1977.

The Official Soap Opera Annual. New York: Ballantine Books, yearly, 1977 to present.

Rouverol, Jean. *Writing for the Soaps*. Cincinnati, Ohio: Digest Books, 1984.

Schemering, Christopher. *The Soap Opera Encyclopedia*. New York: Ballantine Books, 1985.

Soares, Manuela. *The Soap Opera Book*. New York: Harmony Books, 1978.

Van Wormer, Laura. *Dallas: The Complete Ewing Family Saga, including Southfork Ranch, Ewing Oil and the Barnes-Ewing Feud, 1860–1985*. Garden City, N.Y.: Doubleday, 1985.

Wakefield, Dan. *All Her Children*. New York: Doubleday, 1976.

Whitley, Dianna, and Ray Manzella. *Soap Stars: America's 31 Favorite Daytime Actors Speak for Themselves*. Garden City, N.Y.: Doubleday/Dolphin, 1985.

THE SOCIETY FOR THE ERADICATION OF TELEVISION was founded in New Mexico in 1980 by a group of households that did not have television and were anxious to encourage others to remove television receivers from their homes. It was defunct by 1989, presumably having failed in its goal.

THE SOCIETY OF BROADCAST ENGINEERS, INC. was founded in 1963 as the Institute of Broadcast Engineers, with the merger of the Institute of Radio Engineers and the American Institute of Electrical Engineers. It is a non-profit organization, serving the interests of all broadcast engineers, with local chapters throughout the country and abroad, and a membership of 6,000. Since January 1, 1977, it has conducted tests and issued certificates attesting to the competency of members as either Broadcast Engineers or Senior Broadcast Engineers; the certification program is administered by the Ennes Education Foundation of the society.

Address: P.O. Box 20450, Indianapolis, IN 46220.

THE SOCIETY OF CABLE TELEVISION ENGINEERS, INC. was founded in 1969 as a result of an editorial in the November 1968 issue of *Cablecasting* on the lack of recognition awarded cable system engineers. With more than 6,500 members (as of 1990), the non-profit society promotes the sharing of operational and technical knowledge in the fields of cable television and broadband communications.

Address: 669 Exton Commons, Exton, PA 19341.

SOLID-STATE TELEVISION is the name given to television receivers that use solid blocks of crystal or silicon chips for their transistors as opposed to television tubes.

BIBLIOGRAPHY

Davidson, Homer L. *Troubleshooting and Repairing Solid-State TVs*. Blue Ridge Summit, Pa.: TAB Books, 1986.

Hanson, Gerald L. *Introduction to Solid-State Television Systems*. Englewood Cliffs, N.J.: Prentice-Hall, 1969.

SONG ADS CO./SONG AD–FILM–RADIO PRODUCTIONS, headed by Robert Sande, was a Los Angeles–based producer, primarily of television and radio commercials, active in the fifties.

SOUND MASTERS, INC. was a New York–based producer of television commercials, founded in 1937 by Harold E. Wondsel, and active through 1965. A related company was Wondsel, Carlyle & Dunphy, Inc.

SOUTHBROOK TELEVISION DISTRIBUTION CORP. was founded in 1985 by Thomas J. McDermott (1925–1990) and that same year acquired the rights to the *Lone Ranger* and *Lassie* series from the Wrather Corporation. The company was sold in 1987 for a reported $40 million.

Address: 444 Madison Avenue, New York, NY 10022.

SOUTH CAROLINA ETV is an educational television network, created in 1958 to provide programming primarily for classroom use. At its founding, there were accusations that the network was being created to circumvent integration by continuing public education without public schools through making it possible for white parents to turn on the television and keep their children at home.

Address: P.O. Drawer L, Columbia, SC 29250.

BIBLIOGRAPHY

Stucker, Jan Collins, "South Carolina's Educational TV Heads the Class," *New York Times*, March 2, 1975, Arts & Leisure Section, pp. 1, 29.

SOUTH PACIFIC. Aside from Australia and New Zealand, the following is a complete listing of television stations in the South Pacific:

Easter Island—TV Rapanui, Isla de Pascua.

French Polynesia—Société Nationale de Radio Télévision D'Outre Mer, B.P. 125, Papeete.

Galapagos Islands—Telegalapagos, Isla San Cristobal, Galápagos, Ecuador.

Guam—KUAM Television, P.O. Box 368, Agana, Guam 96910.

Micronesia—KPON-TV, Central Micronesia Communications, P.O. Box 460, Kolonia, Pohnpei, 96941/TV-Station TRUK, Truk State, 96942/WAAB-TV, Yap State, 96943.

New Caledonia—RFO-TV, B.P. G3, Noumea Cédex.

Norfolk Island—Norfolk Island Television, New Cascade Road, Norfolk Island, 2899, Australia.

Palau—STV-TV, Koror, Palau, 96940.

Papua New Guinea—EMTV, Media-Niugini Pty. Ltd., P.O. Box 443, Boroko.

Samoa—KVZK-TV, American Samoa Government, Pago Pago, 96799.

SPECIALTY TELEVISION FILMS, INC., founded by Jules B. Weill, was a New York–based distributor to television of twenty-six feature films, active in the fifties and sixties.

"SPECTACULAR" is a word introduced by NBC* president Sylvester L. "Pat" Weaver to describe a special television program designed to create excitement or controversy and broadcast in color. The first NBC spectacular was *Satins and Spurs*, starring Betty Hutton, and broadcast on September 12, 1954. The best example of an NBC spectacular is probably *Peter Pan*, starring Mary Martin, broadcast on March 7, 1955, and, coincidentally, the first network presentation of a Broadway production.
BIBLIOGRAPHY
Lanigan, Betty, "The Year Spectacular Became a Noun," *Television Quarterly*, vol. X, no. 1, Fall 1972, pp. 64–67.

SPELLING, AARON PRODUCTIONS, INC. See AARON SPELLING PRODUCTIONS, INC.

SPELLING/GOLDBERG PRODUCTIONS, INC. was formed in 1972 by producers Aaron Spelling (born 1928) and Leonard Goldberg (born 1934), and produced some of the most popular series of ABC,* including *The Rookies* (1972–1976), *S.W.A.T.* (1975–1976), *Charlie's Angels* (1976–1981), *Hart to Hart* (1979–1984), and *Mod Squad* (1968–1973), whose production it took over from Thomas & Leonard Productions.* Housed initially on the 20th Century–Fox lot, the company moved to the Warner-Hollywood Studios in 1981.

In 1979, complaints were made that profits from *Charlie's Angels* had been diverted to other productions to deprive investors Natalie Wood, Robert Wagner, and writers Ben Roberts and Ivan Goff from their share of profit participation. The matter was investigated by both the Los Angeles District Attorney's Office and the Securities and Exchange Commission, but no charges were ever filed, with the former agency claiming "insufficient grounds."

Spelling/Goldberg Productions was acquired in May 1982 by Columbia Pictures Television for a reported purchase price of between $20 and $25 million.

SPORTS. The first sport to be seen on television was baseball, which had been heard on radio first, over KDKA, on August 5, 1921. The first televised baseball game was of Columbia University versus Princeton, with announcer Bill Stern, seen and heard on NBC* on May 17, 1939. The first major league baseball game to be televised was of the Brooklyn Dodgers versus the Cincinnati Reds on NBC's W2XBS on August 26, 1939. The World Series was first televised, jointly by CBS,* NBC, and DuMont,* in 1947. NBC introduced major league baseball to television on a regular weekly basis in 1972.

The first sport to be seen on television on a regular basis was wrestling, when, in 1944, W6XYZ (later KTLA–Los Angeles*) began broadcasting *Wrestling from the Olympic* [Stadium]. *Gillette Cavalcade of Sports* dominated sports programming on NBC from 1944 (when it was first seen on WNBT–New York) through 1964.

College football was introduced to television on a regular basis with ABC's* *The Game of the Week* (1950–1951). DuMont began carrying professional football in 1953, but it was not seen again on a regular basis until 1959, on ABC, which signed its first contract with the National Football League in 1970. It was ABC that introduced the "Instant Replay" in 1961, under the name of "Video Tape Expander" (VTX), and that same year the network began its long-running *Wide World of Sports*.

Basketball was first seen on NBC in 1948. NBL games began to be televised on a regular basis, on CBS, in 1978. Bowling has been a staple of local television programming since 1950. The most popular of all series devoted to the latter sport is *Bowling for Dollars* (Syndicated, 1970-   ).

Among the individuals whose careers have been advanced or personalities created by commentating on network sportscasts are Howard Cosell, Frank Gifford, Jim Lampley, Jim McKay, John Madden, Don Meredith, Brent Musberger, Pat Summerall, Bob Uecker, and Warner Wolf. Gayle Sierens was the first woman to give play-by-play commentary for an NFL game (Seattle versus the Kansas City Chiefs), on NBC, on December 27, 1987.

BIBLIOGRAPHY

Barber, Red, "We Were Making History—Flying Blind," *TV Guide*, August 24, 1974, pp. 16–17.

Barnett, Steven. *Games and Sets: The Changing Face of Sport on Television*. Indianapolis: Indiana University Press, 1990.

Cosell, Howard. *Like It Is*. Chicago: Playboy Press, 1974.

Cosell, Howard, and Peter Bonventre. *I Never Played the Game*. New York: William Morrow, 1985.

McKay, Jim. *My Wide World*. New York: Macmillan, 1973.

O'Neil, Terry. *The Game behind the Game: High Pressure, High Stakes in Television Sports*. New York: Harper & Row, 1989.

Patton, Phil. *Razzle-Dazzle: The Curious Marriage of Television and Professional Football*. Garden City, N.Y.: Dial Press, 1984.

Powers, Ron. *Supertube: The Rise of Television Sports*. New York: Coward-McCann, 1984.

Rader, Benjamin G. *In Its Own Image: How Television Has Transformed Sports*. New York: Free Press, 1984.

Smith, Curt. *Voices of the Game: The First Full-Scale Overview of Baseball Broadcasting, 1921 to the Present*. South Bend, Ind.: Diamond Communications, 1987.

Wolf, Warner, and William Taafe. *Gimme a Break!* New York: McGraw-Hill, 1983.

SPORTSCHANNEL AMERICA is a joint venture of NBC* and Rainbow Programming Services Corp.,* which began broadcasting on January 3, 1989. Seen by 10 million subscribers, twenty-four hours a day, Sportschannel America is a national sports-programming cable network, which has its origins in the various regional cable sports networks that sprang up in the late seventies, the first of which was SportsChannel New York, founded in 1976 by Cablevision Systems chairman and chief executive officer Charles Dolan. E. James Greiner became the first president of Sportschannel America, in March 1989.

Address: 150 Crossways Park West, Woodbury, NY 11797.

BIBLIOGRAPHY

Snyder, Adam, "Facing Off over Regional Sports," *Channels of Communications*, vol. X, no. 1, January 1990, pp. 62–66.

SPORTS PROGRAMS, INC. was a packager for television of sports programming, founded in 1957 by Edgar J. Scherick, and acquired by ABC* in 1961.

SPORTSVISION, INC. was a San Francisco–based producer of various syndicated sports series, including *All American Game of the Week*, *Big Ten Football Hilites*, *Gridiron Cavalcade*, and *Summer Football*. It was active from the mid-fifties through the mid-sixties, later moving its base to Los Angeles and changing its name to Sports TV, Inc.

SPOTLIGHT was a pay-cable network, providing feature film presentations twenty-four hours a day, and launched in 1981 by the Times Mirror Co. (publisher of the *Los Angeles Times*). In December of that year, four other cable systems, Storer; Cox; Tele-Communications, Inc.;* and Cablevision joined with Times Mirror, but the network was only available on cable systems owned by those companies. In March 1983, Cablevision withdrew from the network, and Spotlight ceased as of January 31, 1984, with its assets being sold to Showtime/The Movie Channel, Inc.*

STAGE FIVE PRODUCTIONS was actor/writer/producer Ozzie Nelson's company, and was responsible for *The Adventures of Ozzie and Harriet* (ABC, 1952–1966).

BIBLIOGRAPHY

Nelson, Ozzie. *Ozzie*. Englewood Cliffs, N.J.: Prentice-Hall, 1973.

THE STATION REPRESENTATIVES ASSOCIATION, INC. was organized in 1947 as the National Association of Radio Station Representatives. It is the trade organization for the representative firms that handle national spot advertising sales for television and radio stations. It has lobbied the FCC* regarding such matters as the Prime Time Access Rule* and the Network Financial Interest and Syndication rules.

Address: 230 Park Avenue, New York, NY 10169.

STAUFFER COMMUNICATIONS, INC. publishes nineteen daily newspapers, and owns five radio stations and nine television stations: KTVS-Sterling, Colorado; WIBW-Topeka, Kansas; WMIZ-Columbia, Missouri; KGWC-Casper, Wyoming; KGWN-Cheyenne, Wyoming; KGWL-Lander, Wyoming; KGWR–Rock Springs, Wyoming; KSTF-Scottsbluff, Nebraska; and KMLT-Amarillo, Texas. The company was founded in 1930 as Stauffer Publications, Inc., and the name was changed in June 1977.

Address: Sixth and Jefferson, Topeka, KS 66607.

STEPHEN J. CANNELL PRODUCTIONS. Stephen J. Cannell was one of the most successful television writers at Universal when he left the studio in 1979 to form Stephen J. Cannell Productions. The company had a five-pilot exclusive deal with ABC,* but its first major success was on NBC* with *The A-Team* (1983–1987). Other Cannell productions include *The Greatest American Hero* (ABC, 1981–1983), *The Rousters* (NBC, 1983–1984), *Hardcastle and McCormick* (ABC, 1983–1986), *Riptide* (NBC, 1984–1986), *Hunter* (NBC, 1984-), *Stingray* (NBC, 1986–1987), *Wise Guy* (CBS, 1987-), and *21 Jump Street* (Fox, 1987-1990).

In 1981, Cannell Music Publishing and S.J.C. Music was formed to handle music rights to the Cannell productions. The company moved to its present Hollywood Boulevard headquarters in the summer of 1983. In 1988, Cannell opened North Shore Studios in Canada, with Cannell Films of Canada Ltd. as its principle tenant, and since then, 75 percent of all Cannell productions have been shot in Canada.

The Cannell Studios was formed in a 1987 reorganization as the holding company for Stephen J. Cannell Productions, with Cannell as its chief executive officer and Michael Dubelko as the president. Two years later, Cannell Communications, Inc. was formed to purchase and manage television broadcast properties. The Cannell Studios has a one-third interest in Televentures, a syndication company co-owned with Tri-Star and Witt-Thomas Productions,* and also owns two television stations, WHNS-Greenville, South Carolina, and WUAB-Cleveland, Ohio.

Address: 7083 Hollywood Boulevard, Hollywood, CA 90028.

BIBLIOGRAPHY

Koch, Neal, "Action-Packed Expansion," *Channels of Communications*, vol. X, no. 4, April 9, 1990, pp. 20–28.

Walsh, James, "Independent Productions," *Los Angeles Business*, May 1990, pp. 147–152.

STEREO. In 1984, the FCC* approved a stereo standard for broadcasters that called for left and right audio channels and a third, separate audio program channel, following the recommendations of the Broadcast Television Systems Committee. The separate audio program channel (SAP) can be used for simulcast audio in a non-English language. Prior to 1984, it was necessary for a television station to utilize also an FM radio station to provide stereophonic sound accompaniment to a television program. Such stereo broadcasts were usually of concerts or live popular music performances, and the first live stereo broadcast was of *Live from Lincoln Center* on PBS* on January 30, 1976.

BIBLIOGRAPHY

Prentiss, Stan. *AM Stereo and TV Stereo: New Sound Dimensions*. Blue Ridge Summit, Pa.: TAB Books, 1985.

Schubin, Mark, "The First Nationwide Live Stereo Simulcast Network," *SMPTE Journal*, vol. LXXXVI, no. 1, January 1977, pp. 9–12.

Snyder, Adam, "Broadcasters Are Waiting with Both Ears Cocked," *Channels of Communications*, vol. VII, no. 11, December 1987, p. 86.

STERLING TELEVISION CO., INC. was the television arm of Sterling Films, Inc. organized in 1946 by Saul J. Turell and Robert Rhoades as a producer and distributor of educational short subjects. The television division was created in 1949 when Bernice Coe joined the company. With over 3,000 short subjects, 28 features, and 176 cartoons, Sterling claimed to be the largest distributor of short subjects in the world. Aside from its shorts, it handled a number of television series, including two 1953 syndicated series, *This Is Charles Laughton* and *Movie Museum*.

The company was merged to form Walter Reade/Sterling, Inc. in July 1963. It was reorganized under Chapter XI of the Bankruptcy Act in May 1981, and acquired by Columbia Pictures Industries, Inc. on January 23, 1986.

STEVEN BOCHCO PRODUCTIONS, INC. was formed in 1988 as an independent production company, with an exclusive contract with ABC* and a distribution deal with 20th Century–Fox, on whose lot the company is located. Its first production was *Doogie Howser, M.D.* (ABC, 1989-   ). The company's logo is an animated, colored photograph of Bochco's father playing the violin.

Address: 10201 West Pico Boulevard, Los Angeles, CA 90035.

BIBLIOGRAPHY

Span, Paula, "Bochco on the Edge," *Esquire*, May 1990, pp. 158–168.

STORER BROADCASTING CO. was started in 1927 by George Butler Storer (1899–1975) with one radio station in Toledo, Ohio. Storer, who had earlier been in business as owner of the Standard Tube Co., was the company's president from 1927 to 1961. In the mid-sixties, the company's profit began to drop. It changed its name to Storer Communications, Inc. in 1983, merged into SCI

Holdings Inc. in 1985, and sold its seven television stations in 1987. The company continues in existence as an operator of cable communications systems.

Address: 1200 Biscayne Boulevard, Miami, FL 33181–2710.

BIBLIOGRAPHY

"The Broadcaster Who Fell from Grace with the Seers," *Fortune*, April 1, 1977, pp. 48–49.

"STRIPING" is the name given to the practice of scheduling a specific program at the same time every day or every week. It is generally used in reference to syndicated programming.

STU BILLETT PRODUCTIONS was founded in 1978 by the former head of development at Hatos-Hall Productions.* It produced two pilots for NBC, *Whodunit?* and *Fantasies Fulfilled*, and then, in 1979, became part of Ralph Edwards Productions.*

STUDIO CITY TV PRODUCTIONS, INC. was the television production subsidiary of Republic Pictures Corporation, headed by Morton W. Scott. Among the series that it produced, all for syndication, were *Stories of the Century* (1954), *The Adventures of Fu Manchu* (1955), and *Frontier Doctor* (1956). Just as Studio City was created to "hide" Republic's involvement in television during a period when the major studios were opposed to the new medium, a second company, Hollywood Television Service, Inc.* was also created by Republic for the television distribution of its product.

STUDIO 8-H is the legendary NBC* studio at the network's 30 Rockefeller Plaza, New York City headquarters. It was built in 1937 for the NBC Symphony Orchestra, which had been formed the previous year under the baton of Arturo Toscanini. Because of its construction, it was often referred to as the only "floating" studio in the world. In 1975, it became the permanent home for NBC's *Saturday Night Live*. NBC introduced a short-lived cultural series, *Live from Studio 8-H*, in the 1979–1980 season.

STUDIO FILMS, INC. (S.A. Costello, president) was a New York–based producer and distributor, active in the fifties. It distributed 1,120 musical shorts to television, and was also responsible for the 1955 thirty-minute syndicated series *Showtime*, with Frankie Fontaine.

STUDIO 3-H was the first fully equipped television studio in the United States, located on the third floor of the RCA* Building at Rockefeller Center. Converted from a radio studio, it was opened by NBC* in January 1944, and merged into Studio 3-K in 1952. Among the programs broadcast from the studio during at least part of their runs were *Kraft Television Theatre*, *Howdy Doody Time*, and *Author Meets Critics*.

BIBLIOGRAPHY
Kalmus, Allan H., "The Little Studio That Could," *Television Quarterly*, vol. XXIII, no. 4, 1988, pp. 39–45.

STV or Subscription Television is a system whereby programs are transmitted in the normal way, but in a scrambled form, which the viewer can only unscramble by way of a rented decoder. Skiatron* was the best-known experimental STV system, and was first offered in 1951, but it was not until 1968 that the FCC* adopted rules permitting STV on a regular basis.

BIBLIOGRAPHY
Nadel, Mark, and Eli Noman, editors. *The Economics of Subscription Television (STV): An Anthology*. New York: Columbia University, Graduate School of Business, 1983.

SUBSCRIPTION TELEVISION was a pay-cable company, offering feature films and sports events to its subscribers, formed by Sylvester L. "Pat" Weaver in 1962, and serving the Los Angeles and San Francisco areas. Opposition by California theatre owners and television stations led to the passage of a November 1964 statewide initiative banning pay television in the state under the banner of "Save Free TV." The California Supreme Court ruled the initiative unconstitutional, but not in time to save Subscription Television, which ceased operations in 1966.

SUPER CHANNEL is a major European satellite cable channel, providing general programming twenty-four hours a day throughout the continent. It was created by the Virgin Group and various independent television networks in the United Kingdom, and began broadcasting on January 30, 1987.

Address: 19–21 Rathbone Place, London W1P 1DS, United Kingdom.

A SUPERSTATION is a local television station that beams its signal up to a satellite and thus makes its programming available throughout the area, usually the entire United States, that is served by that satellite. Major U.S. Superstations are the Turner Broadcasting System* Superstation (WTBS), WGN,* WPIX,* WSBK,* and WWOR.*

SVERIGES TELEVISION (SVT) is Sweden's public television network, with two channels, TV1 and TV2, which are separately operated and managed. Funded through license fees paid by television receiver owners, SVT carries no commercial advertising, and utilizes the PAL* color system. It began broadcasting in the fall of 1956, with stations in Stockholm and Gothenburg, and went nationwide the following year. The second television channel was introduced in 1970. As early as 1938, Svenska Radio AB had broadcast television programming for Christmas shoppers in Stockholm.

Address: S–105/Oxenstiengatan 26–34, Stockholm 10, Sweden.

BIBLIOGRAPHY
Polman, Edward. *Broadcasting in Sweden*. Boston: Routledge & Kegan Paul, 1976.

SWEEPS WEEKS are the most important weeks in the television industry calendar, and constitute the period during which the television audience is measured by the various ratings services. Those ratings affect the rates that the stations and the networks are able to charge for their advertising time. Sweeps weeks are held four times a year, in November, February, May, and July. During sweeps weeks, stations and networks air what they conceive of as their most popular programming, and often resort to considerable hyperbole and crude promotional techniques in order to increase their audience and, consequently, their ratings.

BIBLIOGRAPHY
Beville, Hugh Malcolm, Jr. *Audience Ratings: Radio, Television, and Cable*. Hillsdale, N.J.: Lawrence Erlbaum Associates, 1985.
Christensen, Mark, and Cameron Smith. *The Sweeps: Behind the Scenes in Network Television*. New York: William Morrow, 1984.

SYLVANIA ELECTRIC PRODUCTS, INC. began as a manufacturer of incandescent bulbs—it introduced fluorescent lighting in 1938. Under the direction of Don G. Mitchell (born 1905), Sylvania expanded, adding radio tubes, photoflash bulbs, radios, picture tubes, and television receivers. (Mitchell became vice-president of the company in 1942, president from 1946 to 1953, and chairman of the board from 1953 to 1959.) In keeping with its prominence as a major manufacturer of television receivers, Sylvania also sponsored the Sylvania TV Awards, presented in the fifties in recognition of creative television techniques. On March 5, 1959, the company merged into General Telephone & Electronics Corp.

BIBLIOGRAPHY
"Salesman's Glow," *Time*, June 18, 1951, pp. 93–94.

SYNDICAST SERVICES, INC. was a New York–based syndication distributor active in the seventies and eighties, and headed by Leonard V. Koch. Among the series that it handled were *Black Omnibus* (1975), *The Bobby Vinton Show* (1975–1976), and *Sammy and Company* (1975–1976).

SYNDICATED EXCLUSIVITY was a ruling that required local cable systems to black out programming in order to protect syndicated programming. In other words, if a local television station had the exclusive syndication rights to a television series, such as *I Love Lucy* or *The Donna Reed Show*, the cable system operator in that same area would not be allowed to provide his subscribers with the same shows broadcast on a cable network. The ruling was rescinded by the FCC* in 1980.

SYNDICATION. The FCC* defines syndication as "any program sold, licensed, distributed, or offered to television stations in more than one market within the United States for noninterconnected television broadcast exhibition, but not including live presentations." Syndicated programs are seen on non-network television and are continually "resold" or syndicated. Syndicated shows can include both new programs made specifically for the syndication market and former network shows later released to syndication (and sometimes, but not in recent years, retitled). First-Run Syndication is the name given to programming that has not previously been seen on network television, such as most game shows and many talk shows. Some network programs continue to be produced for first-run syndication after they have been cancelled by their respective networks (for example, *Too Close for Comfort* and *Fame*). Distributors are called syndicators. Some produce the shows themselves, but most purchase the distribution rights from independent producers.

The concept of syndication goes back in the broadcasting field to radio, and before that to the newspaper industry, in which personality columns and comic strips are syndicated. The first major producer and distributor of syndicated television programming was Ziv Television Programs, Inc.,* which had earlier been involved in radio syndication. According to historian Hal Erickson, the first syndicated television program was *Public Prosecutor*, starring John Howard, and produced in 1947 by Jerry Fairbanks Productions.* Probably the most popular network series ever to be syndicated was *I Love Lucy*.

BIBLIOGRAPHY

Eisner, Joel, and David Krinsky. *Television Comedy Series: An Episode Guide to 153 Sitcoms in Syndication*. Jefferson, N.C.: McFarland, 1984.

Erickson, Hal. *Syndicated Television: The First Forty Years, 1947–1987*. Jefferson, N.C.: McFarland, 1989.

Head, Sydney W., and Christopher H. Sterling, "Nonnetwork Programs," in *Broadcasting in America: A Survey of Electronic Media*. Boston: Houghton Mifflin, 1987, pp. 345–369.

Van Petten, Vance Scott, editor. *Television Syndication: A Practical Guide to Business and Legal Issues*. Los Angeles: Los Angeles County Bar Association, 1987.

T

TALENT ASSOCIATES, INC. was founded in 1952 by David Susskind (1920–1987), and became a major producer of television programming with shows as varied as *Mr. Peepers* (NBC, 1952–1955), *Open End* (Syndicated, 1958–1967), *The Play of the Week* (Syndicated, 1959–1960), *Get Smart* (NBC, 1965–1969; CBS, 1969–1970), and *The David Susskind Show* (Syndicated, 1967–1986). The company was acquired by Norton Simon, Inc. in 1970, at which time the name was changed to Talent Associates–Norton Simon. In 1977, the company was purchased by Time-Life Films, Inc. for a reported $3 million.

TALK SHOWS are staple programming for both national and local television. The most prominent seen on national television include *Meet the Press* (NBC, 1947-   ); *That Reminds Me* (ABC, 1948); *America's Town Meeting* (ABC, 1948–1949, 1952); *People's Platform* (CBS, 1948–1950), with Charles Collingwood; *Newsweek Views the News* (DuMont, 1948–1950); *Washington Report* (DuMont, 1951); *Man of the Week* (CBS, 1951–1954); *Person to Person* (CBS, 1953–1961), with Edward R. Murrow and later, Charles Collingwood; *Answers for Americans* (ABC, 1953–1954); *Face the Nation* (CBS, 1954–1961, 1963-   ); *The Mike Wallace Interview* (ABC, 1957–1958); *The Jack Paar Show* (NBC, 1957–1961); *Small World* (CBS, 1958–1959), with Edward R. Murrow; *The David Susskind Show* (Syndicated, 1958–1987); *Washington Conversation* (CBS, 1961–1962); *Kup's Show* (Syndicated, 1962–1975; PBS, 1975-   ), with Irv Kupcinet; *Who in the World* (CBS, 1962), with Warren Hull; *The Tonight Show Starring Johnny Carson* (NBC, 1962-   ); *The Merv Griffin Show* (NBC, 1962–1963; Syndicated, 1965–1969; CBS, 1969–1972; Syndicated, 1972–1986); *Girl Talk* (Syndicated, 1962–1970), with Virginia Graham; *The Pamela Mason Show* (Syndicated, 1963); *The Mike Douglas Show* (Syndicated, 1963–1982); *The Regis Philbin Show* (Syndicated, 1964–1965; NBC, 1981–1982); *The Young Set* (ABC, 1965), with Phyllis Kirk; *The Joe Pyne Show* (Syndicated, 1965–1967); *Book*

Beat (PBS, 1965-   ); *The Hy Gardner Show* (Syndicated, 1965); *Firing Line* (Syndicated, 1966–1971; PBS, 1971-   ), with William F. Buckley, Jr.; *Washington Week in Review* (PBS, 1967-   ); *The Woody Woodbury Show* (Syndicated, 1967); *The Joe Namath Show* (Syndicated, 1969); *The David Frost Show* (Syndicated, 1969–1972); *Dinah's Place* (NBC, 1970–1974), with Dinah Shore; *Donahue* (Syndicated, 1970-   ), with Phil Donahue; *The Virginia Graham Show* (Syndicated, 1970–1972); *Not for Women Only* (Syndicated, 1971–1979); *The Sheila MacRae Show* (Syndicated, 1971); *Dinah!* (Syndicated, 1974–1980), with Dinah Shore; *Jeanne Wolf With* (PBS, 1974–1975); *Conversations with Eric Sevareid* (CBS, 1975); *Headliners with David Frost* (NBC, 1978); *The John Davidson Show* (Syndicated, 1980–1982); *The Larry King Show* (Syndicated, 1983); *Thicke of the Night* (Syndicated, 1983–1984), with Alan Thicke; *Sally Jessy Raphäel* (Syndicated, 1984-   ); *Larry King Live!* (CNN, 1985-   ); *The Late Show with Joan Rivers* (Fox, 1986–1987); *The Oprah Winfrey Show* (Syndicated, 1986-   ); *Geraldo* (Syndicated, 1987-   ), with Geraldo Rivera; and *The Arsenio Hall Show* (Syndicated, 1988-   ).

BIBLIOGRAPHY

Cavett, Dick, and Christopher Porterfield. *Cavett*. New York: Harcourt Brace Jovanovich, 1974.

———. *Eye on Cavett*. New York: Arbor House, 1983.

Donahue, Phil. *Donahue*. New York: Simon and Schuster, 1979.

Downs, Hugh. *On Camera: My 10,000 Hours on Television*. New York: G.P. Putnam's Sons, 1986.

Druxman, Michael. *Merv*. New York: Award Books, 1976.

Franklin, Joe. *A Gift for People*. New York: M. Evans, 1978.

Frischauer, Willi. *Will You Now Welcome . . . David Frost*. New York: Hawthorn Books, 1971.

Galanoy, Terry. *Tonight!* Garden City, N.Y.: Doubleday, 1972.

Griffin, Merv. *Merv*. New York: Simon and Schuster, 1980.

Griffin, Merv, and Peter Barsocchini. *From Where I Sit*. New York: Arbor House, 1982.

Johnson, George. *The Real Jack Paar*. New York: Gold Medal Books, 1962.

King, Larry, with Peter Occhiogrosso. *Tell It to the King*. New York: G.P. Putnam's Sons, 1988.

King, Larry, with Emily Yoffe. *Larry King*. New York: Simon and Schuster, 1982.

King, Norman. *Everybody Loves Oprah!* New York: William Morrow, 1987.

Lardine, Robert. *He-e-e-ere's Johnny*. New York: Award Books, 1975.

Leamer, Lawrence. *King of the Night*. New York: William Morrow, 1989.

Lorence, Douglas. *Johnny Carson*. New York: Drake, 1975.

McMahon, Ed, and Carroll Carroll. *Here's Ed*. New York: G.P. Putnam's Sons, 1976.

Metz, Robert. *The Tonight Show*. New York: Playboy Press, 1980.

Mincer, Richard, and Deanne Mincer. *The Talk Show Book: An Engaging Primer on How To Talk Your Way to Success*. New York: Facts on File, 1982.

Paar, Jack. *I Kid You Not*. Boston: Little, Brown, 1960.

———. *My Saber Is Bent*. New York: Trident Press, 1961.

———. *P.S. Jack Paar*. Garden City, N.Y.: Doubleday, 1979.

Rivers, Joan. *Enter Talking*. New York: Delacorte Press, 1986.

Tennis, Craig. *Johnny Tonight!* New York: Pocket Books, 1980.
Waldron, Robert. *Oprah!* New York: St. Martin's Press, 1987.

"T 'N' A" is the acronym for "Tits and Ass," a term introduced in the mid-seventies to refer to a trend in television toward gratuitous semi-nudity and what was called in the industry "jiggle" (bouncing breasts). Its use in shows such as *Charlie's Angels* (ABC, 1976–1981) led to the growth of the Moral Majority movement, led by the Rev. Jerry Falwell, which sought, in part, to clean up television.

T-BAR-V PRODUCTIONS, INC. was operated from the mid-fifties through the mid-sixties by Donna Fargo. Based in Los Angeles, it listed a number of Western television productions (including *Rodeo Revue*, *T-Bar-V Stories*, *Tom-Tom Tales*, *Trader Lee*, and *Window to the West*), but there is no record indicating that any of these shows was ever produced. They may have been abortive projects or they may have been sold only to a limited Southern television market.

THE TEEVEE COMPANY, headed by Gifford Phillips and Ludlow Flower, Jr., was a Beverly Hills–based producer of the fifties and early sixties. It was responsible for the fifteen-minute *Little Theatre* series (Syndicated, 1951), consisting of two short dramas, and twenty-six episodes of *Tales of Tomorrow* (ABC, 1951–1955).

TELAMERICA, INC., headed by John Whitaker, was a minor New York–based producer of the fifties.

TELE-AMERICA, INC. was a Beverly Hills–based producer, primarily of television commercials, active in the fifties. It was operated by Thor L. Brooks, who was also on the staff of KLAC-Los Angeles.

TELE-COMMUNICATIONS, INC. is the largest American cable systems operator, providing basic cable service to 7.8 million subscribers and pay-cable television service to 5.8 million. It also owns a 22 percent interest in the Turner Broadcasting System,* a 50 percent interest in Showtime/The Movie Channel, Inc.,* a 50 percent interest in The Discovery Channel,* a 50 percent interest in American Movie Classics,* and a 14 percent interest in Black Entertainment Television.* It is a majority shareholder in United Artists Entertainment Co., which owns theatres and cable television systems, and was originally incorporated in 1926 as United Artists Circuit, Inc. Tele-Communications, Inc. was incorporated in August 1968. In October of that year, it acquired Community Tele-Communications, Inc. and Western Tele-Communications, Inc. (which it renamed WestMarc Communications, Inc.).

Address: Regency Plaza One, Suite 600, 4643 South Ulster Street, Denver, CO 80237; P.O. Box 5630, Denver, CO 80217.

THE TELECOMMUNICATIONS CONSUMER COALITION was founded in 1978 as a clearinghouse for information on telecommunications as they affect the consumer.

Address: 105 Madison Avenue, Suite 921, New York, NY 10016.

THE TELECOMMUNICATIONS MUSEUM, located in Stockholm's Tekniska Museum, consists of a collection of equipment illustrating the history of telegraphy, computers, radio, and television in Sweden. A special exhibit shows the history of the Swedish Telecommunications Administration, whose assembly room forms part of the museum. The museum was opened at Karlaplan in 1937, and moved to the Tekniska Museum in December 1975. The portion of the museum devoted to television was not opened until March 1979.

Address: Museivägen 7, 115 27 Stockholm, Sweden.

THE TELECOMMUNICATIONS RESEARCH AND ACTION CENTER, formerly known as the National Citizens Committee for Public Television and the National Citizens Committee for Broadcasting, was founded in 1967, and advocates public action to improve the quality of the communications media.

Address: P.O. Box 12038, Washington, DC 20005.

TELEFILM, INC. was founded in Los Angeles in 1938 by Joe Thomas, Pete Gioga, and Pete Comandini, initially as a 16mm producer of industrial films. It also filmed the final moments of horse races at local tracks in the possibility that a dispute might arise as to the winner. The company became involved in television in 1948, producing television commercials, an early human interest series titled *Screen Snapshots*, and five Spade Cooley 16mm, color, feature-length television Westerns. It ceased operations in 1965 when the company was sold to Nate Lieberman.

TELEFILM ENTERPRISES was a New York–based distributor, active in the fifties. The most important of the series that it distributed was *Fabian of Scotland Yard* (Syndicated, 1955). Owner Charles Wick later changed the company name to Wick Films, Inc.

TELEFIRST. In 1982, ABC* and Sony created TeleFirst, which would transmit recent theatrical features to subscribers' homes late at night, while they were asleep; the films were to be recorded on the subscribers' videocassette recorders (VCRs), for later viewing. The project was test-marketed in Chicago but failed to generate much public interest and was quickly abandoned.

TELEKLEW was founded in 1955 by Lawrence Welk to handle various production responsibilities for *The Lawrence Welk Show*, which was first seen on ABC* on July 2, 1955. In 1957, Teleklew made its first major investment, the purchase of the Harry Von Tilzer Music Publishing Company, which marked the establishment of the Welk Music Group, the assets of which were sold to Polygram International Publishing Companies in 1988. In 1960, the company entered real estate development, initially in Santa Monica, California, and later in Escondido, California, where the Lawrence Welk Resort was created in 1964.

Related companies include Lawrence Welk Syndication, which has been responsible for the airing of *The Lawrence Welk Show* on public television since 1989; Welk Home Entertainment, founded in 1987 to market home videocassettes of the Lawrence Welk shows; the Welk Record Group, which began as Ranwood Records, and includes Vanguard, Hindsight, and Tomato Records; and the Welk Entertainment Group, founded in 1989, which is involved in the production and distribution of various television shows. Lawrence Welk serves as chairman of the board, and his son Larry has been president since 1981. Ted Lennon, who joined Teleklew in 1957 as a talent scout, is executive vice-president, and Margaret Heron, who joined the company in 1961, is its manager.

Address: 1299 Ocean Avenue, Suite 800, Santa Monica, CA 90401.

TELEMATED MOTION PICTURES was founded in New York in 1947 as Telemated Cartoons by Saul S. Taffet. He recalls, "Telemated Cartoons was a name which I contrived from the dual concepts of cartoons which were animated especially for television applications and animated cartoons which were produced to be technically matched or mated to the special requirements of broadcast television." As the company became more involved in the production of live-action commercials rather than animated commercials, the name was changed from Telemated Cartoons, with the company eventually relocating to Florida.

Address: 137 Southwest 54 Street, Cape Coral, FL 33914.

TELEMETER was a pay-television system, marketed by International Telemeter Corporation, a subsidiary of Paramount Pictures. It was first tested over KTLA,* the wholly owned Paramount television station in Los Angeles, in 1951, and later experiments took place in Palm Springs. International Telemeter Corporation remained in existence through 1965, but its pay-television system never came to fruition.

TELEMOUNT PICTURES, INC. was created by Henry B. Donovan for the production of *Cowboy G-Men* (Syndicated, 1952), which Donovan produced, directed, and wrote. The firm continues to the present as owner and distributor of the series.

Address: P.O. Box 1106, Santa Monica, CA 90406.

TELEMUSEUM. See THE TELECOMMUNICATIONS MUSEUM

TELENEWS PRODUCTIONS, INC./TELENEWS FILM CORPORATION was a New York–based production company, headed by Herbert Scheftel, and active in the fifties and sixties. It was responsible for a number of syndicated sports programs: *This Week in Sports* (1953), *Sports Extra* (1953), and *Adventures in Sports* (1956).

TELE-PICTURES, INC., founded by E.J. Baumgarten, was a Los Angeles–based distributor to television of 110 feature films and 13 featurettes. It was active in the fifties.

TELEPROGRAMS, INC. was a New York–based producer of public information programs, owned by Robert Wald, and active in the mid-fifties.

THE TELEPROMPTER is a machine that permits television performers to read their lines from a screen off-camera. The front-lit script appears on the teleprompter on a continuous moving strip of paper. A master control is used to monitor the speed at which the script is moving. The idea originated with actor Fred Barton, who interested two then–20th Century–Fox executives, Hubert J. Schlafly and Irving Kahn. Kahn developed the device with the TelePrompTer Corporation,* and it was first used at the 1952 political conventions. By 1953, the machine was in use in virtually all live television programs as well as the filmed *Dragnet* series.

BIBLIOGRAPHY

Barton, Fred, and H.J. Schlafly, "TelePrompter—New Production Tool," *Journal of the Society of Motion Picture and Television Engineers*, vol. LVIII, no. 6, June 1952, pp. 515–521.
"Mechanical Memorizers," *TV Guide*, December 4, 1953, pp. 18–19.

THE TELEPROMPTER CORPORATION was a major cable television systems operator, founded in 1950 by Irving B. Kahn (born 1917), who was its chairman and president until 1971. In 1960, the company experimented with the Key TV-viewer-selection pay-cable system. The following year, it acquired the Johnstown, Pennsylvania, cable franchise, and expanded its operation rapidly with the acquisition of the cable franchise for upper Manhattan. In 1966, Kahn was accused of bribing Johnstown officials and trading in TelePrompTer shares was briefly suspended. In 1972, TelePrompTer delivered the first pay–sports programming on its Long Island cable system, and in 1979 acquired a half interest in Showtime/The Movie Channel, Inc.* On August 18, 1981, TelePrompTer was acquired by the Westinghouse Electric Corp. for $646 million. At the time of the acquisition, it owned 114 cable systems in thirty-two states.

TelePrompTer is written thus, but the cueing device for actors that it initially marketed is generally written "Teleprompter."

TELEREP was founded in December 1968 as a sales representative for Chris Craft Broadcasting by Al Masini. In 1972, the company was sold to Cox Broadcasting, and as of 1989, TeleRep represented fifty-nine major television stations. For Operation Prime Time, Masini created *Solid Gold '79*, starring Dionne Warwick and Glen Campbell. As part of his plan to create a series from the special, Masini created Television Program Enterprises (TPE). Aside from the syndicated series *Solid Gold* (1980-   ), TPE has also been responsible for *Entertainment Tonight* (1981-   ), *Star Search* (1983-   ), and *Lifestyles of the Rich* *and Famous* (1984–   ), as well as other, shorter lived syndicated series. A second subsidiary company, Teletrib, was created by Masini in 1987 as a barter* sales operation. Its programs include *Charles in Charge* (1987) and *Geraldo* (1987–   ).

Address: 875 Third Avenue, New York, NY 10022.

BIBLIOGRAPHY

"TeleRep: 20 Years of Leadership," *Television/Radio Age*, February 1989, pp. A1–A44.

TELESCENE FILM PRODUCTIONS CO. was a New York–based producer and distributor, active in the fifties and sixties, and responsible for the fifteen-minute syndicated series from the mid-fifties *Pulse of the City*.

TELE-SESSIONS was the name given in 1955 to the closed circuit Theater Television* programming, pioneered by Nathan L. Halpern's Theatre Network Television, Inc.

BIBLIOGRAPHY

Halpern, Nathan L., "Fastest Growing TV," *Television Daily Program Buyers Guide*, 1956, p. 159.

TELETEXT is a one-way system of storing and displaying printed and graphic materials on a home television screen.

See also TEXT SERVICE CABLE NETWORKS.

BIBLIOGRAPHY

Alber, Antone F. *Videotex/Teletext: Principles and Practices*. New York: McGraw-Hill, 1985.

Tydeman, John, Hubert Lipinski, Richard P. Adler, Michael Nyhan, and Lawrence Zwimpfer. *Teletext and Videotex in the United States: Market Potential, Technology, Public Policy Issues*. New York: McGraw-Hill, 1982.

Veith, Richard H. *Television's Teletext*. New York: North-Holland, 1983.

TELETHON. Derived from the words "television" and "marathon," a telethon is defined by Webster's *New World Dictionary* as a lengthy telecast. However, it is virtually always used by the television industry and the television audience to describe a charitable fund-raising event, for which one or a group of television stations have donated their time and services. Most telethons last an entire day, and the most famous is the Labor Day telethon for muscular dystrophy and other muscle diseases, hosted by Jerry Lewis (born 1926). First seen in 1966 on one New York television station, the Muscular Dystrophy Association Jerry Lewis Labor Day Telethon was broadcast in 1990 by approximately 200 stations.

There is no documentation as to the origins of telethons, but Jerry Lewis claims to have hosted his first, in New York, in 1949. The first British telethon was broadcast on Thames Television plc* on October 2, 1980, on behalf of a group of children's charities.

TELEVENTURES is a distributor of television programming in both the United States and abroad. It was founded in 1986 by Tri-Star Pictures, Stephen J. Cannell Productions,* and Witt/Thomas Productions.*
    Address: TeleVentures, 1925 Century Park East, Suite 2140, Los Angeles, CA 90067.

TELEVISA SA is the major, privately owned television network in Mexico, with four channels nationwide and five cable channels in Mexico City. Television was first introduced in Mexico in 1950, and Televisa SA began broadcasting in 1973.
    Address: Av. Chapultepec 18, Mexico City 7 D.F., Mexico.

TELEVISION was promoted as "The World's First Television Journal," and published under the auspices of the Television Society of the United Kingdom from March 1928 through 1932, when it was taken over by the publishers Benn Brothers Ltd. The periodical underwent several name changes after 1935, and is currently published as *Electronic Engineering*.
BIBLIOGRAPHY
Slide, Anthony, editor. *International Film, Radio, and Television Journals*. Westport, Conn.: Greenwood Press, 1985.

TELEVISION AFFILIATES CORP. was a broadcasters' cooperative, serving as a clearinghouse or television program exchange for locally produced informational, cultural, and educational programs. Based in New York, it was founded by Trans-Lux executive Richard Carlton, and operated as a subsidiary of Trans-Lux.

TELEVISION AND RADIO FEATURES OF AMERICA, headed by Oliver W. Nicholl, was a New York–based producer and packager, active in the early fifties.

TELEVISION CLEARING HOUSE, operated by S. Samuel Liggett, was a Los Angeles–based distributor of feature films and series for television, active in the fifties and early sixties.

THE TELEVISION CODE of standards and practices, a form of self-regulation, was first drawn up by the National Association of Broadcasters* (NAB) in 1947 at a meeting in Atlantic City. In June 1951, NBC* made public its own code in Washington, D.C., and, as a result, a new code was drawn up by the NAB and went into effect on March 1, 1952. The code covered "Program Standards" and "Advertising Standards," and, supposedly, television stations violating the code could be (but never were) penalized.
    The code was revised many times, most notably in 1975, when a "Family Viewing Standard," aimed at cutting back on sex and violence in television

programming, was added as a result of pressure from Congress and the FCC.* The code officially ceased to exist in 1983, following a court ruling the previous year that found in favor of the Justice Department's charge that the code's limitations on advertising helped keep advertising rates artificially low.

Each edition of the *International Television Almanac* contains a copy of the code as approved for the year prior to the date of the almanac.

BIBLIOGRAPHY

McGannon, Donald H., "Is the TV Code a Fraud?" *TV Guide*, January 22, 1977, pp. 11–13.

TELEVISION CORPORATION, despite its name, was involved only in the production of theatrical features. It was founded in Colorado in October 1972 by Paul Harrison, Paul Lewis, and Harvey Pergament, and in July 1973 it announced that it had acquired the rights to the properties of writer-producer Philip Yordan.

TELEVISION CORPORATION OF AMERICA (T.C.A.) was formed in 1952 by comedian Lou Costello to handle royalties from *The Abbott and Costello Show* (Syndicated, 1951–1952). It is still extant, and is controlled by the comedian's children. Related Costello companies are Cosman Productions, Inc.* and Exclusive Productions, which was formed to make the 1952 feature film *Jack and the Beanstalk*.

BIBLIOGRAPHY

Costello, Chris, with Raymond Strait. *Lou's on First: A Biography*. New York: St. Martin's Press, 1981.

THE TELEVISION CRITICS ASSOCIATION was founded in June 1977, with its first president being Lee Winfrey of the *Philadelphia Inquirer*. An informal, non-profit organization, funded by annual membership dues from its one hundred or more members, the association represents the interests of its members and presents annual awards. In 1981, it considered but voted down a proposal to present an annual life achievement award.

Address: c/o Michael E. Hill, *Washington Post*, 1150 15 Street, N.W., Washington, DC 20071.

TELEVISION ENTERPRISES CORPORATION was a Los Angeles–based producer and distributor, active in the sixties. It specialized in financing the production of independent theatrical feature films, on the understanding that it would control the television rights. In 1966, it announced the sale of thirteen feature films, eleven of which were still to be made, to the five CBS*–owned television stations, the first time a station group had purchased a block of films prior to production. Television Enterprises Corporation was owned by Harold Goldman, formerly with NTA,* whose other companies included Television Exploitation Company* and Comet Television Films, Inc.

TELEVISIÓN ESPAÑOLA is Spain's official television network, and first began broadcasting on October 29, 1956. A second channel was added in 1967. It is administered by Radio-Televisión Española (RTVE), under the direction of the Ministry of Culture.
    Address: Paseo de la Castellana 109, Madrid 16, Spain.

TELEVISION EXPLOITATION COMPANY was a New York–based distributor of twenty-five feature films to television, founded in 1951 by Harold Goldman, and active through 1966.

THE TELEVISION FILM ASSOCIATION was a Los Angeles–based organization, active in the sixties. According to contemporary publicity, it was created "to maintain a liaison between the producers and distributors of television film, the TV stations, and the companies providing material and services to the TV industry; and to establish better operational practices and to standardize these practices."

THE TELEVISION FILM PRODUCERS ASSOCIATION was a short-lived organization, formed by Hal Roach, Jr. (1919–1972) in 1949. It was one of two rival organizations active in the fifties, with the other being the National Society of Television Producers, founded in 1951 by Louis D. Snader.
BIBLIOGRAPHY
"Roach, Jr., Resists Overtures by Rival TV Prods Assns," *Daily Variety*, September
        14, 1951, p. 8.

TELEVISION FILMS OF AMERICA was a minor Beverly Hills–based production company, operated by Jack Parker, and active in the early fifties.

TELEVISION FOR ALL CHILDREN (TVAC) was created in June 1977 to distribute programming funded by the U.S. Office of Education to local television stations willing to screen the material without commercial interruption. (In 1972, the U.S. Office of Education was required by Congress "to provide money for the production of television shows that would promote integration by giving children greater understanding of and respect for America's diverse racial and cultural heritages.")
BIBLIOGRAPHY
Margulies, Lee, "TVAC Offers New Views in Kidvid," *Los Angeles Times*, October
        26, 1979, part IV, p. 36.

TELEVISION GRAPHICS, INC., founded by Bernard Rubin, was a New York–based producer of television commercials, active in the fifties and sixties.

THE TELEVISION INDEX is a weekly production guide that began publication in 1949 as *Ross Reports: Television*. The latter was intended as a guide for individuals active in the television industry, providing listings of talent agencies, advertising agencies, and the like. It continues as a monthly publication. *Ross Reports: Television* was founded by Wallace A. Ross. Ross sold the publication in the early fifties to Jerry Leicher, who published it until his death in 1988.

Address: 40–29 27 Street, Long Island City, NY 11101.

THE TELEVISION INFORMATION OFFICE was created in October 1959, with financial support from ABC,* CBS,* NBC,* various commercial television stations, and the National Association of Broadcasters,* to provide "a two-way bridge between the television industry and its many publics." Based on New York City's Fifth Avenue, the Television Information Office funded a series of national surveys by the Roper Organization measuring changing public attitudes toward television, maintained a considerable publications program, and provided a research center and reference library. It ceased operations on March 31, 1989, and its research materials were moved to the Museum of Broadcasting.*

TELEVISION INTERNATIONAL CO., founded by Paul N. Robins, was a New York–based distributor to television of fifty-nine feature films, active in the fifties and early sixties.

TELEVISION NEWS, INC. (TVN) was founded in May 1973 by former ABC radio network president Robert Pauley (born 1923) and brewery executive Joseph Coors (born 1917) as a syndicated news service for independent television stations (which up to that time had relied on United Press International Television News, or UPITN, to provide them with news coverage). In January 1975, the company announced plans to use a domestic satellite (DOMSAT*) to distribute its news stories, but ceased operations later that same year, after losing $5 million, and before its plans could become reality.

BIBLIOGRAPHY

" . . . And Now from Our Man in Bangkok," *TV Guide*, June 8, 1974, pp. 21–22.

THE TELEVISION NEWS STUDY CENTER was created with a three-year grant in the fall of 1978 as part of the Audiovisual Department of George Washington University Library. The center (now defunct) provided access to the Vanderbilt Television News Archive,* offering playback facilities for viewing the latter's tapes, and was directed by Fay Schreibman.

THE TELEVISION OPERATORS CAUCUS, founded in 1984, is a professional organization for executives of independent television stations.

Address: c/o 901 31 Street, N.W., Washington, DC 20007.

THE TELEVISION PROGRAM EXPORT ASSOCIATION was formed in 1960 by the U.S. networks to represent their interests abroad. New York–based and headed by John G. McCarthy, the association was created, according to contemporary publicity, "to promote and expand the export of American TV programs throughout the world; to assist American exporters in reducing barriers to foreign distribution; [and] to compile, analyze and disseminate significant statistical information affecting foreign markets for American television programs.'' It ceased operations in 1970.

TELEVISION PROGRAMS OF AMERICA, INC., or TPA, was founded in 1953 by veteran film producer Edward "Eddie" Small (1891–1977), whose career had begun in 1917 and who had created Edward Small Productions in 1938. Associated with Small in the new venture were Milton A. Gordon and Michael M. Sillerman. Among the many syndicated television series distributed by TPA were *Ellery Queen* (1954), *The Count of Monte Cristo* (1955–1956), *Hawkeye and the Last of the Mohicans* (1957), *The New Adventures of Charlie Chan* (1957), *New York Confidential* (1958), *Tugboat Annie* (1958), and *Special Agent 7* (1958).

Arrow Productions, Inc., which had been formed by Small, Milton Gordon, and Leon Fromkess, was absorbed by TPA in the mid-fifties. Arrow had been responsible for the production of *Ramar of the Jungle* (Syndicated, 1952–1953), starring Jon Hall. In 1959, Television Programs of America was absorbed by ITC.*

BIBLIOGRAPHY

"Edward Small Takes Telepix Prod'n Plunge," *Daily Variety*, September 8, 1953, pp. 1, 10.

TELEVISION-RADIO-ENTERPRISES, INC. was founded in 1946 by Hugh Hole for the production of television and radio commercials. It ceased operations in 1948, when Hole became director of radio and television for Brooke, Smith, French & Dorrance, Inc.

TELEVISION SCREEN PRODUCTIONS, INC. was founded in 1948 by Charles J. Basch, Jr., and remained active through the early seventies. Based in New York, it produced and distributed television commercials, industrial films, and television programs, perhaps the best known of which is the 1952 syndicated cartoon series *Jim and Judy in Teleland*.

THE TELEVISION SCRIPT ARCHIVE AT THE ANNENBERG SCHOOL OF COMMUNICATIONS is the largest collection of television scripts in the United States, consisting of more than 24,000 items donated by *TV Guide*, and representing approximately 95 percent of all network programming from 1976 to 1990. Under a long-standing agreement, *TV Guide* will donate an additional 1,500 or more scripts each year. The collection became available for scholarly use in June 1988.

Address: 3620 Walnut Street, Philadelphia, PA 19104–6220.

TELEVISION SNAPSHOTS, INC. was a New York–based distributor and producer, primarily of television commercials, active in the early fifties, and founded by Babette J. Doniger, Dwight Godwin, and Jess Meeker.

TELEVISION WITHOUT FRONTIERS is the title of a directive from the Council of Europe relating to television broadcasts that cross national borders. It requires that the majority of programming be European in origin and that commercials be limited to 15 percent of daily transmission time, and restricts violence, pornography, and racial hatred in programming. The directive was approved at a meeting in Luxembourg in April 1989, and ratified by the council, meeting in Paris, the following month.

The directive resulted in fierce opposition from American producers, led by Jack Valenti, president of the Motion Picture Export Association of America. Not so much because of that opposition, but more because of a failure by the European Community (EC) to agree to what type of quota system it wanted, the Television Without Frontiers directive was rescinded at a June 1989 meeting of EC members.

BIBLIOGRAPHY

Alderman, Bruce, "Lang Sounds Deathknell for Euro TV Quotas; France Mulls Option," *Variety*, July 5, 1989, pp. 1, 2.

Hift, Fred, "European TV Quotas: Angry Yanks and a Community Divided," *Variety*, May 24, 1989, pp. 1, 4.

"Valenti Working on Plan To Counter EC's Quotas on TV Programming," *Variety*, September 16, 1989, p. 5.

TEMPE-PRODUCTIONS, INC. was a Beverly Hills–based producer of animated commercials, founded by Leo A. Minskoff. It was active from 1956 to 1967.

TEN—THE ENTERTAINMENT NETWORK (U.K.) was intended as the British cable equivalent of HBO.* It was formed by a group including Paramount, Universal, and MGM/UA, and began broadcasting in March 1984. Late that same year, the name was changed to The Movie Channel. It ceased operations on June 4, 1985, and was replaced by MirrorVision, whose owner, Robert Maxwell, had acquired a majority share in TEN.

TEN/THE ENTERTAINMENT NETWORK (U.S.) was a Los Angeles–based cable network, specializing in music and variety programming. It was launched in 1983, never showed a profit, and closed following a filing for Chapter XI bankruptcy protection in December 1987. Headed by president and chief executive officer Drew Levin, TEN was involved in a number of co-production activities with the BBC,* notably *Top of the Pops*, a popular music show that had been seen on the BBC since 1964.

BIBLIOGRAPHY

Sanders, Steve, "TEN Upping Prod'n, Distribution," *The Hollywood Reporter*, December 3, 1987, pp. 4, 15.

"TEN Seeks Chapter 11 Protection," *The Hollywood Reporter*, December 22, 1987, pp. 1, 49.

"TERMINAL TELEVISION" is the name by which the phenomenon of coin-operated television sets attached to seats in bus and airport terminals is known. For a small fee, individual viewers are able to watch television programming for a limited time. The concept was first marketed by the Salt Lake City–based company Midwest International in 1969.
BIBLIOGRAPHY
Childress, William, "Now Departing at Gate 4 . . . ," *TV Guide*, July 5, 1975, pp. 11–12.

TEXT SERVICE CABLE NETWORKS. The following is a listing of text-only cable networks, with their addresses and the years in which they first commenced broadcasting:

AP Business Plus (1825 K Street, N.W., Washington, DC 20006; 1986)

AP News Plus (1825 K Street, N.W., Washington, DC 20006; 1984)

AP Sports Plus (1825 K Street, N.W., Washington, DC 20006; 1988)

Cable SportsTracker (Prevue Networks, Inc., 3801 South Sheridan Road, Tulsa, OK 74145; 1984)

EPG/The Electronic Program Guide (Prevue Networks, Inc., 3801 South Sheridan Road, Tulsa, OK 74145; 1982)

FNN Market Watch (1900 South Norfolk Street, Suite 150, San Mateo, CA 94403; 1986)

Storyvision Network, Inc. (1400–191 Lombard Avenue, Winnipeg, Canada R3B 0X1; 1983)

X*PRESS X*Change (4643 South Ulster Street, Suite 340, Denver, CO 80237; 1987)

X*PRESS Executive (4643 South Ulster Street, Suite 340, Denver, CO 80237; 1986).

THAMES TELEVISION plc. Perhaps the best known of all the independent ("commercial") television networks in the United Kingdom, Thames Television provides Monday-through-Friday programming for the London and Home Counties area. The most important and the largest of the independent television networks, Thames was founded by Thorn EMI and British Electric Traction (BET), with the merger of Associated Rediffusion (which had begun broadcasting on September 22, 1955) and ABC (Associated British Cinemas) Television. Thames Television was launched on July 29, 1968.

Among the many Thames productions that have been and continue to be seen on American television are *Rumpole of the Bailey*, *Paradise Postponed*, *The Naked Civil Servant*, *The Benny Hill Show*, *The World at War*, *Hollywood*, and *The Unknown Chaplin*. The company maintains a studio at Teddington, on the outskirts of London, and has two major subsidiary companies, Euston Films Limited* and Cosgrove Hall Productions (Albany House, 8 Albany Road, Chorlton-Cum Hardy, Manchester M21 9BL, United Kingdom). The latter is an animation house, whose series include *Count Duckula*, *Dangermouse*, *The Wind in the Willows*, and *Creepy Crawlies*.

Address: 306–316 Euston Road, London NW1 3BB, United Kingdom.

BIBLIOGRAPHY
"Thames 21st Anniversary," *Variety*, April 12, 1989, pp. 47–77.

THEATER TELEVISION was the name given to entertainment viewed in movie theaters by way of a television system. Immediately following World War II, a number of such systems, including the British Scophony, the Swiss Eidophor,* and the American RCA, were introduced on an experimental basis, but the most practical method was the Paramount intermediate film system, which utilized standard television equipment to receive the video signal at the theater, and then transformed the sound and image on to film. The RCA system was demonstrated in 1947 by both Warner Bros. and 20th Century–Fox, with the latter utilizing it to screen the Joe Louis–Joe Walcott fight at the Fox Theater in Philadelphia. Paramount's system was introduced at the Paramount Theater, Chicago, on June 16, 1948, and the initial presentation included the televising of a vaudeville show and of the audience entering the theatre. A number of Paramount theatres were equipped with Theater Television for the presentation of various sporting and news events through 1951. In the early fifties, two Theater Television networks were established: Theatre Network Television (founded in 1951 by Nathan Halpern) and Box Office Television (founded by Milton Mound). However, Theater Television was never particularly profitable or popular enough to sustain continuous presentations, and from 1955 through to the present, it has been utilized only for occasional presentations of major sporting events (usually boxing).

BIBLIOGRAPHY
Gomery, Douglas, "Theater Television: A History," *SMPTE Journal*, vol. LXXXXVIII, no. 2, February 1989, pp. 120–123.

THEATRE AUTHORITY, INC. represents the interests of the members of the five performers' unions (Actors' Equity, American Guild of Musical Artists, American Guild of Variety Artists, American Federation of Television and Radio Artists, and the Screen Actors Guild) when they donate their talents to live or televised charity-sponsored programs.

THE THEATRE GUILD. U.S. Steel first became involved with the Theatre Guild with its sponsorship of *The Theatre Guild on the Air*, heard on ABC radio from 1945 to 1949. (It was later heard on NBC.) On television, the Theatre Guild produced *The U.S. Steel Hour* (ABC, 1953–1955; CBS, 1955–1963), a dramatic anthology series, in cooperation with the advertising agency of Batten, Barton, Durstine & Osborn (BBDO).

Earlier, in October 1947, the Theatre Guild arranged to present a series of six plays on NBC,* beginning with *John Ferguson* starring Thomas Mitchell. Other plays in the series were *Dinner at Eight*, starring Helen Hayes, and *The Traitor*, starring Tyrone Power.

THOMAS & LEONARD PRODUCTIONS was co-owned by actor Danny Thomas (1914–1991) and writer/director Sheldon Leonard (born 1907), and was based at the Desilu-Cahuenga Studios in Hollywood. It was noted for the creative talent, including Jerry Paris, Carl Reiner, and Melvin Shavelson, involved in its productions (many of which were written and directed by Leonard), including *The Danny Thomas Show* (ABC, 1953–1957; CBS, 1957–1965), *Gomer Pyle, U.S.M.C.* (CBS, 1954–1970), *The Real McCoys* (ABC, 1957–1962; CBS, 1962–1963), *The Andy Griffith Show* (CBS, 1960–1968), *The Dick Van Dyke Show* (CBS, 1961–1966), and *I Spy* (NBC, 1965–1968).
BIBLIOGRAPHY
Whitney, Dwight, "So Who Needs Wall Street?" *TV Guide*, April 25, 1964, pp. 20–23.

THOMAS/SPELLING PRODUCTIONS was formed by actor Danny Thomas (1914–1991) and producer Aaron Spelling (born 1928). It produced a number of made-for-television movies, all for ABC,* including *The Over-the-Hill Gang* (1969), *The Monk* (1969), *The Ballad of Andy Crocker* (1969), *Carter's Army* (1970), *The Love War* (1970), and *The Over-the-Hill Gang Rides Again* (1970).

TIME-LIFE FILMS, INC. was a major distributor of television programming in the seventies, handling exclusive U.S. distribution of BBC* footage from 1970 to 1980. Time-Life Films was initially created in 1969 as a wholly owned subsidiary of Time, Inc. The new division, Time-Life Films, Inc., was founded in January 1973, with the merger of Time-Life Films, Time-Life Video, and Time-Life Education. Peter M. Roebuck, formerly president and managing director of Time-Life Films, was appointed chairman of the new entity.

The first major acquisition of the new company was the library of comedian Harold Lloyd in April 1973. Since 1969, Time-Life Films had been a co-production partner with the BBC, but with the 1977 acquisition of David Susskind's Talent Associates, Inc.,* Time-Life announced an ambitious television production schedule, with Susskind as head of production. (He left the company in 1980.) A motion picture division was formed in 1980, with its first three productions (all 1980) being *Fort Apache, the Bronx, Loving Couples*, and *They All Laughed*.

Following a $9 million loss after taxes in 1980, Time, Inc. entered into discussions with 20th Century–Fox for the latter to acquire Time-Life Films, Inc. The acquisition was abandoned in 1981, but in August of that year, Columbia Pictures Television acquired the assets of Time-Life's television production operations, together with most of its television and feature film library. From that point on, Time-Life Films, Inc. was operated as a part of the Time, Inc. Video Group. In 1985, it became part of HBO,* and licensed syndication rights for its library of 144 television films and 49 features to Procter & Gamble Productions.* In October 1989, Warner Bros. Television took over what remained of the Time-Life Library, but non-theatrical distribution rights remained, as they had for many years, with Kino International.

TIMES MIRROR BROADCASTING is the broadcasting division of The Times Mirror Co., which dates back to an original incorporation in 1884 and publishes the *Los Angeles Times*, *Newsday*, and other publications. It owns KDFW-Dallas; KTBC-Austin; WVTM-Birmingham, Alabama; and KTVI–St. Louis. In 1986, it sold WHTM-Harrisburg, Pennsylvania; WSTM-Syracuse, New York; and WETM-Elmira, New York. It also operates cable television systems.

Address: 20 East Elm Street, Greenwich, CT 06830.

TIMES SQUARE PRODUCTIONS, INC. was a New York–based producer and distributor, headed by Charles W. Curran and active in the fifties.

TIMES TELEVISION CORP., headed by David H. Coplan, was a minor producer of television programming, active in the fifties, with offices in both New York and Los Angeles.

"TINY" FAIRBANKS ENTERPRISES, INC. was a minor New York–based producer of live and filmed television programming, active from the fifties through the mid-seventies. Albert Lincoln "Tiny" Fairbanks (born 1906) was the obese producer and star of his own variety show, called simply *Tiny Fairbanks*, and seen on local New York television as early as 1950.

TITUS PRODUCTIONS was a company owned by Herbert Brodkin (1912–1990), responsible for the series *Shane* (ABC, 1966), the mini-series *Holocaust* (NBC, 1978), the made-for-television movie *Skokie* (CBS, 1981), and other television programming. A related company, owned by Brodkin, was Plautus Productions,* which was responsible for *The Defenders* (CBS, 1961–1965) and *The Nurses* (CBS, 1962–1965).

TNN (THE NASHVILLE NETWORK) is an advertiser-supported basic cable network, offering country music–oriented entertainment from 9:00 A.M. through 3:00 A.M. daily. It was created by Group W Satellite Communications, WSM, Inc. (owners of the Grand Ole Opry), and a related company of Opryland USA Inc., and began broadcasting on March 7, 1983. In April 1988, TNN introduced the annual *TNN Viewers' Choice Awards*, and the following year gained exclusive rights to the formerly syndicated talk show *Crook and Chase*, produced by Jim Owens & Associates. TNN has presented two popular series of black-and-white Western features, *Happy Trails Theater*, hosted by Roy Rogers, and *Melody Ranch Theater*, hosted by Gene Autry. As of 1990, it had 50 million subscribers.

Address: 685 Third Avenue, 20th Floor, New York, NY 10016.

BIBLIOGRAPHY
Hickey, Neil, "Bettin' $50 Million That This Sound's in Tune with America," *TV Guide*,
    February 4, 1984, pp. 24–26.
Moses, Robert, "The Nashville Network Plays It Straight," *Cable Choice*, January 1987,
    pp. 24–25.
"N'Ville Network Set To Make It Formal Today," *Daily Variety*, January 19, 1983,
    pp. 1, 46.
Schneider, Steve, "Country Music Marks a Birthday," *New York Times*, April 13, 1986,
    section 2, p. 32.
Stengel, Richard, "Country Comes to Cable," *Time*, March 21, 1983, p. 68.

TNT (TURNER NETWORK TELEVISION) is a basic cable network, providing twenty-four hour a day programming of classic movies, sports events, children's shows, and original productions for a reported 44.5 million subscribers in 1990. Founded by Robert E. "Ted" Turner (born 1938), and relying heavily on the library of films acquired by Turner Broadcasting System, Inc.,* TNT went on the air on October 3, 1988. Following a taped message of welcome from Ted Turner, the network presented part one of *Gone with the Wind*. Two days later, it presented the world premiere of the documentary *The Making of a Legend: Gone with the Wind*, produced by David O. Selznick's sons Jeffrey and Daniel. One of TNT's first original programs was *A Man for All Seasons* (1989), starring Charlton Heston.

   Address: 1 CNN Center/Box 105366, Atlanta, GA 30348.

BIBLIOGRAPHY
Alexander, Ron, "Movie Buffs Find a Trove on Cable: TNT Has M-G-M's 3,300-Film
    Library," *New York Times*, January 12, 1989, p. B4.
Hall, Jane, "Ted Turner's TNT Exploding onto the Cable Scene," *Los Angeles Times*,
    January 23, 1990, pp. F1, F9.
Huff, Richard, "TNT Is Dynamite with 27-Million Homes; Cable Net Increases Made-
    for Slate," *Variety*, April 26, 1989, p. 206.
Jameson, Richard T., "Life with TNT," *Film Comment*, July/August 1989, pp. 30–39.
Schwartz, Jerry, "Turner Is Hopeful on New Cable Network," *New York Times*, July
    16, 1988, p. 21.
Silden, Isobel, "Turner's Latest Charge," *Emmy*, vol. XI, no. 3, May/June 1989, p. 33.

TOBY ANGUISH MOTION PICTURE PRODUCTIONS was active in the film industry from 1938 and as a producer for television from the forties through the mid-sixties. Based in Los Angeles, it was responsible for the mid-fifties fifteen-minute syndicated series *Adventure Album*. It was Toby Anguish who helped finance production of the last twelve "Hopalong Cassidy" features starring William Boyd (1946–1948), which were some of the first motion picture films "sold" to television.

TOKYO MOVIE SHINSHA (TMS ENTERTAINMENT) is a major Japanese animation house responsible for three 1986 *The Blinkins* television specials. It also worked with Walt Disney to produce the latter's first prime time animated special, *Disney's Fluppy Dogs*, seen on ABC* on November 27, 1986.

   Address: 5–39–1 Kamitakada, Nakano-ku, Tokyo 164, Japan.

TOM BAILEY PRODS., INC. was founded in Tucson, Arizona, in 1952 by Seth (Tom) Bailey, who had earlier launched the Southwest Motion Picture and TV Corp. with Charles Herbert. The company was responsible for the 1953 syndicated series *The Sagebrush Kids*.

TOM J. CORRADINE & ASSOCIATES is a distributor of feature films, short subjects, and series to television, and was founded in 1953. Its first major series for distribution was *The Ruggles* (ABC, 1949–1952), and at one time it boasted having more than 400 feature films and 350 short subjects available; it is currently western representative for a number of companies, including TV Cinema Sales and Weiss Global Enterprises.* A related company, active in the seventies, was Company of Artists Productions, Inc.

TOMORROW ENTERTAINMENT, INC. was formed in 1975 by Roger Gimbel (born 1925) after existing earlier as a subsidiary of General Electric. In June 1976, it merged with EMI to form EMI Television Programs, Inc. In January 1984, the latter became the Peregrine Producers Group, Inc., of which Gimbel was still president. In 1987, Roger Gimbel Productions was created, and the following year it became Carolco/Gimbel Productions, Inc.

Among the many made-for-television movies produced by the company under its various names are *The Amazing Howard Hughes* (CBS, 1977), *Sophia Loren, Her Own Story* (NBC, 1980), *A Question of Honor* (CBS, 1982), *A Piano for Mrs. Cimino* (CBS, 1982), *Deadly Encounter* (CBS, 1982), *Packin' It In* (CBS, 1983), and the mini-series *The Manions of America* (ABC, 1981).

Address: 8439 Sunset Boulevard, 2nd Floor, Los Angeles, CA 90069.

TOWER PRODUCTIONS was the Los Angeles–based producer of the popular children's series *Space Patrol* (ABC, 1950–1955). The series was produced by Frank Moser. Following his death, his widow, Helen L. Moser, continued to operate the company, which remained in existence under the ownership of H.G. and Barbara J. Rhinelander.

Address: 11541 Landale Street, North Hollywood, CA 91602.

TOWERS OF LONDON, LTD. was the production company of Harry Alan Towers (born 1920), also known as Peter Welbeck, whom *Films and Filming* (January 1988) described as "the world's most colorful, yet least-known showman." Between 1945 and 1955, the company produced some 24,000 hours of radio programming. In the fifties, its syndicated television series included *Lilli Palmer Theatre* (1952), *The Scarlet Pimpernel* (1956), and *Dial 999* (1958). Towers abandoned television production in 1960 in order to concentrate on the making of theatrical features.

BIBLIOGRAPHY

Feld, Bruce, "Harry Alan Towers," *Drama-Logue*, October 5, 1989, pp. 26–27.

TRANSFILM, INC. was a New York–based producer of television commercials, founded by William Miesegaes, and active from the forties through the mid-sixties. In 1960, it became Transfilm-Caravel Incorporated, with a subsidiary company, Transfilm-Wylde Animation.

TRANSMODER, a word commonly used in the cable television industry, is a satellite component that receives and retransmits a television signal.

"TRASH TELEVISION" was a term introduced in the 1988–1989 television season to refer to shows, such as those hosted by Geraldo Rivera and Morton Downey, Jr., that utilized shock tactics to offend or outrage their audiences.

THE TRAVEL CHANNEL is a basic cable network, providing twenty-four hour a day business and leisure travel programming to some 14 million subscribers (as of 1990). It was launched in February 1987.
   Address: 1370 Avenue of the Americas, 27th Floor, New York, NY 10019.

TREE AND BRANCH and TREE AND BUSH are two British cable television terms. The former describes a cable system of traditional design, comprising a trunk cable from which each subscriber link is tapped off. Tree and Bush is the term given to the star-configured tree and branch system usually installed in the United Kingdom, involving a number of subscriber drops originating in the same street cabinet.

TRENDEX was a television audience ratings system in use in the fifties. Spot-check, sample telephone calls were made to more than 1,000 homes in fifteen cities to determine what programs viewers were watching.
BIBLIOGRAPHY
"TV Ratings: The Numbers Game," *TV Guide*, October 26, 1957, pp. 24–25.

THE TRIBUNE BROADCASTING CO. is a subsidiary of the Tribune Co. (publisher of the *Chicago Tribune*, the *New York Daily News*, and other publications), which dates back to an original incorporation in 1861. It owns four radio stations and six television stations: KTLA–Los Angeles,* KWGN-Denver, WGNX-Atlanta, WGN-Chicago, WGNO–New Orleans, and WPIX–New York.* Since 1981, the company has been headed by president and chief executive officer James Dowdle.
   Address: 435 North Michigan Avenue, Chicago, IL 60611.
BIBLIOGRAPHY
Heuton, Cheryl, "James Dowdle: Tribune Broadcasting Co.," *Channels of Communications*, vol. X, no. 11, August 13, 1990, pp. 35–37.

TRIBUNE ENTERTAINMENT CO. is a subsidiary of Tribune Co., which was incorporated in 1861 and reincorporated in 1968. The parent company published the *Chicago Tribune*, the *New York Daily News*, and other newspapers.

Tribune Entertainment Co. is responsible for *Geraldo* (Syndicated, 1987-   ) and
The Joan Rivers Show (Syndicated, 1989-   ), as well as a number of specials,
among which the most notorious is *The Mystery of Al Capone's Vault*, hosted
by Geraldo Rivera and seen live on April 8, 1986.

Address: 435 North Michigan Avenue, Suite 1982, Chicago, IL 60611.

THE TRINITY BROADCASTING NETWORK (TBN) is a basic cable television network, broadcasting multidenominational Christian programming
twenty-four hours a day to more than 13 million subscribers (as of 1990).
Launched in April 1978, TBN was founded by Paul F. Crouch (born 1934),
whose avowed mission is to "dispossess the Devil of the airwaves." The major
program on the network is *The Praise the Lord Show*, hosted by Paul and his
wife, Jan Crouch, and seen every weeknight. In 1989, TBN was the subject of
an investigation by the Ethics Committee of the National Religious Broadcasters.
The network is also seen on fourteen UHF* stations that TBN owns (including
two owned by a subsidiary, National Minority Television, Inc.).

Address: 9020 Yates, Westminster, CO 80030.

BIBLIOGRAPHY

Pinksy, Mark I., "Satellites Spread the Scriptures," *Los Angeles Times*, January 26,
    1989, pp. 1, 3, 20–21.
———, "Christian Broadcaster Defends Methods," *Los Angeles Times*, April 9, 1989,
    pp. 27–29.

TRIUMPH ENTERTAINMENT CORP. is a Canadian production company,
responsible for the syndicated series *War of the Worlds* (1989–1990), which it
produced in association with Hometown Films and Paramount Television.*

Address: 940 Lansdowne Avenue, Building 29, Toronto, Ontario M6H 3Z4,
Canada.

TSW—TELEVISION SOUTH-WEST is the British independent ("commercial") television network for the isles of Scilly, Cornwall, Devon, and parts of
Somerset and Dorset. It began broadcasting on January 1, 1982, and replaced
Westward Television (which was launched on April 29, 1961). The network
specializes in the production of local programming (approximately eight hours
a week), and none of its productions has been seen in the United States.

Address: Derry's Cross, Plymouth, Devon PL1 2SP, United Kingdom.

THE TURNER BROADCASTING SYSTEM, INC. is the umbrella company
for the broadcasting activities of Robert E. "Ted" Turner (born 1938), which
developed from the Turner family billboard business in Savannah, Georgia,
which Turner acquired in 1963. In 1970, Turner acquired UHF* station WJRT
in Atlanta. He changed its name first to WTCG and later to WTBS. In December
1976, Turner launched WTBS as a superstation,* programming sports and films
via satellite to cable systems throughout the country. As of 1990, WTBS, now

known simply as TBS, broadcast twenty-four hours a day and had 54 million subscribers.

In 1985, Turner attempted an unsuccessful leveraged buy-out of CBS.* A year later, he acquired the M-G-M library of features and short subjects for $1.2 billion. In 1987, he purchased the RKO Film Library, and in August of that same year, he repurchased the television rights to *Gone with the Wind* (1939) from CBS,* which had held the rights until 1998. Such major purchases left Turner with financial problems. There were unsuccessful negotiations in 1986 for NBC* to acquire a minority interest in the Turner Broadcasting System, but instead, in 1987 a 35 percent share in the company was sold to a consortium of thirty-one cable companies. A book-publishing division, Turner Publishing, Inc., was formed in November 1989.

Address: 1050 Techwood Drive, N.W., Atlanta, GA 30318.

BIBLIOGRAPHY

Cuff, Daniel F., "The Formidable Ted Turner," *New York Times*, April 5, 1985, pp. 25, 38.

Fabrikant, Geraldine, "Some Promising Signs for Turner's Empire," *New York Times*, January 23, 1989, pp. C1, C9.

Harwood, Jim, "Ted Turner: For the Record," *Daily Variety*, March 1, 1989, pp. F10-F12, F14, F16, F18.

Salmans, Sandra, "Television's 'Bad Boy' Makes Good," *New York Times*, August 14, 1983, section 3, p. 1.

Taub, James, "Reaching for Conquest," *Channels of Communications*, vol. III, no. 2, July/August 1983, pp. 26–30, 60–61.

"Turner's Windless Sails," *Newsweek*, February 9, 1987, pp. 46–47.

THE TURNER ENTERTAINMENT CO. was formed in August 1986 to service the library of 1,651 M-G-M, 850 Warner Bros., and 700 RKO feature films (along with 3,500 short subjects), acquired by the Turner Broadcasting System, Inc., and is a wholly owned subsidiary of the latter. Domestic theatrical distribution of the M-G-M and Warner Bros. titles continued to be handled by MGM/UA, and in October 1989, Turner announced that Paramount would handle theatrical release of the RKO films, most of which had been licensed for television to American Movie Classics* prior to their acquisition by Turner. Estimated value of the library is $1.3 billion.

As of August 15, 1986, Roger Mayer (born 1926) was named president and chief administrative officer of Turner Entertainment Co. He had formerly been senior vice-president of administration at M-G-M and president of M-G-M Laboratory.

Address: 10100 Venice Boulevard, Culver City, CA 90232.

BIBLIOGRAPHY

Galbraith, Jane, "MGM Vault Spawns New TBS Subsid," *Daily Variety*, July 18, 1986, pp. 1, 56.

Harwood, Jim, "Ted Turner: For the Record," *Daily Variety*, March 1, 1989, pp. F10-F12, F14, F16, F18.

TV ADS, INC. was a Los Angeles–based producer of television commercials, founded by Doria Balli, and active in the early fifties.

TV-AM. Launched on February 1, 1983, TV-am was the first independent television service, offering early-morning news, information, and current affairs programming in the United Kingdom. Its weekday schedule begins at 6:00 A.M. with *The Morning Programme*, followed by *Good Morning Britain* at 7:00 A.M., and *After Nine* (for women viewers) from 9:00 A.M. through 9:25 A.M. It produces various programs on Saturdays and Sundays, notably *David Frost on Sunday*. (Frost is one of the directors of the company.)

Address: Breakfast Television Centre, Hawley Crescent, London NW1 8EF, United Kingdom.

BIBLIOGRAPHY

Leapman, Michael. *Treachery?: The Power Struggle at TV-am*. London: George Allen & Unwin, 1984.

TV ATTRACTIONS was a New York–based packager of television programming, active from the fifties through the early seventies (by which time the company had relocated to La Jolla, California).

TVB (TELEVISION BUREAU OF ADVERTISING) opened on January 1, 1955, charged by the industry "to secure for television a greater share of advertisers' appropriations, and increase the selling efficiency of the medium." The bureau improves and expands the use of television as an advertising medium, working on both a local and a national level. It organizes an annual convention, presents awards, and sponsors studies and research.

Address: 477 Madison Avenue, New York, NY 10022.

TV GUIDE, with a readership of over 20 million, is believed to be the largest circulation periodical in the world. It is the primary source for information on television listings, providing far more detail than most local newspapers, together with articles and editorial commentary. The publication was created and first published on April 3, 1953, by Walter Annenberg's Triangle Publications with the merger of Philadelphia's *TV Digest*, Chicago's *TV Forecast*, and New York's *TV Guide*. Between July 1979 and May 1981, Walter Annenberg also published *Panorama*, a monthly, quality publication on television. In 1988, Rupert Murdoch's NewsCorp, Ltd. acquired Triangle Publications for $2.8 billion.

Address: Box 400, Radnor, PA 19088.

BIBLIOGRAPHY

Cole, Barry, editor. *Television: A Selection of Readings from TV Guide Magazine*. New York: Free Press, 1970.

Norback, Craig T., and Peter G. Norback. *TV Guide Almanac*. New York: Ballantine Books, 1980.

Slide, Anthony, editor. *International Film, Radio, and Television Journals*. Westport, Conn.: Greenwood Press, 1985.

TV GUILD PRODUCTIONS, INC. (also known as Larchmont TV Studios, Inc.) was a Los Angeles–based producer, primarily of television commercials, headed by Jack Miles, and active from the fifties through the mid-seventies.

TV MARKETEERS, INC. was a New York–based producer and distributor of television programming and commercials, founded in 1950 by Nathan Wynn and active for a couple of years.

TVNZ LTD. (TELEVISION NEW ZEALAND) is the state-run television service of New Zealand, operating two channels, TV1 (from Lower Hutt, near Wellington) and TV2 (from Auckland). Television was introduced in New Zealand between 1959 and 1961: to Auckland in March 1959, Christchurch in June 1961, and Wellington and Dunedin in July 1962. Operated by the Broadcasting Corporation of New Zealand, TVNZ is funded both through advertising and by license fees. Each channel presents at least two days (one of which is Sunday) without commercial interruptions.

Address: 100 Victoria Street/P.O. Box 3819, Auckland, New Zealand.

TVONTARIO (Ontario Educational Communications Authority) was created in 1970. Primarily funded by the government of Ontario (the Ministry of Culture and Communications and the Ministry of Education), it provides educational programming in both English and French. One of its most popular and best-known shows is *Saturday Night at the Movies*, hosted by Elwy Yost. TVOntario is run by a thirteen-member board of directors, appointed by the lieutenant governor.

Since 1982, it has published a monthly program guide titled *Signal*.

Address: Box 200, Station Q, Toronto, Ontario M4T 2T1, Canada.

BIBLIOGRAPHY

"The Ontario Network of TV Ontario," in *International TV & Video Guide 1984*, editor Olli Tuomola. London: Tantivy Press, 1983, pp. 61–64.

TV-Q is the rating of television personalities as to familiarity and popularity, a system devised by Marketing Evaluation Co. Q is the quotient of people recognizing a certain actor or actress, and is often used by network executives to determine casting in a television series. TV-Q has many opponents within the acting fraternity, notably Ed Asner (whose TV-Q is considerably lower than that of "Alf"). As early as 1974, the Screen Actors Guild tried to stop TV-Q ratings, claiming them "an illegal restraint of trade" and protesting that they "interfere with the ability to earn one's living."

BIBLIOGRAPHY

Bierbaum, Tom, "TvQ Popularity Ratings of TV Performers Draws Fire," *Daily Variety*, April 2, 1982, p. 43.

Hurley, Dan, "Those Hush-Hush Q Ratings—Fair or Foul?" *TV Guide*, December 10, 1988, pp. 2–6.

Stabiner, Karen, "Willie Stargell, You're Hot; Shelley Hack, You're Not," *TV Guide*, March 1, 1980, pp. 14–18.

TVRO is the acronym for Television Receive Only, and is the name given to satellite receiving dishes purchased by individuals and set up to receive cable programming from satellites without payment of monthly service fees. Regarded as signal theft by the cable television industry, the use of TVROs led to many cable networks scrambling their signals, beginning in 1986.

BIBLIOGRAPHY

Euston, Anthony T. *The Home Satellite TV Book: How To Put the World in Your Backyard*. New York: Playboy Press, 1982.

Goldberg, Joel. *Satellite Television Reception: A Personal User's Guide*. Englewood Cliffs, N.J.: Prentice-Hall, 1984.

Long, Mark, and Jeffrey Keating. *The World of Satellite Television*. Summertown, Tenn.: Book, 1983.

The Scramble To Scramble: A Satellite Television Dilemma. Washington, D.C.: Television Digest, 1986.

Sutphin, S.E. *Understanding Satellite Television Reception*. Englewood Cliffs, N.J.: Prentice-Hall, 1986.

Traister, Robert J. *Build a Personal Earth Station for World-Wide Satellite TV Reception*. Blue Ridge Summit, Pa.: TAB Books, 1985.

TV SPOTS, INC., founded by Shull Bonsall, was a Los Angeles–based producer of live action and animated television commercials, active in the fifties and sixties.

TV STATIONS, INC. was a New York–based, station-owned and -operated film buying organization, which serviced more than one hundred television stations in the United States and possessions. It was active in the sixties.

TVS TELEVISION is a wholly owned subsidiary of TVS Entertainment plc, the group that owns MTM Enterprises.* TVS Television is the independent ("commercial") television network for the south and southeast of England (Kent, Sussex, parts of Surrey and Hampshire, north to the Thames Valley, west to parts of Dorset, and the Isle of Wight). It began broadcasting on January 1, 1982, and replaced Southern Television (which was launched on August 30, 1958). TVS Television is best known to American viewers for the "Ruth Rendell" mysteries and for the 1989 mini-series *Murderers among Us—The Simon Wiesenthal Story*.

Subsidiary companies of TVS Entertainment plc are Telso Communications, Midem, 21st Century Publishing, Gilson Corporation, and the Button Group.

Address: Television Centre, Southampton SO9 5HZ, United Kingdom.

TVTV was an underground video production group founded in San Francisco in 1972 by Allen Rucker and Michael Shamberg. Initially, the group's videotapes, including *Gerald Ford's America* (1973), were seen only on public access* cable, but in 1976, KCET* commissioned the group to produce a program on the Academy Awards presentation, which was seen on the PBS* network.

BIBLIOGRAPHY

Turchill, Catherine, "TVTV—Tomorrow's Television Today?" *Television Quarterly*, vol. XII, no. 4, 1975, pp. 58–62.

Whitney, Dwight, "Irreverent, Questioning, Perhaps Unfair, but Undoubtedly Provocative," *TV Guide*, September 11, 1976, pp. 21–24.

TV UNLIMITED, INC. (Herbert Rosen, president) was a New York–based producer, active in the fifties.

20TH CENTURY–FOX TELEVISION. In line with the other major studios, 20th Century–Fox refused in the early years of television to license its theatrical features for television broadcast. However, in April 1948 it announced that the Fox Movietone Library would be available for television use. The company's earliest involvement in television appears to have been in 1945, when it leased station W1XG-Boston from General Television Corp.

20th Century–Fox entered television production in 1955 at its Western Avenue lot in Hollywood, where Irving Asher was named general manager of the first television division. The earliest series produced by the company was *My Friend Flicka* (CBS, 1956–1957), based on the 1943 feature of the same name. The television division's biggest expansion was between 1968 and 1974, when William Self (born 1921) was in charge; he was succeeded by Jack Haley, Jr.; Sy Salkowitz; Russell Barry; and finally Harris Katleman. The most popular shows produced by the television division are *Peyton Place* (ABC, 1964–1969), *Daniel Boone* (NBC, 1964–1970), and *M*A*S*H* (CBS, 1972–1983). The studio also produced a series on film history, based in large part on its own library of films, and titled *That's Hollywood* (Syndicated, 1977–1978, 1980–1981). In 1977, 20th Century–Fox became the first major studio to produce specials for cable television.

Address: P.O. Box 900, Beverly Hills, CA 90213.

BIBLIOGRAPHY

Gansberg, Alan L., "Fox Television's Recipe for Success: Quality, Diversity and Innovation," *The Hollywood Reporter*, November 13, 1984, pp. S111-S114.

TYBURN PRODUCTIONS LIMITED was founded in 1971 by Kevin Francis to produce programming for British independent television. It also operates a distribution company, Tyburn Entertainment, and Tyburn Music.

Address: Pinewood Studios, Iver Heath, Bucks, United Kingdom.

TYNE TEES TELEVISION LIMITED is the British independent ("commercial") television network, serving northeast England (from North Yorkshire along the northeast coast and including Northumberland, Durham, and Cleveland). An autonomous private limited company, whose shares are owned by Trident Television Limited (one of whose other subsidiaries is Yorkshire Television Limited*), Tyne Tees Television began broadcasting on January 15, 1959. An associated company is Hadrian Television. Recent dramatic productions from Tyne Tees are Barbara Taylor Bradford's *Act of Will* and C.P. Taylor's *And a Nightingale Sang*, both first broadcast in 1989.

Address: The Television Centre, City Road, Newcastle upon Tyne NE1 2AL, United Kingdom.

U

UBU PRODUCTIONS, INC. was founded in 1981 by Gary David Goldberg, and named after his black Labrador, UBU ROI, who died in 1984. The company, which is located on the Paramount studio lot, enjoyed tremendous success with *Family Ties* (NBC, 1982–1989), and has also been responsible for *The Bronx Zoo* (NBC, 1986–1988), *Duet/Open House* (Fox, 1987-1989), and *Day by Day* (NBC, 1988), among others. In September 1988, it opened a feature film division.

Address: 5555 Melrose Avenue, Hollywood, CA 90038.

BIBLIOGRAPHY

"The Master of 'Video Vérité,' " *Newsweek*, May 9, 1988, p. 77.

UCLA FILM AND TELEVISION ARCHIVE. One of the four major American film archives, UCLA Film and Television Archive is also one of the largest archives of American television programming. In 1965, through the efforts of Robert Lewine, the National Television Library was established at University of California at Los Angeles. It was to be one of three television show repositories created by the Academy of Television Arts and Sciences* (ATAS), but the other two libraries, at American University and New York University, never came to fruition. The name was shortly changed to the ATAS/UCLA Television Archive, but as the UCLA Film and Television Archive expanded, that name was dropped, and by the late eighties, the repository was known as the ATAS Collection at the UCLA Film and Television Archive. Daniel Einstein has been UCLA's television archivist since 1979.

Among the major television holdings at UCLA are the programs of Alcoa, Steve Allen, Jack Benny, "Hallmark Hall of Fame," Loretta Young, and the *Mr. Peepers* series. It also holds copies of programs nominated for national and local Emmys from the early sixties onward. In addition, the UCLA Film and Television Archive holds a collection of Television Technology and Design, created under the guidance of Edwin Reitan. The collection includes black-and-white and color television receivers, television cameras, and various types of video-recording systems.

Address: 1015 North Cahuenga Boulevard, Hollywood, CA 90038.

BIBLIOGRAPHY

ATAS/UCLA Television Archives Catalog: Holdings in the Study Collection of the Academy of Television Arts & Sciences/ University of California, Los Angeles Television Archives. Pleasantville, N.Y.: Redgrave, 1981.

Reitan, Edwin Howard, Jr. "Preserving the History of Television at UCLA," *IEE Transactions on Consumer Electronics*, vol. CE-XXX, no. 2, May 1984.

THE UHF (ULTRA HIGH FREQUENCY) BAND was created in 1952 by the FCC* after it had run out of channels for new stations on the VHF (Very High Frequency) band. It was intended that the two bands would be comparable, but such was not the case, in that the UHF signal does not travel as far as the VHF, and television set manufacturers were unwilling to produce models capable of receiving both VHF and UHF. By the mid-fifties, the FCC had become concerned at the number of UHF stations that were going off the air. In 1962, the All-Channel Act gave the FCC the power to require manufacturers to make television sets capable of receiving both bands, and by April 30, 1964, all receivers had to have that capability. In 1970, the FCC adopted rules to make UHF tuning similar to that of VHF, and major growth took place in the mid-seventies.

The interests of UHF stations are represented by the National UHF Broadcasters Association (220 Adams Street, Rockville, MD 20850).

BIBLIOGRAPHY

Donegan, Frank, "Strike Up the Band . . . Cautiously," *Panorama*, vol. II, no. 3, March 1981, pp. 66–67, 80–82.

Tiven, Kenneth D., "The Sleeping Giant," *Television Quarterly*, vol. IX, no. 1, Winter 1970, pp. 40–49.

ULSTER TELEVISION plc is the British independent ("commercial") television network for Northern Ireland. It began broadcasting on October 31, 1959, and the station was officially opened by chairman Lord Antrim; the governor of Northern Ireland, Lord Wakehurst; and Laurence Olivier. Ulster Television boasts of having produced Britain's first regional magazine program and the first adult education programs, and of being the first regional television company to use satellites.

Address: Havelock House, Ormeau Road, Belfast BT7 1EB, United Kingdom.

BIBLIOGRAPHY

Henderson, Brian, "Ulster Television—A Special 20 Years," *EBU Review*, vol. XXX, no. 5, September 1979.

U.M. & M., INC. is best known for its having removed the Paramount name on all of that studio's shorts and replaced it with its own when it released the library to television. Curiously, U.M. & M. was also responsible for the physical distribution of many television series, including *Sherlock Holmes* (Syndicated, 1954) and *Paris Precinct* (Syndicated, 1955), but it remained anonymous as far as its handling of those series was concerned. The company was founded in 1954 by Charles M. Amory, and was absorbed by NTA* in 1956. The letters U.M. & M. are the first letters of the names of its affiliated companies, United Film Service, Inc. of Kansas City; MPA Service Co., Inc. of New Orleans; and Minot TV, Inc. of New York.

UNIFILMS, INC. (Charles E. Gallagher, president) was a New York–based producer of television commercials, active in the fifties and sixties.

UNITED PRODUCERS-DISTRIBUTORS, operated by Jerry Courneya, was active in the early through mid-fifties as both a producer and a distributor to television. As a producer, it was responsible for *The Chimps* (Syndicated, 1951), which it co-produced; *Noah Beery, Jr.* (Syndicated, 1952); and *World of Adventure* (Syndicated, 1955). It also had a number of features that it released to television.

THE UNITED STATES ADVANCED TELEVISION SYSTEMS COMMITTEE was established in late 1982 by the Joint Committee on Inter-Society Coordination to coordinate and develop voluntary national technical standards for advanced television systems. Its work is divided between two groups, one involved in television distribution and the other in the production of television programs. Charter members of the committee are the Electronic Industries Association, the Institute of Electrical and Electronic Engineers, the National Association of Broadcasters,* the National Cable Television Association,* and the Society of Motion Picture and Television Engineers.
   Address: 1776 K Street, N.W., Suite 300, Washington, DC 20006.

UNITED TELEFILM CO., headed by Jesse L. and Milton L. Stern, was a New York–based distributor of feature films and short subjects to television, active in the early fifties.

UNITED TELEVISION PRODUCTIONS, founded in 1948 by Century Artists, was one of the first major television distributors, with its series including *Sleepy Joe* (ABC, 1949), *Dick Tracy* (ABC, 1950–1951), *The Chimps* (Syndicated, 1951), *Rebound* (ABC, 1952–1953), and *Waterfront* (Syndicated, 1953–1956). It was also responsible for the distribution of all the Bing Crosby–produced film series. The company disappeared in the mid-fifties, with the handling of its programs being taken over by MCA.

UNITED TELEVISION PROGRAMS, INC. was a packager of television programming, founded in 1951 by Milton Blink and Gerald King. King had been responsible for the creation of Standard Radio Transcriptions in 1933. Based in Chicago, with branch offices in New York and Los Angeles, United Television Programs remained active through 1955.

UNITED WORLD FILMS, INC. was active from 1946 to 1967 as the 16mm division of Universal Pictures. In the mid-fifties, it distributed a number of ten- and fifteen-minute syndicated series—*Going Places*, *Animal Fun and Mischief*, and *Stranger Than Fiction*—to television, and was also used by Universal as a television commercial subsidiary.

UNITY TELEVISION CORPORATION was a New York–based company, active in the fifties in the distribution to television of 52 Laurel and Hardy short subjects, 52 Charlie Chase comedies, 300 feature films, 100 cartoons, and 30 serials. It also handled the redistribution of the 1949 March of Time*–produced television series *Crusade in Europe*.

UNIVISION HOLDINGS, INC. provides twenty-four hour a day programming for Hispanic audiences, available as a basic cable network and on UHF* and low power television stations. The company was formed as the Sin Television Network in 1961 by Reynold V. Anselmo, with financial backing from Televisa SA.* Initially, Anselmo acquired two UHF stations in Los Angeles and San Antonio, and from these he created a satellite network of 200 affiliates. A subsidiary company, Spanish International Communications Corp., was created to operate a core group of five UHF stations. The company was sold in 1986 to Hallmark Greetings Cards* and First Capital Corp. of Chicago, and was renamed the Univision Television Network in 1987.

Address: 605 Third Avenue, 12th Floor, New York, NY 10158.

BIBLIOGRAPHY

Critser, Greg, "The Feud That Toppled a TV Empire," *Channels of Communications*, vol. VII, no. 1, January 1987, pp. 24–31.
Silden, Isobel, "The Wages of SIN," *Emmy*, vol. VIII, no. 4, July/August 1986, pp. 110–119.
Walker, Savannah Waring, "In the Grip of SIN," *Channels of Communications*, vol. III, no. 2, July/August 1983, pp. 46–49.

UPA PICTURES, INC. was founded in 1945 by Disney Animator Stephen Bosustow (born 1911) and other former Disney animators (including John Hubley) as United Productions of America. The name was changed to UPA Pictures, Inc. effective January 1, 1956. Originally formed to make educational films, the company was noted for its innovative animation, with its first cartoon to be nominated for an Academy Award being *Robin Hoodlum*, in 1948. UPA introduced two popular characters in 1949, "Gerald McBoing-Boing" and "Mister Magoo." Both were to become favorites on television, with television production on the latter beginning in 1956. *Mr. Magoo's Christmas Carol* (NBC, 1962) was the first made-for-television animated special.

Three cartoons from 1953 illustrate the extraordinary range of UPA's work:

The Emperor's New Clothes (released April 30, 1953), *A Unicorn in the Garden* (released September 24, 1953), and *The Tell Tale Heart* (released December 27, 1953). The last, narrated by James Mason, is probably the first film to recount a horror theme in animated form.

UPA's films were released by Columbia from 1948 onward, and in 1952, the company turned down an offer to become part of Columbia. However, it did open a New York office to handle animation work for Columbia's television subsidiary, Screen Gems.* The New York office closed in 1958, and shortly thereafter Bosustow sold the company to Henry G. Saperstein (born 1918). Saperstein expanded UPA's operations outside the animated field, acquiring the rights to various theatrical features, notably the *Godzilla* series from Japan. In November 1986, he published advertisements in *Daily Variety* offering UPA's assets, including several television series, for sale. The company gained brief publicity in 1990, when it reissued the 1952-produced *Dick Tracy* cartoons to television and was criticized for the series' racist characterizations.

Address: 14101 Valley Heart Drive, Suite 200, Sherman Oaks, CA 91423.

BIBLIOGRAPHY
Langsner, Jules, "UPA," *Arts and Architecture*, December 1954, pp. 12–15.
Lee, Walter W., Jr., "UPA," *Pendulum*, vol. II, no. 2, Spring 1953, pp. 42–50.
Seldes, Gilbert, "Delight in Seven Minutes," *Saturday Review*, May 31, 1952, p. 27.
"Special UPA Issue," *IT*, no. 6, Winter 1956.

THE USA NETWORK is a basic cable network, offering twenty-four hour a day programming to 51.5 million subscribers (as of 1990). It began on September 27, 1977, as the Madison Square Garden Network, founded by Kay Koplovitz, with financial backing from UA-Columbia Cablevision and Madison Square Garden's owner, Gulf + Western Industries (later Paramount Communications, Inc.). Its initial sports programming was available to 750,000 subscribers. Children's programming was introduced in 1978 under the overall title of "Calliope."

To emphasize a change from sports programming to general programming (of feature films, sports events, and specials), the name of the network was changed to USA on April 9, 1980. The network began twenty-four-hour programming in October 1981, and that same month, UA-Columbia Cablevision ceased to be a partner, and was replaced by Time Inc. and MCA, Inc. In 1989, the network's slogan was changed from "America's All Entertainment Network" to "America's Favorite Network."

Address: 1230 Avenue of the Americas, New York, NY 10020.

BIBLIOGRAPHY
Polskin, Howard, "Plodding to Succe$$," *TV Guide*, November 9, 1985, pp. 45–46.
Ross, Chuck, "USA Network Making It Their Own Way," *The Hollywood Reporter*, 56th Anniversary Issue, 1986, pp. 167–168.
Sharbutt, Jay, "USA Cable Network's Potpourri Programming Style Is Paying Off," *Los Angeles Times*, July 13, 1989, part VI, pp. 1, 10.
"USA Network: Ten Years of Excellence," *The Hollywood Reporter*, May 10, 1990, pp. S1–S24.

V

VANDERBILT TELEVISION NEWS ARCHIVE. In 1968, a Nashville businessman, Paul C. Simpson, discovered that the networks were routinely erasing
tapes of their nightly news broadcasts some two weeks after airing. Failing to
interest existing archives in preserving the newscasts, Simpson created the Vanderbilt Television News Archive as a unit of the Jean and Alexander Heard
Library of Vanderbilt University, with James Pilkington appointed its admin-
istrator in 1971.

Since August 5, 1968, the archive has videotaped the evening news broadcasts
of the three networks, along with special news programming such as presidential
press conferences, political conventions, and the Watergate Hearings. Each
month, the archive publishes its *Television News Index and Abstracts*, describing
in detail each item on the news, the date and time it was broadcast, and so forth.
Tapes of the broadcasts are available for in-house study and can also be loaned.
Additionally, the archive is able to compile tapes on specific subjects, providing
a unique record of possible bias or questionable interpretation of the news by
the networks.

Vanderbilt's activities have not been accepted gracefully by the networks. A
lengthy legal battle between CBS* and Vanderbilt took place in the early seventies, and as a result, all networks are now very careful to place copyright
notices on their news broadcasts. As a protest against Vanderbilt's work, CBS
entered into a 1974 agreement with the National Archives and Records Service,
creating an archive of television news broadcasts that would provide taped copies
of the *CBS News* for research use at the National Archives, regional branches
of the National Archives, and presidential libraries.

Address: Vanderbilt University, Nashville, TN 37240.

"A VAST WASTELAND" was first used to describe American television by
Newton Minow when he became chairman of the FCC* on May 9, 1961: "I

invite you to sit down in front of your television set when your station goes on the air ... and keep your eyes glued to that set until the station signs off. I can assure you that you will observe a vast wasteland.''

THE VATICAN TELEVISION CENTER (CTV) handles all video and television activities relating to the papacy, including the videotaping and selling of tapes of papal audiences. The center was founded in 1983 to document the activities of Pope John Paul I.

Address: Vatican City.
BIBLIOGRAPHY
Dionne, E.J., Jr., "The Vatican Is Putting Video To Work," *New York Times*, August 11, 1985, section 2, p. 27.

VERA (Vision Electronic Recording Apparatus) was developed by the BBC* for the recording of television programs on magnetic tape. It was first demonstrated on April 8, 1958.

VH–1 (VIDEO HITS ONE) is a basic cable network, providing twenty-four hour a day music videos for the twenty-five to fifty-four age group. Created by MTV,* it first began broadcasting on January 1, 1985, and as of 1990, had 34.5 million subscribers.

Address: 1775 Broadway, New York, NY 10019.
BIBLIOGRAPHY
Atkinson, Terry, "VH–1: Pop with Pictures for the Parents of the MTV Crowd," *Los Angeles Times Calendar*, March 3, 1985, pp. 58, 60.
Gerard, Jeremy, "An MTV for Grown-Ups Is Seeking Its Audience," *New York Times*, August 7, 1989, p. B3.
Hedegaard, Erik, "New MTV Channel Aims for Older Audience," *Rolling Stone*, October 11, 1984, p. 38.
———, "MTV's Vh–1: Music Video for Housewives," *Rolling Stone*, January 17, 1985, p. 38.
Knoedelseder, William K., Jr., and David Crook, "MTV Plans Cable Channel for the 25-to-49 Age Group," *Los Angeles Times*, August 22, 1984, part IV, pp. 1, 2.
McGuigan, Cathleen, and Linda Tibbetts, "Soft Rock and Hard Talk," *Newsweek*, July 15, 1985, p. 51.
Mitchell, Elvis, "Video Valium: The VH–1 Experience," *Village Voice*, June 4, 1985, p. 39.
Schneider, Steve, "Music Channel Seeks Mature Viewers," *New York Times*, February 24, 1985, section 2, p. 34.
Smith, Sally Bedell, "A New Video Channel for Older Set," *New York Times*, January 1, 1985, p. 17.
Willman, Chris, "Music TV for Adults Grows Up," *Los Angeles Times Calendar*, May 6, 1990, pp. 69, 95.

VIACOM, INC. was founded in June 1971, when an FCC* ruling required CBS* to dispose of its syndication and cable television operations. CBS sold off these operations to its shareholders, and CBS president Frank Stanton chose the name Viacom as a play on "via communications" before he sold it. The company is the largest distributor of television programming in the world, and has also been active as a producer with such series as *Frank's Place* (CBS, 1987–1988) and *Jake and the Fatman* (CBS, 1987-   ).

The company owns five television stations, and in 1985 acquired MTV,* as well as the remaining 50 percent of Showtime/The Movie Channel, Inc.* that it did not already own. Between January 1986 and June 1988, Viacom also owned a 15 percent share of Orion Pictures Corporation. In June 1987, Viacom was acquired by Arsenal Holdings, Inc., which operates the company as five divisions: Viacom Entertainment, Viacom Broadcasting, Viacom Networks, Viacom Cable, and Viacom Pictures.

Addresses: 10 Universal City., Universal City, CA 91608; 1211 Avenue of the Americas, New York, NY 10036.

BIBLIOGRAPHY

Gordon, Meryl, "Fast Company," *Channels of Communications*, vol. VI, no. 1, April 1986, pp. 24–29.

Vaughn, Christopher, and Rich Zahradnik, "Redstone's Arsenal," *Channels of Communications*, vol. VIII, no. 5, May 1988, pp. 46–52.

VI-BAR PRODUCTIONS, INC., owned by Jack Chertok, was responsible for the 1952 syndicated series *Steve Donovan, Western Marshall*.

VIDCAM PICTURES CORP. (Alfred Justin, president) was a New York–based producer, primarily of television commercials, active in the fifties.

VIDEO JUKEBOX NETWORK is the first and only interactive music video channel, enabling viewers to select from over one hundred music videos of all types. Operating twenty-four hours a day, it was launched in December 1985, and has 6.5 million subscribers (as of 1990).

Address: 3550 Biscayne Boulevard, Miami, FL 33137.

"VIDEO NASTIES" is an expression introduced in the United Kingdom in the eighties to refer to material released on videotape and considered offensive because of its violence or sexual content. Under the Video Recordings Act of 1984, all videotapes released in the United Kingdom are required to be certified by the British Board of Film Classification.

BIBLIOGRAPHY

Barker, Martin, editor. *The Video Nasties: Freedom and Censorship in the Media*. London: Pluto Press, 1984.

VIDEO PICTURES, INC., founded by Paul A. Wagner, was a New York–based producer of television commercials, active in the fifties.

VIDEOTAPE. The introduction of videotape brought an immediacy to television production, primarily news programming. Gradually, videotape is replacing film as the medium used in the production of all television programming, but at the same time it has introduced problems in that its life span is limited. There is no exact data for how long a videotape will last before "breaking up," but it is generally thought that its life is no more than twenty years, and probably a lot less. As a result, without preservation (that is, the constant transfer or "dubbing" of videotape to new stock), many television programs will be lost forever.

There are four sizes of videotape: two-inch, one-inch, three-quarter inch, and half-inch. The last is the non-professional, home video gauge. Three-quarter-inch videotape is used for news gathering. One-inch is the professional width for a video master. Two-inch professional-width videotape is largely obsolete, although most video laboratories are still able to handle its transfer to other gauges. Videotape records the image by having the head sweep across the tape from side to side, recording parts of the field in successive passes.

In the late forties, Ampex,* RCA,* the BBC,* and Decca all experimented with the development of videotape as a natural progression from magnetic recording tape. On November 11, 1951, the Electronic Division of Bing Crosby Enterprises, Inc.,* headed by John Mullin, introduced the first working magnetic videotape recorder. In 1955, the BBC introduced the VERA* (Vision Electronic Recording Apparatus), which used a five-foot diameter reel to record a thirty-minute program at a tape speed of 200 inches per second. Finally, the following year, the Model VR–1000 Videotape Recorder was demonstrated by Ampex. It replaced kinescope* recording, and solved problems in delaying East Coast programming for screening to West Coast audiences.

In the sixties, CBS* tried to market its own home video system, Electronic Video Recording* (EVR). In 1972, Sony introduced the first videocassette machine, the VCR, for educational and commercial use. In 1975, Sony introduced its home videocassette machine, the Betamax. A year later, JVC introduced Sony's competitor, the Video Home System (VHS). The VHS cassette is larger than the Beta cassette and has more recording time. The machines are not compatible because the electronic systems are different.

The Videodisc, which does not permit the user to record his own programs, was first demonstrated in Berlin on June 24, 1970, as the Teldec Video Disc, created by AEG-Telefunken and Decca. The system had been developed in 1965 by four German scientists, headed by Horst Redlich and Arthur Haddy, chief engineer of Decca Records, Ltd. In 1978, Magnavox* introduced its laser disc player, followed in 1980 by Matsushita and in 1981 by RCA.

BIBLIOGRAPHY

Anderson, Gary H. *Video Editing and Post-Production: A Professional Guide*. White Plains, N.Y.: Knowledge Industry Publications, 1984.

Fuller, Barry J., Steve Kanaba, and Janyce Brisch-Kanaba. *Single-Camera Video Production*. New York: Prentice-Hall, 1982.

Medoff, Norman J., and Tom Tanquary. *Portable Video: ENG and EFB*. White Plains, N.Y.: Knowledge Industry Publications, 1986.

Millerson, Gerald. *Video Production Handbook*. Boston: Focal Press, 1987.

Murray, Michael. *The Videotape Book*. New York: Bantam Books, 1975.

Patterson, Richard, and Dana White, editors. *Electronic Production Techniques*. Los Angeles: American Cinematographer, n.d. [circa 1984].

Robinson, Joseph F. *Videotape Recording*. Boston: Focal Press, 1982.

Robinson, Joseph F., and P.H. Beards. *Using Videotape*. New York: Hastings House, 1976.

Robinson, Richard. *The Video Primer: Equipment, Production, and Concepts*. New York: Perigree, 1983.

Roizen, Joe, "The History of Videotape Recording," *Television*, February 1976, pp. 15–21.

Rosen, Federic W. *Shooting Video*. Boston: Focal Press, 1984.

Schachtman, Tom, and Harriet Shelare. *Video Power*. New York: Henry Holt, 1988.

Schneider, Arthur. *Electronic Post-Production and Videotape Editing*. Boston: Focal Press, 1989.

Sigel, Efrem, Mark Shubin, and Paul F. Merrill. *Video Discs: The Technology, the Applications and the Future*. White Plains, N.Y.: Knowledge Industry Publications, 1980.

Utz, Peter. *Video User's Handbook*. New York: Prentice-Hall, 1989.

Van Wezel, Ru. *Video Handbook*, edited by Gordon J. King. Boston: Newnes, 1981.

VIDEOTEX is the name given to any marketing system utilizing telecommunications as an interactive device between the "user" and the "provider." Utilizing videotex, with a computer terminal and a television monitor, it is possible to shop, purchase tickets, obtain information, and so forth.

BIBLIOGRAPHY

Alber, Antone F. *Videotex/Teletext: Principles and Practices*. New York: McGraw-Hill, 1985.

Aldrich, Michael. *Videotex: Key to the Wired City*. London: Quiller Press, 1982.

Bretz, Rudy, with Michael Schmidbauer. *Media for Interactive Communication*. Beverly Hills, Calif.: Sage Publications, 1983.

Nugent, Owen, P. J. Peters, and Lee Rockwell *Instructional Development for Videotex: Flowcharts and Scripting*. San Diego: Electronic Text Consortium, San Diego State University, 1984.

Sigel, Efrem. *The Future of Videotext: Worldwide Prospects for Home/Office Electronic Information Services*. White Plains, N.Y.: Knowledge Industry Publications, 1983.

Tydeman, John, Hubert Lipinski, Richard P. Adler, Michael Nyhan, and Laurence Zwimpfer. *Teletext and Videotex in the United States: Market Potential, Technology, Public Policy Issues*. New York: McGraw-Hill, 1982.

Veith, Richard H. *Television's Teletext*. New York: North-Holland, 1983.

The Videotex Marketplace. Bethesda, Md.: Phillips, 1984.

Weaver, David H. *Videotex Journalism: Teletext, Viewdata, and the News*. Hillsdale, N.J.: Lawrence Erlbaum Associates, 1983.

THE VIDEOTEX INDUSTRY ASSOCIATION was founded in 1981 to serve the needs of both individual and corporate members involved in interactive electronic services. It sponsors both a technical committee and a code of rights and conduct committee, organizes meetings, publishes a monthly newsletter, and works with federal regulatory and legislative officials.

Address: 1901 North Fort Myer Drive, Suite 200, Rosslyn, VA 22209,

VIDEO WALLPAPER is a video version of Muzak, developed in the eighties by Nebulae Productions. Each videocassette is intended to provide soothing images for the viewer at home or at the office.
BIBLIOGRAPHY
Jacobs, Frank, "Video Valium," *Panorama*, vol. I, no. 6, July 1980, p. 24.

VIEWER'S CHOICE 1 and VIEWER'S CHOICE 2 are pay-per-view cable networks offering feature films, specials, and sporting events, twenty-four hours a day, to 11.5 million subscribers (as of 1990). Viewer's Choice 1 was launched in November 1985, and Viewer's Choice 2 was first seen in June 1986.
   Address: 909 Third Avenue, 21st Floor, New York, NY 10022.

VISION CHANNEL offers two hours of religious programming a week, intended for Sunday transmission, and distributed to U.K. cable operators on videotape. It was first seen on Swindon Cable in 1986.
   Address: Vision Broadcasting Communications, Shaftesbury Centre, Percy Street, Swindon SN2 2A2, United Kingdom.

VISN (Vision Interfaith Satellite Network) is a basic cable network broadcasting religious and values-based programming with no on-air fund raising. Seen by 7.5 million subscribers (as of 1990), VISN began broadcasting in September 1988, and is on air, daily, from 8:00 A.M. to 2:00 A.M.
   Address: P.O. Box 5630, Denver, CO 80237.

VOLCANO PRODUCTIONS, INC. was a service producer, handling the physical production of television commercials and a number of programs, including *The Adventures of Ozzie and Harriet* (ABC, 1952–1966), *I Married Joan* (NBC, 1952–1955), and *The Mickey Rooney Show* (NBC, 1954–1955). Headed first by Robert Angus and later by James A. Bank, Volcano was active from the fifties through the mid-sixties, and rented space at the General Services Studio in Hollywood.

V[IOLA] S. BECKER PRODUCTIONS was a New York–based producer of television programming and commercials, founded in 1946, and active through 1967.

W

WALTER W. SCHWIMMER, INC. was a Chicago-based television and radio production company, founded in 1945. It specialized in short quiz programs such as *Let's Go to the Races* and *Movie Quick Quiz*, which were popular on syndicated television in the fifties, as well as sports series such as *All Star Golf*, *Championship Bowling*, *Championship Bridge with Charles Goren*, and *World Series of Golf*. Schwimmer also produced the telecast of *The Nobel Prize Awards*, hosted by Alistair Cooke, and seen on ABC* on December 12, 1964. It remained active through 1966.

WALT FRAMER PRODUCTIONS was a New York–based packager of game shows, which had its first big success on radio in 1947 with *Strike It Rich*. The show was later seen on television, on CBS,* from 1951 to 1958. Other Walt Framer shows are *Double or Nothing* (CBS, 1952–1954; NBC, 1953), *The Greatest Man on Earth* (ABC, 1952–1953), *Penny to a Million* (ABC, 1955), and *For Love or Money* (CBS, 1958–1959).

WAR. World War I has never been the subject of an American television series, but in 1979, CBS* aired a television version of Erich Maria Remarque's *All Quiet on the Western Front*. Made-for-television movies and mini-series dealing with World War II include *Inside the Third Reich* (ABC, 1982), *Winds of War* (ABC, 1982), *War and Remembrance* (ABC, 1988–1989), and *The Dirty Dozen* television movies—*The Next Mission* (NBC, 1985), *The Deadly Mission* (NBC, 1987), and *The Fatal Mission* (NBC, 1988). The most popular of the series dealing with World War II are *Combat!* (ABC, 1962–1967) and *Rat Patrol* (ABC, 1966–1968). A humorous view of the war was shown in *McHale's Navy* (ABC, 1962–1966) and *Hogan's Heroes* (CBS, 1965–1971).

A lighthearted look at the Korean War, with occasional serious undertones, was provided by *M*A*S*H* (CBS, 1972–1983). The Vietnam War is the subject of *Tour of Duty* (CBS, 1987-1990) and *China Beach* (ABC, 1988-1991). The best-regarded made-for-television movie on the Vietnam conflict is *Friendly Fire* (ABC, 1979).

A number of British-made documentary series on World Wars I and II have been seen on American television: *War in the Air* (BBC, 1954), *First World War* (ATV, 1961), *The Great War* (BBC, 1964), and *World at War* (Thames, 1973).

See also NUCLEAR WAR.

WARM-UPS are used to put a television audience into a receptive mood prior to a show's being taped or filmed. The tradition is believed to have started in 1951 when producer Jess Oppenheimer persuaded Desi Arnaz to warm up the audience prior to the filming of *I Love Lucy*. Warm-ups are generally handled by comedians not associated with the program as seen by the television viewer but anxious for a break in television. Among those who began their television careers as warm-up comedians are game-show hosts Marc Summers and Ray Combs.

BIBLIOGRAPHY
Waldron, Robert, "Warm-Ups: They Preheat Studio Audiences and Add Sizzle to a Show," *Emmy*, vol. XI, no. 5, September/October, 1989, pp. 28–31.

WARNER BROS. TELEVISION. Warner Bros. entered television production in 1955, with the appointment of William T. Orr (born 1917) as the head of its television division. The studio's first series was *Warner Bros. Presents* (first seen on ABC* on September 3, 1955), comprising three alternating programs, *Casablanca*, *King's Row*, and *Cheyenne*. All the early Warner Bros. television series were seen on ABC, and include: *Sugarfoot* (1957–1961), *Maverick* (1957–1962), *Colt .45* (1957–1960), *Bronco* (1958–1962), *77 Sunset Strip* (1958–1964), *The Lawman* (1958–1962), *Bourbon Street Beat* (1959–1960), *Hawaiian Eye* (1959–1963), *The Alaskans* (1959–1960), *Surfside 6* (1960–1962), *The Roaring 20's* (1960–1962), and *The Gallant Men* (1962–1963).

BIBLIOGRAPHY
Woolley, Lynn, Robert W. Malsbary, and Robert G. Strange, Jr. *Warner Bros. Television: Every Show of the Fifties and Sixties Episode-by-Episode.* Jefferson, N.C.: McFarland, 1985.

THE WEATHER CHANNEL is a basic cable network, providing local, regional, national, and international weather information twenty-four hours a day. Launched in May 1982, The Weather Channel was created by John Coleman (born 1937) with financial backing from Landmark Communications. Coleman resigned as president and chairman in August 1983 after failing to find a new financial backer for the network. Using the STAR system, which it developed, the network gathers all the National Weather Service data into one computer and disseminates it in localized reports several times a day. Advertising-supported, The Weather Channel is seen by 43 million subscribers (as of 1990).

Address: 2600 Cumberland Parkway, Atlanta, GA 30339.

BIBLIOGRAPHY

Beermann, Frank, "Coleman Out at Weather Channel," *Daily Variety*, August 26, 1983, p. 20.

————, "New Prez of Weather Channel Sees Boost in Subs, Nat'l Advertisers," *Daily Variety*, August 16, 1985, p. 18.

Gorman, James, "Will the Weather Channel Save America?" *Discover*, December 1987, pp. 30, 32.

Levy, Stephen, "Weather Channel: When It Rains, It Bores," *Rolling Stone*, October 27, 1983, p. 107.

Sperone, Al J., "The Weather Channel's Moment of Gloria," *Village Voice*, October 8, 1985, p. 44.

WEISS GLOBAL ENTERPRISES is a distributor to television of features and syndicated programming, and was organized in 1974. It is a successor company to Adrian Weiss Productions and Louis Weiss & Co., and responsible for the production of *Craig Kennedy, Criminologist* (Syndicated, 1951) and *The Chuckleheads* (Syndicated, 1962), among others.

Address: 2055 South Saviers Road, Suite 12, Oxnard, CA 93033–3693.

WESTAR was the first domestic communications satellite, launched in the United States by Western Union in April 1974. Manufactured by Hughes Aircraft, it was utilized by PBS.*

WESTERNS. As the following list of the most successful Western series on television indicates, it has been more than a decade since there has been a popular Western production on network television: *The Adventures of Kit Carson* (Syndicated, 1951–1955), *The Adventures of Wild Bill Hickok* (Syndicated, 1951–1958), *Annie Oakley* (Syndicated, 1952–1956), *The Big Valley* (ABC, 1965–1969), *Bonanza* (NBC, 1959–1973), *Bronco* (ABC, 1958–1962), *The Cisco Kid* (Syndicated, 1950–1956), *Daniel Boone* (NBC, 1964–1970), *Death Valley Days* (Syndicated, 1952–1975), *The Deputy* (NBC, 1959–1961), *Dick Powell's Zane Grey Theater* (CBS, 1956–1962), *The Gene Autry Show* (CBS, 1950–1956), *Gunsmoke* (CBS, 1955–1975), *Have Gun Will Travel* (CBS, 1957–1963), *The High Chaparral* (NBC, 1967–1971), *Hopalong Cassidy* (NBC, 1949–1951), *Kung Fu* (ABC, 1972–1975), *Laramie* (NBC, 1959–1963), *The Lawman* (ABC, 1958–1962), *The Life and Legend of Wyatt Earp* (ABC, 1955–1961), *The Lone Ranger* (ABC, 1949–1957), *Maverick* (ABC, 1957–1962), *The Outlaws* (NBC, 1960–1962), *The Range Rider* (Syndicated, 1951–1952), *Rawhide* (CBS, 1959–1966), *The Rebel* (ABC, 1959–1961; NBC, 1962), *The Restless Gun* (NBC, 1957–1959), *The Rifleman* (ABC, 1958–1963), *The Roy Rogers Show* (NBC, 1951–1957), *Sugarfoot* (ABC, 1957–1961), *Tales of Wells Fargo* (NBC, 1957–1962), *The Texan* (CBS, 1958–1960), *Tombstone Territory* (ABC, 1957–1959),

Trackdown (CBS, 1957–1959), *The Virginian* (NBC, 1962–1971), *Wagon Train* (NBC, 1957–1965), *Wichita Town* (NBC, 1959–1960), *The Wild Wild West* (CBS, 1965–1970), and *Zorro* (ABC, 1957–1959).

BIBLIOGRAPHY

Barabas, SuzAnne, and Gabor Barabas. *Gunsmoke: A Complete History and Analysis of the Legendary Broadcast Series.* Jefferson, N.C.: McFarland, 1990.

McDonald, J. Fred. *Who Shot the Sheriff? The Rise and Fall of the Television Western.* New York: Praeger, 1987.

Parks, Rita. *The Western Hero in Film and Television: Mass Media Mythology.* Ann Arbor, Mich.: UMI Research Press, 1982.

West, Richard. *Television Westerns: Major and Minor Series, 1946–1978.* Jefferson, N.C.: McFarland, 1987.

WESTERN TELEVISION CORPORATION was a Chicago-based company created by Ulises A. Sanabria that produced television studio scanners and home televisors. Involved in the field of mechanical television,* the company's most important product was the Visionette Televisor, introduced in 1930, and used to receive programming from its own station, W9XAO, and also the Chicago *Daily News* station, W9XAP, between 1930 and 1933.

WEST HOOKER PRODUCTIONS was a New York–based producer, responsible for two early game shows, *Say It with Acting* (NBC, 1951; ABC, 1951–1952) and *Hold That Camera* (DuMont, 1950). West Hooker also operated a distribution company, Film Network, Inc.

WESTINGHOUSE has for many years been one of the more familiar names in broadcasting. One of the most famous advertising phrases on early television, in reference to Westinghouse household appliances, was, "You can be sure if it's Westinghouse," spoken by Betty Furness on *Westinghouse Studio One* (CBS, 1948–1958). The latter was a major dramatic series from the golden days of television, and just one of many television programs sponsored by Westinghouse. Others include *Westinghouse Desilu Playhouse* (CBS, 1958–1960), hosted by Desi Arnaz; *Westinghouse Playhouse* (NBC, 1961), starring Nanette Fabray; and *Westinghouse Preview Theatre* (NBC, 1961).

Westinghouse Electric Co. was incorporated on January 8, 1886, and adopted its current name of Westinghouse Electric Corp. on May 10, 1945. It was a pioneer in broadcasting, beginning in 1920 with KDKA-Pittsburgh. Television pioneer Vladimir Zworykin (1889–1982) joined Westinghouse in East Pittsburgh in the early twenties, and on December 29, 1923, applied for his first patent covering a complete television system. He left the company in 1929, and joined RCA* as director of the Electronics Research Group.

Among the many "firsts" in radio broadcasting claimed by Westinghouse are the establishment of America's first commercial radio station, KDKA, in 1920. The company was also the first to establish a newsroom, at KDKA, in 1921; the first to broadcast a church service, on KDKA, in 1921; the first to broadcast the world series, via WJZ-Newark and WBZ-Springfield, Massachusetts, in 1922; and the first to broadcast a concert performance by the Boston Pops, on WBZ, in 1927. In the area of television, Westinghouse was the first to construct an all-electronic television receiver, in 1929. Philco's W3XE-Philadelphia, which Westinghouse later acquired and renamed KYW, was the first station to televise a national political convention, in 1940, and the first to televise a commercially sponsored color* program, in 1953.

Westinghouse created Group W as a wholly owned broadcasting and cable division. In 1981, it purchased its first UHF* station, WPCQ-Charlotte, North Carolina, and that same year it also acquired the TelePrompTer Corporation* for $646 million. The corporation, which operated 140 cable systems and served 2.1 million subscribers, was renamed Group W Cable, Inc. The latter was sold in December 1985 (except for two Chicago franchises) for $1.6 billion and assumption of certain tax liabilities to American Television & Communications Corp., Comcast Corp., Tele-Communications, Inc.,* Daniels & Associates, and Century Southwest Communications Corp. In June 1990, Westinghouse disposed of the remaining cable service, Group W Cable in Chicago, to Prime Cable of Austin.

In the area of syndicated programming, the company has been active, notably with *PM Magazine*, which began as *Evening Magazine* in 1976. The name was changed two years later. Other syndicated programming from Westinghouse/ Group W includes *The Mike Douglas Show* (1963–1982), *Hour Magazine* (1980– 1989), and *The Wil Shriner Show* (1987). The company's first network productions were two made-for-television movies, *Lost in London* (NBC, 1985) and *Mafia Princess* (CBS, 1986). In 1981–1982, it was involved with the Walt Disney Company in a joint venture to produce sixteen hours of daily family programming. Also in 1981, Westinghouse established a software programming company, Group W Satellite Communications.

As of 1990, Westinghouse owns twenty-two radio stations and five television stations: WJZ-Baltimore, WBZ-Boston, KYW-Philadelphia, KDKA-Pittsburgh, and KPIX–San Francisco.

Address: 888 Seventh Avenue, New York, NY 10106.

BIBLIOGRAPHY

Fabrikant, Geraldine, "Group W Cable Sold to 5 Buyers," *New York Times*, December 25, 1985, pp. 21, 23.

Schwarz, Michael, and Martin Koughan, "TV's Moral Minority," *Channels of Communications,* vol. IV, no. 2, May/June 1984, pp. 45–47, 66.

WESTWARD PRODUCTIONS, LTD. was a television production company, headed by Samuel Goldwyn, Jr., and extant from the mid-fifties through the mid-sixties. A related company was Formosa Productions, Inc., formed in 1955.

WGBH EDUCATIONAL FOUNDATION holds the licenses for two Boston television stations, WGBH and WGBX; one Boston radio station, WGBH; and one Springfield, Massachusetts, television station, WGBY. All are viewer- and listener-supported public stations. WGBH radio was founded in 1951 by the Lowell Institute Cooperative Broadcasting Council, and WGBH television began in 1955. In its first year, it broadcast the first stereo simulcast* of a Boston Symphony Orchestra concert in cooperation with WGBH-FM. In 1958, WGBH became the first public television station to purchase its own videotape equipment. On October 14, 1961, the station burned to the ground, but it was back on the air within two days.

WGBH is one of the largest public television stations (seen by more than 2 million households), and is generally regarded as the flagship of the public broadcasting service. In fact, it is the source of almost one-third of all prime time programming seen nationwide on public television. The station gained prominence under the leadership of Hartford Gunn, and among its best known series are *The French Chef* (1962–1973), *Evening at Pops* (1970-   ), *Masterpiece Theatre* (1971-   ), *Julia Child & Company* (1978–1979), *This Old House* (1979-   ), *Mystery!* (1980-   ), *Vietnam: A Television History* (1983), and *Frontline* (1983-   ).

One of the station's few failures was a 1978 multimillion-dollar serialization of *The Scarlet Letter*, which resulted in WGBH facing a major deficit for the first time in its history. In 1984, WGBH established the Contemporary Art Television Fund to support experimental video, in association with Boston's Institute of Contemporary Arts. A pioneer in closed captioning for hearing-impaired viewers, WGBH launched a similar innovation, Descriptive Video Service, for visually impaired audiences in 1990.

Address: 125 Western Avenue, Boston, MA 02134.

BIBLIOGRAPHY

Daviss, Ben, "WGBH Boston Presents What Is Arguably the Best Television in the United States," *Emmy*, vol. VII, no. 5, September/October 1985, pp. 48–55.

Efron, Edith, "Boston: Home of the Bean, the Cod and WGBH," *TV Guide*, December 18, 1971, pp. 33–40.

Rifkin, Glenn, "Public TV's WGBH Takes Risks in Pursuit of Provocative Fare," *New York Times*, May 20, 1984, section 2, pp. 29–30.

WGN is Chicago's independent superstation,* offering a variety of programming to 30 million (as of 1990) basic cable subscribers. WGN was launched as a superstation in November 1978.

Address: United Video, 3801 South Sheridan Road, Tulsa, OK 74145.

[CHARLES G.] WHITEHEAD TV PICTURES, INC. was a New York–based producer of television commercials, active in the fifties and early sixties.

WILLIAM ALLAND PRODUCTIONS, founded by William Alland (born 1916) was primarily a producer of theatrical features, but it was also responsible for the 1960 syndicated series *World of Giants*.

WILLIAM BOYD PRODUCTIONS, INC. was formed in 1947 by actor Boyd (1895–1972) and entrepreneur Toby Anguish, and acquired not only the rights but also the use of the name to almost all the ''Hopalong Cassidy'' features (apart from a few that had already been sold off). Between 1947 and 1948, Boyd produced and starred in a further series of ''Hopalong Cassidy'' features, which were some of the first feature-length productions to be sold to television, in 1948. Hopalong Cassidy's creator Clarence Mulford had retained the television rights to the character, and the rights were acquired by William Boyd Productions, with the company producing forty additional films for television betwen 1952 and 1955. The company name was changed to B.B. Productions in 1957, and shortly thereafter William Boyd retired, selling his business interests for a reported $8 million.

BIBLIOGRAPHY

Nevins, Francis M. *The Films of Hopalong Cassidy*. Waynesville, N.C.: The World of Yesterday, 1968.

WILLIAM F. BROIDY PRODUCTIONS, INC. was created in 1946, when Broidy (1915–1959) became an independent producer of theatrical features for Monogram and its successor, Allied Artists. Broidy's best-known television series is *Wild Bill Hickok*, starring Guy Madison (Syndicated, 1951–1958), the rights to which were sold to Screen Gems* in 1957.

[LESLIE] WINIK FILMS CORP. was a New York–based producer of television programming and commercials, active from the fifties through the mid-seventies. The company specialized in sports-related syndicated series, such as *Madison Square Garden* (fifteen- and thirty-minute programs), *Greatest Sports Thrills* (thirty-minute programs), and *Famous Fights* (thirty-minute programs), and also maintained a sports stock-footage library.

WINKLER/RICH PRODUCTIONS, owned by John Rich (born 1925) and actor Henry Winkler (born 1945) produces *MacGyver* (ABC, 1985-   ), and has also been responsible for a 1988 ABC* pilot show, *Second Start*.

Address: 5555 Melrose Avenue, Hollywood, CA 90038.

WITT-THOMAS PRODUCTIONS/WITT-THOMAS-HARRIS PRODUC-TIONS was formed in 1977 by Paul Junger Witt (born 1941), the former head of production for Danny Thomas Productions;* Tony Thomas (born 1948), son of Danny Thomas; and writer Susan Harris. The last individual's name appears as co-producer on the series that she has written and/or conceived: *Soap* (ABC, 1977–1981), *Benson* (ABC, 1979–1986), *Golden Girls* (NBC, 1985-   ), and *Empty Nest* (NBC, 1988-   ). Witt-Thomas co-produced *Beauty and the Beast* (CBS, 1988–1990) with Republic Pictures. It also produced the 1989 theatrical feature *Dead Poet's Society*. Since 1985, the company has had a non-exclusive agreement with the Walt Disney Company.

Address: 846 North Cahuenga Boulevard, Hollywood, CA 90038.

WNET/THIRTEEN is the public television station serving the tri-state area of New York, New Jersey, and Connecticut. Chartered as the Educational Broadcasting Corporation, it is a New York–based non-profit educational corporation, overseen by the Board of Regents of the University of the State of New York, but it is licensed to Newark, New Jersey. Its headquarters (opened in 1985) are at West 58 Street, New York, and its studio facilities (opened in 1981) are in Newark.

The station was created in July 1970 with the merger of NET* and WNDT. The station's first president was James Day, and its initial funding was a $2 million grant from the Ford Foundation.* WNDT ("New Dimensions in Television") began broadcasting on September 16, 1962, and the opening-night program was hosted by Edward R. Murrow. Regular weekday programming did not commence until October of the same year. WNDT was established with the purchase of the station for $6,200,000 from NTA* by a group calling itself Educational Television for the Metropolitan Area, Inc. (ETMA). WNDT's first president was Dr. Samuel Gould, and Richard Heffner was its vice-president and general manager.

WNET grew in stature under the leadership of John Jay Iselin, who joined as general manager in 1971, became president in 1973, and retired in 1987. Among the shows emanating from WNET for the PBS* network are *Great Performances* (1974-), *Dance in America* (1975-), *Live from Lincoln Center* (1976-), *The Adams Chronicles* (1976), *Live from the Met* (1976-), *Creativity with Bill Moyers* (1983), and *The Story of English* (1986). The station began twenty-four hour a day broadcasting in 1987.

Address: 356 West 58 Street, New York, NY 10019.

BIBLIOGRAPHY

Boyer, Peter J., "Life on the Edge at Channel 13," *New York Times*, February 28, 1988, section 2, pp. 1, 31.

Goldstein, Richard, "Mr. Public TV," *Village Voice*, March 3, 1980, p. 31.

————, "Who Stands for WNET?" *Village Voice*, July 6, 1982, pp. 37, 78.

O'Connor, John J., "13: Past, Present, Future," *New York Times*, September 13, 1987, pp. H45, H50.

Taubin, Amy, "WNET Is 25—And Ancient History," *Village Voice*, September 22, 1987, pp. 51–52.

Taylor, Clarke, "Mr. WNET Sums Up PBS Career," *Los Angeles Times*, January 27, 1987, part VI, pp. 1, 9.

Welles, Chris, "Poor Little Rich TV Station," *New York*, October 9, 1978, pp. 51–56.

"WNDT—A Preview," *TV Guide*, September 8, 1962, pp. A4-A5.

[EDWARD] WOLF ASSOCIATES, INC. was a New York–based producer of live game shows, active in the fifties and early sixties (at which time it changed its name to Wolf Presentations, Inc.). The most popular of the company's productions were *Break the Bank* (ABC, 1949; NBC, 1949–1952; CBS, 1952–1953; NBC, 1953; ABC, 1954–1956; NBC, 1956–1957), *Masquerade Party* (NBC, 1952; CBS, 1953–1954; ABC, 1954–1956; NBC, 1957; CBS,

1958; NBC, 1958–1959; CBS, 1959–1960; NBC, 1960), and *Hold That Note* (NBC, 1957).

WOLPER PRODUCTIONS was formed in 1958 by David Lloyd Wolper (born 1928). Quickly it gained a reputation for the production of quality programs utilizing archival film clips, and among the best known of its filmed shows are *Hollywood: The Golden Years* (1960), *Hollywood: The Great Stars* (1962), *Hollywood: The Fabulous Era* (1962), the *Biography* series (1962–1963), the *Hollywood and the Stars* series (1963–1964), *The Legend of Marilyn Monroe* (1964), *Prelude to War* (1965), *The Rise and Fall of the Third Reich* (1966–1967), *The Life and Times of Sophia Loren* (1967), *The Life and Times of Elizabeth Taylor* (1967), and *Bogie* (1967).

In 1966, the company was sold to Metromedia, Inc.,* but two years later, Wolper formed a new company, Wolper Productions, Inc. A related company, Wolper Pictures, Inc., was formed at the same time. Wolper Productions, Inc. was responsible for *Get Christie Love* (ABC, 1974–1975), *Chico and the Man* (NBC, 1974–1978), and *Welcome Back, Kotter* (ABC, 1975–1979). The company experienced a major tragedy on March 14, 1974, when thirty-one members of the cast and crew of "The Primal Man" segment of its series *Struggle for Survival* were killed in a plane crash near Bishop, California.

Wolper Productions, Inc. was sold to Warner Bros. in January 1977, and was replaced by yet another organization, the Wolper Organization, Inc. It was closely associated with Warner Bros. (and located on its studio lot), and Wolper signed a seven-year exclusive contract with that company in July 1988.

Wolper's next group of productions included his most famous endeavor, *Roots* (ABC, 1977), which was followed by a second mini-series, *Roots II: The Next Generation* (ABC, 1979). Other mini-series and movies-for-television produced by Wolper include *Moviola* (NBC, 1980), *The Thorn Birds* (ABC, 1983), *The Mystic Warrior* (ABC, 1984), *North & South* (ABC, 1984), and *North & South, Book II* (ABC, 1986).

In addition, Wolper received worldwide praise for his production of two outdoor events, the opening of the Twenty-Third Olympiad in Los Angeles in 1984 and the Statue of Liberty Centennial Celebration in 1986.

Address: The Wolper Organization, Inc., 4000 Warner Boulevard, Burbank, CA 91522.

BIBLIOGRAPHY

Mann, Arnold, "David Wolper: The Extraordinary Ordinary Man," *Emmy*, vol. VIII, no. 6, November/December 1986, pp. 22–33.

WOMEN IN CABLE was founded on July 20, 1979, as a support group for women, aimed at expanding the role of women in the cable television industry. Since 1987, it has sponsored the Women in Cable/University of Denver Certificate in Cable Management Program and the Betsy Magness Executive Development Seminars.

Address: 500 North Michigan Avenue, Suite 1400, Chicago, IL 60611.

WORLDNET, sponsored by the United States Information Agency (USIA), is a cable network providing U.S. news and information to European viewers. It was first seen in April 1985.

Address: U.S. Embassy, 24 Grosvenor Square, London W1A 1AE, United Kingdom.

WORLD TELEVISION ALLIANCE (WTA) was a pretentious and abortive 1987 proposal by producer Charles W. Fries to "provide the world's viewers with free access to international TV programs in local languages anywhere on the planet." WTA was to lead to the creation of the Universal Television System (UTS), the first member of which was to be the United States Television Alliance, founded and headed by Fries. WTA was also intended to establish the World Teleresearch Center.

BIBLIOGRAPHY
Chunovic, Louis, "Fries Unveils Plan for Worldwide TV," *The Hollywood Reporter*, July 9, 1987, pp. 1, 8.

WORLD TELEVISION RELEASING CORPORATION was founded in December 1976 by Mickey Roth to syndicate feature films and television programming worldwide.

WORLDVISION ENTERPRISES was a major distributor of television programming, formed on March 23, 1973, by Kevin O'Sullivan, former president of ABC Films, Inc.* Quickly it acquired distribution rights to such major series as *Little House on the Prairie* (from NBC*), *The Love Boat* (from Aaron Spelling Productions, Inc.*) and *Dallas* and *Eight Is Enough* (from Lorimar Television*). It also distributed many feature film packages, including the Selznick Classics collection. In September 1979, Worldvision merged with Taft Broadcasting, and, subsequently, in July 1988, it merged with Aaron Spelling Productions, Inc.* under the new name of Spelling Inc.

BIBLIOGRAPHY
Gansberg, Alan L., "Worldvision: More than a Decade of Success," *The Hollywood Reporter*, April 20, 1984, pp. W5-W9.

WPIX is one of two New York independent superstations,* offering a variety of programming to 10 million (as of 1990) basic cable subscribers. WPIX was launched as a superstation in May 1984.

Address: United Video, 3801 South Sheridan Road, Tulsa, OK 74145.

WQED is the public television station for the Pittsburgh area, operated by Metropolitan Pittsburgh Public Broadcasting, Inc. It began broadcasting on April 1, 1954. The two best-known series originating from WQED are *National Geographic Specials* (1975-) and *Mister Rogers' Neighborhood* (1967-). The latter, which was off the air from 1975 to 1979, is the longest running program on PBS,* and is hosted by Fred Rogers, a Presbyterian minister from Pittsburgh.

Address: 4802 Fifth Avenue, Pittsburgh, PA 15213.

BIBLIOGRAPHY

Margulies, Lee, "Visionary TV via Pittsburgh," *Los Angeles Times*, January 18, 1977, part IV, p. 13.

WRATHER TELEVISION PRODUCTIONS, INC. was an offshoot of Jack Wrather Pictures, Inc., which was formed in 1946. Based in Beverly Hills, it was one of a number of companies organized by businessman Jack D. Wrather (1918–1984), who gained prominence in 1954 with his acquisition of the rights to the "Lone Ranger" character. Wrather had started to acquire television stations in 1952. In 1959, he purchased Transcontinent Television, but sold it three years later to Taft. Wrather was also a major shareholder in the TelePrompTer Corporation* from 1965 to 1981.

WSBK is Boston's independent superstation,* offering a variety of programming to 2 million (as of 1990) basic cable subscribers. WSBK was launched as a superstation in February 1988.

Address: Eastern Microwave, 112 Northern Concourse/P.O. Box 4872, Syracuse, NY 13221.

WWOR is one of two New York independent superstations,* offering a variety of programming (including 350 live sporting events a year), available to 13 million (as of 1990) basic cable subscribers. WWOR was launched as a superstation in April 1979.

Address: Eastern Microwave, 112 Northern Concourse/P.O. Box 4872, Syracuse, NY 13221.

_____ **Y** _____

YORKSHIRE TELEVISION LIMITED is the independent ("commercial") television network for the area of Britain extending from North Yorkshire to Lincoln in the south and from the east coast to the Pennines. A private, limited company, wholly owned by Trident Television Limited, Yorkshire Television began broadcasting on July 29, 1968. It is perhaps best known to American television viewers for the production of two comedy series, *Rising Damp* and *Only When I Laugh*.

Address: The Television Centre, Leeds LS3 1JS, United Kingdom.

THE YOUNG BLACK PROGRAMMERS COALITION, founded in 1976, represents the interests of black professionals in all areas of the communications industry. It offers scholarships, maintains a publications program, lobbies for the interests of its members, and presents awards.

Address: P.O. Box 11243, Jackson, MS 39213.

Z

ZACH BAYM FILMS was a New York–based producer and distributor of the fifties, responsible for the 1955 syndicated series of thirty- and fifteen-minute programs titled *World Close-Up*. It also distributed features and Westerns to television.

ZAPPING and ZIPPING are names given to popular methods used by television viewers to avoid commercials. The former is used in reference to changing channels by remote control in order to avoid a commercial break. Zipping is used to refer to the practice of fast-forwarding past commercials when playing back a program recorded on videotape.

THE Z CHANNEL was the first subscription movie channel in the Los Angeles area, created in 1974 by Theta Cable, a subsidiary of the TelePrompTer Corporation.* It broadcast only two feature films a day—with the first two being *Save the Tiger* and *Play It Again Sam*—but within a few months, Z became the largest pay-cable channel in the country. Z Channel's success is generally credited to Jerry Harvey (1949–1988), who began programming films there in 1980 and introduced a policy of screening uncut or original versions of features that had not previously been accessible. After many ownership changes, the Z Channel was acquired, in March 1989, by Cablevision's Rainbow Programming Services Corp.,* which, on June 1, 1989, changed Z's name to Sports Channel Los Angeles and commenced an all-sports format.

BIBLIOGRAPHY

Margulies, Lee, "The Pay Channel That No One Disconnects," *Channels of Communications*, vol. IV, no. 3, September/October 1984, pp. 38–39.
Parisi, Paula, "Z Channel Fading to Black amid Film Industry Tributes," *The Hollywood Reporter*, April 27, 1989, pp. 1, 18, 21.

ZDF (Zweites Deutsches Fernsehen) is one of the two German nationwide public television networks—the other is ARD.* ZDF was formed in 1961, and began broadcasting in 1963. It is funded through advertising revenues and licensing fees.

Address: P.O. Box 4040, B–6000 500, Mainz, Germany.

ZENITH PRODUCTIONS LTD. was created in 1984 by Central Independent Television* to produce films for the home and international markets. It began operations officially on October 1, 1984, with its first film being *The Hit*, directed by Stephen Frears. (*The Hit* was also released theatrically, in 1984.)

Address: 8 Great Titchfield Street, London W1, United Kingdom.

ZENITH RADIO CORPORATION is a major manufacturer of television receivers; it introduced its first color television sets in August 1961. The company was incorporated on July 5, 1923, and changed its name to Zenith Electronics Corp. on April 24, 1984. Zenith also operated station W9X2V-WTZR (Chicago), one of nine active television stations in 1945.

Address: 1000 Milwaukee Avenue, Glenview, IL 60025.

ZIV TELEVISION PROGRAMS, INC. was one of the best-known names in the production and distribution of syndicated television series in the fifties. The company was founded in Cincinnati in 1937 as a producer and distributor of radio programming by Frederick W. Ziv. He entered television syndication in February 1948 with the purchase for $240,000 of the General Film Library, consisting of 10 million feet of film, which was used in the production of fifteen-minute compilation programs such as *Yesterday's Newsreel*.

Among the more than seventy-five series produced for syndication by Ziv are *The Cisco Kid* (1950–1955), *Boston Blackie* (1951–1952), *My Favorite Story* (1952–1953), *The Unexpected* (1952), *I Led Three Lives* (1953–1955), *Mister District Attorney* (1954), *Meet Corliss Archer* (1954), *Highway Patrol* (1955–1959), *The Eddie Cantor Comedy Theatre* (1955), *Science Fiction Theatre* (1955–1956), *The Man Called X* (1956), *Dr. Christian* (1956), *Harbor Command* (1957), *Dial 999* (1958), *Sea Hunt* (1958–1961), *Target* (1958), *Bold Venture* (1959), *Lock-Up* (1959–1960), *This Man Dawson* (1959), *Home Run Derby* (1959–1961), *Tombstone Territory* (1959), and *The Case of the Dangerous Robin* (1960).

Leaving its Cincinnati headquarters, the company moved its head office to Hollywood in 1950, and its logo, "Your Outstanding Source of *Dependable* Programming," became a familiar term to program purchasers at independent stations. Ziv Television Programs was purchased by United Artists in 1960. The Ziv Archive is located in the Division of Broadcasting at the University of Cincinnati.

BIBLIOGRAPHY

Onosko, Tim, "The Ziv Tradition," in *The Ultimate Television Book*, editor Judy Fire-
    man. New York: Workman, 1977, pp. 77–78.
Silden, Isobel, "The Ziv Reunion," *Emmy*, vol. VIII, no. 5, September/October 1986,
    pp. 70–78.

Appendix

LEONARD H. (HARRY) GOLDENSON (Born December 7, 1905). Although not its founder, Leonard H. Goldenson is the key figure in the history of the American Broadcasting Company from 1950 through its sale to Capital Cities Communications, Inc. in 1985. Goldenson began his career as a law clerk, after earning an LL.B. degree from Harvard Law School in 1930. Three years later, he was selected to help in the reorganization of Paramount's New England theatres, and this led to a long-term relationship with the Paramount theatre chain. Following the 1948 U.S. government–ordered divestiture by the motion picture studios of their theatre chains, Goldenson became president of the former Paramount theatre circuit, now renamed United Paramount Theatres, Inc.

In 1950, Goldenson negotiated the merger of United Paramount Theatres, Inc. with Edward J. Noble's American Broadcasting Company. The Federal Communications Commission approved the merger in 1953, and the new company was initially named American Broadcasting Paramount Theatres, Inc.; the name was changed to ABC, Inc. in 1965. Goldenson was president and chief executive officer of the company, taking the title of chairman of the board in 1954.

Goldenson was instrumental in the diversification of ABC's corporate activities, beginning in 1955 with the creation of a subsidiary, Am-Par Record Corporation, to produce phonograph records. Later, the company branched out into publishing and the establishment of amusement parks. In 1956, Goldenson took personal charge of the reorganization of the company's television division, following the resignation of division president Robert Kintner. In 1985, Goldenson negotiated the acquisition of ABC, Inc. by Thomas S. Murphy's Capital Cities Communications, Inc.

In 1987, Goldenson was elected to the Academy of Television Arts and Sciences Hall of Fame, and in 1990, he received the academy's highest honor, the Governors Award. He is involved in a number of charitable activities, notably the co-founding of the United Cerebral Palsy Association in 1950,

WILLIAM S. PALEY (September 28, 1901–October 26, 1990). The man most associated with CBS, Inc., and its largest stockholder, William S. Paley is often hailed as a visionary, although the programming on his radio and television networks is perhaps more indicative of an astute businessman able to understand the public's need. Critic David Halberstein has written in the *Atlantic* (January 1975), "He achieved a power over American taste and wrought an effect on American culture and sociology that had never been envisioned before."

Born in Chicago, Paley entered his father's business, the Congress Cigar Co., at the age of twenty-one. His interest in radio stemmed from his buying of advertising time for La Palina cigars on radio station WCAU-Philadelphia. In 1928, Paley acquired a controlling interest in a radio network, the Columbia Broadcasting System, which had been formed the previous year. He became president of the company, and adopted a hands-on policy regarding its programming. Paley's business acumen and his desire to give the public what it wanted is evidenced by his successfully luring away of some of NBC's biggest stars, including Jack Benny, Red Skelton, Amos 'n' Andy, and Edgar Bergen, in 1948.

Throughout his career, Paley demonstrated an inability to relinquish control of the CBS radio and television networks. He groomed many successors but the successions never took place. President from 1928 to 1946, Paley became chairman of the board from 1946 to 1983, and in 1983 he accepted the title of founding chairman. When his ultimate successor, Thomas H. Wyman, was forced to resign in 1986, Paley returned as acting chairman, and was reappointed chairman of the board the following year.

Following a divorce from his first wife, Dorothy Hart Hearst, Paley married the well-known New York socialite Barbara (Babe) Cushing in 1947; she died of cancer in 1978. William S. Paley was active on the board of the Museum of Modern Art as a trustee from 1937 to 1968, as its president from 1968 to 1973, and as chairman of the board from 1972 until his death. In 1976, he founded the Museum of Broadcasting, and remained chairman of its board until his death. He received the George Foster Peabody awards in 1958 and 1961, and the *TV Guide* Life Achievement Award in 1984. He was the first recipient, in 1978, of the Governors Award, the highest honor from the Academy of Television Arts and Sciences, and in 1984 was elected to the academy's Television Hall of Fame.

DAVID SARNOFF (February 27, 1891–December 12, 1971). While coming far from a far humbler background than Goldenson and Paley, and lacking their financial clout, David Sarnoff is the only member of the triumvirate of radio and television industry pioneers actually responsible for the creation of a radio and television network, NBC. Born in western Russia, Sarnoff came with his parents to the United States in 1900. He left school at the age of fifteen and obtained his first job as a messenger boy for the Commercial Cable Company. Later that same year, 1906, he joined the Marconi Wireless Telegraph Company, also as an office boy, but later became a wireless operator. In that capacity, on

April 14, 1912, he received the first distress signal from the doomed passenger liner, the *Titanic*.

In 1919, American Marconi became Radio Corporation of America (RCA), and in 1921, Sarnoff became the new company's general manager. A year later, he was appointed vice-president and general manager, and in 1929, he became executive vice-president. In 1930, David Sarnoff was named president of RCA, a position he was to hold until 1947. It made him the head of America's largest communications conglomerate, including not only RCA, but also NBC (which Sarnoff had created in 1926) and RKO Radio Pictures (founded in 1929). In 1947, David Sarnoff was named chairman of the board of RCA, a position that he held until 1970, when he retired and accepted the life title of honorary chairman.

Sarnoff is often referred to as "the General," in acknowledgment of his appointment as brigadier general by General Dwight D. Eisenhower, whose communications consultant Sarnoff served as during and after the Normandy invasion. He was also decorated with the Legion of Merit in 1944; in 1946, as president of RCA, he received the Medal for Merit in recognition of his corporation's services to the nation from 1942 to 1944.

Television Reference:
———— A Bibliography ————

Abramson, Albert. *The History of Television, 1880–1941*. Jefferson, N.C.: McFarland,
    1987.
Bailey, Robert Lee. *An Examination of Prime Time Network Television Special Programs,
    1948 to 1966*. New York: Arno Press, 1980.
Barnouw, Eric. *A Tower of Babel: The History of Broadcasting in the United States to
    1933*. New York: Oxford University Press, 1966.
————. *The Golden Web: The History of Broadcasting in the United States, 1933–1953*.
    New York: Oxford University Press, 1968.
————. *The Image Empire: The History of Broadcasting in the United States from 1953*.
    New York: Oxford University Press, 1970.
Beitman, Morris N. *Television Cyclopedia*. Chicago: Supreme Publications, 1939.
Blum, Daniel. *Pictorial History of Television*. Philadelphia: Chilton, 1959.
Brooks, Tim, and Earle Marsh. *The Complete Directory to Prime Time Network TV
    Shows, 1946–Present*. New York: Ballantine Books, 1988.
Brown, Les. *Les Brown's Encyclopedia of Television*. New York: Zoetrope, 1983.
Campbell, Robert. *The Golden Years of Broadcasting*. New York: Charles Scribner's
    Sons, 1976.
Cassata, Mary, and Thomas Skill. *Television: A Guide to the Literature*. Phoenix, Ariz.:
    Oryx, 1985.
Castleman, Harry, and Walter J. Podrazik. *The TV Schedule Book: Four Decades of
    Network Programming from Sign-On to Sign-Off*. New York: McGraw-Hill, 1984.
David, Nina, compiler. *TV Season: 74–75*. Phoenix, Ariz.: Oryx,1976.
————. *TV Season: 75–76*. Phoenix, Ariz.: Oryx, 1977.
————. *TV Season: 76–77*. Phoenix, Ariz.: Oryx, 1978.
————. *TV Season: 77–78*. Phoenix, Ariz.: Oryx, 1979.
Einstein, Daniel. *Special Edition: A Guide to Network Television Documentary Series
    and Special News Reports, 1955–1979*. Metuchen, N.J.: Scarecrow Press, 1987.
Erickson, Hal. *Syndicated Television: The First Forty Years, 1947–1987*. Jefferson, N.C.:
    McFarland, 1989.
Fireman, Judy, editor. *TV Book: The Ultimate Television Book*. New York: Workman,
    1977.

Gianakos, Larry James. *Television Drama Series Programming: A Comprehensive Chronicle, 1959–1975*. Metuchen, N.J.: Scarecrow Press, 1978.

————. *Television Drama Series Programming: A Comprehensive Chronicle, 1947–1959*. Metuchen, N.J.: Scarecrow Press, 1980.

————. *Television Drama Series Programming: A Comprehensive Chronicle, 1975–1980*. Metuchen, N.J.: Scarecrow Press, 1981.

————. *Television Drama Series Programming: A Comprehensive Chronicle, 1980–1982*. Metuchen, N.J.: Scarecrow Press, 1983.

————. *Television Drama Series Programming: A Comprehensive Chronicle, 1982–. 1984*. Metuchen, N.J.: Scarecrow Press, 1987.

Godfrey, Donald G. *A Directory of Broadcast Archives*. Washington, D.C.: Broadcast Education Association, 1983.

Goldberg, Lee. *Unsold Television Pilots, 1955–1989*. Jefferson, N.C.: McFarland, 1990.

Goldstein, Fred, and Stan Goldstein. *Prime Time Television: A Pictorial History from Milton Berle to "Falcon Crest"*. New York: Crown, 1983.

Greenfield, Jeff. *Television: The First Fifty Years*. New York: Harry Abrams, 1977.

Grossman, Gary H. *Saturday Morning TV*. New York: Dell, 1981.

Harris, Jay. *TV Guide: The First 25 Years*. New York: Simon and Schuster, 1978.

Hawes, William. *American Television Drama: The Experimental Years*. University, Ala.: University of Alabama Press, 1986.

Head, Sydney W., and Christopher H. Sterling. *Broadcasting in America: A Survey of Television, Radio, and New Technologies*. Boston: Houghton Mifflin, 1982.

Henson, Robert. *Television Weathercasting: A History*. Jefferson, N.C.: McFarland, 1990.

Hubbell, Richard F. *4000 Years of Television*. New York: G.P. Putnam's Sons, 1942.

Johnson, Catherine. *TV Guide Index: 1978–1982*. Radnor, Pa.: Triangle Publications, 1983.

Kempner, Stanley, editor. *Television Encyclopedia*. New York: Fairchild, 1948.

McCavitt, William E. *Radio and Television: A Selected, Annotated Bibliography*. Metuchen, N.J.: Scarecrow Press, 1978.

————. *Radio and Television: A Selected, Annotated Bibliography, Supplement One: 1977–1981*. Metuchen, N.J.: Scarecrow Press, 1982.

McNeil, Alex. *Total Television: A Comprehensive Guide to Programming from 1948 to the Present*. New York: Penguin, 1984.

Marill, Alvin H. *Movies Made for Television: The Telefeature and the Mini-Series, 1964–1984*. New York: Zoetrope, 1984.

Norback, Craig T., and Peter G. *TV Guide Almanac*. New York: Ballantine Books, 1980.

Norman, Bruce. *Here's Looking at You: The Story of British Television, 1908–1939*. London: BBC/Royal Television Society, 1984.

Parish, James Robert, and Vincent Terrace. *The Complete Actors' Television Credits, 1948–1988*. Metuchen, N.J.: Scarecrow Press, 1989.

Passingham, Kenneth. *The Guinness Book of TV Facts and Feats*. Enfield, U.K.: Guinness, 1984.

Paul, Michael, and James Robert Parish. *The Emmy Awards: A Pictorial History*. New York: Crown, 1970.

Post, Joyce. *TV Guide 25 Year Index, April 3, 1953–December 31, 1977*. Radnor, Pa.: Triangle Publications, 1979.

Pringle, Peter K., and Helen E. Clinton. *Radio and Television: A Selected, Annotated*

Bibliography: Supplement Two: 1982–1986. Metuchen, N.J.: Scarecrow Press, 1989.

Prouty, Howard K., editor. *Variety Television Reviews, 1923–1988*. New York: Garland, 1989.

Rose, Brian G. *Television and the Performing Arts: A Handbook and Reference Guide to American Cultural Programming*. Westport, Conn.: Greenwood Press, 1986.

————, editor. *TV Genres: A Handbook and Reference Guide*. Westport, Conn.: Greenwood Press, 1985.

Scheuer, Steven H. *TV: The Television Annual, 1978–79*. New York: Macmillan, 1979.

————. *Who's Who in Television and Cable*. New York: Facts on File, 1983.

Schreibman, Fay C., and Peter J. Bukalski. *Broadcast Television: A Research Guide*. Frederick, Md.: University Publications of America, 1983.

Settel, Irving. *A Pictorial History of Television*. New York: Frederick Ungar, 1983.

Shapiro, Mitchell E. *Television Network Prime-Time Programming, 1948–1988*. Jefferson, N.C.: McFarland, 1989.

Shulman, Arthur, and Roger Youman. *How Sweet It Was!* New York: Bonanza Books, 1966.

Steinberg, Cobbett. *TV Facts*. New York: Facts on File, 1980.

Sturcken, Frank. *Live Television: The Golden Age of 1946–1958 in New York*. Jefferson, N.C.: McFarland, 1990.

Terrace, Vincent. *Encyclopedia of Television: Series, Pilots and Specials*. New York: Zoetrope, 1986.

Thomey, Ted. *The Glorious Decade*. New York: Ace, 1970.

Udelson, Joseph. *The Great Television Race: A History of the American Television Industry, 1925–1941*. University, Ala.: University of Alabama Press, 1982.

Wheen, Francis. *Television: A History*. London: Century, 1985.

Who's Who on Television. London: Independent Television Books, 1980.

Wilk, Max. *The Golden Age of Television*. New York: Delacorte Press, 1976.

Winship, Michael. *Television*. New York: Random House, 1988.

Name Index

Numbers in **bold** indicate location of main entry.

Program Index

About the Author

ANTHONY SLIDE has held executive positions with both the Academy of Motion Picture Arts and Sciences and the American Film Institute. The author or editor of more than forty books on the history of popular entertainment, he has been called "a one-man publishing phenomenon" (by the Los Angeles Times and "a meticulous scholar" (by Variety). Beginning in 1970 with Early American Cinema, many of Slide's books have been devoted to the silent cinema, earning for him the accolade from Lillian Gish of "Our Preeminent Historian of the Silent Era." Aside from his activities as a writer, Anthony Slide is also the editor of the "Filmmakers" series, and has produced and directed documentaries on Blanche Sweet, Viola Dana, Karl Brown, and early women directors. In 1990, he was awarded an Honorary Doctorate of Letters from Bowling Green University.